PRENTICE HALL STUDIES IN INTERNATIONAL RELATIONS

ENDURING QUESTIONS IN CHANGING TIMES

Charles W. Kegley, Jr., *Series Editor*

In the era of globalization in the twenty-first century, people cannot afford to ignore the impact of international relations on their future. From the value of one's investments to the quality of the air one breathes, international relations matter. The instantaneous spread of communications throughout the world is making for the internationalization of all phenomena, while the distinction between the domestic and the foreign, the public and the private, and the national and the international is vanishing. Globalization is an accelerating trend that is transforming how virtually every field of study in the social sciences is being investigated and taught.

Contemporary scholarship has made bold advances in understanding the many facets of international relations. It has also laid a firm foundation for interpreting the major forces and factors that are shaping the global future.

To introduce the latest research findings and theoretical commentary, a new publication series has been launched. *Prentice Hall Studies in International Relations: Enduring Questions in Changing Times* presents books that focus on the issues, controversies, and trends that are defining the central topics dominating discussion about international relations.

The Elusive
Quest Continues

Theory and Global Politics

YALE H. FERGUSON
RICHARD W. MANSBACH

Upper Saddle River, NJ 07458

Library of Congress Cataloging-in-Publication Data

Ferguson, Yale H.
  The elusive quest continues : theory and global politics / by Yale H. Ferguson and
Richard W. Mansbach.
    p.   cm.
  Includes bibliographical references and index.
  ISBN 0–13–099279–8 (alk. paper)
  1. International relations.   I. Mansbach, Richard W., (date)   II. Title.

JZ1242 .F47   2002
327.1′01—dc21   2002021662

Senior Acquisitions Editor: *Heather Shelstad*
Associate Editor: *Brian Prybella*
Editorial Assistant: *Jessica Drew*
Project Manager: *Merrill Peterson*
Cover Director: *Jayne Conte*
Cover Designer: *Kiwi Design*
Marketing Manager: *Claire Bitting*
Marketing Assistant: *Jennifer Bryant*
Prepress and Manufacturing Buyer: *Ben Smith*

This book was set in 10/11 New Baskerville by DM Cradle Associates
and was printed and bound by Courier Companies, Inc.
The cover was printed by Coral Graphics.

© 2003 by Pearson Education, Inc.
Upper Saddle River, New Jersey 07458

Printed in the United States of America

10 9 8 7 6 5 4 3 2 1

ISBN 0-13-099279-8

Pearson Education LTD., London
Pearson Education Australia PTY, Limited, Sydney
Pearson Education Singapore, Pte. Ltd
Pearson Education North Asia Ltd, Hong Kong
Pearson Education Canada Ltd., Toronto
Pearson Educación de Mexico, S.A. de C.V.
Pearson Education—Japan, Tokyo
Pearson Education Malaysia, Pte. Ltd
Pearson Education, Upper Saddle River, New Jersey

In loving memory of our parents
Florence Appel Mansbach and Milton Mansbach
and
Marion Hicks Ferguson and Phil Mass Ferguson

Contents

PART II: CONCEPTUAL ANARCHY

Preface

When *The Elusive Quest* appeared in 1988, we were pessimistic about the future of international relations theory. We declared the book a very personal one that, in some respects, contradicted our previous work and presented assumptions that were at odds with those we and most scholars of global politics had held previously. As we predicted at the time, *The Elusive Quest* was controversial because it raised questions about epistemological issues that had been fundamental to much of the research conducted during previous decades. Our conclusions implicitly (and in some instances explicitly) questioned the utility of much of this research. Since then, epistemological and ontological issues have become increasingly central to theoretical discourse in the field.

Much has changed since the book first appeared. The Cold War came to an end, the Soviet Union collapsed, and Russia became increasingly ungovernable, raising concerns about its nuclear weapons stockpile. A major war was fought over Iraq's occupation of Kuwait, and as 2001 came to an end, Islamism and Islamic fanaticism were stirring conflict. Elsewhere, states crumbled in Africa and the Balkans and weakened everywhere, and civil strife provided new euphemisms for conflict—"ethnic cleansing," "failed states," "humanitarian intervention." Perhaps most important, the United States experienced war in the heart of Manhattan, and "9/11" will forever alter Americans' sense of security at home. Dramatic changes in technology, especially in microelectronics, provided people with front-row seats to major events everywhere, degraded the significance of distance and territory, and forced us to rethink the basic meaning of political space. Finally, a new buzzword—globalization—that few understood or could define appeared on everyone's lips as an effort to explain myriad other changes.

Changes such as these necessarily intensified the quest for new theory and new "thinking spaces." Postmodernism, postpositivism, constructivism, critical feminism, prospect theory, scientific realism, and various other "neos" and "isms" questioned the uses and abuses of science and gained their own loyal followings. Like the specific puzzles they addressed, these approaches combined old problems with new names (for example, "agent-structure"), recycled insights, and produced at least a few genuinely novel formulations. Although grounds for pessimism have hardly disappeared, there are signs of an intellectual spring that, in the end, may lead to an integrated field of politics. Indeed, growing appreciation that the Westphalian interstate system and the leviathans that constituted it do not exhaust all we need to learn about has led us to substitute "global" in many cases where we used "international" in 1988. In many respects, the world is, to use James Rosenau's felicitous phrase, "postinternational."

We did not intend *The Elusive Quest* to signify the end of an intellectual trek. Instead, it represented an important initial step in looking at global-politics theory from a different perspective. It was the opening statement in what we hoped would prove to be a comprehensive and thematic analysis of the history and evolution of ideas about global politics. Before proceeding with such analysis, however, it was necessary to ask two key questions: (1) Why do we think what we do about the world around us? and (2) How do these ideas change? *The Elusive Quest* was our effort to address these questions, and the publication of *Polities: Authority, Identities, and Change* was a further down payment on this effort. Our forthcoming book, *Remapping Global Politics*, will represent a further step.

We wish to thank Rhoda and Rachael Mansbach and Kitty, Colin, Duff, and Caitlin Ferguson, who have contributed beyond measure with their sustaining love.

Grateful acknowledgment is made to the University of Chicago Press for permission to quote from Bertrand Badie and Pierre Birnbaum's *The Sociology of the State,* © *1983* by The University of Chicago.

Introduction

Taking Stock

We, like many students of global politics, were once convinced that we were participants in a quest for theory that would, in time, unravel the arcane secrets of global politics. That quest would deepen our theoretical insights as we tested our ideas according to the canons of science. Knowledge and understanding would be accumulated gradually and cumulatively, but, in the end, they might even enable us to overcome age-old political scourges like war.

In subsequent decades, those dreams were dashed. We have witnessed changes in discourse in our field, the development of intriguing and ingenious methodologies, the creation of new forms of data, and the diffusion of American social-science techniques throughout the world. Yet, our understanding of key phenomena is expanding only very modestly, if at all, and scholarly attention shifts back and forth among these phenomena with almost faddish regularity. If insight is to be understood as "the capacity of the mind for making a path through time and complexity,"[1] then little is evident in our field. "New" theories, often dressed in novel jargon, turn out upon close examination to be restatements of old ideas, and they enjoy only fleeting moments of academic adulation because fashions soon change again.[2] Graduate students are repeatedly forced to return to "a kind of 'old theories' home"[3] in which the lineage of the theories they meet is rarely revealed to them; the wheel is regularly rediscovered. Perhaps it is just as well that practitioners find themselves unable to understand the scholarly literature in global politics and, therefore, make little use of it. Otherwise, they might decide that the emperor is indeed naked. Its exponential growth and profusion have rendered the literature unmanageable; there is too much to consume.

One historian has observed that

a number of currents converged to create a type of social inquiry whose methodological distinctiveness was a commitment to quantitative research. Underlying the application of quantification was the assumption that such a methodology could illuminate and explain social phenomena. Consequently, . . . social commentators became preoccupied with the development of elaborate classification systems capable of ordering a seemingly infinite variety of statistical data.[4]

Although this quotation could be a splendid description of trends in the study of political science in general and global politics in particular beginning in the 1960s, it actually refers to research in psychiatric epidemiology after 1800. The analysis goes on to explain why these methodological innovations failed to advance psychiatric understanding to any appreciable extent:

Epidemiology, of course, required in part clear classes or categories of disease in order to facilitate the collection of statistical data. Prevailing nineteenth century psychiatric nosologies, however, did not lend themselves to any kind of precision.[5]

In other words, the conceptual apparatus of this field was inadequate for major theoretical advances to occur. Muddy concepts also precluded operationalizations that would permit valid measurement. The situation is much the same in contemporary global politics, where the presence of muddy concepts and the absence of conceptual consensus or clarity, perhaps more than any other factors, account for the appearance of theoretical gridlock.

In 1988, we were not merely disappointed with the slow progress that had been made in transforming the field of global politics into a scientific discipline. More importantly, we were uncertain whether such a transformation was possible at all. We argued then that, like the nineteenth-century epidemiologists who were dedicated to applying their understanding "to a series of pressing social problems that seemed to threaten the very fabric of American society,"[6] the research of global-politics scholars is, apparently inevitably, conditioned by deep normative commitments. Today, we are convinced that we were correct and, as we shall see, many international relations scholars with little else in common have reached the same conclusion. Normative commitments, which effectively determine the research agenda, vary by time and place and, consequently, so do the key concepts in the field. In effect, then, global-politics scholarship grows out of the social milieu in which it occurs and, since that milieu is constantly in flux, linear theoretical growth is impossible. Unfortunately, for some, recognition of the inevitable normative content of theory has meant a flight from empiricism and a descent into unalloyed relativism.

The degree to which the intellectual enterprise is dependent upon social context is reflected in many ways. The political needs and preferences of political practitioners and the funding practices of government institutions constantly reshape research orientations and the normative predilections of scholars (themselves facts of note). The latter especially account for the pseudo-scientific bent of American global-politics scholarship. Like our epidemiologists, who utilized statistical data "to establish the legitimacy of public mental hospitals and build broad support among state officials and the public,"[7] contemporary global-politics scholars often focus on methodology at the expense of theory in order to legitimize their field as a discipline and coax greater resources from government and university sources.

By 1988, the quest on which we embarked at the outset of our careers seemed to have become increasingly elusive. The time had come for us to address these concerns directly and to ask ourselves whether the intellectual map we expected to follow offered any prospect for reaching our destination. In order to do this, we assessed the state of theory in global politics at the time and the progress we had made in apprehending the essence of our subject. We also sought to explain the reasons for the condition in which the field found itself, if indeed it were a field.

The Elusive Quest Continues returns to many of the same questions we asked in 1988 in light of the sometimes dramatic changes in theory and reality that have taken place since then. On the one hand, we were enthused by several shifts in approach augured by Yosef Lapid's "Third Debate," especially the renewed concern with epistemological and ontological issues, the (re)turn toward subjectivity, the reuniting of facts and values, and the renewed interest in using history to make sense of the present and future. On the other hand, we were less pleased by the overreaction of some colleagues who turned their backs squarely on empiricism of any sort, threatening to make the field even more remote from real-world threats to and promises for human survival and well-being than had been the case when the field was under the sway of rigid positivism. Finally, we were delighted by the willingness on the part of at least a few of the wisest among us, often those outside of political science or outside of the American mainstream to pose bold challenges and return to "big" questions.

After all, whatever the advantages or failings of islands of theory and limited ambitions, they made for far more tedious reading than the intellectual excitement generated by the Lasswells, Deutschs, Sprouts, Carrs, Bulls, or Wrights. On reflection, it is clear that by 1988 the field had become boring, perhaps the worst of all offenses it might commit.

The following chapter summaries are offered as a map to help readers descry more easily the path that we have taken on our journey.

PART I: SOURCES OF THEORY

In the first four chapters of the book, we elaborate our analysis of how theory construction takes place in the field of global politics.

1. Paradigms and Theoretical Growth in Global Politics. In this chapter we review Kuhn's and Popper's versions of scientific advancement and assess their applicability to the social sciences in general and to the study of global politics in particular. We argue that, in view of the noncumulative nature of the social sciences, the Kuhnian paradigm proved irresistibly seductive. We show that efforts to apply that framework to global politics, however, have not been successful, nor is there any agreement as to what constitutes a paradigm in that field or in other social sciences.

2. Values and Paradigm Change in Global Politics. We observe that significant differences exist between theory in the natural sciences and in global politics, notably regarding the role of values in formulating the latter. We contend that ideas in global politics are contextual and emerge from and are dependent upon social norms. They, therefore, evolve in a manner quite uncharacteristic of the Kuhnian model. Theoretical controversies in global politics are shown to be less debates over objective truths than over normative commitments and political preferences. We proceed to elaborate the sources of social norms and the means by which they develop and change.

3. Changing Norms and Theory: The Middle Ages to Machiavelli. The manner in which theory evolves in global politics is illustrated in this chapter, which reviews key ideas about global politics and changes in them from the early medieval period in Europe until the Renaissance. The relationship between changing conditions, norms, and theory is revealed in the ideas of such thinkers as St. Augustine, John of Salisbury, St. Thomas Aquinas, Dante Alighieri, Pierre Dubois, Marsilio of Padua, and Niccolò Machiavelli. Dramatic differences exist among the normative commitments of such scholars and publicists, and we elaborate the unique concatenation of conditions that underlies each of them.

4. The Vicissitudes of Norms and Theory: Realism and Idealism. In this chapter we suggest that those schools of thought labeled "realism" and "idealism" are less coherent bodies of theory than they are competing bundles of norms. A historical analysis of this competition, we argue, reveals that the relative influence of each set of norms and, therefore, of the theories that reflect those norms has fluctuated in reaction to changing sociopolitical conditions. We briefly review the manner in which norms have oscillated from the founding of the modern state in Europe through the nineteenth century, then pay close attention to changing norms and theory in the present century. The rise of idealism after World War I and its subsequent decline along with the ascent of realism after World War II are analyzed and explained. Finally, we review the waning of realism in the 1970s and its partial reemergence the following decade.

PART II: CONCEPTUAL ANARCHY

In the second section of the book, we illustrate the inadequacy of concepts in global politics for constructing theory and assess the present state of theory in the field as well as its future prospects.

5. The State as an Obstacle to Understanding Global Politics. The central purpose of this chapter is to illustrate the degree to which confusion about the concept of state acts as a barrier to constructing theory in the field. Not only have many international relations theorists tended to universalize what is a concept anchored in time and space, but they have also failed to take account of the changed nature of states at the end of the millennium or to make critical distinctions among real states. We introduce and illustrate the general problem of the subjectivity of concepts in global politics by reference to the state concept. The dimensions of the problem are portrayed by efforts to understand the state concept as a historical phenomenon. Sharp disagreements about the origins and evolution of the phenomenon, we argue, reflect incompatible normative perspectives. Efforts to identify a Platonic state confront the same difficulties. We illustrate the resulting confusion about the concept and the explanation for that confusion through a brief discussion of ten distinct conceptualizations of the state along with the normative intent underlying each.

6. The Uncertain Bounds of Bounded Rationality. This chapter explains the central role played by the concept of rationality in the development of foreign policy theory and explores the consequences and implications of abandoning or weakening the concept. Realist approaches to the field, we show, virtually depend upon some assumption of rationality and, without it, are severely circumscribed. But growing disillusionment surrounding American foreign policy in the 1960s and 1970s produced a lack of confidence in existing models of policy formulation and encouraged models that no longer assumed rational decisionmakers. We then review a number of efforts to develop theoretically attractive alternatives to the assumption of rationality. Most of these, we argue, have severe conceptual and data problems. Insights derived from them cannot be generalized and are unlikely to produce coherent or consensual bodies of theory. Efforts in recent years to advance our understanding of rationality, especially by application of mathematical modeling, have not overcome earlier problems, and the postpositivist stream of the field has attacked the assumption with greater relish than did earlier critics.

7. *Quo Vadis* Foreign Policy? This chapter analyzes how the retreat from realism and its assumption of rationality encouraged scholars to scrutinize their traditional claim that unitary nation-states are the key explanatory units in foreign policy. A survey of a number of alternative models reveals that, as in the case of the retreat from rationality, abandoning the unitary state-as-actor perspective has not produced coherent and generalizable theory. Key perspectives we review are the elites, shared images, groupthink, cybernetics, and governmental (bureaucratic) politics approaches to foreign policy. Efforts to integrate some of the insights from them—especially in the comparative study of foreign policy—have been disappointing. We conclude that the overall result of this proliferation of approaches has been to increase confusion rather than coherence in the field.

8. The Challenge of Anarchy and the Search for Order. In this chapter we review a final pair of concepts central to global politics—anarchy and cooperation. These two concepts, we argue, really represent the realist-idealist antinomy and the resulting conflict in normative commitments and perspectives. Anarchy traditionally has been regarded as the defining characteristic of the field (though the implications of this claim increasingly have been challenged by constructivists and others in recent years), even as the existence of social bonds in global politics and linked fates among actors are receiving ever greater recognition. The 1970s, however, marked a retreat from the anarchy concept and an effort to raise the standard of interdependence (a concept no less muddy than anarchy). The anarchy-interdependence debate is not of recent vintage. Efforts to modify the assumption of anarchy include the systems approach and integration and development theory. All proved effective competitors with realism for a time until their popularity waned. Recent successors to these approaches are regime theory and globalization perspectives, but the latter are largely old wine in new bottles and have been no more successful than anarchy in producing explanatory theory. Ultimately, the concepts of anarchy, interdependence, and their ilk are nontheoretical and are unlikely to prove effective building blocks for theory.

9. The End of the Elusive Quest? This chapter summarizes the reasons for the failure of a scientific approach to meet its promises in theory construction in global politics. We go on to discuss and evaluate new (and not-so-new) approaches in the field that take seriously the criticisms of science, and more importantly, of the empirical method itself. The various postpositivist perspectives associated with the Third Debate, though very different in detail, raise sharp epistemological and onto-logical questions regarding what we know and whether we know what we think we do. Postmodernists, for their part, reject empiricism and in some cases even the pos-sibility of gaining access to a reality outside oneself, while emphasizing the critical role of norms and subjectivity more generally in political life and thought. They do not seek to explain and recall the Dadaists of an earlier era. Some of their insights are a healthy corrective to the unquestioned faith in science of earlier scholars, but few of their concepts and views are as original as they would like to think. Ironically, their emphasis on power in some ways mirrors the views of early realists, whom they thoroughly dislike. The several schools of constructivism go in various directions but, overall, retain a view of reality more akin to that of the traditionalists who lost the academic wars of the 1950s and 1960s. Like postmodernists, constructivists restore the subjective dimension of politics to the center of concern but assume a less original position than younger students of the field believe. Some are in the realist and others in the idealist tradition, and all owe a debt to earlier scholars who took psychology and sociology seriously.

10. The Quest Continues. In this chapter we sum up and look ahead. We suggest why the nature of theory in global politics and the manner in which it evolves, along with the subjectivity of concepts in the field, make progress in the-ory construction difficult. We point out that the historical record reinforces the analysis leading to this pessimistic conclusion. We do, however, describe the out-lines of a potentially constructive epistemology arising out of a limited empiri-cism that emphasizes contest, contingency, and history. We also point to developments that give grounds for optimism, especially insights into the dynam-ics of identity as a possible means of uniting the field of politics to an extent not possible since the field became focused on studying states and their relations.

NOTES

1. Gerald Abrahams, *The Chess Mind* (Baltimore: Penguin Books, 1960), 15.
2. An observer may detect changing fashion in academics from professional conferences, doctoral dissertations, "obligatory" footnotes, and editorial decisions of leading journals.
3. Ronald Rogowski, "Rationalist Theories of Politics: A Midterm Report," *World Politics* 30, no. 2 (1978), 306.
4. Gerald N. Grob, "The Origins of American Psychiatric Epidemiology," *American Journal of Public Health* 75, no. 3 (1985), 229.
5. Ibid., 230.
6. Ibid., 231.
7. Ibid., 229.

CHAPTER 1

Paradigms and Theoretical Growth in Global Politics

The theme of this book, like its predecessor, is similar to that articulated by Michael Brecher in his provocative 1999 presidential address to the International Studies Association:

> As the twentieth century draws to a close, it seems time to reflect on "where have we gone wrong?" The question is not new, but it continues to perplex. The answers, unfortunately, are as numerous as our contentious schools, divided by epistemology, methodology, and ideology, along with idiosyncratic elements like personality. Realism and Neo-Realism, traditional and Neo-Institutionalism, Critical Theory, Post-Modernism, Post-Positivism, Rational Choice Theory, Cognitive Psychology, the English school, Neo-Marxism, World System, Feminist IR, and Constructivism would offer different reasons for the malaise of International Studies.[1]

Brecher concludes that "our field . . . has not yet . . . crystallized into a mature social science discipline."[2] Implicit in this conclusion is the belief that such maturity is possible if only we will avoid the five shortcomings that he identifies: intolerance, closed-mindedness, tendency to research fads, retreat from science, and the low value placed on cumulation of knowledge.

Where we part company with Brecher is the last two reasons. He seems to argue that if only we had done it better and remained faithful to the canons of science and the optimism of an aging generation of scientists we would have attained the Promised Land. Indeed, it was precisely the Panglossian faith in science and the confusion of method and theory that produced a theoretical dead end.[3] We do, however, agree with Brecher that the material we are examining and the way we examine it do not constitute a discipline. In our view, a discipline must have a reasonably coherent and widely accepted set of concepts and questions, as well as a shared ontology. Since these provided the boundaries necessary to define a discipline, realists, focusing on the question of the causes of interstate war, could imagine themselves as companions on a single disciplinary path. Today, by contrast, there are no discernible limits to the questions, concepts, actors, behaviors, or structures that constitute our common enterprise, so we refer to it as a "field" rather than a "discipline." And the field is "global" rather than "international" politics partly because it entails far more than interactions among sovereign states; most importantly, it involves the allocation of values among people who associate with one another in an almost infinite variety of ways to achieve greater value satisfaction. Finally, although political science remains central to the field of global politics, understanding can be derived only by borrowing from sociology, economics, geography, history, psychology, and, increasingly, from humanities such as literary criticism and ethics.[4]

If we place little value on cumulation in the field, it is because there has been so little. Our disillusionment mirrors that of Donald Puchala when he writes:

> Behavioralism in international relations . . . has . . . hit an epistemological iceberg that has been floating in its intellectual waters since the beginning. In its rush to "go scientific" in the 1960s, practitioners of behavioralist international relations rather uncritically adopted from political science the logical positivistic epistemology that political science, in its haste to move away from public law and government, rather uncritically adopted from sociology.[5]

From a pragmatic perspective, little of the theorizing or research undertaken in recent decades in global politics has been very useful to practitioners, and much of it seems largely irrelevant to understanding real events in the real world. In fact, as we shall argue later, far from practitioners learning from theorists, theorists often faddishly try to give practitioners what they seem to want.

The very ontology of much of global politics—or "international politics" as it is usually and significantly termed—is misplaced. " 'Ontology,'" as David Dessler observes, "refers to the concrete referents of an explanatory discourse. A theory's ontology consists of the real-world structures (things, entities) and processes posited by the theory and invoked in the theory's explanations."[6] Using the language employed by Imre Lakatos to evaluate research programs, the state centric assumptions of much of international relations have been sufficiently undermined to threaten the hard core of conventional international relations.[7] Any ontology that focuses exclusively on states in a state system must fail to account for much of what is important in the world today. For this reason, "international" no longer does justice to the issues we seek to understand, any more than Hans Morgenthau's effort to exclude economics and define an autonomous "international politics" provided an adequate description of the field's boundaries.

The growing pluralism and apparent incoherence in theorizing about global politics, as well as other social sciences, helps account for the warm welcome accorded Thomas Kuhn's paradigm concept when it appeared in 1964.[8] That concept seemed to explain why theorists had failed to make the great strides of the natural sciences in understanding the essentials of their field. Either we were poor scientists, or the field was not susceptible to the scientific method as described by those like Karl Popper and Ernest Nagel. Instead, the field, far from constituting a genuine discipline, was divided into competing camps with few, if any, accepted truths. With Kuhn, however, the answer became clear, especially for the rationalists who dominated the field: global politics lacked a paradigm to organize research. The idea of a paradigm was itself part of a welcome paradigm shift that revealed the shortcomings of existing ideas about scientific accumulation.[9]

Thereafter, it became difficult to find a major work in global politics that did not either urge that the field synthesize a new paradigm or did not itself offer such a synthesis.[10] "The tasks of the normal scientist," declared James N. Rosenau, "can be undertaken only after her revolutionary counterpart has paved the way—to use Thomas Kuhn's distinction."[11] Moreover, a change in research agendas "does not represent a haphazard sequence of theoretical or topical 'fads' but is rooted in a 'core concern' or a set of puzzles which give coherence and identity to this field of study."[12]

Implicit in such claims was an assumption that the "constellation of beliefs, values, techniques . . . shared by members"[13] of the global politics fraternity was evolving in a manner similar to that of the natural sciences as depicted by Kuhn. In other words, our understanding of the world around us putatively was growing even as theoretical consensus was breaking down. Indeed, Kuhn argued that the breakdown of consensus may even signal step-level progress in such understanding. Both the absence of scientific progress and the growing eclecticism in theory and method heightened suspicions about the accessibility of truths in global politics. A combination of accelerating change in global reality and greater attention to the subjective dimension in global politics implied, at a minimum, that whatever truths were accessible might be tentative, even ephemeral. At its extreme, this meant, in Bunge's words, that "truth" was "coextensive with consensus."[14] To the extent that such a view spread within the field, the founding of new schools entailed incommensurable criteria for determining truth. It is precisely because the field failed to develop by a process of incremental or continuous theoretical growth that partly explains the magnetic effect Kuhn's model exerted on global-politics scholars.

One of Kuhn's central concerns was the barrier posed by differing premises regarding the nature of evidence. Before the end of World War II, the study of global politics had been largely the domain of political philosophers, historians, lawyers, and diplomats. Accumulated knowledge, then, consisted of a welter of legal commentaries, diplomatic reminiscences, historical case studies, and ethical and theological tracts. Although a variety of theoretical orientations was identifiable, each with its own classical referents, the field lacked the attributes of a discipline. It lacked any consensus regarding the proper questions to be confronted, what methods or concepts were appropriate to the subject matter, and even what that subject matter was. Because the field lacked identifiable boundaries, it was not even clear who was part of it and who was not.[15]

After World War II a generation of scholars emerged that was determined to bring more order to the field and unite around the concept of power. These scholars were hardly dispassionate seekers after truth but were instead the product of a particular political and social context. Their impetus was normative, the implications of which were scarcely recognized at the time. They explicitly blamed global-politics theorists, especially those in the Anglo-American tradition, and the practitioners who were their clients for having failed to prevent the war by adopting utopian assumptions about the way the world worked. Instead, they demanded a return to reality by adopting the assumptions of the continental Europeans power tradition. In turn, these realists were succeeded by another generation that accepted realist assumptions but were committed to forging a discipline of global politics and were attracted to the methods of the natural sciences. Analyses of international phenomena were to be made systematic and to be built on empirical observation.[16] Sociopolitical phenomena, like the subject matter of the natural sciences, were assumed to be part of the natural world with natural causes whose discovery was impeded only by the absence of suitable data, methods, and tools. Nothing was, in principle, unknowable if the search for patterned behavior was undertaken in systematic fashion.

In retrospect, it is odd that anyone could believe that a single methodology or set of assumptions, however suitable in one field of inquiry, might be bodily transported to another or that a single set of questions and methods might be suitable within political science. Even in the natural sciences, after all, one studies and thinks about quarks differently than one studies and thinks about ecosystems or black holes.

This so-called behavioral revolution in political science was a self-conscious effort to break with previous tradition and quite explicitly assumed an ahistorical posture. New ideas regarding global politics, for instance, could not be viewed—as discoveries in the natural sciences before Kuhn had been—"as the developing achievement of the successive commentators on Aristotle," nor were they the outcome of "a continuous development of Western thought."[17] Global politics lacked a consensual set of beliefs and theories that could be regarded as the culmination of the analyses of previous generations. Nor did the history of the field reveal a process of persistent theoretical refinement consonant with Karl Popper's view of falsification and refutation.[18]

To social scientists, wrestling with the claims of critics who pointed out the noncumulative nature of their enterprise, Kuhn's critique of the accepted view of progress in the natural sciences was a jeu d'esprit. Kuhn questioned whether "the cognitive development of science is a rational process governed by timeless rules of procedure" and argued, instead, that the growth in scientific knowledge was the product of "a succession of points of view—each point of view constituting a self-authenticating tradition of thought."[19] Thus, critical experiments of the sort on which scientists depend to select among competing theories are precluded because of fundamental differences in assumptions and ontologies. Kuhn's idea that knowledge systems evolve by a process that is at once dynamic and unpredictable, marked by discontinuities and dramatic shifts, seemed to contrast starkly with the perspective that science evolves in a gradual but linear manner. Kuhn's claim that new theories and methods are not merely incremental adaptations of older ones, modified to incorporate new facts and findings, was eagerly accepted as legitimizing the revolutionary nature of the behavioral enterprise in the social sciences.

PARADIGMS, SCIENTIFIC REVOLUTIONS, AND THE SOCIAL SCIENCES

The central concept in Kuhn's framework, the "paradigm," was inevitably a magnet for scholars seeking to abolish tradition rather than to build upon it. Kuhn perceived science as evolving by means of a succession of comprehensive and mutually exclusive metatheories or paradigms that embrace and redefine disciplines, set new research agendas and boundaries, guide scholarly inquiry, and provide new criteria for theoretical acceptance. Despite the ambiguity of this concept, it appeared to legitimize abrupt intellectual shifts and the abandonment of traditional ways of viewing things.[20] Genuine paradigms, according to Kuhn, do not provide answers to specific research questions. Rather, the assumptions they incorporate define those problems, inform the scholar as to how solutions should be sought, and so generate theory. Commonly, the dominant paradigm is incorporated in a single work or "exemplar." As Kuhn stated:

> Aristotle's *Physica*, Ptolemy's *Almagest*, Newton's *Principia* and *Opticks*, Franklin's *Electricity*, Lavoisier's *Chemistry*, and Lyell's *Geology*—these and many other works served for a time implicitly to define the legitimate problems and methods of a research field for succeeding generations of practitioners. They were able to do so because they shared two essential characteristics. Their achievement was sufficiently unprecedented to attract an enduring group of adherents away from competing modes of scientific activity. Simultaneously, it was sufficiently open-ended to leave all sorts of problems for the redefined group of practitioners to resolve.[21]

In other words, paradigms "do not so much confront the facts as tell us what we should see in the facts."[22] Social scientists, however, "see" normative, ideological, and, yes, personal implications "in the facts." And anyone who doubted this before should reassess the question in light of September 11, 2001.

Kuhn called scholarship that follows paradigm assumptions and carries out the research agenda set by a paradigm "normal science." Such scholarship does not aspire to theoretical originality but seeks to realize the promise of the paradigm by extending understanding of the facts toward which the paradigm points "by increasing the extent of the match between those facts and the paradigm's predictions, and by further articulation of the paradigm itself."[23] This largely involves efforts to solve the numerous puzzles toward which the paradigm directs attention.[24] Normal science attempts to force nature to conform to the assumptions of the dominant paradigm; scholars who do not share these assumptions and eschew puzzle solving are regarded as pariahs by the dominant scientific community. Paradigm shifts occur because normal science will, in time, reveal puzzles for which the dominant paradigm affords no solution, and "their assimilation requires the elaboration of another set of rules. Such puzzles, which entail observations that are inconsistent with the assumptions of the dominant paradigm, are termed "anomalies" by Kuhn. In these conditions, there is growing recognition "that nature has somehow violated the paradigm-induced expectations that govern normal science."[25] If such anomalies persist, it becomes at least possible that normal scientific activity will cease and the discipline will enter a period of crisis. Disciplines are, then, "intermittently shaken by collective nervous break-downs followed by restored mental health."[26] Such crises, argued Kuhn, must be resolved in one of three ways:

> Sometimes normal science ultimately proves able to handle the crisis-provoking problem. . . . On other occasions the problem resists even apparently radical new approaches. Then scientists may conclude that no solution may be forthcoming in the present state of their field. The problem is labeled and set aside for a future

generation with more developed tools. Or, finally . . . a crisis may end with the emergence of a new candidate for paradigm and with the ensuing battle over its acceptance.[27]

An existing paradigm is discarded only when an alternative is available. The latter must predict novel experimental outcomes, explain the unrefuted content of its predecessor, and succeed in corroborating some of its new predictions.[28] These requirements are what, in Kuhn's eyes, ensures progress in a science rather than perpetual conflict.[29]

"Scientific revolution" is, for Kuhn, the transition from crisis to the acceptance of a new paradigm, during which time a field is fundamentally reconstructed. While progressive, such a process is not cumulative in the conventional sense, even though those who triumph may wish it to appear so. In fact, earlier paradigms are either banished or regarded as historical curiosities by subsequent generations of scholars. "Why," asks Kuhn, "should the student of physics . . . read the works of Newton, Faraday, Einstein, or Schrodinger, when everything he needs to know about these works is recapitulated in a far briefer, more precise, and more systematic form in a number of up-to-date textbooks?"[30] Such a perspective fits precisely the aspirations of postwar social scientists, who saw little reason to study directly the likes of Freud, Smith, Machiavelli, and so forth. As modern social scientists, they were the heirs but not the linear descendants of these great figures.

For communities of social scientists aspiring to disciplinary status, seeking to emulate their counterparts in the natural sciences yet unable to point to an unbroken history of progressive knowledge accumulation, Kuhn's analysis appeared at the right time. Their critics seemed not to appreciate that "during a pre-paradigm period, when there is a multiplicity of competing schools, evidence of progress is very hard to find," and "during periods of revolution . . . doubts are repeatedly expressed about the very possibility of continued progress if one or another of the opposed paradigms is adopted."[31] Many social scientists believed that their revolution was underway and that, in joining it, they had nothing to lose except the chains of tradition. Those who had crossed the revolutionary divide, like the behavioralists in political science, could not expect their critics to understand them. The nature of discourse had been altered, and opponents were bound to speak past one another. Old language was being used in new ways. As "the proponents of competing paradigms," they were practicing "their trades in different worlds," thereby dooming them to "see different things" and to see them "in different relations one to the other."[32]

The Kuhnian approach served the interests of social scientists who were in the midst of declaring the scientific status of their fields. No longer would they have to apologize for the patently noncumulative histories of their disciplines. The paradigm concept was a tonic for social scientists who were seeking to map out the future direction of their professions and demarcate the boundaries of their disciplines in a period of unprecedented institutional growth.[33] In order to sustain proliferating graduate programs and enhanced government funding, social scientists felt compelled to jettison the image that they constituted no more than loose congeries of relatively independent and isolated scholars interested in vaguely similar problems. Considerations of professional status encouraged them to depict themselves as marching in unison toward the solution of commonly held problems; they wished to constitute themselves into disciplines, not merely fields or subjects. In order to do so, social scientists had to identify their paradigms, for as Kuhn observed, it is "sometimes just its reception of a paradigm that transforms a group previously interested in the study of nature into a profession or, at least, a discipline." Social scientists could achieve the prestige of their cousins in the natural sciences if they could but fit the Kuhnian mold. "In the sciences," Kuhn argued, "the formation of specialized journals, the foundation of specialists' societies, and the claim for a special place in the curriculum have usually been associated with a group's first reception of a single paradigm."[34]

Less publicly discussed were some of the other rewards of being on the side of the paradigm "winners." Professional prestige and status, government grants, promotions, departmental and disciplinary power, the awe of graduate students, and all the other signs and accoutrements of academic success beckoned paradigm advocates. And to speak of normal science meant to control a field's research agenda as well as the human and financial resources necessary to carry out that agenda.

Social scientists also believed that acceptance of dominant paradigms would bring order into fields historically rent by quarrels over beliefs, values, and expectations. With paradigms, scholars would no longer have to start afresh from first principles, repeatedly defining and justifying concepts necessary for theory construction and elaboration. For these reasons, social scientists set out to identify comprehensive metatheories that at first blush could fulfill the criteria of Kuhnian paradigms.

To date, however, the success of paradigm advocates has been modest at best. For the most part, there has been little agreement in any of the social sciences as to what have been or currently are their dominant paradigms. There exists considerable uncertainty as to whether paradigms must dominate entire disciplines or merely subareas within disciplines. Finally, the social sciences simply do not resemble Kuhn's scientific communities. At best, some of the social sciences have identified research traditions, consisting of sets "of general assumptions about the entities and processes" in subareas.[35] This leads Brecher to write of "the dismal paradigm state of International Studies" in which "the paucity of serious attempts at synthesis, or at least complementarity, among contending paradigms is an indicator of deep malaise."[36] But did paradigm adherents really want "complementarity"? Probably not, in the end, because it would dim their own place in the sun.

There may be different schools of thought within the social sciences, but these do not function as communities working within their own distinct traditions. Instead they tend to act like partisan bands, with followers feuding among themselves as well as with the partisans of other schools of thought over norms, concepts, methods, and so forth. Particular partisan bands that distinguish themselves from departments elsewhere and seek to recruit graduate students by promulgating the superiority of their school of thought from time to time seize individual academic departments. The prospective students must decide whether, for example, they wish an education in traditional, behavioral, or postbehavioral political science, as their counterparts in economics might have to decide to be a Keynesian or a disciple of Milton Friedman. Schools of thought are often so narrow that they are identified with individual institutions or scholars—the "Michigan" or "Rochester" schools of political science, Straussian political philosophy, and the like. It would surely be generous to describe these as "islands of theory," to use Harold Guetzkow's felicitous metaphor, which "are seldom synthesized."[37] After all, as Kuhn himself recognized, the criterion for deciding whether or not a research program is progressive is "irreducibly sociological."[38]

Having once selected an institutional affiliation, graduate students will have defined their future professional friends and adversaries, and they will select their professional journals, associations, and even association panels at annual meetings to ensure a minimum of communication with those outside their school of thought.[39] Thereafter, they will communicate largely with those with whom they already are in agreement, and they and their colleagues will minister to and reinforce each other. Electronic mail only aggravates this situation.

Sociology typifies the effort of the social sciences to make use of Kuhn. In order to identify paradigms, sociologists, like other social scientists, tend to loosen the fairly rigid criteria of a Kuhnian paradigm. Thus, "the term comes most often to mean no more than a general theoretical perspective, or even . . . a collection of elements from several more or less distinct perspectives," and paradigms become "nebulous, shifting entities, indicating whatever one wishes them to indicate . . . limited only by the theorist's imagination." Douglas Lee Eckberg and Lester Hill Jr. identify twelve different groups of authors "who view the organization of sociology in at least ten fundamentally different ways—each claiming to present 'Kuhnian paradigms.' "[40] Are structural-functionalism, operationalism, and ecological-interactionalism the three great paradigms of sociology,[41] or should it be divided among social facts, social behavior, and social definitions"?[42] Does the discipline host many paradigms, each with its own disciples and distinct constellations of values, axioms, concepts, and methods, or does it remain in an immature and preparadigmatic state?[43] Alternatively, do sociologists use the term "paradigm" to legitimize parochial perspectives and mask the situation described by Eckberg and Hill:

> What we often actually find is research modeled upon no other research at all, upon a short, soon-extinguished line of research or upon a single theorist's speculations. There is little extended puzzle solving. There are few instances in the literature where an important puzzle has been solved. Indeed there are few puzzles, mostly problems. If a problem is considered important, it is never solved at all, but serves as a point of contention among variant perspectives. We find constant arguing, bickering, and debate, but very little agreement. This lack of agreement affects operationalization and manipulation of concepts, such that different research requires different, often incommensurable data. The concepts themselves seem to change from study to study.[44]

Other "protosciences" also, sought to avail themselves of the Kuhnian framework, with similar results—or lack thereof. For instance, "appeal to paradigmatic reasoning quickly became a regular feature of controversies in economics and 'paradigm' is now the byword of every historian of economic thought."[45] As for historians, "Not since the publication of R. G. Collingwood's

Idea of History has a work of 'theory' won from historians the amount of interest recently accorded Thomas S. Kuhn's *The Structure of Scientific Revolutions.*[46] Like sociologists, neither economists nor historians have been able to agree on what their paradigms are or on how to "fit" the paradigm concept to the development of their fields.[47] Again, part of the problem lies in Kuhn's own ambiguity and the willingness of his readers to interpret him in ways that suit their own claims. As a consequence, one economist argues in exasperation "that the term 'paradigm' ought to be banished from economic literature, unless surrounded by inverted commas."[48]

Yet theorists persist in trying to apply Kuhn in truncated form in order to provide a non-Popperian version of progress for the field they represent. Declares David Hollinger:

> While not "a science," the discipline of history is at least an academically organized branch of inquiry; it resembles Kuhn's scientific communities more obviously than do many of the cultural units that are said to partake of the same pattern of historical development. Increasingly, historians offer new interpretations, or suggestions for new research, as "paradigm-proposals" and historians have begun to regard basic changes in common outlook as "paradigm-shifts."[49]

In an especially ingenuous effort, political philosopher Sheldon Wolin argues that, although political theory is not a science, "political theories can best be understood as paradigms."[50] He proposes that political society itself be conceived as an operative paradigm which is reflected in its institutions and practices. Crises in societies serve, for Wolin, as Kuhnian anomalies, and if such crises cannot be accounted for by existing theory, they produce novel theories. Wolin is really employing paradigm as a metaphor but, although his usage is basically un-Kuhnian, its emphasis on factors *outside* the community of scholars provides an excellent starting place for analyzing the evolution of political ideas.

> Many of the great theories of the past arose in response to a crisis in the world, not in the community of theorists. . . . In each case political crisis was not the product of the theorist's hyper-active imagination but of the actual state of affairs. . . . In the natural course of its history a society undergoes changes which impose strains upon the existing paradigm. A society may find the paradigm being challenged directly, or it may experience difficulty in coping with the results of change. New social classes may have developed; or new racial or religious patterns may have appeared. In much the same way that a scientific community will seek to adjust its paradigm to account for "novelty," a political society will seek to adapt its system to the new developments brought by change.[51]

As this brief discussion implies, there are a number of inherent difficulties in transplanting the Kuhnian framework from the natural sciences to less congenial areas. For such a framework to be usable, genuine communities of scholars must be identified. Gary Gutting is on the mark when he argues:

> Kuhn's account of the natural sciences emphasizes the fact that their scientific status depends essentially on the emergence of a consensus among the community of practitioners as to the authority of a given paradigm. Since this consensus is remark-

ably absent in the social sciences, there should be no question of Kuhn's account supporting the scientific status of these disciplines. . . . The very existence of so many attempts by social scientists to use Kuhn's work to arrive at a basic understanding of what is going on in their disciplines shows that they have no consensus in Kuhn's sense.[52]

In addition, social scientists are hard put to identify dominant areas of research in which they engage in normal science by generating and resolving puzzles. Quite to the contrary, research areas in the social sciences typically bear little resemblance to one another, individual lines of research tend to be pursued in relative isolation, and idiosyncratic speculation remains the norm. Scholars remain embroiled in controversies over first principles, consensual operational concepts are rare, and data are often incommensurable. Little wonder that Kuhn denied that he had intended to guide social scientists in their quest for scientific status: "I claim no therapy to assist the transformation of a protoscience to a science. . . . If . . . some social scientists take from me the view that they can improve the status of their field by first legislating agreement on fundamentals and then turning to puzzle solving, they are badly misconstruing my point."[53]

GLOBAL POLITICS AND THE CUMULATION OF KNOWLEDGE

For scholars of global politics, as for other social scientists, Kuhn's work was highly seductive. The 1960s and early 1970s were decades of intellectual ferment in the field during which realist doctrine was under assault and halloes were raised in the name of science. Increasingly, global-politics scholars subscribed to James Rosenau's claim that "the same methods that unraveled the mysteries of atomic structure can reveal the dynamics of societal behavior."[54] Thus, it was widely believed to be critical that "scholars, who seek to solve the same puzzles, build on their colleagues' findings."[55]

The claim that global politics is or could become a science entails more than a methodological controversy. It is at once an article of faith and a matter of some desperation. Underlying it is a widespread belief that such acknowledgment is necessary in order to sustain professional and institutional well-being in the face of theoretical disarray and disciplinary adversity.

As we have maintained, the Kuhnian framework was a device that allowed global-politics scholars to see progress in their field while surrounded by theoretical incoherence.[56] It provided criteria for the establishment and maintenance of a discipline and a means to argue that, although global politics had not experienced linear development, the subject was still equivalent to a natural science. It promised that global politics could become cumulative as scholars came to recognize a common set of puzzles needing solution and a set of rules that both defined the steps to achieve such solutions and provided criteria for their acceptability. For global-politics scholars, the concept of paradigm came to be, in Richard Ashley's words

A vaguely envisioned utopian destination which, like Hilton's Shangri-La, is not marked on any map. Of the little that is known of this destination, its most alluring feature is its orderliness . . . the Rousseauesque orderliness that comes when consensually shared beliefs, values, and expectations motivate a society's members to serve common ends by common means. It is widely believed that in a paradigmatic society each member's labor constitutes a cumulative contribution to the society's product, for each member is certain of the form that the product has taken and is taking. The member is not nagged by doubts about the sturdiness of the prior contributions upon which he builds; after all, these have been subjected to reliable quality controls that screen out those contributions in which he should not be confident. He even knows the general form that his contribution must take, if it is to "fit."[57]

Global politics has not, however, agreed on a set of puzzles requiring solution, and it is at least as difficult as it is in economics or sociology to discern genuine paradigms.[58] Kuhn, as already noted, viewed such puzzles as determining acceptable research and as prerequisites for cumulation through normal science. In a word, they are necessary for drawing the boundaries of a discipline and imposing orthodoxy upon it. Consequently, "the primary obstacle to cumulation in global politics research," as P. Terrence Hopmann observes, "seems to be that we have lacked any broadly shared conceptualizations of the important puzzles or problems to be solved and any adequate theory to guide us in the solution of those problems."[59]

Surely part of the problem is the nature of the beast itself. The study of politics—that "master art" in Aristotle's view—is relatively unamenable to "hard" empiricism. Its concepts, as we shall emphasize later, lack objective referents and tend to be highly abstract, and their meaning does not exist independently of those who use them. As such they defy consensual definition. In a number of ways, especially in the core role of norms, political science probably requires a less demanding set of empirical criteria than physics for instance, does. To the degree it is genuinely architectonic the study of politics necessarily encompasses ideas, concepts, and perspectives from other disciplines—psychology, biology, economics, sociology, and anthropology, to name a few.

But, for whatever reason, far from having institutionalized a consensual set of puzzles, global-politics theorists continue to debate basic concepts and pursue idiosyncratic lines of research with scant reference to prior achievements or research being pursued by others. Idiosyncratic research is commonly justified by reference to the putative rewards of "middle range" theory in contrast to the impracticality of building "grand" theory. Paradoxically, normal science—ostensibly the clearest reflection of maturity in a discipline—is eschewed by global-politics scholars and their students because "someone who tests or builds on someone else's theory receives less credit than someone who can claim to have developed his own."[60] After all, few of our colleagues see much of a future in being relegated to what Kuhn calls "mopping up operations."[61] Far from cumulation, then, the field is consistently in the grip of fads that, like novas, light up the scholarly heavens for a brief time and then disappear. Along with Richard Ashley,

We are disturbed by the scarcity of firm theoretical propositions on which to build. We are concerned by the absence of cooperation: the disregard that others seem to have for our contributions, the vaporous qualities of others' contributions. . . . We are confused and perplexed by the number of competing blueprints and the fact that each is incomplete. We often conclude that, by the standards set by our vision, our progress has been dismal.[62]

Despite the absence of a well-defined set of puzzles, global-politics theorists are largely unwilling to concede that theirs may be less a discipline than a limited convergence of scholarly interests—that is, a field. Many believe that there has been some cumulation of knowledge, although they disagree on the extent to which this has occurred. This disagreement reflects their varying usage of Kuhn's concept of paradigm, their competing versions of how cumulation should be defined, their confusion between methodological and theoretical progress, and the enormous difficulty in evaluating progress itself. G. R. Boynton is probably correct, then, in declaring that "cumulativeness in any discipline is, at least in part, a frame of mind of the practitioners of the field."[63]

The growing suspicion that cumulation was, at best, occurring in painfully slow fashion and, at worst, occurring not at all increased the attractiveness of the Kuhnian framework. Arguably, some cumulation has occurred in a few sub-areas where replication does take place and as regards selected puzzles, for example, the conditions for successful deterrence and the "democratic peace." However, the efforts have not been sustained. Instead, as the editors of a volume dedicated to the question of cumulation in global politics declare, "the absence of substantial cumulation is particularly disappointing,"[64] and the same theme was echoed by other contributors in describing their own subfields. Among those who study war, for example, "there is a pronounced tendency to concep-tualize current research orientations without recognizing the way in which these relate to previous research."[65] Brian Job in his assessment of the lack of progress in understanding alliances reveals the disappointment many of us share when he concludes that "international relations research is highly sus-ceptible to fads and . . . the appeal of studying alliance was just another passing fancy in the late sixties and early seventies."[66] "In conclusion," declare the edi-tors, "all these articles indicate that cumulative development of international conflict research still leaves much to be desired."[67] Yet, even in the absence of cumulation, the Kuhnian framework allowed scholars to sustain their belief in the possibility of progress.

Disagreement over the degree of cumulation in global politics results in part from confusion about the meaning of Kuhn's "scientific revolution." Richard Smith Beal suggests, "Scientific revolutions are, by their very nature, noncumulative developments. They are radical breaks with past paradigms; they are possible only insofar as they destroy the very foundations upon which the previous paradigm was based."[68] Sheldon Wolin offers a similar interpretation, arguing that, for Kuhn, cumulation takes place only through the process of nor-mal science.[69] Yet while Kuhn's model emphasizes the discontinuous and nonin-cremental nature of progress, it should be stressed that the successful confrontation of anomalies, the solution of previously unsolved puzzles, and the generation of new sets of puzzles demanding solution imply step-level, if uneven, knowledge accumulation. The natural sciences, at least, have surely "progressed" in the sense of an ability to exercise greater control over nature. For Kuhn, progress in science, though not the product of "a rational process governed by timeless rules of procedure" is assured "by its social character—by the nature of science as a social system." Hence, although there is a significant element of ideological, professional, and political contention in the confrontation between rival paradigms even in the natural sciences, as Wolin suggests, it is apparent that what takes place is more than "an adversary proceeding."[70] Indeed, since Kuhn argues that normal science does not even try "to produce major novelties, conceptual or phenomenal,"[71] there is arguably no place in his scheme for theoretical advances to take place except during periods of revolution and paradigm transition.

In light of the divergent meanings given to Kuhn's work, it is hardly surprising that there also exist several not entirely compatible views among global-politics scholars as to what constitutes cumulation. Differing views are also encouraged because of the absence of cumulation in global politics in the conventional sense expressed by Boynton:

> The most obvious characteristic of cumulative thinking is that it is a temporal frame of reference which incorporates the past, present, and the future. From this perspective it is assumed that the present research could not have been done except for the work that preceded it. . . . [I]t also sees past and current research as leading to research in the future. . . . It is sometimes asserted that cumulativeness means that current research *builds* on previous research. But the more stark characterization, *that without which this work could not be done*, . . . may be a clearer way to present what is basic to the cumulative perspective.[72]

Ashley suggests two forms of cumulation, "which can occur at confidence levels much below those demanded in our paradigm image" and which he terms "expansive" and "selective" cumulation. The former produces "an expanding, commonly perceived catalogue of models, concepts, variables, indices, relationships, data, and techniques"; the latter he describes "as a process of evolving shared *expectations* about models, relationships, variables, techniques, etc., such that a group of scientists' selections among these increasingly will be informed by prior experiences, including empirical research." "Expansive cumulation," which Ashley sees as characterizing global politics, is closer to our notion of theoretical proliferation than cumulation in the standard sense and seems disturbingly antiparadigmatic in nature. This leads Ashley to conclude that "the field is not truly divisible into paradigms."[73]

Dina Zinnes dichotomizes cumulation rather differently than Ashley does, distinguishing between "additive" and "integrative" versions. By the former she means that "one study adds some information to the existing literature on the subject" and by the latter "that a study ties together and *explains a set* of research findings."[74] It is difficult to see precisely where this dichotomy leads us. At first reading, it might appear that what Zinnes characterizes as "additive cumulation" is similar to Kuhn's normal science. Yet the mere accretion of facts is not equivalent to genuine puzzle solving and should not be considered cumulation in a theoretical sense. "Integrative cumulation, of which Zinnes sees little in global politics, appears to be equivalent to theory itself, at least as conceived by Kenneth Waltz: "A theory is not the occurrences seen and the associations recorded, but is instead the explanation of them." Waltz argues that the "longest process of painful trial and error will not lead to the construction of a theory unless at some point a brilliant intuition flashes, a creative idea emerges."[75] He thus would presumably agree with

Zinnes's criticism of what she calls "the additive mentality" as an impediment to cumulation in global politics:

> The principal characteristic of the additive mentality is its belief that integrative cumulation will occur of its own accord through the simple process of adding more and more facts and relations to a body of knowledge. It is assumed that integrative cumulation is the consequence of a sufficient quantity of additive cumulation; the bits and pieces will in effect arrange themselves into meaningful packages, if only enough parts of the puzzle are supplied. . . . The problem is, as many philosophers of science have noted and a careful scrutiny of the physical sciences shows, we cannot achieve explanation through induction. At some point someone must make the leap and *propose* an explanation.[76]

The Zinnes/Waltz conception of theory construction is precisely what was largely absent from the behavioral revolution in global politics. With them, we suggest that theory consists of more than strategic simplification or the linking of tested hypotheses. Such formulaic definitions rob theory of any independent meaning. Theory for us consists of claims that point to what is important and what is unimportant for us to examine if we are to explain that which matters to us. Necessarily, then, all theory spotlights some factors while leaving much in gloom or darkness. Theories are, as Puchala felicitously describes them, "accomplishments in holistic image-building—feats of imagination." Theorists "are first and foremost conceptualizers, symbolizers, synthesizers and abstract organizers" who paint "for us bold-stroked, broad-brushed pictures of social reality" and tell us "that the real world is like their pictures."[77]

Ironically, the behavioralists rose to prominence on the claim that traditional global politics had failed to produce cumulative knowledge because theorists had been content with assertions that were in principle untestable and unfalsifiable.[78] "Until systematic observation, operationally derived evidence, and replicable analytical procedures were introduced," declared J. David Singer, "skillful rhetoric and academic gamesmanship often carried the day."[79] The absence of procedures for empirical verification and testable hypotheses had precluded the possibility of resolving conflicting claims or of establishing the reliable foundation of knowledge that behavioralists considered essential for cumulation to take place. Thus, charged behavioralists, traditional scholarship in global politics assured that no controversy could ever be resolved in final fashion. By contrast, systematic testing and replication of operationalized hypotheses utilizing quantitative data promised orderly, cumulative knowledge. To paraphrase Puchala, that which was unverifiable was regarded as untrue.[80]

For these reasons, the ascendance of behavioralism in political science was itself perceived by some scholars as a paradigm revolution. Wolin declared:

> In striking ways, the behavioural movement satisfies most of Kuhn's specifications for a successful paradigm. It has come to dominate the curricula of many political science departments throughout the country; a new generation of students is being taught the new methods of survey analysis, data processing, and scaling; and there are even signs that the past is being reinterpreted in order to demonstrate that the revolution is merely the culmination of "trends" in political science over the past few decades.[81]

Arend Lijphart saw behavioralism as playing this role in global politics and as having succeeded a traditional paradigm whose core was the concepts of state sovereignty and international anarchy.[82]

What such enthusiasts did not understand is that the behavioralists in global politics lacked the sort of dominant theory that might have allowed them to deduce hypotheses that would have served as Kuhnian puzzles. The absence of an overarching theoretical framework necessarily reduced the relevance, impact, and richness of the empirical effort.[83] The "revolution" was largely methodological, not theoretical, and so encouraged practitioners to set off without a common and coherent research agenda. Accordingly, they were to develop and use a variety of new tools to study problems that were not inherently linked. Induction was confused with theory construction, and probabilism—or, more accurately, possibilism or even "maybeism"—was confused with explanation. P. Terrence Hopmann, himself a persuasive proponent of increasing the scientific content of global-politics theory, posed the issue rather well:

> [T]he development of cumulative global politics theory is not likely to come through purely inductive data gathering or through beginning with descriptions unencumbered by explanatory or predictive theory. Unless the standard of logical interrelatedness is upheld, the solution of one problem or puzzle will tell one nothing about where to turn next. The testing and subsequent confirmation or disconfirmation of an ad hoc proposition tells us nothing about what should be investigated next and *hence provides no basis for cumulative research.* On the other hand, the deductive interdependence upon which scientific theories depend should suggest the logical nature of the interrelationships among puzzles. This means that the solution of one puzzle may suggest new puzzles to be solved. . . . It is . . . through the logical interrelationships of these puzzles provided by a fundamental set of axioms that research is likely to become cumulative, since the answer which one researcher obtains to his or her particular puzzle will have important implications for himself or herself as well as for other researchers in solving other puzzles and in suggesting new puzzles which require solution.[84]

Although packaged as a paradigm, behavioral scholarship is preoccupied by questions of methodology rather than theory,[85] and its practitioners have had little impact on the ways in which international phenomena are conceived. Significantly, behavioral scholars tacitly accepted many of the assumptions of those traditionalists whom they vigorously criticized. As John Vasquez has persuasively argued, much of the behavioral research of the 1950s and 1960s employed realist axioms. Using Hans Morgenthau as his exemplar, Vasquez described these as the centrality of nation-states as actors, the bifurcation of domestic and global politics, and the dominance of the struggle for power and peace.[86] Boynton makes much the same point as Vasquez: "Political scientists have been busy testing hypotheses for more than 20 years, and . . . there has been little theoretical development in coordination with research findings." This led Boynton to "question the utility of hypothesis testing, in and of itself, as a road to theory."[87]

Dissatisfied with the blanket critique of behavioral methods, Vasquez updated his findings about realism in the 1998 edition of *The Power of Power Politics.* Analyzing nonbehavioral analyses of global politics starting with Waltz's 1979 *Theory of International Politics* to the present, he stated, "One of the major conclusions of this study is that the neo-traditional theorizing and policy analysis ... has proven no more able to provide clear evidence in favor of the realist paradigm than did the earlier quantitative research that tested the paradigm."[88] While reinforcing doubts about realist analysis, this finding does *not* alter our basic conclusions about the impact of science on the study of global politics. Indeed, it is only the ebbing of the scientific tide that permitted serious theorizing about the subjective dimension of global politics that is so promising today.

A number of seriously debilitating consequences flowed from the fetish with data and quantitative methods. The most important of these was the propensity to confuse correlative findings with genuine theoretical explanation, despite the repeated caution that correlation is not causation. Indeed, scholars even tried to construct hypotheses *after* obtaining the sort of statistical results they sought. As Zinnes contends:

> The computer printout, with the addition of a few sentences indicating how the data were collected and a summary paragraph of interpretation, became a fast and easy publication in a world of publish or perish. We began to succumb more and more to the belief that explanations were found in amounts of variance explained or in levels of significance. Even our hypotheses now became products of statistical results—when bivariate correlations were significant, we then formulated the relevant hypotheses.[89]

However robust their statistical associations, scholars could be certain neither that critical causal factors were absent nor that their operational procedures did not encourage tautology. More importantly, in the absence of prior theorizing, it is possible to subject even the relatively few hypotheses that have not been falsified to a variety of explanations depending upon the theoretical perspective employed.

Certain sophisticated statistical procedures actually encouraged theoretical anarchy. The naming of factors in the course of factor analysis, for example, permitted researchers to impose their own theoretical predispositions upon data without having to spell out the assumptions with which they were working. The same data could be manipulated endlessly in a search for different outcomes.[90] In a deeper sense, this manipulation reflected a propensity to view data and data collection as ends in themselves and to confuse data with truth itself. "We began to believe in our data sets," admits Zinnes, "as if they contained some kind of objective truth, forgetting that someone had to make decisions on what was to be measured and how."[91] Statistical analysis can reveal patterns in data, but such analysis cannot in itself point to patterns that have theoretical significance unless observations are conditioned by a sophisticated theoretical scheme.

And what of the data themselves? Here we come upon a paradox: the more ingenious the data creation became, the farther away global-politics scholars moved from the behavior in which they were interested. Behaviorialism was intended as a focus upon people rather than institutions or abstractions.[92] Yet, neither what leaders say (content analysis) nor what the media report that actors do (events data) constitutes actual behavior. At best, they are the consequences or traces of decisions and behavior; at worst, they are pale reflections of behavior filtered through processes that homogenize the behavior itself.

Event data, for example, *necessarily* incorporate the perceptions and prejudices of a journalistic profession characterized by a set of interests and preferences. A researcher who uses such data is surrendering much of the task of making theoretical choices to the media whose reports he or she studies. To the degree that events data collection is limited to the media of a single country or set of countries owing to resource constraints (including language skills), the impact of cultural and social diversity is lost. Indeed, the impact of sociocultural and psychological factors in a heterogeneous world is attenuated by researchers' need to impose a single set of standards on a data set. Yet the meaning of specific terms (e.g., "war," "peace," "truth," and so forth) varies by culture and is probably culturally determined; superficially identical acts also have different meanings in different cultures (e.g., the function of "lying" or "corruption" in Eastern versus Western societies).

There have been other, though perhaps more remediable, consequences of the behavioralists' fetish for data collection and analysis. One consequence is the propensity to study phenomena for which data are already available or can be constructed with relative ease. As we have argued before, this problem contributes to an unwillingness to study actors other than sovereign nation-states and imposes an unwarranted conservatism and ethnocentricity on theoretical speculation.[93] Whatever the relative impact of actors other than states or governments on world politics, the objects of human loyalties appear to vary in both time and place. Thus, contemporary violence in the Middle East, Asia, and Africa often entails fierce tribal and ethnic collisions rather than conventional interstate politics.

All too often the availability of data and a desire to use a particular methodology have determined the theoretical framework. It is almost as though "data collectors have virtually attributed the characteristics of a paradigm to data collection and analysis techniques themselves."[94] Reversing the horse and cart in this manner not only runs the risk of generating trivial research but of trivializing the field as a whole.

CONCLUSION

Efforts to impose a Kuhnian framework upon global politics, although no more successful than they were in other social sciences, did for a time boost the morale of a generation of scholars who thought they had been provided a guide to disciplinary maturity. For some, notably realists and later neorealists, sustaining the putative paradigm became more important than "providing new insight."[95] Although it is increasingly apparent that behavioralism itself does not constitute a Kuhnian paradigm, the field has not surrendered its disciplinary vision, and the search continues for paradigm candidates. For some, that search entails efforts to fuse elements from diverse frameworks into a synthetic paradigm of "shreds and patches." Such efforts, however, entail a fundamental misunderstanding of the paradigm concept because, in Braillard's words, "although one can hope to integrate within a common model the various aspects of global politics channeled by the paradigms, that integration can be effected only by dissociating those aspects from the philosophical and ideological framework within which they appear."[96] Whether, as we suggest, global politics is inherently unamenable to a Kuhnian perspective or whether the solution is simply a matter of one day prescribing the right theoretical lenses, at the present time we do look, as Singer declares, "painfully like our friends the historians or perhaps even the couturiers. We are almost as trendy, and seem willing to scrap and return to our paradigms with the same alacrity as historical revisionists or fashion designers."[97]

CHAPTER 2

Values and Paradigm Change in Global Politics

In the preceding chapter, we suggested that one consequence of the behavioral revolution in global politics was to evoke unrealistic expectations of cumulative progress in understanding global politics. Yet, even in the absence of cumulation, acceptance of Thomas Kuhn's epistemology permitted optimism. The repeated invocation of Kuhn especially encouraged the belief—often unarticulated—that our understanding of the world around us was advancing almost dialectically. If progress had previously been imperceptible, this was no longer the case because science itself constituted something of a revolution in the field, which would as a consequence shortly enter a stage of "normal science." In other words, science itself was something of a paradigm.

Our intention is not to reopen the stale and unrewarding science-versus-traditionalist controversy,[1] nor do our views fall neatly on one or the other side of the positivist-postpositivist divide. We will argue that among the reasons for theoretical stagnation in the field are the materialist bias of Western science and the European tradition of global politics. This leads us to conclude that there are crucial differences between the evolution of theory in the social sciences (including global politics) and Kuhn's version of the natural sciences that render much of his analysis inapplicable to the former. If that is the case, perceptions of progress in global politics may be unwarranted and illusory. Indeed, it shall become apparent that ideas emerge and compete in global-politics scholarship in a most un-Kuhnian manner.

THE SOURCE AND ROLE OF VALUES

Kuhn himself highlighted the most significant difference between the natural and social sciences when he wrote of "the unparalleled insulation of mature scientific communities from the demands of the laity and of everyday life." "In this respect . . . the contrast between natural scientists and many social scientists proves instructive. The latter often tend, as the former almost never do, to defend their choice of a research problem . . . chiefly in terms of the social importance of achieving a solution."[2]

In other words, the work of social scientists is generally infused by a commitment to serve the needs of the society of which they are is a members, and such a commitment is routinely reinforced or weakened by government and community norms and incentives. For global-politics scholars, research is exciting because, in the words of Patrick McGowan and Howard Shapiro, they "find it dramatic, gratifying, or fearsome, as well as puzzling. . . ."[3] They summarize well the impossibility of freeing research from its normative roots—although they shy away from the full consequences of this—and make the critical point that even the quest to separate facts from values reflects a normative claim:

> If normative preferences are not explicitly stated, then they are always implicit in the research—for even the desire to do a "scientific" study is a normative decision. In addition, scholarship is a social process that in the end must justify its cost to society by the benefits it creates. Many social scientists feel today that social science is a tool in the struggle for a better world—for example, a world with a more equitable distribution of wealth and less violence. . . . For many, then, their systematic orientation to the study of foreign policy derives from their normative interests in policy evaluation and prescription.[4]

Indeed, one of the founders of modern realism, E. H. Carr, was fully aware of the normative underpinning of the scientific enterprise in global politics, including his own antipathy toward norm-made illusion. It was, after all, the dolorous consequences of a "twenty years' crisis" as much as any rationalist disagreement that led him to write as he did:

> The science of global politics has . . . come into being in response to a popular demand. It has been created to serve a purpose. . . . At first sight, this pattern may appear illogical. Our first business, it will be said, is to collect, classify, and analyse our facts and draw out inferences; and we shall then be ready to investigate the purpose to which our facts and our deductions can be put. The processes of the human mind do not, however, appear to develop in this logical order. . . . Purpose, which should logically follow analysis, is required to give it both its initial impulse and its direction.[5]

The facts that scholars amass and the phenomena that preoccupy them are selections derived initially from a set of specific value-based concerns. Those concerns lead them to focus attention at selected facts and phenomena at the expense of others. Thus, their version of reality necessarily spotlights some aspects of the world while keeping others in shadow. Hence, until recent decades, history was the story of kings and politics the story of men involved in "public" affairs. If the theorist chooses to take cognizance at a future date of what previously has been ignored, that choice reflects a shift in normative concerns rather than a paradigm change in the Kuhnian sense.[6] Carr sees this to some extent as a condition of the physical sciences as well, but notes correctly how much more difficult it is to isolate facts from values in the social sciences:

The purpose of research in global politics is not, as some claim of the physical sciences, irrelevant to the investigation and separable from it: it is itself one of the facts. In principle, a distinction may doubtless be drawn between the role of the investigator who establishes the facts and the role of the practitioner who considers the right course of action. In practice, one role shades imperceptibly into the other. Purpose and analysis become part and parcel of a single process.[7]

For the most part, both natural and social scientists are aware of the intrusion of their values into the research process and make efforts to control their impact. But it is far more difficult for social scientists to do so successfully because of the pervasive influence of society upon them and their perceptions. The relative absence of objective concepts confounds the task even more, and policy preferences are routinely clothed in the garb of abstraction. Although natural scientists hope their theoretical insights may *in the end* have an impact upon society, social scientists hope for such an impact, but as soon as possible. There are few equivalents to *Foreign Policy* or *Foreign Affairs* in the natural sciences, though a few like *Scientific American* do advocate policy.

The synthesis of purpose and analysis is evident in R. J. Rummel's autobiographical reflection, which could probably be echoed by many in our profession. "My lifelong superordinate goal," Rummel declares, "has been to eliminate war and social violence; only by understanding this goal's genesis and enveloping cognitive structure can DON's [Dimensionality of Nations project] research and my current re-orientation be grasped. For to me science or quantitative research are not the aims, but tools to be pragmatically applied to doing something about war."[8] How different than this was the normative commitment of German historian Heinrich von Treitschke, who equated war with the "grandeur of history." And how well do these contrasting admissions reveal the starkly different normative climates of the societies in which they were written! It is not uncommon for pundits in impoverished or subjugated societies to devalue peace in the name of goals such as prosperity and independence and to promulgate theories that would achieve these ends through violence. At root, these preferences can be debated, but no final proof can be offered as to the inherent superiority of one set of values over the other. Given such divergences in purpose and commitment, it is hardly surprising that cumulation has not occurred in global politics.

Jacob Bronowski's arguments against the "naturalistic fallacy" in the natural sciences are, if anything, even more germane to the social sciences. Bronowski suggests that normative consequences inhere in scientific discovery for at least three reasons. The first is that discovery reveals that certain forms of conduct are "obviously ridiculous" and that one ought to tailor one's own actions so as not to be ridiculous. The second is that science informs us of our capabilities as human beings and "that it is right that we should practice those gifts." Finally, and most importantly for Bronowski, scientists must behave in certain ways in order to learn what is true, which is the object of their calling: "What is the good of talking about what is, when in fact you are told how to behave in order to discover what is true. "Ought" is dictated by "is" in the actual inquiry for knowledge. Knowledge cannot be gained unless you behave in certain ways."[9]

It is hardly surprising, then, that theoretical debates among political scientists reflect different normative commitments that are indirectly revealed in competing claims over which actors should be studied, which level of analysis[10] is

most appropriate, which variables are critical, and which issues are most pressing. Thus, assertion of structural primacy over agency is hardly acceptable to
those dissatisfied with the status quo any more than advocating limiting the franchise to propertied classes in the name of stability is acceptable to "diggers" or
"levelers."

What is striking about these debates, and what distinguishes them from
debates in the natural sciences, is that essentially the same arguments and
emphases tend to recur through time despite superficial changes in concepts
and language. And, as we shall suggest, such debates recur because they revolve
around enduring normative themes.[11] The key assertions and themes of realism
and idealism, for example, have been present in intellectual discourse about
global politics at least since Thucydides (see chapter 4). In this sense, realism
and idealism (or liberalism) are *Gestalten* with more or less clear ontologies
rather than specified paradigms or theories as defined by scientists. As such, they
are inevitably value laden, and their normative implications are often better
refined and structured than their predictions or explanations.

Thucydides' *Melian Dialogue* and Thrasymachus's argument with Socrates
in Plato's *Republic* are enduring reflections of the antinomy between power and
justice. Sophocles' *Antigone* confronts this tension directly. Centuries of
European political theorists served the roles of realists and idealists. Machiavelli
and those later known as Machiavellians consciously propounded their versions
of realism in contrast to the so-called idealists of their time.[12] In this country, the
same antinomy was evident in the debates between Alexander Hamilton and
Thomas Jefferson regarding whether the young United States should aid revolutionary France in 1793, with the former dismissing gratitude and invoking
power in opposition to American intervention and the latter taking the
"utopian" position. The old realist-idealist debate is currently manifested in
debates among structural realists and liberal institutionalists, on the one hand,
against unrepentant neofunctionalists, postmodernists, and constructivists on
the other. (However liberal or reformist, no theorist wishes to be labeled
"utopian.")

Such debates are no less value laden than their precursors. Leading schools
of thought in global politics are as much a part of the *Zeitgeist* of their age as are
dominant theories of art and literature; all are part of the *ductus* of a culture.[13]
Indeed, the continuing devotion to science in global politics is a phenomenon that
will always be associated with late-twentieth-century America and the numerous
symbols of its "modernity"—pragmatism, technology, nonrepresentational art,
functional architecture, and so forth. All reflect a similar ethos, fully as much as
did *The Trojan Women* of Euripides and Thucydides, *History*.

Changing fashions in art and literature, changing social values, and the
wrenching nature of such shifts are commonly reflected in fierce, though often
arcane, conflicts over aesthetics and purpose.[14] The triumph of baroque forms,
for instance, gave testimony to a growing belief in human perfectibility and
rationality, whereas the ascendance of nonrepresentational art was but one of
many clues that society had come to sense the growing impact of the unconscious
and the nonrational on human behavior. More obviously, we are repeatedly
reminded of the unbreakable link between art and political ideology—both the
reflections of more fundamental social values—in the legacies of great artists such

as Pablo Picasso and Francisco Goya and of authors like Rudyard Kipling (imperialism), Maxim Gorky (socialist realism), and many others. The values reflected in their work reveal the social context in which they were formed and allow us to glimpse the collective values of their time and place. The intimate relationship between politics, and art and music has been appreciated and commented upon by successive generations of scholars; Plato, Hegel, Kant, and Marx are but a few of those who have been preoccupied by this relationship. Ultimately, art, like political theory, reflects choices among competing value systems. Thus, Pierre Bourdieu's analysis of the consumers of culture might be applied equally well to consumers of political ideas: "The science of taste and cultural consumption begins with a transgression that is in no way aesthetic: it has to abolish the sacred frontier which makes legitimate culture a separate universe, in order to discover the intelligible relations which unite apparently incommensurable 'choices,' such as preference in music and food, painting and sport, literature and hairstyle."[15]

But what are the source and nature of the values to which we have been alluding?[16] Values are abstract aspirations for improving the human condition that may be pursued only indirectly through the acquisition of scarce objects that serve as stakes in political contests. In this way, stakes are the building blocks of what political scientists, especially realists and neorealists, call "interests." When perceived in this way, interests are less ends in themselves (as realists and neorealists claim), than they are reflections of the values that underlie them. In this sense, then, politics may be regarded as an unending quest for value satisfaction and as a process in which values are allocated and reallocated. Abstract values are sought as consummatory ends with intrinsic worth, while the stakes that represent them are merely instrumental in terms of value satisfaction. The former are universal or nearly so, while the latter are subject to significant sociocultural variation.[17]

The definition of individual or group interests, derived from values, is the core of self-identity, and bundles of different interests necessarily produce multiple identities. Context, of which the key element at issue is defined in terms of "what is at stake," largely determines the individual identity that is triggered and actuated at any moment and, therefore, the direction and intensity of individual loyalty. On some occasions, multiple identities are triggered by a single issue, thereby producing loyalty contests that may lead to cognitive inconsistency or inertia. For the most part, however, multiple identities coexist harmoniously.

Although values are largely universal, value hierarchies periodically change in response to contextual and situational factors that heighten perceptions of deprivation of some values and reduce anxieties about others. In this way interests, far from being static, continually evolve. Such shifts may be slow and imperceptible, resulting from evolutionary or secular environmental changes (e.g., technological development and ecological change), or they may be sharp and clear as a consequence of cataclysmic events (for example, wars, plagues, and famines).[18] Although individual value hierarchies vary, they can largely be deduced from socially specific collective norms. Thus, individual Americans, however different their backgrounds and experiences, do as a rule value material well-being more than do Burmese or Tibetans. The collectivity determines the limits of what is culturally and socially acceptable and legitimizes certain values at the expense of others.

Value hierarchies represent *collective* perceptions of value deprivation (though there may be variation among individuals) and reflect *collective* experiences and neuroses. Their collective nature is institutionalized and reinforced by mechanisms of socialization, including family, education, and role. Political leaders must share and articulate key values and, in turn, seek to anchor them ever more firmly in order to foster cohesion and consensus. The scope and domain of such hierarchies are determined by additional factors such as the extent to which environmental changes or cataclysmic events are shared symmetrically and the degree to which peoples are interdependent or isolated. Thus, the Black Death, which afflicted all of Europe, had a profound impact on the value hierarchy of all who witnessed it. Ignorant of the causes of the plague, Christian Europe regarded it as the wrath of God:

> The general acceptance of this view created an expanded sense of guilt, for if the plague were punishment there had to be terrible sin to have occasioned it. What sins were on the 14th century conscience? Primarily greed, the sin of avarice, followed by usury, worldliness, adultery, blasphemy, falsehood, luxury, irreligion. . . . The result was an underground lake of guilt in the soul that the plague now tapped.[19]

And the disappearance of the plague "did much perhaps to revive a spirit of optimism in European affairs."[20]

Value and identity hierarchies find expression in the normative temper of a society and an era, which in turn conditions intellectual direction and philosophic predisposition.[21] Theories of human nature, for instance, which are commonly the bases of elaborate theoretical edifices, are among the most obvious manifestations of changing value hierarchies and consequent normative predispositions. The "timeless" commentaries on human nature by the early Christian scholars or by the likes of Rousseau, Locke, and Hobbes are not timeless at all; they are concrete articulations of the value hierarchies of particular eras and places. Thus, Hans Morgenthau's bleak realist view of human nature flowed from the atrocities of World War II: "There is no escape from the evil of power, regardless of what one does. Whenever we act with reference to our fellow men, we must sin, and we must still sin when we refuse to act; for the refusal to be involved in the evil of action carries with it the breach of the obligation to do one's duty."[22]

Whatever the prospects, then, for applying scientific methods to studying political phenomena, political science will continue to develop more like one of the arts than one of the sciences unless or until political scientists can isolate themselves from the milieu whose problems they seek to address. This, we believe, is an impossible task and therefore not one even worth attempting.

THE NORMATIVE BASIS OF THEORY

Although a feedback loop of sorts is involved, political dialogue is most accurately seen as a *reflection*, rather than a *cause*, of the normative temper of an era. And it is the shift in that temper, rather than the appearance of Kuhnian anomalies, that stimulates what are characterized as paradigm shifts in global-politics theory. Such shifts occur under conditions of rapid change and stressful events that generate an atmosphere of unpredictability and instability, a sense that somehow new and baleful forces are at work that will alter existing conditions in ways as yet not fully apprehended. In these circumstances, prior patterns of behavior and standard procedures either no longer seem able to perform the tasks for which they were established or appear unsuited for new tasks that are identified. What James Rosenau has felicitously termed the "habit pool . . . that is fed and sustained by the diverse wellsprings of human experience"[23] is dramatically changed during such times.

Although the causal sequence remains unclear, such periods seem to be associated with the genesis of sharply different individual and collective identities and norms that constitute a very different subjective environment than in the time preceding them. This environment may be characterized by new or changed religious, scientific, social, or ideological concepts. The emergence of Christianity and Islam and the collective self-identity of groups of people as Christians and Muslims accompanied sharply etched normative climates that altered the political bases of the worlds in which they occurred. The scientific ideas of Hippocrates, Galileo, Darwin and Einstein, among others, forced the reconsideration of humanity's place in the cosmos and fostered the emergence of powerful, normatively infused political doctrines and movements.

Changes in the subjective environment may be triggered by and may in turn trigger qualitative technological and economic shifts and major unanticipated events, especially wars and environmental disasters. Often the subjective and objective worlds change simultaneously, though this is not necessarily the case. Fifth-century Greece was one such period. This era witnessed the development of tragedy as a literary form by the Athenian poets, the philosophic relativism of the Sophists, the introduction of empirical diagnosis by Hippocrates of Cos, the development of mining at Mount Laurion (which provided precious metals for a monied economy), the earthquake and helot revolt in Sparta (464 B.C.), the plague in Athens (430 B.C.), and the Peloponnesian War. These events provided the framework for Thucydides' view of the world. The late fifteenth through early seventeenth centuries in Europe was another tumultuous period that witnessed a renewal of the plague; the rise of Protestantism; the ideas of Brahe, Galileo, and Kepler regarding the physical universe; the spread of movable type; the rifling of guns and the boring of cannon; and, finally, the Thirty Years' War—all combined to constitute a sharp break with the past and to usher in fundamental revisions of the normative order. In recent years, the revolution in microelectronics, with its implications for overcoming distance and devaluing territory, has had a similar effect. Changes of such magnitude point to new issues in need of resolution, new opportunities to be exploited, or both.

More recently, two types of changes have taken place in the subjective dimension of global politics. On the one hand, the decline of Marxism-Leninism was followed by the proliferation of free-market and modernist cultural self-conceptions, which have accompanied and reinforced globalization while undermining territorially limited conceptions of state citizenship.[24] On the other hand, there has been a veritable explosion of ethnic, religious, tribal, and even "civilizational" self-identities—some historical and some new—that also compete with citizenship identities and threaten existing sovereign territorial arrangements. The consequences have been most dramatic in the developing world, where statist identities imposed by colonialists have yielded to prestatist identities, resulting in conflicts that threaten state survival. These events are examples of what Rosenau calls "the breakdown of traditional norms and the authority crises into which states have entered."[25]

> It is in the deterioration of habit that authority crises originate: the more a membership moves away from automatic acceptance and toward outright rejection, the more is an authority relationship subjected to strain. Indeed, the beginnings of a crisis are signaled by a breakdown in the compliance habits of the members or the units of a collectivity. As the habits wane, the crisis deepens, until either the habits are restored through effective bargaining or they collapse altogether *and are redirected toward other collectivities.*[26]

Thus, ours is an "era marked by shifting boundaries, emergent authorities, weakened states, and proliferating nongovernmental organizations (NGOs) at local, provincial, national, transnational, international, and global levels of community."[27] All of these changes are facilitated by the microelectronic revolution that has overcome the limitations of time and distance.

Typically, major authority crises are accompanied by revisions in identity hierarchies and in the nature of political communities. As we shall see, contemporary authority crises are also related to the declining importance of "citizen" as an identity and the erosion of the territorial state as the dominant form of political organization. In earlier centuries, the authority crisis accompanying the European Reformation and religious wars was associated with the emergence and maturation of the territorial dynastic state, legitimated by "the notion of personal sovereignty to buttress traditional divine right doctrine."[28] New norms produced new identities: "Against king and particularistic privilege," revolutionary leaders invoked "the 'rights of man and the citizen,' 'justice,' 'liberty, equality, fraternity,' and citizenship for the 'people' and 'nation.'"[29] "Citizen" succeeded "subject" as a core identity with the wedding of nation and state during the French Revolution and in the nineteenth century, the growing activism of the European bourgeoisie and the extension of the suffrage—the emergence of what Hall calls "national-sovereign identity."[30]

This process is hardly limited to Europe, however. An authority crisis within Arabian tribal society was associated with the emergence of Islam in the seventh century. Islam and Islamic identities constituted a new and revolutionary normative order associated with a theocratic empire that at its peak stretched from Spain to the Oxus River of central Asia. In addition, the collision between tribal and religious identities that began with the Shi'a-Sunni split and the establishment of the Umayyads in Damascus continues in the present.[31]

Authority crises reflect revisions in the normative order. Intervening between changing identities and political communities on the one hand, and revision of the normative order on the other, are perceptions of linkages among stakes at issue in the global arena and the hierarchy of issues on the global agenda.[32] Fears of value deprivation, identification of new opportunities for value satisfaction, or both occur as old stakes disappear and new ones emerge. Although these processes are continuous, they are especially intense during periods of potential or actual shifts in the global status hierarchy, when the enfeeblement of high-status actors encourages challenges to an existing distribution of stakes and the energizing of low-status actors spurs their ambition.[33] For instance, the dramatic increase in German industrial and military strength and the significant advances in medical science during the second half of the nineteenth century, coupled with the relative decline of Great Britain and France, made available as stakes territories in Africa that previously had been seen as preempted or qualitatively inaccessible. Similarly, the decline of traditional trade unions in the West and the growing obsolescence of traditional industries at a time of recession and high unemployment in the 1980s transformed into stakes many social and economic benefits and entitlements that until then had been regarded as sacrosanct.

As new stakes become available for contention and old ones are removed from contention, new issues emerge, old ones are redefined, and the salience of issues on the global agenda may be revised dramatically.[34] Changes in issue salience redirect attention toward the values that underlie the newly important issues and away from values that are associated with declining issues. Accordingly, the value of prosperity, which in the United States had dominated the value hierarchy during the Great Depression, became a secondary concern with the outbreak of World War II and its aftermath, during which time physical security and freedom became principal preoccupations. As memories of the war receded in the 1960s and 1970s and the relative salience of key issues continued to change, values such as peace, health, and human dignity assumed greater importance.

KEY NORMATIVE DIMENSIONS

Changes in the global agenda of issues and in the value hierarchy underlying that agenda invariably produce new normative emphases, which are reflected in what we have called the normative temper of an era. Normative shifts occur along several dimensions, often at the same time. Among the most important of these are mutability/immutability, optimism/pessimism, competitiveness/community, and elitism/nonelitism.

Mutability/immutability is the degree to which it is believed that human affairs and the conditions that shape them can or will be purposefully modified. In traditional cultures the status quo in human affairs is accepted as inevitable and unchanging, and the conditions in which people find themselves are viewed as beyond control or manipulation. Arguments that attribute behavior to the supernatural, to human nature, or sometimes, to structural conditions commonly assume immutability. By contrast, modern Western science assumes almost unlimited mutability.

The normative implication of a belief in immutability is that efforts to change the human condition are at best a waste of time and at worst dangerous and illusory. In any event, such efforts ought not to be made. Political realism in its several versions tends to view political conditions as relatively immutable, whether owing to "human nature" (Morgenthau), "original sin" (Niebuhr), "death instinct" (Freud), or "system anarchy" (Waltz). Following Hegel, such theorists believe that the dilemmas of politics "cannot be rejuvenated, but only known."[35] Although realists and neorealists accept that alterations in the distribution of power continuously occur, they see the struggle for power as a permanent feature of the international landscape. It is power theorists to whom Robert Gilpin is referring when he writes of "the Western bias in the study of international relations" as an obstacle to analysis of political change.[36] Nowhere is this emphasis on immutability more succinctly expressed than in Hans Morgenthau's observation:

> Human nature, in which the laws of politics have their roots, has not changed since the classical philosophies of China, India, and Greece endeavored to discover these laws. Hence novelty is not necessarily a virtue in political theory, nor is old age a defect.[37]

For Waltz, global structure rather than human nature is the source of immutability. Although he admits the possibility that the global system could be transformed from anarchy to hierarchy, such transformation is highly improbable because states mimic one another's behavior, most importantly in acting to balance one another's power.[38] Thus, John Ruggie concludes that "Waltz's theory of 'society' contains only a reproductive logic, but no transformational logic," and "continuity . . . is a product of premise even before it is hypothesized as an outcome."[39] Realists and neorealists, argues Robert Cox, "have tended to adopt the fixed ahistorical view of the framework for action characteristic of problem-solving theory, rather than standing back from this framework, . . . and treating it as historically conditioned and thus susceptible to change."[40]

This emphasis leads political realists to criticize those who seek to reform prevailing conditions, claiming that such individuals are "divorced from the facts . . . and informed by prejudice and wishful thinking," and that the laws of politics, rooted as they are in human nature, are "impervious to our preferences."[41] In the United States and Europe, at least, such an emphasis on immutability found ready acceptance after World War II with the apparent failure of bold experiments like the League of Nations. Those who sought to make fundamental changes were dismissed as idealists. Even Marxism-Leninism, with its putative belief in the march of history and the uplifting of humanity, seemed to have lost its vigor in Stalin's conservative empire. Since experimentation entailed an element of peril, prudence became the prescriptive hallmark of political realism. The prudent leader would understand the immutability of historical laws and eschew bold efforts to transform humankind or the global system.

In contrast to realists, those whom realists dismiss as idealists blame "the failure of the social order to measure up to the rational standards on lack of knowledge and understanding, obsolescent social institutions or the depravity of certain isolated individuals or groups."[42] For them, social engineering is both possible and morally compelling. Constructivists, for example, allow for changing meanings and identities that can entail fundamental transformations of global politics and for cultural changes that produce such altered meanings and identities. Over time, interaction can produce changed interests and identities.[43] For their part, liberals allow for shifting state preferences—"the fundamental social purposes underlying the strategic calculations of governments"[44]—emerging from experience with international cooperation and shifting domestic interests, norms, and ideas.

Unlike the realist/neorealist world in which human nature, structure, or both produce negative feedback that keeps on reproducing the same old world, liberal theory allows for nonlinear change owing to "a disproportion between the magnitude of the cause and the results, which will depend on the system as a whole."[45] Moravcsik continues:

> *Liberal theory offers a plausible explanation for historical change in the international system.* The static quality of both realist and institutionalist theory—their lack of an explanation for fundamental long-term change in the nature of international politics—is a recognized weakness. In particular, global economic development over the past five hundred years has been closely related to greater per capita wealth, democratization, education systems that reinforce new collective identities, and greater incentives for transborder economic transactions.[46]

Specifically, as more and more key actors share similar domestic values and institutions, their behavior, according to liberals, will converge.[47] In this way, domestic change can produce trust and cooperative relations that succeed conflict and vice versa. This, according to liberals, explains the end of the Cold War. "[T]he demise of Soviet-style communism," declares Wade Huntley, "is clearly consistent with the long-term patterns of change in international politics given in Kant's approach. In particular, against assessments of the Cold War put in strictly strategic terms, Kantian analysis points to the decisive advantages provided to the Western states by their liberal governments and societies. Communism's collapse must be sought in "the 'legitimation crisis' . . . at the core of its economic decline."[48]

Optimism/pessimism constitutes a second critical normative dimension. Unlike mutability/immutability, which describes the degree to which it is believed that change can be engineered by human intervention, optimism/pessimism refers to the direction in which change is headed and whether such change is the consequence of purposeful modification or not. More simply, it describes the answer given to the question: "Are conditions likely to improve or not?" Nevertheless, as the previous discussion of realism suggests, those who see conditions as relatively immutable are also likely to view change in a distinctly pessimistic light. After all, if the forces of change cannot be governed and directed, change itself is likely to be fickle, unpredictable and, ultimately, dangerous. There are, of course, significant exceptions to this intellectual propensity. Classical Marxists, for example, view history itself as an engine of progress governed by laws of economic development that will in time improve the human condition. And, as Waltz points out, even those who start from an assumption that human nature is relatively immutable can be divided into optimists and pessimists.[49] There are obviously degrees of immutability that allow for varying assessments of the potential for change.

Overall, however, optimism is at least partly a function of belief in mutability. Natural and behavioral scientists and social reformers share an acceptance of the possibility that the cumulation of knowledge and the application of that knowledge can improve conditions and behavior. (This claim emerges from the passages cited earlier from Bronowski.) The implication of such optimism is that it is the obligation of those with knowledge and insight to apply these for the benefit of humanity.[50] In the context of political life, liberalism tends to be associated with optimism and conservatism with pessimism.[51] Since degrees of optimism or pessimism would appear to be associated with discernible psychological profiles, it may be possible to predict the future political and scholarly orientations of individuals by suitable tests administered during their formative years.

Jeremy Bentham, who sought to deduce a universal ethic, typifies the synthesis of optimism and mutability through the application of reason. Buoyed by the apparently limitless prospects opened by the industrial revolution, Bentham decreed that, since humans sought pleasure, "the greatest happiness of the greatest number" was the only possible guideline for collectivities. Such a guideline could be followed only by cooperation, and its content could be determined only by informed public opinion. Hence, Bentham and James Mill lauded the egalitarian effects that they saw as flowing from education, public knowledge, and by inference, political democracy.[52] And it was this dedication to the cause of democracy that, perhaps more than any other factor, characterized nineteenth- and early-twentieth-century idealism. Since individuals sought their own happiness and since peace was instrumental to achieving this, only democracies could assure international peace, as only this form of government could accurately reflect popular interests and sentiments.[53]

It is no coincidence that intellectual optimism and scientific advances are associated with eras and places where the norms of the culture were characterized by waves of optimism—Renaissance Italy, late-eighteenth-century France, Edwardian England, and pre-Depression America. Whereas pessimism encourages political conservatism and inertia, waves of optimism inspire great efforts to give history a nudge. Political revolutions, for example, generally occur in the context of growing optimism, or at least a belief that the improvement of conditions is probable once the weight of existing institutions is swept away. As historian George Soule observed:

> When the people are in their most desperate and miserable condition, they are often least inclined to revolt, for then they are hopeless. . . . Only after their position is somewhat improved and they have sensed the possibility of change, do they revolt effectively against oppression and injustice. What touches off insurrection is hope, not lack of it, rising confidence, not bleak suffering."[54]

Wordsworth's ecstatic description of his feelings at the time of the French Revolution captures perfectly the optimism of that era:

> Bliss was it in that dawn to be alive
> But to be young was very heaven! (*The Prelude*)

Not surprisingly, advances in natural science suggest to laymen that optimism is not misplaced.[55]

In the context of global-politics theory, the postwar ascendance of political realism in part reflected a rejection of the prevailing optimism of the 1920s and early 1930s. Yet realism is not a doctrine of unrelieved gloom. Realists do see the possibility of ameliorating the effects of international conflict by the judicious management of power, especially its balancing. Indeed, some neorealists (or structural realists), such as Waltz, can be regarded as cautiously optimistic.[56] As a whole, advocates of a scientific approach to the discipline in the 1960s and

1970s, while retaining many critical assumptions of realism, reflected an increasing optimism about the prospects for overcoming the most dangerous problems of global politics insofar as the methods of the natural sciences were to be applied to an understanding of them.[57] However, growing fears about environmental, political, and economic trends in the early 1970s produced a renewal of pessimism that was perhaps most vividly reflected in Robert Heilbroner's *An Inquiry into the Human Prospect:*

> At this final stage of our inquiry, with the full spectacle of the human prospect before us, the spirit quails and the will falters. We find ourselves pressed to the very limit of our personal capacities, not alone in summoning up the courage to look squarely at the dimensions of the impending predicament, but in finding words that can offer some plausible relief in a situation so bleak. There is now nowhere to turn other than to those private beliefs and disbeliefs that guide each of us through life.[58]

And although perhaps not quite so extreme, the pessimism of the 1970s was a significant aspect of the revolt against realism, a new emphasis on "spaceship Earth," and the reemergence of doubts regarding the ultimate prospects for a science of global politics. Not surprisingly, this revolt accelerated after the end of the Cold War.

A third normative variable that is central to global-politics theory is that of *competitiveness/community,* that is, the degree to which welfare and deprivation are perceived in relative or absolute terms. "[P]ower," declares Waltz, "has to be defined in terms of the distribution of capabilities."[59] Are evaluations of status and value satisfaction made in comparison to others, or are they made in terms of an absolute level that changes over time? The former emphasizes competition for scarce resources and the latter, linked fates and interdependence. When evaluation is made in relative terms, it implies that greater value satisfaction can be achieved only at the expense of others; changes in the absolute level of well-being matter less than the distribution of costs and benefits among competitors.[60] Outcomes are viewed in zero-sum, rather than positive- or negative-sum terms.

Emphasis on competition intensifies as perceptions of scarcity grow. This connection is vividly articulated in Sheldon Wolin's description of Renaissance political life:

> Minds that knew no repose, ambitions that were boundless, an insatiable pride, a restless species of political man which, when not bedeviled by ambition, was stirred by sheer boredom—all of these considerations conspired to shrink political space, to create a dense and overcrowded world. A terrain with few areas open for unrestricted movement left one course for the politically ambitious: to dislodge those already occupying specific areas.[61]

One need not, however, necessarily assume such a convenient relationship between the two dimensions. Highly competitive doctrines such as Adam Smith's version of capitalism or late-nineteenth-century social Darwinism became popular in exuberantly expansionist eras. By contrast, theories of interdependence and "limits to growth," which are at least in part based on perceptions of scarcity, emphasize the shared condition of humankind and the absolute nature of value enhancement and deprivation. Nor does there seem to be any *necessary* connection between competitiveness/community and optimism/pessimism, despite the common assertion that pessimism encourages competitive evaluations.

Political realism, with its emphasis on national interest, falls on the competitive end of the spectrum, and it is hardly surprising that this tradition took root in Europe after the Middle Ages, when numerous small states found themselves cheek to jowl. Morgenthau's definition of global politics "as a continuing effort to maintain and to increase the power of one's own nation and to keep in check or reduce the power of other nations"[62] highlights the realist emphasis on the relative nature of status and security in the global system. Although there is no implication that a scarcity of political goods conditions the intensity of competition, it is the assumption of an absence of central power and trust that is fundamental to this analysis. In other words, scarce political space creates pressure toward zero-sum relationships. Efforts to equate the national interest with a global interest through international law and organization are dismissed as "legalistic-moralistic,"[63] "too wildly improbable"[64] or, more generally, idealistic. Efforts to achieve justice must, in the realist vision, give way to the more basic search for security that can limit the prospect of relative loss with scant possibility for universal gain.[65] "Global politics is," declared Kenneth Thompson, "the study of rivalry among nations and the conditions and institutions which ameliorate or exacerbate these relationships."[66] The competitive world that political realists see is not anarchic, however, though it has the potential to become so. Classical realists from Thucydides on have seen their task as preventing such potential anarchy from becoming reality. The prevention of unrestrained violence in the international system and the management of the sources of such violence are key values that loom behind realist claims of the inevitability of interstate conflict.

For neorealists, anarchy is the most important source of conflict in global politics. As a result of anarchy, competition is, for Waltz, "pervasive,"[67] and competition, in turn, induces rational competitors to emulate the most successful among them. Anarchy in realist/neorealist thinking permits only one interpretation because it is a condition in which betrayal is always possible and trust, therefore, never complete.

By contrast, those whom realists label idealists have argued that informed reason reveals a harmony of interests that can be sustained only by cooperation. Peace, for instance, constitutes a public good that cannot survive intense competition and parochial rivalries. "I believe," declared John Stuart Mill, "that the good of no country can be obtained by any means but such as tend to that of all countries, nor ought to be sought otherwise, even if obtainable."[68] Since democracies share the same values, there is no reason for conflict among them, and it is these values—nurtured and disseminated by education and a free press—that, to many so-called idealists, provide the real bases for a world community even in the presence of sovereign states.

In practice, emphasizing competitive elements in global politics necessitates undervaluing prospects for international, supranational, or transnational organization, whether formal or informal. Actors that are more powerful, wealthier, or more skillful should, it is implied, see to their own well-being and security before concerning themselves with some "abstract" global good unless it can somehow be shown that the two are identical.[69] The global good may be secured but only in the manner of Smith's "invisible hand" if actors follow the dictates of national interest.

By contrast, idealists perceive individual and collective good as identical and, in any event, believe that the former must give way to the latter if they are somehow incompatible. It is not the interests of states—fictitious corporations—that hold their attention, but rather the shared interests of the individuals who constitute them. "If it were not for extraneous interference, and a remediable measure of ignorance and misunderstanding," wrote Arnold Wolfers of this perspective, "there would be harmony, peace, and a complete absence of concern for national power."[70]

The devaluation of the norm of equality by those who emphasize competition tends as well to make them relatively *elitist* in their perceptions of global politics. This normative dimension entails perceptions of who ought to be involved in the making of decisions and the management of issues. Elitists emphasize that the possession of some attribute—for example, wealth, power, or skill—renders some individuals or groups legitimate leaders (and others, followers).

Among global-politics theorists, elitism takes the form of an assertion that certain actors in the global system are and ought to be responsible for significant outcomes that affect the system as a whole. An elitist emphasis can be manifested at different levels of analysis. At the system level, for instance, it may assume the form of claims that the discipline should limit its focus to "sovereign" entities and exclude nongovernmental and transnational interactions. In a more extreme form, it may implicitly or explicitly entail the assertion that only the governments of "great powers" or "superpowers" matter and that the interests and aspirations of minor states can (and by implication, ought to) be ignored except in unusual circumstances. This realist bias is, in part, a reflection of a belief that order and stability are best assured in a system governed by a few who share common norms and are relatively satisfied with their status.

Realist admiration for the virtues of the eighteenth-century European state system, which was characterized by a shared value consensus within the narrow stratum of rulers and professional diplomats, is elitist in this sense. Among contemporary scholars, Waltz's unabashed preference for bipolarity is perhaps the clearest expression of the elitist norm.[71] Writing before the collapse of the Soviet conglomerate, Waltz believed that the world had remained fundamentally bipolar since 1945 and, more importantly, thought that this was a virtue. He argues persuasively that bipolarity assures greater stability than any alternative structure and appears to restrict himself to empirical and prescriptive analysis. There always was a clear, if unstated, normative position underlying the analysis, however. For both Waltz and realists in general, the avoidance of catastrophic war is the most important of values. In order to secure this, they are prepared to assume as irrational the value hierarchies of those for whom the risks of war might be preferable to the perpetuation of unbearable political, economic, and social conditions. They assume that the great powers are somehow more responsible than lesser powers, presumably because the former have so much more to lose than the latter. The poor or the weak might be tempted to behave rashly and promote instability in order to improve their status. Whether this argument takes the form of opposition to nuclear proliferation or praise for the ability of the balance of power to preserve the independence of major states, it is profoundly conservative and elitist.[72] In effect, it is an international version of the argument that there should be a property or educational qualification as a prerequisite for enfranchisement.

The Wilsonian critique of balance-of-power politics was dismissed by realists as utopian because it did not take sufficient account of the role of power in global politics. Yet however "unscientific" Woodrow Wilson's analysis of global politics, what probably incensed realists most was his denunciation of the prevailing elitist ethic. It is not simply that Wilson denounced aristocratic rule within states but also that he rejected a condominium of the great powers. His assertion of the rights of nationalities and ethnic minorities, along with his praise of democracy and the rights of small states, constituted a brief in favor of greater participation at all levels of global decisionmaking. There is an added irony in the fact that, although Wilson was accused of being naive for advocating such participation, he effectively predicted what has become an elemental process in the global politics of the late twentieth century.

At a different level of analysis, elitism may also take the form of assertions that foreign policy should be left in the hands of small coteries of professional diplomats. Such arguments are often made in the context of expressions of concern about the allegedly injurious impact of public opinion or shifting electoral majorities on the possibility for formulating consistent and farsighted foreign policy. Walter Lippmann, for instance, saw the "devitalization of the governing power" as "the malady of democratic states,"[73] and Alexis de Tocqueville concluded that "a democracy can only with great difficulty regulate the details of an important undertaking, persevere in a fixed design, and work out its execution in spite of serious obstacles."[74] For their part, realists consistently lament the passing of the age of the professional diplomat and the onset of the era of mass politics. George Kennan believes that "a good deal of our trouble seems to have stemmed from the extent to which the executive has felt itself beholden to short-term trends of public opinion in the country and from . . . the erratic and subjective nature of public reaction to foreign-policy questions,"[75] and Morgenthau cites as one of his "four fundamental rules" that "[t]he government is the leader of public opinion, not its slave."[76] In sum, the elitist bias of political realists is characteristic of their perception of all levels of analysis just as Wilson's anti-elitist bent was present in his views of both internal and external political life.

CONCLUSION

This brief analysis of the sources and nature of evolving theory in global politics is pessimistic about the prospects both for developing a cumulative science in the discipline and for paradigm advances of a Kuhnian sort. Notwithstanding significant advances in data collection and method, our analysis views the discipline as mired in an unceasing set of theoretical debates in which competing empirical assertions grow out of competing normative emphases that have their roots in a broader sociocultural milieu. Dominant norms tend to vary through time in concert with shifts in perceptions of the sources of value deprivation and satisfaction; and such norms, therefore, reflect the hierarchy of issues on the global political agenda. In effect, social norms mediate between circumstances and events and the perceptions of analysts and practitioners.

Our analysis suggests, furthermore, that dominant theories of an age are more the products of ideology and fashion than of science in the Kuhnian sense. Their sources are relentlessly subjective. If the natural sciences somehow evolve in linear fashion regardless of their social and cultural contexts, knowledge generation in the social sciences—including global politics—may more closely resemble that in the humanities, which is inevitably infused by the ethos of the era. Global politics will, therefore, continue to be characterized by a welter of competing theories that reflect significant political, subjective and normative differences.[77] Only when the global system enters a period of rapid and stressful change will a dominant theory *superficially* resembling a Kuhnian paradigm possibly emerge for some period of time. In all likelihood that "new" theory will be old wine in a new bottle. It will reflect a changing normative environment and will yield pride of place once that environment again changes.

CHAPTER 3

Changing Norms and Theory

The Middle Ages to Machiavelli

We have suggested that prevailing theory in global politics—the way in which we explain the world around us—is an epiphenomenon of the normative temper of an era and that social norms evolve in response to changing perceptions of reality. In contrast to models of progressive paradigm shifts, this perspective assumes that global-politics theory is closer to what is conventionally conceived of as ideology and intersubjective perceptions rather than an intersubjective body of knowledge. In this chapter, we shall examine this assumption in the context of the evolution of "reality," norms, and theory from medieval Europe to the Renaissance.

Norms tend to evolve in leisurely fashion so that significant shifts—their sources and their impact—may become visible only after a prolonged time, and past norms tend to become embedded in and identified with a culture, reappearing repeatedly in new contexts. This is evident in the enduring impact of the world's great religions and their periodic revival. For this reason, a historical approach of the sort we have selected to use in the following pages is very useful.

MEDIEVAL GLOBAL POLITICS

Medieval ideas about global politics are, at first blush, almost unrecognizable to contemporary theorists. In contrast to the European interstate experience of the eighteenth and nineteenth centuries, the Middle Ages has been largely ignored by global-politics theorists, partly because of the absence of a clear differentiation between politics within communities versus among them. This is to be regretted, because all five of the trends that Hedley Bull identified in 1977 as harbingers of a new medievalism—regional integration of states, disintegration of states, restoration of private international violence, transnational organizations, and technological unification of the world[1]—have greatly accelerated in the intervening years.

It is also ironic that little is recalled of this epoch. First, the absence of a clear domestic arena during much of the period entailed a "purer" and more completely "anarchic" arena than was the case before or after; second, the erosion of the boundary between the domestic and international realms in contemporary politics has played a major role in undermining acceptance of traditional theories about global politics. Indeed, one of the most compelling characteristics of the medieval period was the gradual evolution of territorial entities and the rediscovery of the boundary between those two arenas. As realities changed, so too did ideas about global politics, and by the end of the period it was a relatively brief journey to the "modern" ideas of Machiavelli, Bodin, and Hobbes.

Prior to the emergence of a system of sovereign territorial states characterized by complex overlapping jurisdictions, European political life featured the absence of clear conceptions of private property, exclusive territorial control, or a distinction between public and private spheres and goods.[2] Multiple loci of authority produced a system that was "decentralized even by the standards of similar regimes elsewhere,"[3] in which, at least in Europe itself, "inside" was virtually indistinguishable from "outside." For example, at the height of their power, the Avignon popes constituted something of a cultural center for Europe as a whole and had the administrative status of a genuine international organization. H. G. Koenigsberger writes:

> They pronounced on matters of faith and doctrine with complete authority. They extended papal taxation of the clergy and perfected their financial control. They appointed bishops and abbots all over Christendom. They called up cases from ecclesiastical courts to the curia. By exercising the papal "plenitude of power," the right to bind and loose, which included release from oaths, the popes could and did set aside electoral promises which they had made in conclave before being chosen. Personal absolutism could go no further.[4]

Yet for all their power, the popes were themselves dependent on the resources of Italian bankers, who alone "had the network of representatives necessary for financial dealings on a European scale" and "the reserves of cash at Avignon and in Italy to finance papal operations."[5]

The apparent absence of the sorts of explanatory factors on which many contemporary global theorists and practitioners focus—nation-states, state bureaucracies, and so forth—seems to divorce the period from contemporary global problems to a greater extent than the earlier epochs of classical Greece and Rome, which at least had rudimentary conceptions of citizenship and domestic versus interstate. In the eyes of statist theorists, medieval Europe, emerging from the demise of Rome and the competition that Michael Mann describes as between "the immanent morale of the Roman ruling class" and "the transcendent power of Christianity,"[6] seems politically regressive. Such views betray an unspoken Eurocentric belief that the state and state system were somehow historically destined. There is also a seeming reluctance to give full credit to "private" power, innovations, and authority. Few recall the important role of the Peace and Truce of God in ameliorating feudal conflicts or the fact that companies created the "transnational" institution of the medieval fair and a network of resident missions rivaling those of governments. Firms were the first to establish the diplomatic role of consul (the origin of "consulate"), who represented their interests abroad and with the local ruler formed a "mixed tribunal" to adjudicate disputes with citizens in the host community.[7]

In fact, all the elements of global politics as we understand them today—autonomous actors, violence and war, system solidarity and culture, and supranational organization—were present in medieval Europe and were topics of great moment to scholars of the period. There existed a corpus of ideas about these issues that, while not systematically articulated and presented in a manner remote to contemporary empiricists, reflected the social and cultural realities of the period. For an empiricist, it is difficult to tease out many of these ideas because much of medieval theory is self-consciously normative, revealing the operation of the system only indirectly in expressing aspirations for order and universality quite at odds with the disorder and fragmentation that actually existed.

CHRISTIAN UNIVERSALISM AND THE CHRISTIAN COMMONWEALTH

The dominant medieval myth—that latinized Europe constituted a special community distinct from the pagan world—was an inheritance partly from pagan Rome that had been reinforced by Jewish tradition, biblical scripture, and Roman persecution. "The identity of Christendom," as Mann observes, "was transnational, based not on territory or locality" and "provided both a common humanity and a framework for common divisions among Europeans."[8] "The church," argues Hendrik Spruyt, "saw itself as a community of believers with no geographic limit to its authority."[9] Only Christian believers, argued St. Augustine, could guide the universal family of peoples to the inevitable City of God. The disappearance of the Roman Empire of the West and the schism between the Latin Church and Byzantium institutionalized this sense of exclusivity and isolation. With the waning of Byzantine authority, the Roman Church increasingly assumed temporal as well as spiritual authority.[10]

In fact, the idea of a unified Christian commonwealth, which made its appearance as the Roman Empire faded, coincided with the breakdown of central authority during which territorial rulership on any significant scale virtually disappeared. If, as we shall suggest later, the idea of anarchy that came to characterize so much of international relations theory during the era of the sovereign territorial state entailed overstatement for purposes of drama, anarchy—in the sense of chaos—was a close approximation of Europe in the early Middle Ages. In this sense, the period was an archetypal international, if not interstate, system.

Rome had been a centrally governed territorial polity characterized by relatively clear frontiers, a central army supported by taxation of the community, and centralized civil and military bureaucracies. A clear delineation existed between international war and internal disturbances. "In principle," declares Philippe Contamine, "by using a continuous line of defence around Roman territory, it had been expected that peace would reign within the Empire and that there would be no reason for bearing arms, that violence would be illegal and recourse to justice would be the normal means of resolving litigious questions whatever they concerned."[11] By contrast, early medieval

society witnessed the virtual disappearance of direct taxation, central bureaucracy, and regular armies:

> The resources of monarchies were largely absorbed by the immediate private
> expenses of kings and their entourages. The idea of a frontier (*limes*) was almost
> completely lost. At a stroke insecurity became general; no region was able to claim
> immunity from war. Each individual, every social or family group, had to look to
> their own security, to defend their rights and interest by arms. . . . The differences
> were obliterated between public warfare and private violence, between the feud or
> vendetta and a conflict waged by the king in the name of his people.[12]

The inability of Byzantium to screen Italy from the eighth-century invasion
of the Lombards confirmed western Europe's isolation and produced an alliance
between the Latin Church and the Frankish Empire of Charlemagne. The
Carolingians, having united Gaul, western Germany, and other western territories, became the second pillar of Christian Europe and enabled the Roman
Church to distance itself from Byzantium with relative impunity. The Franks, as
the new protectors of the western Christian tradition, were induced to accept the
idea of the Christian community. Frankish emperors viewed themselves as the
heirs of the Roman emperors and founded the Holy Roman Empire. What
evolved thereafter was an acceptance of unity and diversity—a society based on
an amalgam of German tribal traditions and law, Roman law, and church writings and law. Until the demise of the Frankish Empire, the imperial-papal duop-
oly restored a measure of centralized rule to the West.

The myth of a unified Christian commonwealth was fostered by the continued expansion of Latin Christianity even after the Frankish Empire waned.
Poland, Hungary, Scandinavia, Spain, and Sicily were progressively added to this
commonwealth, which achieved its greatest extent with the temporary establishment of latinized enclaves in the Middle East in the course of the crusades.
Paradoxically, however, this expansion was accompanied by the increasing dissolution of central authority within that commonwealth. This tendency was accelerated
by the technology of warfare, most importantly the heavily armored horseman and
the stone fortification. Contamine succinctly describes the extent of this fragmentation and the degree to which it contrasted with the myth of unity:

> It is true that between the tenth and twelfth centuries some relatively powerful, uni-
> fied states survived or were created. . . . In France, however, as well as in the Empire,
> . . . duchies, marquisates, counties, baronies or simple lordships multiplied. All
> formed political units enjoying increased autonomy, even quasi-sovereignty. Even
> more than the relationships between one man and another, the rites of homage
> and vassalship, this is the outstanding feature of that complex phenomenon which
> historians call feudalism. In tens and hundreds, principalities of every size became
> centres of independent military systems, including, in addition to specific means of
> attack and defence, the right and power to declare, pursue and terminate war.
> From this sprang that multitude of skirmishes, sieges, raids, burnings, encounters
> and battles . . . whose recital constitutes the daily fare of contemporary annalists
> and chroniclers.[13]

France in the tenth century, for example, witnessed first the proliferation
of local principalities and then the growing autonomy of these from king and

emperor. The extent of this phenomenon is extraordinary; from A.D 900 to a.d 975 the number of relatively independent counts and viscounts in southern France grew from about 12 to 150.[14]

PUBLIC VERSUS PRIVATE SPHERES

The idea of a homogeneous and unified Christian community masked the very real heterogeneity of those who lived within it and the existence of innumerable autonomous units that constituted it and vied for power and prestige within it. There could be no autonomous political units because politics itself was not viewed as separate from theology. Rather than being a human construct, government was seen as an extension of God's will, and God anointed emperors and kings. The private interests and property of kings and emperors were poorly demarcated from their public responsibilities. Within an imperial framework, the demarcation of the public from the private realm was murky at best. "With the collapse of Rome," writes van Creveld, "the public sphere . . . all but disappeared. In medieval Latin the term *dominium*—from *domus,* house or residence—could stand either for a prince's private property or for the country that he ruled, and indeed lawyers often argued as to which was the correct usage."[15]

The confusion of public and private was partly a consequence of the mixing of several legal traditions. Roman law, for instance, reinforced by canon law, promoted a sense of community and implied a single domestic arena, but it had to coexist alongside the traditions of the Germanic tribes that conquered Rome. For these tribes, law was largely an accretion of customary rights and duties that initially varied by tribal group and, as previously nomadic tribes settled down, became associated with territory. As described by one legal scholar, "Laws and systems of law became local. And the lines of division between them came to correspond roughly with the Roman provincial frontiers."[16] As instances of customary law, tribal norms and mores were personal in the sense of applying to individuals by virtue of their membership in the tribal group. The stubborn persistence of such local law assured diversity within the empire and was the soil from which nationalism grew and could flourish.

It was not merely the diversity assured by customary law that worked against political centralization, but also the idea that such law was not decreed from above but rather percolated up from below. In theory, legislation as understood today did not take place. Rather, law represented the codification of customary behavior that had been "discovered" and systematized. Law, therefore, though ultimately divine, derived from the people who, at least tacitly, had to give it their consent. And, in principle, rulers were subject to the same customary law. Overall, the effect was to enshrine tradition and impose upon society a rigid conservatism based on inherited inequalities. Thus, custom and, in consequence, the law served to perpetuate privileges and immunities determined by inherited status, and no authority, however august, dared tamper with these. In this manner, as well as for practical reasons of communication, limited coercive capability, and geographic inaccessibility, the theoretical centralization of power implicit in the hierarchical organization of the system was extremely limited, at least on a day-to-day basis. As tacit consent was the basis of law, so too was it the basis of rulership. In time, the role of inheritance grew on the more local levels, but electorship remained the basis for selecting popes and Holy Roman Emperors.[17]

In contrast to the rudimentary national consciousness and localism fostered by customary law, the elaboration of canon law functioned to institutionalize the idea of a Christian commonwealth. Canon law, heir to Roman law, developed by the accretion of decrees of church leaders and the writings of religious scholars. The papal-Carolingian alliance encouraged the codification of canon law, a process that from the ninth through the twelfth centuries produced roughly forty systematic collections. All inhabitants, however noble or mean, were subject to canon law, with the threat of eternal damnation as its major sanction. Ecclesiastical courts located in each diocese under papal authority administered the law.

For the most part, canon law was concerned with matters of faith and Christian ethics and, while in principle this separated it from secular law, its ethical content made it germane to otherwise secular issues such as slavery, individual human rights, and contracts. It was only as the authority of the papacy waned and quarrels arose with increasing frequency between the pope, on the one hand, and the emperor or local kings and princes, on the other, that canon law began to lose its grip upon Europe. This development coincided with the waning of the Middle Ages and the emergence of territorial states. The Hussite Revolt and the Protestant Reformation that followed continued the process of secularization of the law, and Martin Luther explicitly renounced claims for the role of religion in secular affairs. While canon law thrived, however, it bridged both the private and public spheres and provided an ideological basis for European unity. In Bozeman's words:

> The international character of the canon law, which had been apparent in the law's double function as a general European system of public and private law applicable with equal force to each separate region and to each individual and as a set of norms guiding the relations between the separate Christian governments, derived, in the last analysis, from the recognition that the individual Christian, regardless of his residence or status, was the chief subject of the law's concern. As long, then, as the papacy could treat monarchs as individual Christians, the canon law could influence the relations between the kingdoms represented by the monarchs. But when the Christian kings became conscious of the unchristian sources of their own power, the papacy was left to fight its political battles without the aid and comfort of objective norms, and the canon law lost its character as a regulatory force in the relations between governments.[18]

However complex and amorphous may appear the overlapping of public and private realms and the coexistence of several sources of law and authority, these features accurately reflected the political, economic, and social circumstances of feudalism. Although that system (or more correctly systems) developed unequally in western Europe, certain key features of it may be identified.[19] Fundamental was that feudalism was a system in which only the most local forms of direct rule were possible. The decline in systems of transportation and communication after the fall of Rome and the limited coercive means available to those with pretensions to rule made local communities the foci of political attention. The economy was agricultural, and wealth was based on land and labor. Political power, therefore, was inextricably connected with landholding and territory, and the complex hierarchical system of rights and obligations and indirect authority associated with feudalism reflected this. It was only with the emergence of trading cities after the twelfth century and the concentration of political power in the hands of temporal kings that direct political control was enlarged beyond the local community.

It is this extreme localism that makes feudalism appear so unlike the version of global politics to which we have become accustomed. Essential relationships were those among local communities and between local landholders and those who could provide them with some measure of security. It was in the latter relationship that the overlap between public and private obligations was most pronounced. Although he might exercise a substantial degree of local control, the local landholder in effect turned over formal ownership of the land and rendered services to a lord in return for protection, and this was repeated to the apex of the feudal pyramid. Medieval kingdoms constituted states of a sort, but monarchs, like the barons who served them and the emperor and pope whom they all supposedly served, largely exercised authority indirectly and were rigidly constrained by their dependence upon others, as well as by customary and canon law. Military power was the lord's chief asset; he provided protection to those below him and reaped the profits of the land held in trust for his monarch, to whom, in turn, he was obligated to provide troops if the need arose. However great the formal authority of those on top, they depended upon those below them for economic and military wherewithal, and that authority could be exercised only in indirect fashion. A monarch, for example, had a personal contractual relationship with those who were entrusted with his lands at the same time as he represented the apogee of public authority, and the two roles implied different rights and obligations. The combination of private property relations and public obligations—reinforced by customary law that ensured the perpetuation of individual status—produced a system of global politics in Europe that gave unusual rein to the individual as actor.

The clear distinction between the public and private realms that came to characterize modern states evolved only gradually. It was not until Hobbes's "commonwealth" that we come across a secular and artificial state separate from its sovereign and the sovereign's private interests. Thereafter, the distinction between the public and private realms was increasingly demarcated, and the vertical boundaries separating states grew harder and harder even as the horizontal boundaries among classes grew more permeable.

It was not until the seventeenth century in Europe that bureaucrats employed and paid by the state, as opposed to nobles employed by the king, began to appear. Reasonably accurate maps became available late in the eighteenth century, when triangulation became possible, allowing state boundaries to be formalized rather than merely guessed or estimated; and the population censuses necessary for governments to know whom they ruled were instituted at about the same time.[20] Differentiation of a monarch's private finances from the public finances of the state began to appear in the sixteenth century, but depending upon the country, the process would not be complete for several hundred years. Even the "state's monopoly on external violence came very late and through a process spanning several centuries"[21] that was not completed until the nineteenth century. Finally, it was not until the end of the Thirty Years' War that organized interstate warfare replaced what van Creveld describes as "a free-for-all in which Emperor, kings, territorial rulers of various ranks, religious leagues, free cities, and commissioned and noncommissioned military entrepreneurs (many of them scarcely distinguishable from robbers and, unless willing to change sides, often treated as such) fought each other with every means at their disposal."[22]

THE FOREIGN-DOMESTIC DICHOTOMY

The overriding ideal of a unified Christian community and the absence of a clear conception of the difference between the public and private realms made it impossible for medieval thinkers to conceive of relations among autonomous princes as contemporary theorists do of relations between states. In the circumstances of what Rodney Bruce Hall calls "the medieval-feudal theocratic order," "a primary source of personal identity for most mature and reflective early-modern Europeans would be a religious, and specifically confessional Christian self-identification."[23] Indeed, "inclusion in the feudal structure was not defined by physical location," and "territory was not determinative of identity and loyalty."[24] Nevertheless, medieval political relations were characterized by many of the same dilemmas that we associate with contemporary global politics, including war.

In practice, the ideal of Christian unity starkly contrasted with the genuine decentralization of feudalism. Owing to the absence of any authority with the means to enforce peace, local lords not infrequently resorted to military force to resolve contested jurisdictions or other conflicts of interest, especially after tribunals had failed to satisfy claims arising from incompatible rights and prerogatives. Such wars were regarded by the papacy as private and, for the most part, unjust (unless waged by the papacy itself). Thus, the boundary between legitimate violence and crime was virtually nonexistent. Wars were, nevertheless, widely seen as necessary for adjudicating disputes and as welcome opportunities for armed vassals to exhibit military prowess. For the latter, violence was a profession and a major source of income. If loot or ransom could be obtained in the course of wars sanctioned by higher authority, so much the better. In the absence of such wars, resorting to theft and pillage was common.

The nature of violence in the Middle Ages within Christian Europe made it difficult to categorize as clearly public or private. On the one hand, wars were waged among kings. Yet treaties were considered the personal contracts of monarchs assumed under oath, rather than commitments by kingdoms, and were regulated in this fashion by canon law. On the other hand, murder, personal vengeance, and brigandage, especially after the decline of the Carolingian dynasty, were the most common threats to order and peace and the major sources of universal insecurity. Kings were expected to protect those who depended upon them and to maintain peace in their realms, but their ability to do so varied dramatically as their personal power and the loyalty they commanded waxed or waned.

It was in those areas of Europe where monarchical power had ebbed and personal acts of violence had become most vexatious that movements arose to limit and regulate the nature of conflict.[25] Such efforts, the most important consequences of which were the Peace of God and the Truce of God, were initially associated with local bishops and, temporarily at least, led to various forms of arms control. By the eleventh century, for instance, southern and central France had come to lack any strong local power of the sort that was exercised by princes in Flanders or Normandy. It was here that local agitation produced the clearest articulation of limits on conflict. The Truce of God outlawed fighting on selected days prior to the weekend and on holidays, and the Peace of God sought to protect various classes of people as well as religious and economic enterprises from the ravages of violence. To the degree that such efforts succeeded, they did so for reasons of common benefit, especially the maintenance of those sources of prosperity upon which entire regions depended. On occasion, princes sought to ally themselves with peace movements or associations, but for the most part such efforts enjoyed only limited success. Especially in cases where efforts to enforce limits on violence led to the organization or arming of elements of the population, feudal nobles reacted harshly to what they feared were threats to their prerogatives and powers.

In contrast to wars within the Christian community of Europe, wars between that community and outsiders, or wars waged to repress heretics (Albigensians, Cathars, and Waldensians), were regarded as public and deemed to be just. Such wars were considered crusades and were initiated for the most part with papal approbation between the end of the eleventh and the thirteenth centuries to stem the tide of Islam and recover the Holy Land. If judged according to these objectives, the crusades were dismal failures, not only because they failed to secure and retain Jerusalem, but also because they hastened the collapse of the Byzantine Empire. Jerusalem had fallen to Islam in 1187. It was not restored to Christian rule until 1229 when Emperor Frederick II, despite papal opposition, succeeded in negotiating its peaceful return. The restoration was only temporary, however, as disunion among Christian leaders assured its fall once more in 1244.

If, however, the crusades are viewed as a means of pacifying Europe itself by exporting violence, they may be judged more kindly. Medieval European nobility constituted a warrior caste that, as noted earlier, posed a constant threat to the "domestic" peace and prosperity of the Christian commonwealth. Improvements in armaments, including the introduction of the stirrup, the heavy lance, and more effective armor, limited the number of individuals who could join the military profession, increased the need for wealth for those who practiced it, and made it difficult for societies to control the activities of its members, especially after the tenth century. Boredom and the constant need for funds encouraged the nobility to seek profit either through war or brigandage, and neither the sorts of arms control described previously nor the efforts to substitute symbolic equivalents for violence like tournaments was adequate to assure peace within western Europe. These warriors were attracted to wherever there arose an opportunity for excitement and profit.

[They] helped the native Christians in Spain to reconquer the northern part of the peninsula from Islam; they set up the Norman states in southern Italy; even before the First Crusade they enlisted as mercenaries in the service of Byzantium and fought against its eastern foes; finally, they found in the conquest and defence of the Tomb of Christ their chosen field of action. Whether in Spain or in Syria, the holy war offered the dual attraction of an adventure and a work of piety.[26]

Even more important, as in contemporary "failed states," "fighting was also, and perhaps above all, a source of profit—in fact, the nobleman's chief industry," and "the finest gift the chief could bestow was the right to a share of the plunder."[27] Popes and monarchs repeatedly found it in their interest to purge their own societies of the energy and destructiveness of these noble warriors by declaring crusades that would export violence overseas. Knights were summoned to fulfill their duty as Christians and vassals and were afforded a legitimized opportunity for glory, booty, and salvation. In this sense, the crusades were functional, in that "a common Christian cause against a declared enemy of all the Christians would defer fraternal bloodshed in Western Europe more effectively than any specially instituted Truce or Peace of God."[28] "[T]he bloodletting thus practiced abroad by the most turbulent groups in the West saved its civilization from being extinguished by guerrilla warfare. The chroniclers were well aware that at the start of a crusade the people at home in the old countries always breathed more freely, because now they could once more enjoy a little peace."[29]

THE SACERDOTAL AND THE TEMPORAL

The crusades were but one aspect of medieval society in which the secular and the religious merged. Indeed, an outstanding characteristic of the period was an omnipresent preoccupation with the hereafter. All aspects of medieval thought were infused with religion, and the idealized unity of the European commonwealth grew out of the belief that a Christian empire had succeeded the Roman one.

During the early Middle Ages, reality tended to mirror this ideal in political life despite the relative autonomy of local institutions. The Frankish-papal condominium, the unifying effect of canon law, and the combining of secular and religious authority in the persons of bishop-nobles in large measure precluded friction between the temporal and the sacerdotal. Early Christian thought, especially as articulated by St. Augustine, was highly individualistic, distinguishing only between the spiritual and temporal aspects of men but not between two authorities. However, the division of Christianity into Eastern and Western churches and the flowering of the Frankish Empire necessitated inquiry into the relationship between these two authorities.[30] From the end of the fifth until the ninth century, the answer was contained in the Gelasian doctrine or the "doctrine of the two swords," which admitted the existence of two authorities, each with its own exclusive jurisdiction. Although the emperor was expected to give way in matters of faith, it was declared, no one after Christ could exercise dominion in both realms, and both authorities were sanctioned directly by God. Potential friction, then, was diffused by the sense that, while each hierarchy was supreme in its own arena, each was simultaneously and inevitably dependent upon the other. What remained unresolved was the question of who was to determine whether a matter was spiritual or temporal.

In practice, however, during the period in which the Gelasian doctrine proved adequate, the empire tended to wield greater influence than the papacy; the latter, after all, remained dependent on the former for protection and resources, a condition that made it clear to Charlemagne, for instance, that he was responsible for both hierarchies. After the ninth century, the gradual growth in papal self-sufficiency and the weakening of the empire began to erode the equilibrium represented by the Gelasian doctrine. Increasingly, the church began to demand that its norms and laws govern the temporal as well as the spiritual realm and that its voice be determinant in the selection of secular leaders. Thus, one Giles of Rome declared that princes' "domains belong to the church more than to you."[31] This tendency was strengthened, in the first instance, by the publication of forgeries (the Pseudo-Isidorian Decretals) in the ninth century, intended to enhance the authority of bishops at the expense of archbishops, who were more beholden to secular authorities, and to expand the jurisdiction of the papal court. Their effect was to centralize the Roman Church and, therefore, to reduce its dependence on secular authorities. A century later a new source of energy and political influence was made available to the Roman Church in the reform movement associated with Cluny. The latter erected a semiautonomous and tightly organized system of abbeys that sought to purify the Roman Church and strengthen papal control of the ecclesiastical hierarchy.

Imperial-papal friction almost inevitably intensified as the Roman Church acquired the trappings of a territorial principality. For centuries individual clergymen had been landowners and, as such, had exercised secular power in the feudal system. This fusion of temporal and religious functions had been encouraged as well by making bishops in several areas responsible for local defenses; especially in Italy, such bishops had themselves become lords. Fusion was further reflected in the orders of knighthood—the Templars, the Hospitallers of St. John of Jerusalem, the Teutonic Order—that grew up to conquer the infidels. By the eleventh century, however, "the church had acquired the characteristics of an earthly empire: it claimed all Italy with Corsica and Sardinia as 'states of the church,' Spain because it supposedly belonged of old to St. Peter, Hungary as a gift from King Stephen, Saxony as a Carolingian bequest, and the entire Christian Roman Empire as a fief of Rome."[32]

And by this time the higher clergy had become so enmeshed in secular affairs as individual nobles that it had become virtually impossible to draw a clear distinction between Europe's religious and temporal hierarchies. The higher clergy had both temporal and spiritual responsibilities and, consequently, divided loyalties. Especially between the middle of the eleventh and the thirteenth centuries, the church enjoyed immense secular authority. According to van Creveld:

> From about A.D. 1100 on, it possessed, apart from the power to lay down and interpret divine law, the right to nominate and promote its own officials; immunity from secular justice . . . ; the right to judge and punish both its own personnel and, in cases involving the care of souls, laymen; the right to offer asylum to fugitives from secular justice; the right to absolve subjects from their oaths to their rulers; and, to support the lot, immense landed estates, a separate system of taxation, and, here and there, the right to strike money as well.[33]

The first great clash between pope and emperor erupted at the end of the eleventh century when Pope Gregory VII sought to prohibit the lay investiture of bishops. The subsequent quarrel pitted the pope against Emperor Henry IV. The papal claim for the superiority of the Roman Church entailed arguing that Peter had given both swords to the popes. More importantly, it was argued that the church was responsible for regulating the ethical lives of all Christians and that, at least in spiritual matters, this included the emperor himself. In excommunicating Henry IV, then, Gregory was also asserting an authority to depose the emperor. The implication was that, although the church conceded temporal jurisdiction to the emperor, it could act as the highest court to determine the legitimacy of imperial behavior.

Perhaps John of Salisbury, a twelfth-century English clergyman and close friend of Pope Adrian IV and Thomas à Becket, voiced the most persuasive argument in favor of papal supremacy. In *Policraticus* ("The statesman's book"), John declared that princes received their authority from the church. Elaborating an organic theory of society in which each person had a distinct function, John concluded "since the soul is . . . the prince of the body, and has rulership over the whole thereof, so those whom our author calls the prefects of religion preside over the entire body."[34]

Supporters of the emperor, for their part, argued for retaining the Gelasian doctrine which, in practice, meant conceding to the emperor significant influence in the selection of the pope and other high clergy. The emperor's argument was that both he and the pope were granted authority directly by God so the temporal and spiritual hierarchies had to be kept separate and independent of each other. This claim, however, was fast losing its conviction. However steeped in tradition was the Gelasian doctrine, the very real decline in imperial fortunes, especially the growing incapacity of the emperor to control and command lesser princes, undermined imperial pretensions. Even though the Holy Roman Empire had continued to expand after Charlemagne, no later emperor enjoyed as much authority as had that great leader. The legatees of the emperor's authority were, in a sense, local princes.

Conflict between a waxing papacy and a waning empire persisted for several hundred years, made more complex as the dispute came to involve the delineation of jurisdictions between other secular princes and the papacy. Indeed, this issue—with which most political thinkers were preoccupied—was not resolved until the emergence of autonomous territorial kingdoms and city-states. Arguments regarding the questions raised in the conflicts must be regarded as major elements of global-politics theory of the period and were the harbingers of later theory associated with the birth of the system of sovereign states lacking an overarching authority.

The proliferation of theory intended to buttress papal claims to universal rulership went hand in hand with changes in papal organization and policy in the Middle Ages. The Clunaic movement, which began in the tenth century, provided a model of globalism that the papacy sought to emulate. Clunaic clergy established themselves throughout Europe and were unwilling to be supervised by any but papal authority. In time the movement "was recognized generally as the chief support of the public peace, the most effective agency for the rallying of public opinion against feudal violence, a well-equipped bureau of information for the dissemination of Christian ideas, and a smoothly operating political machine that was to be ultimately responsible for the establishment of papal supremacy."[35] With the assistance of Cluny, papal power grew dramatically after the tenth century. Bozeman describes the consequences of this as follows: "Under Innocent III the church had become an international state. It had the power to set large armies in motion, to create and destroy coalitions, to control the mighty and the meek, to raise funds by direct taxation, and to bring offenders to justice. It controlled education, propaganda, social welfare, and the courts, and it wielded the awesome power of external life and death."[36]

As part of its effort to achieve global supremacy, the papacy assembled intelligence agents, propagandists, lawyers, and diplomats; and it maintained a central archival system. At its peak, papal power was not merely theoretical. For example, Innocent III

> laid an interdict upon France and withheld all rites of the church from the lands that were subject to France, until King Philip Augustus agreed to take back a Danish wife whom, in the pope's opinion, he had repudiated unjustly. He gave the empire to Otto of Brunswick and forced him to renounce his chief imperial claims in Italy (1201). A few years later (1211) he deposed Otto for perjury and placed Frederick II of Hohenstauffen upon the imperial throne. And by sentence of interdict, excommunication, and deposition he forced King John of England to surrender his crown in order to receive it as a vassal of the pope.[37]

It was by playing off emperor and pope that local kings could attain greater autonomy for themselves.

MEDIEVAL SCHOLARS

Some of the most gifted of the medieval scholars sought to dispute papal pretensions, even during the period in which that institution enjoyed its greatest predominance. The flowering of scholarship, especially in the twelfth and thirteenth centuries, was associated with the Italian Renaissance, the universities of Paris and Oxford, and the Dominican and Franciscan orders and was able to take advantage of the rediscovery of Roman law and the work of Aristotle. Thus the Donation of Constantine, described by van Creveld as "one of the key documents used by the papacy to justify its claim to monarchical power over Rome, Italy, and the West," was exposed as a forgery in 1440 by Lorenzo Valla, who was able to do so by "exercising his knowledge of classical Latin."[38]

It was scholars' reliance on Aristotelian precepts and reason (revolutionary at the time) combined with their use of theological argument that make medieval discourse and method appear so remote to contemporary empiricists. The Platonic preoccupation with the ideal society, which was highly compatible with Christian revelation, was overshadowed by Aristotelian secularism and rationalism, fueling growing doubts about the superiority of the spiritual to the temporal realm and challenging the tradition that had dominated Christian thought until the thirteenth century. It also began to undermine the belief that the temporal state was no more than the consequence of human sin.

St. Thomas Aquinas, for example, argued for reinstating the Gelasian doctrine on the premise that the universe constituted a hierarchy with God at its apex, in which every creature sought its own perfection. Within this hierarchy, the lower was obliged to serve the higher, and God himself had entrusted the emperor to govern the temporal realm. Applying Aristotelian reasoning, St. Thomas saw human law as articulating for humankind the principles of order inherent in natural and divine law. In tone and substance, his Aristotelian humanism represented a dramatic departure from earlier Christian thinkers such as Tertullian and St. Augustine. Temporal authority flowed naturally from humans' social nature rather than from sin. Imperial prerogatives were of double practical significance, as far as St. Thomas was concerned, because of the growing claims of lesser princes and because of the growing propensity of the papacy itself to behave in ways similar to those princes. In consequence, politics within the Christian commonwealth was becoming less stable and was beginning to take on the attributes of a decentralized political system. Notwithstanding these developments, St. Thomas remained firmly attached to the ideal of a unified Christian community. Despite his effort to revive the Gelasian tradition, he continued to regard the Roman Church as the basis of human unity.

Like St. Thomas, the great Italian poet Dante Alighieri also retained the vision of a united Christian commonwealth since it was "the intention of God that all created things should represent the likeness of God, so far as their proper nature will admit." But, unlike St. Thomas, he declared that such unity must be based on the temporal empire rather than the church; humankind could not be united "except when it is subject to one prince."[39] Of course such an empire had never existed. The source of Dante's concern was the conflict in Italy between papal and imperial parties; he, like many other Italians, feared the secular pretensions emanating from Rome. That conflict was manifested both in the internal politics of the maturing Italian city-states and in the politics among those actors; the demarcation of interstate from intrastate politics had begun to emerge but was far from complete at the time Dante wrote. The bases of wealth had begun to change, and a bourgeoisie had emerged in Italy to challenge both the clergy and the feudal nobility.

The theoretical side of Dante's argument proceeded from the claim that Christ himself had declared that his kingdom was not a temporal one and that only a secular monarch could provide the peace necessary for subjects to realize their full potential. Such had been the case during the Roman Empire, and the Holy Roman Emperor, as the heir to the Roman imperium, was the only possible candidate to impose unity and peace. The practical source of Dante's position, however, arose from his partisanship as a member of the imperial faction in the city of Florence and his exile from that city during a time when his political foes had achieved political ascendancy.

In reality, Dante's advocacy of a unified temporal empire was something of an anachronism because the Hohenstauffen heirs to the imperial throne had already become impotent servants of the territorial princes whom they in theory governed. In his effort to unite traditional Christian theology with Aristotelian assumptions and in his belief in the unity of a Christian community, Dante stood with St. Thomas even while taking the opposite side in the papal-imperial controversy. They agreed, declares George Sabine,

> that the distinguishing mark of human nature is its combination of a spiritual and a physical principle, each requiring an appropriate kind of authority. The government of the world is therefore shared between a spiritual and a temporal power. . . . This single world-wide society may be called . . . either a commonwealth or a

church. Whether in church or state, power is justified ultimately as a factor in the moral or religious government of the world, and yet is equally a factor in the life of a self-sufficing human community. . . . The controlling social conception is that of an organic community in which the various classes are functioning parts.[40]

Dante's "De Monarchia" was written almost a decade after the climactic collision between Pope Boniface VIII and the French king, Philip IV; yet, in its analysis of papal and imperial claims, it belonged to an earlier world. The chief competitors were no longer pope and emperor but rather pope and the secular princes of the emerging territorial states of western Europe, most importantly the kings of France and England (especially after the Norman Conquest of 1066). This collision began to intensify at that moment when it appeared that papal authority was at its acme; the empire was in a state of progressive decay, and territorial princes were only beginning to appreciate the strength they possessed. Between 1150 and 1300 the kings of France and England had pacified their realms to a degree not seen for hundreds of years and had achieved significant visibility through their service in the crusades. Papal efforts to enlist such princes in opposition to imperial pretensions had, ironically, heightened the sensitivity of monarchs to any abridgement of their own autonomy. Nascent nationalism was beginning to prove an ally of the princes, and theorists like Pierre Dubois and John of Paris, an advisor to Philip the Fair, reflected both the new nationalist ethos and the willingness to assert national independence from both the empire and the papacy.

For instance, Dubois, a French lawyer, was something of a harbinger of Jean Bodin. He argued that all those who believed in the possibility of a universal ruler were looking hopelessly to the past. If a semblance of peace were to be provided for Europe, papal authority in secular matters had to be eliminated and the equivalent of a collective security system consisting of independent princes would have to be constructed:

> No sane man could really believe that at this period of the world's history one individual could rule the whole world as a temporal monarch, with all men obeying him as their superior. If a tendency in this direction did appear, there would be wars and revolutions without end. No man could put them down because of the huge populations involved, the distance and diversity of the countries, and the natural propensity of human beings to quarrel.[41]

The controversy between papacy and princes that erupted at the end of the thirteenth century was triggered by a conflict over control of taxation. Initiated by a papal claim that secular officials had no authority over the clergy and could not tax church property, the ensuing struggle dramatically reduced papal power and confirmed the central place of territorial states in the new order of things. Papal claims were anathema to the monarchs of France and England because of their dependence on revenue from church property; both refused to accede and could not be coerced into doing so. In 1302 Boniface issued a papal bull (*Unam Sanctam Ecclesiam*) that declared his authority supreme in both the spiritual and temporal realms; only the pope, who could be judged by God above, could judge princes. Philip of France was excommunicated, and the king then summoned a royal council—which included the

French high clergy—that indicted Boniface for a series of alleged crimes. Philip subsequently undertook an abortive effort to kidnap the pope, who died shortly thereafter. Boniface's immediate successors, Benedict VI and Clement V, abandoned their predecessor's bold claims, and Clement, a French cleric, came to reside at Avignon rather than in Rome. There followed a long period of papal decline. Between 1305 and 1378, successive popes resided at Avignon ("the Babylonian captivity"), and for almost forty years thereafter rival popes resided at Avignon and Rome ("the Great Schism"). The feeble attempts by popes between 1323 and 1347 to reverse this decline, especially their efforts to intervene in imperial elections, were singularly unsuccessful. In sum, the papacy at the peak of its power had confronted incipient nationalism and had been humbled by it.

The end of the conflict for all intents and purposes finally dispelled the medieval myth of universal monarchy and community. This dramatic shift was most clearly reflected in the ideas of a Franciscan monk, Marsilio of Padua.[42] His *Defensor Pacis* (The Defender of Peace), which appeared in 1324, was conditioned by trends such as the rise of a new commercial middle class and the growing autonomy of territorial states. One emergent result of these trends was a fundamental transformation in the nature of the European political system, which was increasingly characterized by behavior and norms quite unlike those of the medieval imperium.

Like the period in which he lived, Marsilio's ideas represent something of a bridge from the medieval system to the Renaissance and the Protestant Reformation. The transitional nature of his thought is reflected in the combining of what is an essentially medieval mode of discourse with self-conscious advocacy of emergent nationalism and the prerogatives of dynastic states. Like St. Thomas and Dante, Marsilio retained Aristotelian forms but abandoned the myth of Christian unity. Of equal importance was his propensity to legitimize authority on the basis of consent from below. Authority, for Marsilio, was legitimized by the will of the community in whose name and for whose benefit it existed. In this, Marsilio at once echoed early medieval conceptions of the law and later conceptualizations of national sovereignty. Strikingly absent from his ideas were those conceptions of divine and canon law that constituted the pillars upon which the myth of Christian unity had been erected.

Not only did Marsilio reject the universal pretensions of the papacy, but he also declared that bishops and the pope alike were responsible to and derived their authority from the community of believers. Any additional claims by them, he believed, represented efforts to usurp the authority of secular rulers. Nor were they entitled to exercise coercive power, even over heretics; the authority to do so belonged entirely to secular officials in this world and to God in the hereafter. Indeed, religious officials, he argued, should constitute no more than one of many functional classes within civil society and should be governed by temporal authorities like all such classes in order to maximize the peace and well-being of the communities of which they were a part. Religion, like agriculture or commerce, had social consequences and, therefore, logically must be regulated by those responsible for maintaining public order. Papal usurpation of temporal authority was, for Marsilio, the single greatest obstacle to peace and order:

This wrong opinion of certain Roman bishops, and also perhaps their perverted desire for rulership, which they assert is owed to them because of the plenitude of power given to them, as they say, by Christ—this is that singular cause which we have said produces the intranquillity of discord of the city or state.[43]

THE MACHIAVELLIAN REVOLUTION: GLOBAL POLITICS IN THE RENAISSANCE

In the evolution of global-politics theory from the medieval imperium to the European state system of the seventeenth and eighteenth centuries, Niccolò Machiavelli, like the Renaissance itself, must be regarded as transitional. He at once echoed the ideas of Marsilio and forecast the ideas of later balance-of-power and power-oriented theorists. Not quite a realist in the contemporary sense, he was a progenitor of realist thought. Having decisively rejected the Aristotelian rationalism of the late Middle Ages, he was an empiricist who sought lessons from classical history. Like Hobbes and later political theorists, Machiavelli was thoroughly secular in his approach to politics, but unlike them, he could not differentiate between the state as an autonomous entity and those who ruled it.

Like his medieval predecessors, Machiavelli was the product of his time and place, and he was conscious of the transitional nature of the period in which he was living. He understood that the myth of political and religious universalism had been eclipsed by the emergence of princely territorial states, and he knew, too, that Italy and its system of city-states were in transition between two political ages. He was at once an Italian patriot in the tradition of Marsilio and a theorist who sought to construct an autonomous model of politics. Thus, he sought simultaneously to rid Italy of its fiercely competitive parochialism and to provide a secular and timeless theory of political power.

Machiavelli was a political practitioner as well as a theorist, and his writings were self-consciously animated by and directed toward both audiences. He was politically active between 1498 and 1512, following the ouster of the Medicis from his native Florence, and was a partisan of Piero Soderini. His participation in the government of Florence, most especially in its effort to reconquer the city of Pisa, and his preoccupation with the condition of Italy following the French invasion of 1494 made him keenly aware of the rapidly changing international environment and conditioned his political ideas. Those ideas are, of course, staples in all courses in the history of political thought, and Machiavelli is perhaps most readily—though somewhat inaccurately—recalled as the archetypal political amoralist. Hence, Marlowe has him speak of himself in the prologue to *The Jew of Malta:*

To some perhaps my name is odious,
But such as love me guard me from their tongues;
And let them know that I am Machiavel, And weigh not men, and therefore not men's words. Admired I am of those that hate me most. Though some speak openly against my books, Yet they will read me, and thereby attain to Peter's chair; and when they cast me off, are poisoned by my climbing followers.[44]

Postwar realists commonly cite Machiavelli's ideas as evidence for their assumptions and method.[45] Waltz virtually credits Machiavelli with having found

Realpolitik: "Ever since Machiavelli, interest and necessity . . . have remained the key concepts of *Realpolitik.* From Machiavelli through Meinecke and Morgenthau the elements of the approach and the reasoning remain constant." E. H. Carr views him as "the first important political realist." From the other end of the intellectual spectrum, a British scholar of international law, J. L. Brierly, declares that "Machiavelli's *Prince* . . . had already given to the world a relentless analysis of the art of government based on the conception of the state as an entity entirely self-sufficing and non-moral."[46] How redolent of what later theorists would term realism is Machiavelli's declaration of independence from his predecessors:

> I fear that my writing . . . may be deemed presumptuous, differing as I do . . . from the opinions of others. But my intention being to write something of use to those who understand, it appears to me more proper to go to the real truth of the matter than to its imagination; and many have imagined republics and principalities which have never been seen or known to exist in reality; for how we live is so far removed from how we ought to live, that he who abandons what is done for what ought to be done, will rather learn to bring about his own ruin than his preservation. A man who wishes to make a profession of goodness in everything must necessarily come to grief among so many who are not good.[47]

In other words, counsels Machiavelli, observe what *really* exists, not what one would wish into existence.

The International System of Renaissance Italy

Although it was clear to Machiavelli, writing in the early sixteenth century, that the independent city-states of Italy had become anomalies in the face of the large territorial states of western Europe,[48] the relatively long period in which those polities had developed had produced fertile soil in which his ideas might germinate and flourish. Except in the south, feudalism had not taken hold as fully in Italy as elsewhere in Europe. "Sometime during and after the final decades of the Hohenstauffen empire," writes Winfried Franke, "the Italian regional states and city-states coalesced, so to speak, from a multitude of politically rather 'atomized' and disjointed entities into several sets of regional actors and finally into one system of interlocking, independent states." By the fifteenth century, city-states such as Venice, Milan, Genoa, Florence, and the Papal States had already enjoyed several hundred years of political independence and commercial development and had accumulated significant experience in "balance-of-power" politics. Indeed, Venetian diplomatic method served as a model for the emerging territorial states of Europe.[49]

International trade and commerce, bourgeois political influence, and urban habits of life developed earlier and faster in Italy than elsewhere in Europe. It was also in Italy, as reflected in the thought of Dante and Marsilio, that recognition of and resistance to the secular pretensions of the Roman Church took root most deeply. By the time of Machiavelli, then, the city-states of Italy had considerable experience with a decentralized system in which independent actors were sufficiently powerful to retain their autonomy but over which no one of them could exercise hegemony. Bozeman's description of that system resembles descriptions of the so-called European balance-of-power system of large sovereign states of the eighteenth century: "It was characterized by a plurality of city-states among which Milan, Florence, Naples, the Papacy, and Venice were the strongest. Each of these five claimed to be sovereign, yet none could muster the necessary strength to realize its particular aspirations independently."[50]

Yet despite their early assertion of autonomy, the growth of the Italian city-states—as Machiavelli realized—had fallen well behind that of the territorial monarchies of western Europe by the end of the fifteenth century. The city-states remained sufficiently small that no clear distinction could be drawn between the interstate and intrastate realms. As noted earlier, the Guelph/(papal)–Ghibelline/(imperial) quarrels of Dante's era raged both within and among the city-states, and the tight linkage of internal and interstate conflicts continued to characterize Italian politics during the Renaissance. In Bozeman's words:

> The struggle for supremacy within the state was . . . seldom confined to the local scene. For since the Italian cities were closely related to each other both physically and culturally, aspirants to power were always tempted to seek the supplementary strength they needed by conspiring with governments or factions in neighboring communities. The area of diplomatic activities, already disturbed as a result of the uneasy distribution of power in the Italian region as a whole, was thus still further confused by the espionage, intrigues and betrayals in which conspiring partisans engaged incessantly across the boundaries of their native states.[51]

To this extent, Italian politics stood somewhere between what we think of as gangster politics and the politics of sovereign states. The autonomy of the city-states had come early, but by the end of the fifteenth century, nationalism in Italy was rudimentary indeed in comparison to that in England and France.

Had Machiavelli not appreciated the anomalous nature of Italian politics before, he certainly did so after a French army under Charles VIII, with artillery and Swiss mercenaries, descended on Italy in 1494. In the words of his contemporary, historian Francesco Guicciardini:

> [H]is passage into Italy not only gave rise to changes in dominions, subversion of kingdoms, desolation of countries, destruction of cities and the cruelest massacres, but also new fashions, new customs, new and bloody ways of waging warfare, and diseases which had been unknown up to that time. Furthermore, his incursion introduced so much disorder into Italian ways of governing and maintaining harmony, that we have never since been able to re-establish order, thus opening the possibility to other foreign nations and barbarous armies to trample upon our institutions and miserably oppress us.[52]

The effect of the French and Spanish invasion of Italy, the decline in the independence of city-states like Naples and Milan, the overthrow of the Florentine republic, and the triumphs of those whom Italians looked upon as cultural upstarts infused Machiavelli with passionate nationalism and brought him to demand his country's unification so that it might restore and maintain its independence. He saw his country as "more enslaved than the Hebrews, more oppressed than the Persians, and more scattered than the Athenians; without a head, without order, beaten, despoiled, lacerated, and overrun."[53]

The French invasion of Italy not only impressed upon Machiavelli the advantages of the large territorial state over competing political forms like the Italian city-states, but brought him to recognize the absolutely central role of military power in global politics, a belief handed down to subsequent generations of realist theorists and practitioners. In *The Prince,* he declared that the "chief foundations of all states . . . are good laws and good arms," neither of which could exist without the other (XII) and that a prince should "have no other aim or thought . . . but war and its organisation and discipline, for that is the only art that is necessary to one who commands. . ." (XIV).[54] And Machiavelli's understanding of warfare, like politics, was conditioned by his recognition of the relationship among changes in technology, economics, and society.

In the technological sphere, the introduction of firearms, gunpowder, and artillery had undermined the military role of the medieval knight and, consequently, his political and social status. The feudal system itself was a victim of these changes, as the knight could no longer perform his legal functions. But it was not merely technological changes that doomed the feudal system, but the growth of commerce and the spread of money. This shift in the economic basis of society weakened the religious and legal bonds that had constituted the bases of political loyalty and increasingly depreciated the centrality of landholding as a political-economic power factor. "It was primarily in the military field," declares Felix Gilbert, "that those who were the protagonists of the new economic developments—the cities and the wealthy overlords—could make greatest use of the new opportunities: namely, to accept money payments instead of services, or to secure services by money rewards and salaries."[55] Urban elites, then, were able to assemble professional armies, the *condottieri,* in which allegiance was based on pay rather than vassalage. This revolution in the nature of military organization started earliest and proceeded fastest in Italy, where economic changes were most advanced.

The effect of these changes in technology and organization was to create the potential for more destructive and longer wars. Where medieval armies were largely recruited from the narrow caste of noble knights who served only for short periods of time, mercenary armies had a larger pool of manpower from which to draw. Artillery especially was responsible for degrading the defensive capacity of isolated strongholds and high-walled castles, the bastions of medieval knights. Mercenaries were willing to serve as long as they were paid. That this potential was not realized until the end of the fifteenth century was due largely to the reluctance of mercenary commanders to squander their military resources in fierce campaigns and their preference for more leisurely and indecisive conflicts that would earn them greater profits. In addition, such mercenaries—unmoved by a higher cause—were rarely inclined to die for their employers. The French invasion of Italy seemed to change all this with dramatic ferocity. In Guicciardini's passionate description,

> The effects of the invasion spread over Italy like a wildfire or like a pestilence, overthrowing not only the ruling powers, but changing also the methods of government and the methods of war. Previously there had been five leading states in Italy . . . ; and the foremost interest of all these states had been to maintain the status quo. . . . When war broke out, the forces were equal, the military organization slow and the artillery cumbersome, so that usually the entire summer was

spent on the siege of one castle; the wars lasted very long and the battles ended with small losses or no losses at all. Through the invasion of the French, everything was thrown upside down, as though by a sudden hurricane. . . . Now the wars became quick and violent, a kingdom was devastated and conquered more quickly than previously a small village; the sieges of cities were very short and were successfully completed in days and hours instead of in months; the battles became embittered and bloody. Not subtle negotiations and the cleverness of diplomats, but military campaigns and the fist of the soldier decided over the fate of the states.[56]

Almost overnight, the Italian city-states had been reduced to pawns in Europe's emerging interstate system, as the citadels upon which they had relied for protection against each other fell swiftly before the French onslaught.

Military disaster had a decisive effect on Machiavelli's political outlook. Not only did he come to appreciate the coming hegemony of large, centrally organized, and secular territorial states, but also he came to understand instinctively the political and military necessity of popular support and legitimacy. It was no longer possible, he believed, for a narrow elite unilaterally to make itself responsible for the masses; the former could only survive if it enlisted the latter. Repeatedly he ridiculed the fighting prowess of paid mercenaries in contrast to citizen-armies:

The mercenaries and auxiliaries are useless and dangerous, and if any one supports his state by the arms of mercenaries, he will never stand firm or sure, as they are disunited, ambitious, without discipline, faithless, bold amongst friends, cowardly amongst enemies, they have no fear of God, and keep no faith with men. Ruin is only deferred as long as the assault is postponed; in peace you are despoiled by them, and in war by the enemy. *The cause of this is that they have no love or other motive to keep them in the field beyond a trifling wage, which is not enough to make them ready to die for you.* They are quite willing to be your soldiers so long as you do not make war.[57]

Only if the sort of nationalist spirit based on citizen identities dimly perceived earlier by Marsilio could be harnessed to the defense of the state would it be possible for Italy to regain its former independence. Translated into military practice, this meant that Machiavelli advocated reliance upon citizen-militias rather than paid mercenaries despite his own disappointment in such a militia during the defense of Florence against the return of the Medicis. It was his belief in the efficacy of the citizen-soldier motivated by love of country that led him to downplay the importance of money in war. Overall, Machiavelli predicted by almost three centuries the military consequences of revolution in France, that tremendous infusion of martial energy and spirit that so frightened Clausewitz.

It was, moreover, the French invasion and Machiavelli's analysis of the reasons for Italian weakness that led him to his key idea that there existed a public morality of states and rulers different than and independent of the conventional or private morality of individuals. "Although deceit is detestable in all other things," he argued, "yet in the conduct of war it is laudable and honorable."[58] In effect, Machiavelli was articulating the primacy of states' interests and the compelling proposition that the ends justify the means.

The Primacy and Autonomy of Politics and Power

If, during the Middle Ages, the temporal and spiritual represented two sides of the same coin and were inextricably woven together, Machiavelli reflected the new reality in which the two realms were clearly demarcated.[59] Increasingly, political leaders were no longer subject to spiritual authority and no longer sought to play dual roles. Indeed, like Hobbes later, Machiavelli dismissed the independent role of religion in politics as "illusion." Throughout Europe the previously unlimited rights of the clergy were being narrowed. Even the popes had come to respect and participate in the ebb and flow of balance-of-power politics.

Especially in Italy, political leadership was no longer based on ascription or law but on the ability of parvenus to seize and hold the reins of government. Finally, the universalist ideal of the Middle Ages had surrendered to the clash of state egoisms; the apparent permanence of the past had given way to a scene of apparently ceaseless and turbulent change. Machiavelli's prince was, in Sheldon Wolin's apt phrase, "the offspring of an age of restless ambition, of the rapid transformation of institutions and quick shifts in power among the elite groups."[60] His skills were those of manipulation of symbols and people; his "right" to rule was confirmed by his ability to do so. Ethics, like religion, were instrumental rather than ends in themselves. For Machiavelli, observes Carr, "politics are not . . . a function of ethics, but ethics of politics. . . . Morality is the product of power."[61] In Machiavelli's eyes medieval rulership, like medieval theory, was obsolete—an idealist illusion of no theoretical value for Renaissance practitioners.[62]

Like later realists, Machiavelli's ideas flowed from a gloomy assessment of human nature, especially that of political man, and he argued that "human desires are insatiable (because their nature is to have and to do everything whilst fortune limits their possessions and capacity of enjoyment), this gives rise to a constant discontent in the human mind."[63] The ambition that inevitably flowed from such discontent implied a perpetual scarcity of power among individuals as well as among states. This in turn implied a constant clash of wills and interests. In contrast to his medieval predecessors, then, Machiavelli viewed conflict and preparations for conflict as the norm rather than as exceptions to the norm. History was the repetition of cause and effect in which conflict was the motor force; it was no more possible to will away the dilemmas inherent in scarcity than to will away history itself. As the product of cause and effect, rather than the whim of God, history for Machiavelli could be and had to be approached empirically, as a science. It was the politician's task to do so, always sensitive, however, to those unpredictable elements that Machiavelli labeled *"fortuna"* and always aware that political outcomes were as dependent on the actions of others as on his own decisions.

If for Machiavelli there existed an autonomous science of politics based on an understanding of history, then it followed that states, as the products of history, must be guided by principles of behavior and morality unique to them. States had interests that were not merely the sum of the interests of their citizens. To pursue these interests effectively in conflict with others, it followed that they must be guided by a corporate reason of state. And although reason of state consisted of certain very general common principles, it must also incorporate specific instructions determined by context and situation, especially the distribution of power. Later theorists would refine these assumptions and deduce what they would call the national interest.

In the Middle Ages, the idea of reason of state could not evolve because the concept of the secular state itself was boxed in by competing concepts such as divine law and religious obligation; and Machiavelli's own later conception remained limited owing to the immaturity of the city-state and the European state system. Yet he tapped its essence by combining his three master concepts of virtue, fortune, and necessity. The first was that quality of heroic commitment that distinguished successful rulers from common men and was a prerequisite to the founding of a state. That act, which was to Machiavelli a supreme achievement, could not be accomplished by blind obedience to conventional norms and should not be judged by such norms. Machiavelli's treatment of the myth of Romulus, in contrast to St. Augustine's treatment thereof, as Wolin observes, reflects the step-level shift in thinking between ages: "For Augustine the vile acts committed by Romulus in laying the foundations of Roman power constituted a political version of the drama of original sin. . . . Machiavelli . . . argued that the ends of national greatness legitimized Romulus' deeds: crimes committed by political actors fell under the judgments of history not morality."[64]

For Machiavelli the great task of princes was to instill virtue in their subjects, imbuing them with a healthy patriotism that created and sustained institutions. A high level of social virtue was the prerequisite of republics, which Machiavelli deemed superior to principalities. Like Romulus, a prince with virtue was responsive to something greater than his personal interests and was, therefore, not to be constrained by ordinary morality. "And because it [virtue] was for him the higher world," declared historian Friedrich Meinecke, "so it could be permitted to trespass and encroach on the moral world in order to achieve its aims."[65]

The state and its rulers are, however, constantly assailed by fortune, which to Machiavelli consists of factors and events beyond deliberate control and rational planning.[66] While fortune cannot be overcome, its effects can be modified and constrained by rulers and states that have virtue. Fortune creates necessity, which provides, in Meinecke's words, "the causal pressure, the means of bringing the sluggish masses into the form required by virtu."[67] Necessity encourages virtue and, like the invasion of Italy, demands heroic actions: "virtue has more sway where labor is the result of necessity rather than of choice."[68] The state and its rulers must be responsive to the dictates of necessity even if such response flagrantly violates conventional morality; necessity; in other words, is the basis of reason of state, and it is in this sense that, for Machiavelli, the end justifies the means.

From this equation, Machiavelli deduced a relativist morality for states and their rulers. Declaring that everyone would wish a prince to possess good qualities, he quickly adds, "but as they cannot all be possessed or observed, human conditions not permitting of it," it is necessary for rulers to do what they must if the state is endangered. Necessity, then, may require force and fraud if the state is to survive and prosper,[69] but the idea of reason of state is, for Machiavelli, a prudential and "utilitarian middle way"[70] between good and evil; it is realism as opposed to idealism. Politics consistently requires, the confrontation of dilemmas, and reason of state entails the selection of the lesser of evils that will ensure state survival.[71] All this is summed up in that most "realist" of Machiavelli's conclusions: "For where the very safety of the country depends upon the resolution to be taken, no considerations of justice or injustice, humanity or cruelty, nor of glory or of shame, should be allowed to prevail. But putting all other considerations aside, the only question should be? What course will save the life and liberty of the country?"[72]

CONCLUSION: MEDIEVAL IDEALISM AND MACHIAVELLIAN REALISM

In this brief review of medieval and Machiavellian ideas, it has become clear that both were responses to social conditions and social norms. While it is difficult to generalize about the medieval millennium, the thrust of much of its theory reflected a world characterized by an economically and socially stratified universe in which political and military power were local and limited, obligations and loyalties were personal, and differentiation between individual and collective interests and wills and between domestic and global politics was virtually nonexistent. Theory tended to reflect these realities in a number of ways, most importantly the myth of individuals united in a universal imperium and the dichotomy between the relative immutability of temporal conditions and the ultimate perfectibility of humanity as a spiritual collectivity. The strong religious component and the very real authority of the Roman Church imbued theorists with deeply held norms and produced what seems like idealism among them; especially those influenced by Platonism.

The dominance of Christianity itself was a reality that tended to overshadow pervasive conflict and economic and social stagnation. Christian belief in spiritual perfectibility bred optimism about the course of human affairs as part of a divine plan. It fostered, too, a belief in the community and equality of Christians in the face of a temporal reality that was at once disunited, competitive, and hierarchical.

As the Middle Ages drew to a close, the underlying conditions that had evoked medieval idealism began to shift. The early decline of the Holy Roman Empire and the subsequent decline of the church as both a spiritual and temporal force inevitably stimulated new and radically different ideas about the political universe. The rise of the large and centrally administered territorial state, shifts in the bases of economic and military power, the breakdown of feudal social constraints, and growing secularization through the recovery of the classics—especially Aristotle's writings—and advances in science produced a new spirit that was evident in Marsilio and dominant in Machiavelli.

All of these great changes are reflected in Machiavelli's historical empiricism, as well as in the substance of his ideas. Large territorial states governed by secular princes in the absence of any higher authority whose independence was ensured by force of arms and nascent nationalism were the focus of his attention. Written in what Jacob Burckhardt described as an "age of bastards"—the era of the Borgias—Machiavelli's ideas reflected the insecurity, the rapid shifts in political power, and the demise of traditional bases of authority that he saw all around him. Machiavelli's political realism reflected a belief in the immutability of the security dilemma while allowing for the waxing and waning of individual states and leaders.

From this belief and from his assumptions about human nature flowed a fundamental pessimism about the human condition. Individual heroes were capable of creative political acts just as were individual artists and scientists, and an individual state could, at least for a time, encourage sufficient virtue among its citizens for them to prosper; all could not do so at once. Machiavelli's world was one of intense competition and turbulence in which the power and prosperity of individual leaders and states could be measured only in relation to one another. Finally, Machiavelli's ideas reflected elitism in the sense that only a relatively few individuals possessed the virtue of a prince, yet this elitism was tempered by his belief in the importance of republican legitimacy, his skepticism toward ascriptive bases of authority, and his rejection of a hierarchical international system.

Our analysis suggests, furthermore, that what we have termed idealism and realism are not theories in the scientific meaning of that term but rather conceptual and normatively inspired prisms through which scholars and practitioners view the political world around them. These prisms, in turn, provide the assumptions on which decisions are made and from which specific hypotheses are generated in particular eras. With this perspective, it becomes easier to appreciate why it is so difficult for theorists to progress toward some abstract truth. For global-politics scholars, history itself provides the raw data from which inspiration is born. Yet, in the fundamental sense we have outlined, their data and its interpretation remain prisoners of history.

CHAPTER 4

The Vicissitudes of Norms and Theory

Realism and Idealism

Scholars of global politics who have sought to depict the evolution of theory in their field in accordance with the Kuhnian model almost inevitably point to realist theory as the discipline's outstanding paradigm. They argue as though postwar realism were a revolution, a reaction to anomalies associated with what they describe as interwar idealism. Their argument is strengthened, they believe, by the subsequent decline of realism, especially in the 1970s, which they offer as evidence that the paradigm process in global politics remains healthy and continues to operate as they would have predicted.

Postwar realists such as Hans J. Morgenthau, Kenneth Thompson, Reinhold Niebuhr, and E. H. Carr themselves contributed to the illusion by emphasizing the novelty of their ideas and depicting them as the antitheses of idealism. Although they recognized their debt to earlier scholars like Thucydides, Machiavelli, Han Fei-tzu, and Kautilya, they were more concerned with fundamentally reorienting the foreign policies of their countries and so tended to claim more for themselves than was justly theirs.

Yet realism, as we suggested earlier, is less a theory than it is a set of normative emphases that shape theory.[1] Boiled down to essentials, it is a self-contained syllogism whose premises are these:

1. As long as human beings are organized into sovereign states, their survival and security can be assured by only acting according to the dictates of power.
2. Sovereign states are permanent features of the political landscape.
3. Ergo, competitive power politics, realist-style, is the alpha and omega of global politics, and any alternative system of thought is incompatible with reality.

This is a closed system of analysis. Relying implicitly or explicitly upon such a syllogism condemns the theory to the same conclusion regardless of methodology and reduces analysis to the level of ideology. Balance of power, for example, is merely a logical corollary, not an empirical fact, and history can be rummaged to support (or falsify) the claim. No allowance is made for the possibility that realist assumptions themselves constitute empirical claims and that the underlying phenomena on which these assumptions are based (e.g., the territorial nation-state) are the products of historical evolution rather than being timeless or universal constructs. Little effort is therefore made to hypothesize the conditions for further evolution. Moreover, when the behavior of leaders or collectivities fails to obey this iron law, realists explain such deviance as utopian or, worse, suicidal stupidity. Unfortunately, such condemnation reveals the iron law to be no law at all but merely prescription laced with a good deal of subjectivism. Under these circumstances, the prospects for genuine theoretical breakthroughs are remote, especially since even much of contemporary behavioral analysis remains in the grip of this ideology.[2]

Historically, most societies have been characterized by the presence of several normative strains simultaneously competing with one another.[3] For this reason, theories of global politics that reflect one or another extreme have rarely monopolized scholarly discourse. For every self-professed Machiavellian, there has been an anti-Machiavellian; Jeremy Bentham and Richard Cobden flourished alongside the nineteenth-century advocates of balance of power and imperialism. As illustrated in the preceding chapter, however, the normative temper of any era is likely to have distinct emphases. Typically, if these are extreme in one period, a compensatory shift will take place during an ensuing period, especially in the face of policy failures. These shifts are reflected in changing fashions and fads in the social sciences, including global politics.

Realists have often recognized their own role in this ancient drama, and they have themselves pointed to the shifting nature of ideas in their field. For realist John Herz, this takes the form of movement between extremes: "a utopian and often chiliastic Political Idealism, or—when disillusionment with the ideal's ability to mold the 'realist' facts frustrates expectations—it [the ideal] has taken refuge in an equally extreme power-political and power-glorifying Political Realism."[4] Realists have also been prepared to describe in clear and forceful terms the repeated collision between themselves and their putatively idealist adversaries, and have provided histories of foreign policy that depict the cyclical domination of one or the other set of normative claims.[5]

Earlier we described the key normative continua along which conflicting theories of global politics are distributed and suggested the circumstances under which shifts tend to occur. Although it is not easy to predict which emphases will dominate at a particular moment, two observations are in order at this point: Self-styled realists and idealists are prone to identify different aspects of the same phenomena as evidence for their positions, and it is a profound error to accept the realist contention that their adversaries are merely misty-minded dreamers and utopians with no sense of the "real" conditions that shape human behavior and the *condition humaine* more generally. The first of these observations helps to explain why realist and idealist theoretical strains coexist in time and place regardless of which is dominant, and the second is essentially a corollary of the first.

Scholars whose theories emphasize immutability, pessimism, competition, or elitism (e.g., realists) are fundamentally conservative in politics and outlook.

They are alert to the perils posed by the inherent unpredictability of change and are fearful of its consequences either for them personally or for their polities. For them, the great challenge is to control and manipulate the forces of change against human error, stupidity, and avarice. Theirs is a world of limited resources and unlimited ambition. Those conditions, in their view, are immutable. Older realists like Morgenthau stress the immutability of human nature, whereas neo-realists like Waltz stress the immutability of structural factors (the manner in which actors are arranged vis-à-vis one another[6]), especially anarchy.

In contrast to realists, those whose theories reflect mutability, optimism, community, and nonelitism (e.g., idealists or, more accurately, liberals) see the forces of change as opportunities for reducing stupidity and avarice and for expanding spiritual and material resources. Consider Richard Rosecrance in whose recent work, *The Rise of the Virtual State*, these idealist norms are admirably reflected. He writes:

> This book asserts that, despite retrogressions that capture our attention, the world is making steady progress toward peace and economic security. It argues that as factors of labor, capital, and information triumph over the old factor of land, nations no longer need and in time will not covet additional territory.[7]

For Rosecrance, the world is changing for the better in ways that should promote egalitarianism and general prosperity—views offered after the Cold War, at a time of accelerating technological change and little interstate violence.

In the view of realists, the calamities of major wars provide evidence of the failure to use violence scientifically, the risk of unleashing human passions, and the folly of reformist zeal. For idealists, such tragedies reflect the futility of prevailing rules of the game and afford opportunities to alter these rules. The former regard technological innovation as providing new and often dangerous capabilities with which struggles may be waged, whereas the latter view science and technology as means for enlarging the resource pie and overcoming the superstitions, ignorance, and parochialism that they see as sources of conflict. To some extent, both are correct, just as iterated non-zero-sum games provide evidence for the virtues both of cooperative and noncooperative strategies. From time to time, one or the other normative strand will appear to have triumphed, because the values that preoccupy its adherents most seem—temporarily—at greater risk; yet neither can triumph in any permanent way.

OSCILLATING NORMS

Realism and idealism, as we have portrayed them to this point, appear antithetical, and it might be inferred that we are proposing a simple theoretical dichotomy. This is not of course the case, as scholars rarely place themselves at one or the other extreme. Just as Morgenthau and Machiavelli were prepared to admit of the role of law and justice, so Wilsonians were not ignorant of the importance of national power and ambition.[8] For us, realism and idealism represent logical extremes or Weberian ideal types, much as Clausewitz, influenced by Kant, distinguished between "absolute" and "real" war. The insightful theorist sees the pitfalls and virtues of both and refuses to embrace either without reservation.

So it is that the apparent realist Thucydides gives voice to Pericles' Funeral Oration and depicts the tragedy of the *hubris* of Athens' undiluted policy of power in its dealings with Melos and its subsequent Sicilian expedition. And, although pointing to the changing distribution of power between Athens and Sparta as the chief cause of the Peloponnesian War, Thucydides later identifies a variety of other causes and repeatedly points to the relevance of domestic factors in explaining behavior. In other words, Thucydides, like most great thinkers, refuses to be pigeonholed.

In paying homage to Thucydides, Sir Alfred Zimmern also expressed more eloquently than we could have a key theme of the present book: "All great art is like a ghost seeking to express more than it can utter and beckoning to regions beyond. This is as true in history . . . as in poetry or any more personal art."[9] This was only partly understood by German historian Friedrich Meinecke when he described the "compromise" that seventeenth-century thinkers professed to find between Machiavelli's creed and natural law:

> The immense power of the old tradition of Natural law is shown by the fact that even the most emancipated thinkers of the century lay under its spell and made no attempt to grasp the handhold which the doctrine of raison d'état offered towards a new empirical doctrine of the state. But, being great and profound thinkers, besides imbibing the old tradition they also mentally digested the living reality of state life.[10]

Yet there is oscillation among the norms that condition theory in global politics. We have seen this to be the case in the evolution of medieval theory and in its transition to the realism of Machiavelli. Such oscillation does not necessarily reflect major shifts in the subjects that preoccupy theorists and practitioners of global politics as much as it does changes in the salience of those subjects and in strategies for coping with them. At any given moment, "reality," as defined by the external world and the situation of the observer, conditions the observer to notice some phenomena while omitting or ignoring others. Thus, Thucydides' *History* makes sense only when we understand that it was written by a former general who was witnessing the decline of his beloved Athens. Still, at a general level there is a remarkable consistency in some of the subjects that the global-politics literature treats. As expressed by Arnold Wolfers and Laurence Martin:

> The problems of self-preservation in the light of external danger, of expansion into new territories or of contraction, of intervention in the affairs of others, of alliances, peace-making, and the conduct of wars are as much matters of concern and controversy as they were when a More, Hume or Bentham put their minds to them.[11]

Are their observations necessarily inconsistent? No. Instead, we are over and over again confronted with theoretical "novelties" that on close inspection turn out to be rediscoveries of old ideas, themes, and hypotheses. These reappear as conditions evoke similar normative emphases.

That historical and geopolitical circumstances at least partly determine theoretical outlook is borne out by the distinct intellectual traditions of continental Europe and the Anglo-Saxon world. Historically, realist doctrines appear to have enjoyed greater prominence and to have become more firmly anchored in the former, owing to geographic factors and the consequent presence of powerful countries, bordering and all posing potential threats to one another. By contrast, the longtime isolation and greater sense of security enjoyed by the United States and Great Britain produced more fertile ground for ideas of an optimistic liberal stripe.[12] Even during the Cold War, the relatively greater realism, even cynicism, of Soviet than American leaders was partly the legacy of historical insecurity and seemed strangely at odds with the optimism of classical Marxism. Anglo-Saxon theorists and practitioners, then, typically have viewed themselves as enjoying greater latitude in foreign affairs than their continental brethren, who saw themselves as under the spell of Machiavelli's "necessity." The traditional faith of Americans in the benefits of science and technology, their optimism about the future and the prospects for improving the human condition, and their general problem-solving ethos are products of the United States' unique historical experience, especially its abundant resources and secure geographical location.

There have, of course, been notable Anglo-Saxon realists as well as continental idealists. What is singular about them is that they seem to have emerged in exceptional historical periods. Thomas Hobbes, for example, must be understood as the product of a period of civil war in England, and Alexander Hamilton was at once the product of the American Revolution and the relatively brief era of extreme American vulnerability to European power that followed the revolution; in any event, the Federalist ascendancy was brief, followed by an era of Jeffersonian optimism.

At root, mature realism and the theories and doctrines of global politics and foreign affairs that emerged from it entail an acceptance, even an endorsement, of the system of territorial states as a permanent and universal phenomenon. The relationship between this acceptance and the norm of competitiveness is evident. What is more important, however, is the realist/neorealist propensity to view the state as something greater than the sum of its parts, as an organic entity endowed with personality and interests that are not to be understood as the mere sum of individual personalities and interests. This propensity partly explains the elitist bias in realist theory. Some such premise is also necessary to conceptualize a national interest or to view economics through a neomercantilist lens as a means of serving state power.

By contrast, political, empirical, or normative challenges to state claims of authority over individuals domestically or to the state system internationally are viewed by realists with suspicion and even fear. This accounts in part for the neorealist's preference for system-level analyses and antipathy to "reductionist" theory.[13] Consequently, individualism is equated with utopianism; individual preferences, interests, and ethics are regarded as inconsistent and feckless and are therefore dangerous, especially to political and social stability. In this manner, the realist tends to equate currents of thought or political movements that threaten revolution within states with transnational and supranational currents that threaten the state system itself. Commonly, such movements prove to be individualist in content and are associated with norms of harmony and equality. This is reflected in Edmund Burke's reaction to the French Revolution.

Clashes between these competing norms historically have produced remarkable ironies. Some of the more interesting of these grew out of the great philosophical and political conflicts that enveloped Europe during the Protestant

Reformation. In its most general sense, Protestantism was a doctrine of individual conscience and personal piety, yet the outcome of the Reformation was to free princes from papal and imperial authority, strengthen temporal monarchies, affirm the doctrine of state sovereignty, and usher in the halcyon era of Realpolitik. This generalization, however, masks specific consequences that were even more paradoxical. Martin Luther, for instance, espoused a highly personal and individual doctrine of faith; yet, upon discovering that the secular German princes could, for their own reasons, serve as the instruments of this faith, he opposed the peasants' revolt, denounced resistance to state authority, and legitimized princely tyranny as God's vengeance for sin.[14] By contrast, John Calvin and his followers, especially John Knox, were more inclined to see the state as a secular instrument for imposing and sustaining religious purity. Yet, the force of circumstances in France, Holland, and Scotland transformed Calvinism into a fundamentally revolutionary movement that legitimized individual resistance against those states and monarchs that failed to adopt Protestant reforms. In a word, where Protestantism found acceptance, it became allied with the state, and where it did not, it reaffirmed either feudal localism or individual conscience against the power of states.[15]

Given the association between the evolution of the state system and the emergence of a tradition of power politics, it is not surprising that the doctrine gained new adherents following the articulation of the doctrine of state sovereignty. It was in France, the country that served as Machiavelli's model of the emerging territorial state, where the latter doctrine was born. Between 1562 and 1598 the French state was splintered by religious strife. Caught between the extremist Catholic League, aided by Spain, and Protestant Huguenots supported by coreligionists in England and Holland, the French monarchy increasingly saw its authority circumscribed. For their part, the Huguenots allied themselves with centrifugal forces that threatened the dismemberment of the state and became spokesmen for the feudal privileges of cities and provinces.

It was to bring an end to civil disunion and restore the majesty of the monarchy that Jean Bodin, a member of the moderate Catholic *Politiques* published, in 1576, *Six Books on the State*. Bodin defined sovereignty as "the absolute and perpetual power of the state, that is, the greatest power to command," and as the authority to appoint public officials, wage war and peace, mint currency, and provide justice. Sovereignty, as Bodin used the concept, was an attribute neither of government nor of individual monarchs, but rather a permanent characteristic of the state itself as an entity apart from and greater than the inhabitants of the realm.[16] The doctrine was directed equally against those subnational forces that threatened the state from within and those transnational and supranational forces of religion and empire that threatened it from without. Bodin's sovereign power could neither be divided nor delegated, so that the sort of shared authority characteristic of feudalism was incompatible with it. As we shall see in the following chapter, the doctrine of sovereignty became the rallying cry of state-centric theorists.[17]

The defeat of the Huguenots and the triumph of the monarchy in France set in train a process that culminated in the centralized state of Louis XIV and the doctrine of divine right of kings. And it was the Peace of Westphalia of 1648, which ended the Thirty Years' War, that ratified the state system internationally and the absolute power of the state over its subjects. It also ushered in the period known as the "classical balance of power" to which power theorists point with such approbation. In a sense, the state system and the balance of power were indivisible.

> A balance of power apparatus could not function without the existence of a state system.[18]

> Balance of power theorists assumed, first of all, the existence of a *state system,* that is, a group of independent "neighboring states more or less connected with one another."[19]

Generations of global-politics scholars, especially realists, have virtually defined their field in terms of sovereign states, thereby seeking to build an empirical discipline on the weak reed of what was for Bodin an aspiration rather than a reality. Even the "model" French state only briefly and imperfectly resembled the sovereign monolith described by Bodin and Hobbes. Indeed, the French state began to tax its citizens directly and eliminated internal customs duties only after the French Revolution. Neither of the key claims of the doctrine of sovereignty—absolute power of the state domestically and legal equality of states internationally—has been an accurate depiction of the global community.[20] Their increasing irrelevance, along with the erosion of sovereign boundaries and growing authority of nonsovereign polities at the present time, accounts for the apparently unreal and backwater quality of much contemporary scholarship in public international law. Historically, sovereignty was a potent psychological symbol, but it is hyperbole indeed to term the symbol, as does one scholar, "a source of vitality for the state."[21]

Yet the apparent congruence between the ideal world of sovereign states and the real world of eighteenth-century Europe led that period to become the "age of realism." It was an era of absolutist monarchy and intense interstate competition featuring transitory alliances and limited wars, as well as a period of cosmopolitan diplomacy and political stability. The entire edifice was reinforced by a rejection of the political and religious extremism that had characterized the bloody centuries preceding it. Statesmen of the era, like generations of realists that followed, could believe with Sir Harold Nicolson that "the worst kind of diplomatists are missionaries, fanatics and lawyers; the best kind are the reasonable and humane sceptics."[22]

The normative transition that had already begun would generate some very different ideas about politics. Cosmopolitan humanists, especially French philosophers such as Voltaire, Montesquieu, and Diderot, gave voice to a new individualism, a belief in the brotherhood and harmony of humankind, and a dedication to applying enlightened rationalism to overcoming social and political woes. It was this resurgent emphasis on the potential for human mutability, cooperation, and equality that constitutes the Age of Enlightenment, and it was sufficiently strong that it persuaded even monarchs like Catherine the Great and Frederick the Great to attempt novel experiments to foster the cultural and economic well-being of their subjects. It was also a prerequisite for the great surge of idealistic optimism that culminated in the American and French revolutions. Writing of the latter, Thomas Paine expressed the optimism of this mood and its consequences for the system in which it had been fostered.

> Monarchical sovereignty, the enemy of mankind and the source of misery, is abolished; and sovereignty itself is restored to its natural and original place, the nation. Were this the case through-out Europe, the cause of war would be taken away.[23]

And when Crane Brinton defined the Enlightenment as characterized by "the belief that all human beings can attain here on this earth a state of perfection hitherto in the West thought to be possible only for Christians in a state of grace, and for them only after death,"[24] he, too, captured the optimism and belief in mutability characterizing the tremendous burst of energy that engulfed all of Europe at the time of the French Revolution and France's effort to export its newfound creed.[25]

The French Revolution and the Napoleonic Wars placed in great peril the European state system itself; yet, as if an additional irony were needed, the fusion of state and nation brought about by the revolution seemed to give further evidence of the durability, even permanence, of the state concept. With Rousseau came the "general will and the state as a corporate entity," and with the French Revolution what Rodney Bruce Hall calls "national-sovereign identity," which "problematized ethnic, linguistic and cultural minorities, territorial integrity and security, migration, titular claims to dynastic lands, and the integrity and identity of polyglot states."[26]

The full potential of this fusion was not realized until the end of the nineteenth century with the flowering of political romanticism, especially in Germany. In the interim, skilled statesmen such as Metternich, Talleyrand, Castlereagh, and later Bismarck postponed this development as they sought to reestablish the beneficent dynastic system that had existed prior to the French Revolution, buttressed by the institutional framework of the Concert of Europe and reinforced by a conservative ideological harmony. That they appreciated the dangers of national fervor wedded to state power was revealed in their "condemnation of the revolutionary principle"[27] at the Congress of Vienna and their strong endorsement of the "legitimacy principle" as the basis of the new order. Fearful of abrupt change either within or between states and advocates of a highly elitist international system run by professional diplomats in the service of conservative monarchs, the architects of the Concert were by instinct and training cautious realists. And, at least in the years immediately after the Napoleonic Wars, their conservative philosophy reflected the prevailing mood. As Richard Rosecrance observes:

> The Concert of Europe was created at a uniquely favorable time. The ravages of war and revolution demanded a new effort for peace and domestic stability. . . . Even the philosophic fashions of the age railed at the doctrinaire rationalism of the Enlightenment and fostered a new attention to traditionalism and romanticism. . . . Even the peoples themselves were ready for a period of stability and order.[28]

This mood was transitory, however, and the implications of fusing the ideas of nation and state could not long be delayed. Within a few years of the Congress of Vienna, the national idea swept Europe and left in its wake the wreckage of those institutions established in 1818. In some cases, the effects were relatively benign, as in the liberalization of British institutions, including broadening the franchise, which had the effect of a withdrawal of British support for the Concert mechanism that Britain had helped to construct. In many cases, violence and revolution accompanied nationalist agitation: Spain (1820); Naples (1820); Moldavia and Wallachia (1821); Greece (1821); Sardinia (1821); France (1830); Belgium (1830); and France, Austria, Prussia, and the German states (1848). Many of these upheavals were unsuccessful, but their overall effect was synergistic. Nationalism became a doctrine of both liberals (e.g., Mazzini) and reactionaries (e.g., Tsar Alexander I), but its overall impact was to strengthen greatly the vertical cleavages among states, to provoke imperialism and to generate ideologies of national idolatry. The national idea was further institutionalized by the successive wars of German unification (1863, 1866, and 1870) and by the unification of Italy (1861). And, notwithstanding Bismarck's efforts to impose a realist solution to Europe's instability after 1870, the sense of cosmopolitan solidarity and elite harmony of interests that underlay both the eighteenth-century balance of power and the later Concert was gradually but persistently eroded.

Perhaps the greatest irony of eighteenth- and early-nineteenth-century European realism was that, although a doctrine that assumed a world of fiercely competitive states, it prospered in an environment of cosmopolitan concern for the survival of the system as a whole and of the major state entities that constituted it. It was the very conditions of the eighteenth century—relative tolerance, cosmopolitanism, economic growth, scientific advance, and relative peace—that were prerequisites for the belief in the possibilities of change and the spirit of optimism that pervaded political thought. Sovereign boundaries had not yet hardened as they would a century later when nation and state merged, and the continuing personal, dynastic, and class linkages that did not heed national boundaries were vital to the spirit of the age. This was shortly to change. "As the classical theory had its limitations," observed John Bowle, "romanticism had its dangers, in the loss of political realism and of the old sense of European order."[29]

As the nineteenth century advanced, societies were infected by a romanticism that glorified state and nation and, especially in Germany, power-politics theory deteriorated into a crude parody of itself. As leading victims of French expansionism, the peoples of the disunited German states were eager recipients of the national idea that Napoleon's armies brought with them.[30] It was there as well that the romantic image of the nation developed and took root. This process was intensified by the frustration of German liberalism in 1848.

Johann Gottfried Herder presaged this romantic obsession with the nation—the *Volk*—as a historical and cultural organism arising from a distant past and exhibiting personality and consciousness. Rejecting Enlightenment exaltation of reason, Herder, like other early Romantics, saw the state as an individual cultural being.[31] Only the people constituted a natural entity, united in blood and a common history; all other interests, whether of individuals, groups, or humankind as a whole, were artificial, parochial, transitory, or chimerical and so must give way to the interests of the historical nation. And the political imagery of nationalist romanticism was but a part of broader intellectual currents. "It was," in Bowle's words, "bound up with the new philology, with the study of ancient languages; embodied in Percy's *Reliques,* in Macpherson's *Ossian* and in weird Scandinavian mythology."[32] It was also influenced by Montesquieu's political geography and by the botany of Linnaeus, with its predilection for taxonomy and classification.

The political imagery of this romantic movement was, in Herder's version, relatively benign. In contrast to some of those who followed him, he perceived the possibility of nations living in harmony. But nationalist imagery grew more dangerous when seized upon first by Fichte and then by Hegel. Transformed into a German nationalist by Prussia's defeat in 1806, Johann Gottlieb Fichte added to Herder's romantic historicism the belief in a strong state. Individual freedom, in his view, could be secured only through such a state, not apart from it. In his *Addresses to the German Nation,* Fichte portrayed Germany, as Liah Greenfeld puts it, "as the object of supreme loyalty," "the embodiment of true individuality, the moral totality, the eternal in this world."[33]

Georg Wilhelm Friedrich Hegel went a step further: "He endowed the state with a dangerous glamour and lacked the salutary suspicion of power which has inspired more realist thinkers."[34] For Hegel, world history was the story of the awakening, growth, clash, and decay of states as the agents of the dialectic. "For him," declares Greenfeld, "the state was an organism, and 'ethical totality,' and the only vehicle through which the true individuality of any particular human being, that is, one's humanity, could be expressed."[35]

Widely read and highly influential, Hegel's ideas, especially in relation to the international sphere, seemed to endorse perpetual and unlimited conflict among nations, unrelieved by any vision of individual or collective well-being. As Bowle observes:

> Here . . . is a manifestation of romantic early nineteenth-century nationalism; the cult of the Volk; the cult, of course, of Germany. And Hegel gives the nation a charter which would have made Bodin shudder. "The Nation State," he writes, "is mind in its substantive rationality and immediate actuality, and is . . . absolute power on earth." This hideous remark is followed by a joyful acceptance of war.[36]

War, to Hegel, was the means by which the will of each nation could be asserted as it sought domination. Law and ethics were, he believed, mere artifacts having no moderating role to play in the collision of national destinies; and not society nor government nor individuals had any reality or interest apart from the collective destiny. Thus, war was the means by which the state remained an ethical whole, more than "a mere aggregate of private interests organized around the principle of civil society,"[37] as Kant seemed to regard it.

Hegel, and more importantly, his cruder imitators and popularizers, both reflected the broad upsurge of nationalism in Europe in the first half of the nineteenth century and provided intellectual legitimacy for its intensification in the second half. Theirs was a dark and fundamentally reactionary philosophy, in contrast to the liberal nationalism of Mazzini, Garibaldi, and Kossuth; and it was this darker strain that persisted, especially in Germany but elsewhere as well, after the failure of the 1848 revolutions. The more liberal nationalism that saw the realization of self-determination and democracy as ushering in an era of individual freedom and international peace was aborted by the events of that year. If the spirit of the earlier period found expression in the music of Beethoven and the art of Delacroix, the spirit of the latter was reflected in the older Wagner.[38]

Despite the ultimate failure of the revolutions of 1848, conservative leaders increasingly found it necessary to appeal to and appease nationalist fantasies in order to justify their continuance in office. The dynastic legitimacy principle no longer sufficed, as cultural myths increasingly hardened state boundaries and deepened "we-they" cleavages across those boundaries. Both public and elite opinion in Europe became captive to nationalist doctrine of one or another stripe. Consequently, however much traditional realist leaders may have remained convinced of the need to retain a cosmopolitan balance-of-power system, they found themselves increasingly compelled to violate its principles. Even Bismarck, who after the final unification of Germany sought to restore such a system, played the nationalist card in 1871 when he seized and retained the provinces of Alsace and Lorraine from France. From that point until his ouster in 1890, the realism of the German chancellor was bedeviled by nationalist resentments in France and Russia,[39] as well as pan-German sentiments at home.

The intellectual and practical consequences of the fusion of nation and state were increasingly in evidence as the nineteenth century waned and the world began its descent toward World War I. A crude and violent nationalist philosophy—typified by the work of Heinrich von Treitschke—combined with social Darwinism, imperialism, and outright racism to produce a climate in which war was regarded as a necessary engine of social change and a vehicle by which nations could prove their vitality and superiority. "Popular bourgeois culture," declares Hall, "had quickly reached into Darwin's ideas on natural selection and, discarding the kernel of Darwin's thought, extracted the chaff of the Victorian pseudo-science of philology and racist pseudo-scientific variants of eugenics."[40] This violently nationalist ideology retained something of the trappings of classical power-politics theory in its emphases on national sovereignty and international competition, but at root it was a perverse caricature of the genuine article. It represented an unbridled egoism and lacked any vestige of the cosmopolitan sense of responsibility and prudence that characterized the Machiavellian tradition.

Treitschke, for instance, cited Machiavelli to justify his claim that war is natural and inevitable and that international law is chimerical. However, whereas Machiavelli and his followers appreciated the necessity of mechanisms such as the balance of power to limit the effects of the anarchy they believed to exist, Treitschke glorified war. "The State," he argued, "is power;"[41] it may not "renounce the 'I' in its sovereignty." "War," he continued, "is justified because the great national personalities can suffer no compelling force superior to themselves, and because history must always be in constant flux; war . . . must be taken as part of the divinely appointed order."[42] Neither peace nor international solidarity held any attraction for Treitschke: "Brave peoples alone have an existence, an evolution or a future; the weak and cowardly perish, and perish justly. The grandeur of history lies in the perpetual conflict of nations, and it is simply foolish to desire the suppression of their rivalry."[43]

It was this ethos that influenced German foreign policy after Bismarck, a policy inimical to the ideas of the cautious realists who had created the Concert of Europe. In general, this ethos appealed to those whom Michael Mann calls "superloyalists" and was integral to late-nineteenth-century imperialism and militarism. Who were the superloyalists? Mann argues that Europe's "much-maligned petite bourgeoisie" was relatively unaffected by aggressive nationalism and that it was civilian and military administrators who "provided most of the core of extreme nationalism." Hall is less charitable to the bourgeoisie, attributing the new wave of imperialism to "bourgeois status anxiety."[44]

If there was a popular alternative to the unbridled and perverse realism that dominated European thinking in the final decades of the nineteenth and first decade of the twentieth centuries, it was Marxist socialism. Indeed, Marxism may be regarded as an idealist variant in its vision of a world in which states would wither away, its belief in the limitless mutability of human beings, and its optimistic and egalitarian biases. Marxists saw classes, not nations, as the bases of historical analysis and not only rejected the static assumptions of realist theory, but insisted upon the inevitability of change owing to the evolution of modes of production.[45] From the standpoint of global politics, at least, a paradox is apparent here. Political philosophers regard Hegelians as Idealists owing to their metaphysical version of the dialectic. Yet they were more firmly rooted in the realist tradition than the Marxist materialists were. For their part, as Bowle observes, "Marx and Engels were at heart revolutionary romantics, in the tradition of 1789."[46]

Like the worshipers of the state, the Marxists reflected social and cultural currents of their time, most importantly the rapid industrialization of the late nineteenth century and its companions, the urbanization and proletarianization of societies. Ultimately, the currents of nationalism proved stronger, and the Marxist prediction of class solidarity against war proved baseless in 1914. Even in Russia, where Marxism triumphed in 1917, Lenin and later Stalin found nationalism a more congenial ally than internationalism and rapidly abandoned any notion of dismantling the state.

THE TWENTIETH CENTURY: IDEALISM ASCENDANT

The futile bloodletting of World War I produced an atmosphere very congenial to a resurgence of an idealist ethos. One effect was to intensify demands that the study and practice of global politics and foreign affairs be opened to greater popular participation. The bloody waste that had just come to an end suggested that issues of war and peace were too important to be left to professional diplomats and soldiers. Diplomats' virtual abdication of responsibility to the generals and their military plans in 1914 and the overblown rhetoric that accompanied the intensification of the war contributed to this disillusionment. The consequences of inverting Clausewitz's formula of the relationship between politics and war proved to be very dangerous indeed. Agitation focused especially on secret treaties and on so-called merchants of death, and in general reflected a revulsion against "the Old Diplomacy."[47] The new ethos entailed a rejection of elitism in foreign affairs and the belief that the arcane issues of global politics could be left safely in the hands of a narrow stratum of professionals.[48] Woodrow Wilson and Colonel House, ignoring their own State Department, fostered this culture, and professional diplomacy, especially in the United States, has never recovered the status it lost at that time.

Nineteenth-century developments such as mass education, yellow journalism and inexpensive books, and the broadening of electorates in the West had already begun the process of democratizing foreign affairs, but the war dramatically increased public mistrust in the capacity and wisdom of foreign policy establishments. In addition, changing technology (e.g., machine guns, barbed wire) had debased the value of cavalry and had transformed World War I into a struggle of attrition in which infantry, recruited largely from lower-middle and working classes, played the principal role. This had a significant social leveling effect, as the cavalry had traditionally been the "gentlemen's service." At home, too, the increasing involvement of civilians in the war effort and their increasing vulnerability to enemy action (e.g., the use of zeppelins in the bombing of London) generated antielitist sentiment.

Under these conditions, scholars entered a new idealist phase characterized by optimism (at least until the Depression and the rise of Hitler), a belief in social and political mutability, an emphasis on global interests and cooperation through international law and organization, and a renewed faith in public opinion.[49] Science and reason were regarded as tools that could be applied to understanding the causes of war as the first step toward engineering international society in ways that would prevent war's recurrence.

Dr. Lewis Richardson exemplified this new spirit as it was manifested in the social sciences. Richardson pioneered in the application of mathematical modeling to identify patterns and sequences of interstate behavior associated with the outbreak of war in order to "improve public debate by making it easier to discern the likely consequences for peace of various proposed policies and thus to create peace plans actually more likely to promote peace than to incite war."[50] Richardson's approach assumed that the human condition was malleable, and his faith in the efficacy of science was adopted by a generation of his followers, especially in the United States. They believed science and reason combined could uncover the conditions necessary for realizing the harmony of interests to which idealist scholars aspired. "The scholar's purpose," declares John Vasquez, "was to reveal this fundamental truth and to delineate those conditions so that it would be possible to establish a set of institutions that by their very structure would force nations to act peacefully and thereby cause a revolution in the way global politics was conducted."[51]

Scholars, then, looked to history as the great data source that would reveal errors of the past in order that people could avoid their recurrence. Thus, the first two occupants of the Chair of Global Politics at the University College of Wales—the first of its kind—were diplomatic historians (Professors Alfred Zimmern and C. K. Webster). Describing the study of global politics at this time, Kenneth Thompson suggested that "what most distinguishes this period is the high level of historical accuracy and the faithful attention to the canons of historiography and historical method by which it was characterized."[52]

The widespread belief that global harmony would exist if the system of competitive nation-states could be modified and reformed provided an impetus to the study of international law and organization. Indeed, of the twenty-four scholars of global politics who had attained the rank of professor by 1930, eighteen were specialists in law and organization. The purposes of such analysis were "the stimulation and advancement of international cooperation and good will among the world's people."[53] As this description suggests, global-politics scholarship in the years after World War I had decidedly antinationalist and antistate biases. Peoples, not states, were viewed as the key units of analysis. States were impediments to the achievement of a natural harmony of interests and to an understanding of the degree to which the fates of individuals everywhere were linked. It was believed that public opinion, channeled by supranational organizations such as the League of Nations and the Permanent Court of International Justice, would generate pacifist pressures sufficient to prevent the outbreak of war.[54]

Woodrow Wilson contributed significantly to the scholarly mood in the years after 1918. As noted earlier, global-politics scholars regularly seek cues from political practitioners, and the latter play a major role, intentionally and unintentionally, in structuring scholarly research agendas. This was as much the case in post–World War I America as it had been during the late-nineteenth-century era of imperial expansion and would prove to be during the Cold War and thereafter. Wilson shared the optimism that inspired industrialist Andrew Carnegie to instruct the trustees of Carnegie Endowment for International Peace: "When . . . war is discarded as disgraceful to civilized man, the trustees will please then consider what is the next most degrading evil or evils whose banishment . . . would most advance the progress, elevation, and happiness of man."[55]

War was merely one of many problems confronting civilized people that could be conquered if sufficient zeal and energy were applied. Wilson's optimism and belief in mutability are conveyed in Hedley Bull's description of the president's conviction that

> the system of global politics that had given rise to the First World War was capable of being transformed into a fundamentally more peaceful and just world order; that under the impact of the awakening of democracy, the growth of the 'international mind,' the development of the League, the good works of men of peace or the enlightenment spread by their own teachings, it was in fact being transformed; and that the responsibility of students of global politics was to assist this march of progress to overcome the ignorance, the prejudices, the ill-will and the sinister interests that stood in its way.[56]

Wilson's belief in the culpability of narrow nationalism, authoritarianism, and selfish interest reveals an antipathy toward competitiveness and elitism. Thus, democracies shared an obligation "to turn wars from the object of the narrowly defined safety of the state into crusades to establish the conditions under which all states can coexist in perpetual peace."[57] Only democracies could prevent preemption of the common interest by willful minorities that might benefit from war. This is clearly conveyed in Wilson's message to Congress asking that war be declared against Germany:

> A steadfast concern for peace can never be maintained except by a partnership of democratic states. . . . [O]nly free people can hold their purpose and their honor steady to a common end and prefer the interests of mankind to any narrow interest of their own.[58]

And if some miscreant state initiated war in defiance of the common will of humankind, the United States and the other democracies would take up the burden of that common will:

> All the peoples of the world are . . . partners in this interest, and for our part we see very clearly that unless justice be done to others it will not be done to us. The program of the world's peace, therefore, is our program.[59]

Although Wilson did not share the Marxist vision of ultimately eliminating nation-states, his conception of states was vastly different than that of the nineteenth-century practitioners and theorists of Realpolitik. States were not in his view anthropomorphic entities with interests greater than those of their citizens. Governments were established to represent those individual interests rather than to mobilize them in the name of parochial elites. It was this conception of the state that allowed idealists to draw upon domestic analogies in analyzing global politics.[60]

Public opinion was not something to be feared as an impediment to rational decisionmaking but was something to be revered as a source of rationality and good sense. Individuals, not corporate entities called states, were the key units of analysis. It was this last assumption, so different than that of realists, which allowed Wilson to predict that once democracy were universally established, the peace of the world would rest on "the organized major force of mankind," which would constitute "a community of power" rather than a balance of power. Public opinion was a more certain guarantor of peace than were national armies. "What we seek," declared Wilson, "is the reign of law, based upon the consent of the governed and sustained by the organized opinion of mankind."[61]

So different a conception of the state would *alone* have made it difficult for Wilson and other so-called idealists to communicate with classical realists. Basic definitions reveal ideological predispositions, and differences among them reflect much more than the scientific immaturity that many global-politics scholars expect shortly to be overcome.

Realists have argued repeatedly that idealist scholarship, unlike their own, consists of "normative and prescriptive analysis."[62] E. H. Carr perhaps most eloquently articulated this claim in his critique of idealism, *The Twenty Years' Crisis.* Carr argued that idealists had confounded aspiration with reality and that it was necessary to understand how things really were before a science of politics could be developed. In this, Carr echoed his great realist predecessor, Machiavelli.[63] In this way, realists set the agenda for the debate they proposed to have with their idealist adversaries, just as Machiavelli had done four centuries earlier.[64]

But in successfully setting the agenda, realists also succeeded in perpetuating a false dichotomy; that is, that—in contrast to their quixotic adversaries— they were hard-headed empiricists whose close reading of history enabled them to discern general laws of politics by means of induction. In fact, the general laws that realists propounded were value-laden assumptions buttressed by a ransacking of history. And those assumptions reflect normative commitments antithetical to the beliefs of idealists. It is not that idealist analyses were more "normative and prescriptive," but that they were more *overtly* so.

Despite the realists' repeated invocation of idealist strawmen, twentieth-century realists, like those they criticized, were less concerned with imposing a new methodology on a discipline than with reorienting foreign policy. While realists rarely articulated clearly the norms that guided them, they were not at all shy about prescribing "correct" and "prudent" foreign policy behavior. Indeed, in providing advice to practitioners, realists implicitly recognized that idealism was not merely a mode of scholarship. Rather, especially in the United States, it represented a broad mood of optimism that came with the end of World War I and was sustained by booming economic conditions. Within a relatively short time, Wilsonian internationalism was replaced by isolationism tinged with pacifism, but the mood remained optimistic.

Post–World War I political, economic, and social conditions suggested to many Americans that their time had come to assume world leadership and that the examples and practices of Europe, which they believed had been shown as failures, could be safely ignored. Americans, including many in the scholarly community, assumed that the practices of business leaders and lawyers—practices that had built the United States—could be applied internationally. What was termed isolationism was, in reality, a disavowal of the practices of power politics—political and military intervention in the name of a balance of power—accompanied by economic globalism. Underlying this partial isolationism was a sense that global peace and prosperity required the conditions of a free market and that interventionism would distort this market. This belief system constituted a unique blend of nationalism and internationalism, the former manifested as a belief in the superiority of the American system and the latter as a belief that American interests and world interests were identical.

Realists have suggested that this mood was responsible for the failures of the 1930s. On one level, they are correct; America's political and military noninvolvement made it difficult to contain German and Japanese revisionism. But what realists call American idealism did not take root in Europe (except in some British circles). European pacifism and failure to confront Hitler in timely fashion had very different sources than did American isolationism. In Europe, this behavior was largely the product of a mood of pessimism and cynicism and an absence of self-confidence produced by the fearful waste of World War I, the Bolshevik Revolution in Russia, and America's earlier refusal to incur the obligations of collective security. British and French leaders repeatedly sought to apply the principles of balance of power, but they at once lacked available alliance partners and did not grasp that Hitler would not play by the prudential rules of realism.

THE REALIST "PARADIGM"

Western inability to cope effectively with German and Japanese revisionism and the catastrophe of World War II brought on an eclipse of idealism and set the stage for the reascension of realist perspectives. The international institutions that had been established after 1919 did not evolve as Wilsonians had anticipated and achieved neither the political nor functional ends for which they had been created. The 1930s and 1940s seemed to be dominated by a "struggle for power." Following E. H. Carr, realists argued that self-abnegation in the face of growing German and Japanese power had culminated in the disasters of the 1930s. But Hitler, as we have observed, was no more in the tradition of classical Realpolitik than were the most ardent of idealists. Would the postwar experiments have succeeded if the German Army had seized power or if the world had not been gripped by economic depression? We shall never know.

In a more general sense, the end of World War II witnessed the migration of global politics to the United States. A number of reasons account for this. One was the fact that, in comparison to Europeans, Americans were well behind the learning curve in the field, having previously followed either Europeans in the great power tradition or the Anglo-Saxon liberal tradition. Both of these seemed bankrupt. American government and academe were acutely conscious of their status in light of the superpower status that was suddenly thrust upon American elites.

Secondly, some of Europe's most self-conscious scholars, such as Morgenthau, had been forced to flee their continent before or during the war and, like German rocket scientists, were available to provide intellectual leadership. Yet a third reason was the growing link between academe and Washington that made large infusions of wealth available to universities and policy-relevant research. Funded research concerning war, strategy, deterrence, bargaining, and so forth accompanied the need to confront these as serious questions in the global arena. And the range of puzzles extended geometrically as Washington assumed responsibility for everything from economic and political development in former colonial arenas to stabilizing monetary and trade flows.

Increasingly, American approaches to global politics turned away from institutions and toward behavior, and away from descriptive history toward science (which forms a major part of the story we are telling). Insulated by growing government funding and gigantic and prosperous universities and academic communities, traditional American faith in technology and pragmatism reasserted itself and increasingly seduced mathematicians, economists, biologists, and others who brought with them a profound belief in the capacity of the scientific method to solve puzzles. This belief contrasted vividly with European historical and descriptive inclinations. In Great Britain, for example, where classicists and philosophers were more highly esteemed than physicists and engineers, American approaches found little sympathy among those associated with the so-called "English school." The latter, in Ole Waever's words, "is a respectable, traditional approach which includes quasi-philosophical and historical reflection, and especially it interrogates deep institutions in the system."[65] Members of this school, notably Hedley Bull, Herbert Butterfield, and Martin Wight were profoundly interested in the interaction between facts and values, an interest explicitly rejected by American scientists. Finally, European scholarship could not compete with the explosion of huge American publishing firms and well-endowed scholarly journals intended to serve the growing American market of undergraduate and graduate students and faculty. As we shall see, however, the last decade or so has witnessed a revival of European scholarship in global politics, resulting particularly from the reaction against science, the infusion of new ideas from European humanists like Foucault and Derrida, a modest shift away from highly limited research questions to broader theories and perspectives, and a revival of interest in history and philosophy.

In any event, the experience of World War II and the onset of the Cold War provided fertile soil for the reassertion of realist doctrine and its application in the United States in the form of containing the Soviet Union and negotiating from a position of strength. As initial postwar optimism gave way to a growing pessimism that accompanied Soviet triumphs in Eastern Europe and Asia, realist assumptions once more found public and intellectual acceptance. So dominant did realism become in academic and policymaking circles in the 1950s and 1960s that to many global-politics scholars it assumed the status of a genuine Kuhnian paradigm. Postwar realism even seemed to have an "exemplar" in Hans J. Morgenthau's *Politics among Nations* (1948), and until the end of the 1960s, most textbooks tended to share realist assumptions.[66] Morgenthau, as Vasquez declares, "best expressed, promulgated and synthesized" postwar realism and was the "single most important vehicle for establishing the dominance of the realist paradigm within the field."[67]

Realist theory, especially as articulated by Morgenthau, was at once elegant and parsimonious, emphasizing national goals and objectives in the context of a global distribution of power. But—and this cannot be stressed strongly enough—the reason the doctrine gained ascendance was *not* because it was able to account for anomalies that its competitors had failed to explain. In fact, idealist and Marxist theories can explain the outbreak of World War II quite as persuasively as can realism. The ascendance of realism merely revealed once more that although the facts of history do not change, scholars are free to select from among them in constructing plausible explanations. Consequently, dominant explanations vary as some facts are emphasized and others de-emphasized and as phenomena are viewed through changing normative lenses. The inevitable disputes that arise in academic circles as norms shift are anchored in genuine policy quarrels among practitioners preoccupied with life-and-death issues; they are *not* the stuff of ivory towers alone.[68] Interestingly, realists' blanket criticism of interwar scholars and practitioners is an implicit recognition of how tightly they assume theory and policy to be linked.

Realists accused Western statesmen of the interwar period of having "deprecated" power in favor of legal and moral solutions to the problems of their time (for example, the 1928 Kellogg-Briand Treaty that outlawed war). In doing so, according to realists, idealists confused theory with practice and confounded scientific with normative analysis. Yet, for the most part, the supposedly offending statesmen were quite as aware of the balance-of-power concept as their realist critics but were in practice as unable as are contemporary analysts to assess that balance in a manner that could provide clear policy guidelines.

Power, as most of us acknowledge, is an elusive concept that has become increasingly difficult to measure as the pace of technological change has accelerated. It is relational and contextual and, therefore, essentially unmeasurable except by inference from results or capabilities. National power (as capability), as Morgenthau himself notes, includes such unmeasurable elements as "national character," "national morale," "the quality of diplomacy," and "the quality of government." In their efforts to formulate policy interwar diplomats sought to account for these several factors, yet realist criticisms of these efforts come perilously near to focusing only on military factors. Ultimately, Morgenthau admits that the calculation of national power "is an ideal task and, hence, incapable of achievement,"[69] and this admission forces us to ask why realists think they could have done better. Ironically, the factor that was least understood by interwar politicians was one for which realists cannot account either, the motives and personality of Hitler, who refused to behave according to the dictates of balance of power. In short, realists would have been unable to explain or predict the behavior of a leader who did not act according to the dictates of realist rationality. History revealed to the realists (and to many of the practitioners of that time as well) that the interwar statesmen *should* have acted differently. Unfortunately, theory that can provide answers only retrospectively is of limited value. The iron laws of realism and neorealism are brittle indeed.

The manner in which realism triumphed after World War II reveals again that theory in global politics evolves in a significantly different fashion than the almost dialectical manner of Kuhnian paradigm change in the natural sciences.[70] The revival of realism was not merely a product of what Kuhn described as "the recognition that nature has somehow violated the paradigm-induced expectations,"[71] but also represented a condemnation of earlier norms brought about by the revolutionary effects of World War II and the onset of the Cold War. For Kuhn, a paradigm shift occurs *not* because the natural universe itself changes, but because something about the universe becomes manifest for which the existing paradigm cannot account. In global politics, the essential fact is that change, while sometimes accelerating and sometimes showing, is continuous. Realism triumphed precisely because the political universe that had existed in the interwar period had been shattered and replaced by a dramatically different one in which the United States was pressed to play a leading role.

The outbreak of World War II served less to reveal anomalies in an existing paradigm than to provide legitimacy for the claims of power thinkers who had been competing with liberal rivals for centuries. In the same way, World War I previously had provided normative justification for Wilsonians to assert the bankruptcy of narrow nationalism and the superiority of moral universalism. Thus, the early interwar period seemed to represent a final victory for the Gladstone-Cobden school over the adherents of Disraeli. It was in each and every case, of course, only temporary—a Pyrrhic victory.

In fact, twentieth-century realists were not especially innovative theoretically. We have noted their debt to their predecessors, eighteenth-century European political practice, and the ideas of early American power theorists such as Alexander Hamilton.[72] It was not, then, that realists could account for anomalies in an existing body of thought but that they eloquently asserted the normative superiority of the national interest over universalism and globalism. The key to their victory lay less in the power of their assumptions or logic than in the climate of the times, as well as the claim that their work was, in Morgenthau's words, "abstract but empirical and pragmatic" and that they could discern a "science of global politics."[73] For a number of reasons, this claim exercised a powerful normative and prescriptive attraction in the years after World War II; the soil was fertile for what Morgenthau declared to be "another great debate." Realism entailed a rejection of ideologies such as those that had legitimized the excesses of the previous years, as well as of those institutional and legal efforts to eliminate world conflict that had failed in the 1920s and 1930s. Moreover, realism meshed nicely with America's self-image at a time when the United States had so clearly emerged as *primus inter pares* in the global system.[74]

American scientific knowhow and economic productivity had won the war, and the atom bomb would secure the peace. Munich and Pearl Harbor were symbols of obsolete thinking and a discredited past. Of course, pragmatism, positivism, faith in scientific advancement, and free enterprise themselves constituted an ideology, but one that appeared objective and rational. In this context, realism was especially attractive because it, too, appeared to offer an alternative to ideological and moralistic analysis. "Intellectually," declared Morgenthau, "the political realist maintains the autonomy of the political sphere, as the economist, the lawyer, the moralist maintain theirs."[75] This claim seemed to serve the paradigmatic purpose of providing disciplinary boundaries. Although, like Machiavelli, realists were accused of being amoral; like Machiavelli, they in fact provided a rather clear set of moral and prescriptive dicta that constituted the obligations of official decisionmakers seeking to serve the national interest. Indeed, one of the ironies of their triumph is that realists were able to make a powerful moral case against their intellectual adversaries by asserting the value-free nature of their theories while simultaneously providing moral and prescriptive guidelines for a generation of scholars and statesmen.

Surveys have shown that Morgenthau is the political theorist whose ideas have been most familiar to U.S. policymakers.[76] Among other reasons, his derogation of moral concerns has appealed to them. Thus, Bernard Brodie writes of a strong "professional tradition" among American practitioners that views the intrusion of moral considerations into policymaking as "inherently mischievous, that is, . . . likely to cause the warping of what otherwise would be trimly correct thinking about foreign affairs."[77] Richard J. Barnet summarizes this position: "Those who run nations cannot be unselfish, generous, or even honest in the jungle world of global politics because such impulses are not reciprocated. To recognize external limits on discretion is to compromise the interests of the American people and of future generations for whom the statesman is supposed to act as trustee." To the realist, he continues, "What was expedient also became right. . . . Neither God, law, world opinion, right reason, or any other outside standard was recognized as a limit on their own discretion, for that discretion, they convinced themselves, would be exercised in pursuit of the highest moral values."[78]

In justifying expediency, realism neatly reinforced the ideological core of pragmatism that has been central to American culture and to policymakers who are the product of that culture. For instance, David Halberstam reports:

> In the early days of the [Kennedy] Administration [the word pragmatism] had been used so frequently that David Brinkley, writing the introduction of an early book of portraits of the Kennedy people, would dwell on that single word, and note that at an early Washington cocktail party a woman had gone around the room asking each of the hundred people there if he was a pragmatist.[79]

Pragmatism is an example of what might be termed "the attitude of ideology toward itself," advancing as it does the proposition that "practical" responses to the "real world" should take precedence over the dictates of ideology (other than pragmatism). It is, as Steve Smith summarizes it, "the *via tertia* between empiricism and rationalism, in that it attempts to combine the notion that the mind is always active in interpreting experience and observation, with the thought that revisions in our beliefs are to be made as a result of experience."[80]

Pragmatism has regularly allowed decisionmakers, especially American ones, to conceal from themselves the ideological premises behind their policies and, less often, to congratulate themselves on the "rightness" of their policies when the dictates of ideology and the demands of the real world have seemed to coincide. The concealing function of pragmatism has been enhanced by its links to the realist concept of the national interest, which purports to provide an objective standard for national policy. Of course, as numerous critics have pointed out, this supposed standard is so vague that its interpretation cannot but involve a highly subjective judgment. As Arnold Wolfers declares:

> When political formulas such as "national interest" or "national security" gain popularity they need to be scrutinized with particular care. They may not mean the same thing to different people. They may not have any precise meaning at all. Thus,

while appearing to offer guidance and a basis for broad consensus, they may be permitting everyone to label whatever policy he favors with an attractive and possibly deceptive name.[81]

Realism thus provided the legerdemain through which the sow's ear of the pragmatist's expediency could be converted into the silk purse of the pursuit of the national interest. The realist's association of the national interest concept with a struggle for power, in turn, has reinforced yet another aspect of what Richard Barnet sees as part of the American tradition, a phenomenon that he terms "bureaucratic machismo." "One of the first lessons a national security manager learns after a day in the bureaucratic climate of the Pentagon, State Department, White House, or CIA is that toughness is the most highly prized virtue." U.S. officials have customarily adopted a self-consciously "tough," "hard-nosed" brand of decisionmaking and have evidenced a profound distrust of policies favored by "soft-headed" "liberal," "idealists," and "intellectuals."[82] Thus, when the label "wimp" stuck to President George Bush Sr. during the 1992 presidential campaign, it proved a virtually insurmountable impediment to his re-election.

Many intellectuals, too, were influenced by realism. Realism's apparent rejection of institutional and legal mechanisms and its assertion of the value-free nature of theory were instrumental in encouraging the behavioral and scientific revolutions in global politics. Morgenthau's assertion that realism "requires . . . a sharp distinction between the desirable and the possible"[83] was repeated by a generation of 1960s scholars who believed that it was possible to isolate values from the analysis of political phenomena. While retaining the assumptions of realism, these scholars performed something approaching the task of normal science in the Kuhnian sense.[84] Their contributions were primarily methodological rather than theoretical and unwittingly served to institutionalize and legitimize many of realism's key assumptions.

NEW NORMS AND OLD THEORY IN THE LINGERING DECLINE OF REALISM

The 1970s witnessed a concerted assault on several realist assumptions—the centrality of the unitary state-as-actor, the autonomy of the international and domestic realms of politics, and the existence of a single issue of managing power—accompanied by an implicit "declaration of independence" from the doctrine.

Among the principal lines of attack were those that highlighted nonrational sources of decisionmakers' behavior, the impact of changing situations on decisionmaking, the importance of bureaucratic politics and organizational behavior, the significance of transnationalism and interdependence, the role of nonstate actors, and the influence of issues on behavior.[85] In a word, realism was no longer a "disciplinary matrix."[86]

None of the phenomena identified by these scholars as detracting from realism was new, and none was in any sense discovered in the 1970s. For example, even as realism was in ascendance the ideas of Freud about nonrational sources of behavior entered the discipline;[87] the evolution of the containment policy and the reorganization of the American defense and foreign policy establishments provided clear case examples of the impact of situation and bureaucracies on policy;[88] the integration of western Europe revealed some of the implications of interdependence and transnationalism;[89] the emergence of revolutionary and anticolonial movements and of multinational corporations reflected the potential roles of nonstate actors; and the appearance of a North-South axis alongside an East-West axis illustrated the role of issues.[90]

What had really changed most dramatically were scholars' frame of reference and the ethos of the societies in which they were working. Many factors were involved in bringing about these changes. The decline in American hegemony symbolized by Vietnam, the growing salience of problems with an economic or environmental rather than military focus, and growing fears of nuclear war all encouraged scholarly criticisms that were grounded in an unarticulated dissatisfaction with realist norms.

The Vietnam debacle suggested that the elements of power were far more complex and murky than had been realized, that national power was contextual, and that military capabilities had limited utility. Recognition of the limits of American power—perceived by some as a process of decline and by others as the restoration of normalcy after a unique and unnatural era of postwar hegemony[91]—was especially important in shifting the scholarly agenda in the United States from how American power could be utilized unilaterally to shape world events in U.S. interests to how relatively uncontrollable forces in an interdependent world could be channeled and tamed by multilateral cooperation.[92] Successive energy crises highlighted the fragility of economic interdependence and the finite nature of key resources. Endemic stagflation in the West pointed to the central role of economics in national power, reinforced the growing sense of interdependence, and focused attention upon issues without any evident military dimension. In many ways, the process of détente and successive environmental traumas had the same effects. Finally, the demise of détente in the late 1970s and early 1980s and the achievement of techno-military breakthroughs unleashed dormant fears in the United States and Europe regarding the adequacy of nuclear deterrence as a formula for managing conflict.[93]

These and other events produced a shift in the nature of political vocabulary and dialogue. That altered vocabulary emphasized the linked fate of humanity as a whole, processes and interactions only partly controlled by national decisionmakers, and potential outcomes in which the differences between winning and losing were unclear. For the most part, these were precisely the concerns that had motivated political thinkers after 1919 and had shaped their vocabulary and dialogue. The ethos had come full cycle, and no one seemed to notice.

Such a shift was well under way by the early 1970s. In its postwar heyday, realism emphasized immutability, pessimism, competitiveness, and elitism. These emphases were at least partly the product of a global preoccupation with the value of security in the wake of World War II, and this preoccupation was manifested in the overriding salience of a single critical issue, the Cold War.[94] Having emerged from a catastrophic conflict that had been inflicted by the aggressive behavior of a small group of dissatisfied and expansionist actors, publics and governments were ready to embrace policies and theories that focused upon the prevention of war through strength.

By the 1970s, the salience of the Cold War issue had begun to recede, permitting renewed attention to a host of other global issues that had been neglected in the previous years. These issues involved disputes and concerns around global resource allocation, the maintenance of postwar prosperity, and environmental decay. Many, of course, were not new issues but old issues that had been quietly managed after the war by international institutions and regimes that had been elaborated largely by American efforts. The growing prominence of these issues in the 1970s, however, coincided with a decline in the preoccupation with security in a military sense that accompanied the flowering of détente, along with an intensified sense of potential deprivation of other base values. In a more general sense, their prominence grew as the United States found itself increasingly less able to dominate unilaterally in key international arenas like oil and money.

In this climate, realism and the norms it reflected seemed less relevant than before.[95] The decline in Cold War anxieties was largely responsible for reducing, at least in the West, the belief in human immutability and competitiveness, and the apparent emergence of power centers other than Washington and Moscow necessarily diluted the atmosphere of postwar elitism. There was, however, little change along the dimension of optimism/pessimism because, even as acute anxieties concerning some survival issues eased, new anxieties about other survival issues increased.

This change in the global agenda and shift in normative emphases was mirrored by the breakdown of consensus about global-politics theory and the proliferation of new approaches, frameworks, and theories that rejected some or all of the realist assumptions. There was a retreat from grand theory and an impulse to the investigation of specific issues and cases in inductive fashion. The nonmilitary nature of many issues encouraged the introduction of concepts and ideas from allied disciplines, especially economics, psychology, biology, and sociology; and such borrowings increased doubts about the disciplinary autonomy of political science. Although the heterogeneity and ecumenical nature of postrealist global-politics scholarship makes generalization difficult, some of the nonrealist concepts that attracted attention were linkage, interdependence, regimes, political economy, and transnationalism.[96] Relatively greater attention was still paid to power factors, but there was a marked de-emphasis of the unitary state-as-actor.

The shift in normative emphases that accompanied the erosion of the realist consensus was perhaps epitomized in the work of Robert Keohane, who explicitly sought to graft nonrealist concepts onto realist insights about power.[97] Keohane is interesting especially because he was a prolific writer during the 1970s and 1980s, has been refreshingly self-conscious and candid regarding the evolution of his ideas, and has openly discussed the normative content of those ideas. Keohane regarded global politics as more mutable than did realists, viewing a significant degree of cooperation among actors through international regimes as both possible and desirable. And, although cautious, he argued that such cooperation could bring about fundamental changes in political behavior. He was relatively sanguine about postwar developments while taking pains to preclude accusations of idealism, and he viewed global society through a less elitist and competitive lens than did his realist precursors. Keohane was variously labeled a structural realist, an institutionalist, and a neoliberal institutionalist but deservedly eludes categorization.

Keohane's concepts and ideas did not provide the bases for a paradigm for global politics in the Kuhnian sense any more than had realism. Even as major syntheses of postrealist theory emerged, such as Keohane's *After Hegemony,* the agenda of global issues was once more in transition, with military security concerns and East-West relations assuming greater salience in the late 1970s and the election of Ronald Reagan in 1980. Concomitantly, an upturn in economic conditions in the West and a prolonged oil glut reduced anxieties about economic matters, even though the global economic system continued to face serious threats from trade imbalances, monetary instability, and debts.

Keohane's own work offered considerable latitude for a renewed emphasis on realist assumptions. While retaining some of the language and insights of scholars who had predicted decline in the autonomy of nation-states, the growing irrelevance of military security issues, and the inevitable growth of regional and global cooperation on functional or neofunctional lines, he carefully asserted his debt to realism:

> My analysis has assumed that governments calculate their interests minutely on every issue facing them. It has not relied at all on assumptions about the "public interest" or the General Will; no idealism whatever is posited.[98]

The waxing and waning appeal of realist norms owed much to yet another shift in the global agenda of critical issues. That shift was less a product of new scholarly insights than of political change in the United States and the preferences of political leaders. Jimmy Carter had sought to emphasize human rights and to focus attention both at home and abroad on global resource and economic issues. His successful negotiation of the Panama Canal Treaty, his initial attitude toward the Nicaraguan and Iranian revolutions, the apartheid issue, and the developing world in general reflected his belief that American power was declining and that the United States had to learn to function as a "normal" country in an interdependent world. And in large measure Carter succeeded in reorienting the agenda of the academic community. Then he "rediscovered" the Cold War following events in Afghanistan and, in the waning days of his administration, gave much more attention to the East-West and military side of the global equation. SALT II was frozen, and Nicaragua became more of a concern with the Sandinistas' consolidation of power and the escalation of guerrilla violence in El Salvador.

Carter's successor, Ronald Reagan, was predisposed to emphasize realist issues in any event. Open hostility toward the Sandinistas and Angolan Marxists replaced Carter's relatively flexible attitude. The symbols of the Reagan administration were Euromissiles, the Strategic Defense Initiative, aid to the Nicaraguan contras, antiterrorism, and an upgrading of American military and intelligence capabilities. He was at once less prepared than Carter to see evidence of American decline, except as an argument for greater military spending, and more prepared to see America act unilaterally. As had occurred before, the scholarly agenda followed this official shift in perception. *International Security* replaced *International Organization* as a journal of preferred publication, and the Jeanne Kirkpatrick–Edward Luttwack–John Mearsheimer[99] school of academia replaced the intellectual courtiers of the Carter years.

Although specific events helped to trigger these policy and intellectual metamorphoses, the basic issues they reflected were relatively constant. Those East-West relations in which realists were most interested did not disappear in the Carter years; nor did North-South relations and nonmilitary concerns, of interest especially to theorists of interdependence and political economy, vanish after 1980. National and international moods, however, did change and were orchestrated by leaders. As in the past, intellectual fashion dutifully responded to these shifting social and political currents.

The reference to the Reagan years and, indeed, this entire analysis suggests that realist norms (in whatever guise) can return in periods of high tension (as in the months after 9/11), major war, or some other systemwide catastrophe. Their resurgence in the 1980s was reflected in the impact of Waltz's *Theory of International Politics* and its reassertion of the primacy of structural or neorealism on the discipline when it appeared in 1979.[100] Influenced by Rousseau's stag-hare parable,[101] Waltz sought to develop a system-level version of realism that relies heavily on a microeconomic view of global politics with the state being analogous to the firm and anarchy being analogous to the free market. In Waltz's highly parsimonious effort, unitary states seek security and survival in conditions determined largely by capability distribution.[102] The arrangement or position of the units—hierarchical or anarchical—is Waltz's key structural property, and it largely determines their behavior.[103] Under anarchy, competition is pervasive, and, since Waltz sees virtually no likelihood of its disappearance, it is also perpetual and effectively universal.

The brief resurgence of realism ended with the end of the Cold War, although its influence lingers in various quarters. Some realists and neorealists, such as John Mearsheimer and Waltz, engaged in ad hoc theorizing to wage a vigorous rearguard effort, arguing that nothing had changed and that realism was at least as relevant as ever in a multipolar world.[104] As Rey Koslowski and Friedrich Kratochwil felicitously express it:

> Since the end of the cold war had the potential of representing a crucial case for the corroboration or refutation of the structural realist research program, its exponents have resorted to various gambits to shelter neorealism's theoretical core. Thus, the recent transformation is treated as an anomaly, while it is suggested that the international system is, according to John Mearsheimer "back to the future."[105]

Nevertheless, the end of the Cold War, the demise of the Soviet bloc, the explosion of identity-based cleavages, and the growing globalization of markets had two critical implications. The first was that, far from being immutable, global politics could be transformed and that at the heart of such transformation was identity politics.[106] Thus, the Soviet Union, formerly the spearhead of Marxist revolution worldwide, became Russia, an aspiring capitalist and protodemocratic society, and citizens of states as disparate as Afghanistan and Rwanda redefined themselves in terms of tribe, ethnicity, or religion. Writing of Mearsheimer's and other realists' efforts to explain global changes, John Vasquez concludes that the work "reflects both the indeterminate logic of power politics, as well as its tendency to protect itself from empirical falsification by chameleon protean shifts that camouflage its nonconformity with the evidence."[107]

Under such conditions, schools of thought such as constructivism and liberalism that, unlike realism and neorealism, allow for change and transformation moved into the academic mainstream, and empiricists turned their firepower toward studying the "democratic peace." "The strikingly rapid collapse of communist ideology and Soviet authority," wrote Wade Huntley, "marks an historic threshold between two eras of international relations. Neorealism cannot account for this transformation—nor does it claim to, as structure does not initiate structural change."[108]

It should be stressed, however, that both Keohanian liberal institutionalism and that strain of constructivist theory associated with the work of Alexander Wendt remain as firmly anchored in a realist state-as-primary-actor political universe as the writings of Hedley Bull decades earlier. The shared conservatism of realists, neorealists, institutionalists, and state-centric constructivists has rarely been as clear as in a 1995 mini-symposium in *International Security* (vol. 20, no. 1, 1995). Keohane and Lisa L. Martin acknowledge that Mearsheimer "correctly asserts that liberal institutionalists treat states as rational egoists operating in a world in which agreements cannot be hierarchically enforced, and that institutionalists only expect interstate cooperation to occur if states have significant common interests."[109] Wendt similarly comments, "I share all five of Mearsheimer's 'realist' assumptions . . . that international politics is anarchic, and that states have offensive capabilities, cannot be 100 percent certain about others' intentions, wish to survive, and are rational. We even share two more: a commitment to states as units of analysis, and to the importance of systemic or 'third-image' theorizing."[110]

CONCLUSION

Three conclusions emerge from the foregoing analysis:

1. There has been a tendency historically for dominant normative emphases to move back and forth along the dimensions described earlier, and as a consequence, for so-called realist and idealist theories to alternate as the nearest thing to paradigms in global politics.
2. Shifting terminology notwithstanding, genuinely new theoretical visions regarding global politics have been few and far between.
3. Intellectuals and practitioners in any era tend to reinforce one another's theoretical preferences, and their relationship is generally more intimate than contemporary social scientists care to believe.

Perhaps the most important reason for the alternation between realist and idealist dominance in global-politics thought and practice has been the key role played by unanticipated and disillusioning events in producing revisions in the dominant normative order of an era. Examples of such events include the Peloponnesian War and its impact on Thucydides; the fall of Rome; the French invasion of Italy of 1498 that so influenced Machiavelli; the destructive religious wars of the sixteenth and seventeenth centuries that weighed heavily on Bodin,

Hobbes, and others; the French Revolution and the Napoleonic Wars; the two world wars; the Vietnam War; the seizure of American hostages in Iran; and the end of the Cold War. Following each, there has been a tendency to place the blame on existing values and modes of thought and to embrace "new" norms and theories.

These dramatic shifts, however, have rarely produced genuinely new visions. Instead, they hastened a return to earlier values and the consequent rediscovery of earlier theories enhanced by new vocabularies. A survey of most grand theories of global politics reveals them to be built upon bundles of social and political preferences that grow out of shifting political and social contexts. The more fundamental the restructuring of existing institutions, the more likely that dominant theories will be—at least temporarily—abandoned.

That this should occur is in no way surprising in light of the relationship between pundits and practitioners. With few exceptions, the former represent specific social and political interests and may even seek the patronage (or, at a minimum, the passive approval) of those in authority. Machiavelli sought the protection of the Medicis in a world undergoing revolutionary political change; Hobbes desired royal patronage (but frightened both royalists and their foes); and Locke was spokesman for the newly empowered bourgeoisie. Even Hegel, after the metaphysical debris has been cleared, is revealed to have concluded that imperial Prussia represented the ultimate stage in historical evolution. In return, intellectuals structure and articulate the perspectives of practitioners, and legitimize their behavior. On the other hand, as Charles Lindblom and David Cohen observe, contemporary practitioners, even when not directly utilizing the work of social scientists, "may take the whole organizing framework or perspective for their work from academic social science."[111] Additionally, practitioners crave theoretical justification for what they intend to do in any case, and they have the means today, as in the past, to encourage this.[112] Social science even more than natural science is, as Bernard Barber declares, "a social activity" that has "determinate connections . . . with the different parts of a society, for example, with political authority . . . and with cultural ideas and values."[113]

Behavioral research, while failing to produce the cumulative knowledge to which its pioneers aspired, has had the important consequence of disconfirming many of the assumed verities of the past and producing healthy scholarly skepticism about such verities. It has also contributed to theoretical disarray by undermining existing general theories yet has failed to generate any of its own. Part of the problem is that the stable of concepts available to us cannot easily sustain theory construction. It is to some of these concepts that we turn in the next part.

CHAPTER 5

The State as an Obstacle to Understanding Global Politics

Almost two decades ago, Martin Wight addressed the question, "Why is there no international theory?" in an article bearing that title. His answer was that political theory traditionally had focused on "speculation about the state."[1] Humanity lived within states; at least so it was believed after the European epoch in global politics began around 1648. Since citizens do not live in the interstices between states or in a "state of nature," necessarily analyses of global politics could be no more than logical extensions of the study of the state. Thus, in their relatively modest excursions into global politics, theorists such as Locke, Hobbes, Marx, Hume, Rousseau, Kant, and Hegel all began from their peculiarly Eurocentric understanding of the state as an autonomous and sovereign actor in a condition with no authority above it.[2]

"If political theory," Wight reasoned, "is the tradition of speculation about the state, then international theory may be supposed to be a tradition of speculation about the society of states, or the family of nations, or the international community."[3] In other words, it became altogether too natural "to think of global politics as the untidy fringe of domestic politics."[4] Hobbes and Marx, for example, directed their attention to global politics only briefly, extrapolating conclusions about the global community from observations about the relations of individuals within states. The absence of the sort of sovereign power that constrained human passions within states led Hobbes to posit global anarchy. For his part, Marx and his followers viewed states as extensions of class domination that must logically vanish with the establishment of classless societies.

Wight's analysis highlights one reason why global-politics theorists, unlike other self-conscious communities of scholars, have been unable to establish an autonomous discipline. Even today, the most fundamental concepts in the field—its linguistic building blocks—are derivative. The very notion of international, for instance, can be understood only in respect of that which is *not* national or domestic. The same, of course, is true of concepts like transnational, interstate, and foreign policy. Governments have bureaucratic specialists who look at other states and specialists who deal only in domestic issues, and, until recently, few were trained to plan for or manage issues that existed along what Rosenau terms "the domestic-foreign frontier."[5] A field whose concepts can only be defined negatively can scarcely aspire to disciplinary status. Nor, as we shall argue, does there exist any agreement about the meaning of the state concept or, for that matter, about most other core concepts in global politics. And, if we conclude that global politics is more comprehensive than an interstate system; that inter-, intra-, and trans-state politics are all of a piece; or that the boundaries between "inside" and "outside" states have substantially collapsed, what is left of a field called "international politics"?[6]

Even postwar realism, which leans so heavily upon the state concept, exhibits confusion with regard to the meaning of "state." Hans J. Morgenthau, for example, uses "state" interchangeably with "nation," and the waters are further muddied by the equating of "national interest" with the "struggle for national power."[7] And Inis Claude, having suggested that states are "those important political, legal, and administrative units into which the world is divided,"[8] proceeds to inform us in some detail of what the state is *not*, while never informing us of what its attributes *are*.[9]

CONCEPTUAL ANARCHY

An autonomous discipline requires a stable of concepts unique to it and over which there is substantial agreement. In the absence of such concepts, global politics will remain a derivative field of study. Unique and consensual concepts are the bases of disciplinary boundaries and are prerequisites to identifying a common set of problems and puzzles that constitute the raisons d'être of its practitioners. In the absence of such boundaries, it is not even clear who is in the field and who is not. The moral theologian, the psychiatrist, the agricultural specialist, and many others may equally and plausibly claim to be undertaking research in global politics. Under these conditions, individual scholars or groups of scholars will continue to pursue idiosyncratic lines of research, often in isolation. They will continue to contemplate different, even unrelated, problems or, even worse, may believe that they are addressing the same problem only to discover that this is not the case. Put differently, global-politics specialists commonly discover that they are giving the same names to quite different phenomena; if they fail to recognize this, they will inevitably speak past each other. Quarrels over satisfactory operational definitions may mask deeper divisions over meaning; thereby aborting the voyage of discovery even before it is launched. Competing methodological claims will continue to obscure more fundamental questions of meaning and language.

Global politics, then, remains in a condition of conceptual anarchy; and, owing to the normative core of theory (whether or not admitted); it is unlikely that the field will transcend this condition in the foreseeable future. In Justice Benjamin Cardozo's words: "We may try to see things as objectively as we please. None the less, we can never see them with any eyes except our own."[10]

Normatively infused theory is the inevitable product of normatively infused concepts, and the meaning of concepts is bound to change along with the changing normative temper of society. Like other political concepts that have been "invented" by scholars and practitioners, the meaning of the state concept does not exist apart from the conditions in which it is used. In this, it is like the concept of human dignity as described by Justice William Brennan: "The precise rules by which we have protected fundamental human dignity have been transformed over time in response to both transformations of social conditions and evolution of our concepts of human dignity."[11] In other words, the value of human dignity has remained prominent in American thinking for two hundred years, but its content and meaning have changed dramatically. The reference to jurisprudence is instructive. For the most part, concepts in global politics evolve in a manner similar to that of law as described by Justice Holmes:

> The life of the law has not been logic: it has been experience. The felt necessities of the time, the prevalent moral and political theories, intuitions of public policy, avowed or unconscious, even the prejudices which judges share with their fellow men, have had a good deal more to do than the syllogism in determining the rules by which men should be governed.[12]

Concepts such as state are forged and reforged in accordance with shifting life habits and critical global issues, and the process of interaction among them. As social mores evolve in response to perceptions of necessity and social utility, the fundamental meanings associated with the sorts of abstract and artificial concepts inherent in political science are bound to change as well. Justice Cardozo's analysis of the changing meaning of liberty could easily be applied to the state concept:

> Does liberty mean the same thing for successive generations? May restraints that were arbitrary yesterday be useful and rational and therefore lawful today? May restraints that are arbitrary today become useful and rational and therefore lawful tomorrow? I have no doubt that the answer to these questions must be yes. . . . The same fluid and dynamic conception that underlies the modern notion of liberty . . . must also underlie the cognate notion of equality. . . . From all this it results that the content of constitutional immunities is not constant, but varies from age to age.[13]

The general conceptual problems of the field are epitomized by the state concept,[14] "one of the most contested in the literatures of constitutional law, political science, and international relations," according to Kalevi Holsti.[15] That concept has been so central to the study of international politics for more than three centuries that there has been virtually no possibility of developing unified and cumulative theory in the absence of universal agreement as to what the concept connotes.[16] Historically, however, the state has had widely different connotations for scholars. Mainly for this reason, no doubt, they have not been in agreement as to when the state or the modern state emerged or even as to whether all contemporary sovereign entities are true states. To the extent that the state has multiple meanings, it is difficult to imagine the development of the sort of general theory that many of us keep hoping will someday, somehow evolve.

Historically, as we have already implied, efforts to define the state have inevitably combined views of what it is with what it ought to be, views conditioned by context-bound issues of practical significance. For Aristotle, the notion of the state was inseparable from that of the Greek *polis*. For Romans, the state evolved from the city of Rome itself into a vast empire with an emperor who in later stages was seen by many as being both above the law and divine. For St. Thomas Aquinas and his contemporaries during Europe's medieval era, there were in a sense many overlapping states or none—diffuse, overlapping, and fragmented hierarchies of authority, ranging from pope and emperor (or perhaps God alone) at the pinnacle through local monarchs down to the humblest manor, town, or cloister. Machiavelli's idea of the state and its prince was derived from the small Medici Italian city-polity universe in which he lived and, perhaps more immediately, from his desire for a job at court—although the French occupation of Italy subsequently convinced him of the need for republican, limited government. As for Bodin, the lawyer and *politique* (in contrast to *fanatique*) who is usually credited with having articulated the first full-blown notion of state sovereignty, the state was essentially dynastic property; and, under the conditions of religious war, sovereignty was essentially aspirational. As F. H. Hinsley explains: "Bodin's book was a direct outcome of the confusion brought about by civil and religious wars in a France which had known no peace between the conflicts arising from the dissolution of its feudalized segmentary structure and the onset of the Reformation in the form of a new kind of rebellion against the state."[17] Likewise, Hobbes's *Leviathan,* including its rejection of the relevance of religion to politics, was the product of his preoccupation with civil strife in England and his desire to see it bought to an end.

The meaning usually given the concept by international-relations scholars as an abstract entity separate from the personality of its ruler did not exist prior to its "invention" after the 1648 Westphalian Treaty ended the Thirty Years' War. "To their contemporaries," argues Martin van Creveld, "the territories of Lodovico Sforza, Francis I, Charles V, and the rest were known as marquisates, countries, duchies, kingdoms, and of course the Empire. Each such territorial unit might contain 'states' (French *états*): such as the aristocratic one, the ecclesiastical one, and the common one. . . . They themselves, though, came to be called states only during the first half of the seventeenth century."[18] And the Spanish writer Francisco Suarez, author of *Treatise on Laws and God as Legislator,* which appeared in 1612, along with Hugo Grotius, in his *De Jure Belli ac Pacis Libri Tres* ("Three books on the law of war and peace"), which appeared in 1625, were among the first theorists to contemplate law between, as opposed to above, states. Both implicitly acknowledged state sovereignty by regarding law as a voluntary institution derived from state custom and treaties.

The first time the term "the state" actually came into general use in England was during the era of Oliver Cromwell when the crown's properties were seized and the followers of Cromwell scratched their round heads trying to decide to whom or what the properties now belonged. John Locke, Adam Smith, and others adopted the perspective of a liberal state in which the people reigned, which perspective neatly coincided with the political and economic interests of a rising middle class—and of upper-class revolutionaries and capitalists in America. (Contract became the watchword in more ways than one!) Karl Marx, on the other hand, regarded the state as a potential instrument (until it would wither away) of the urban proletariat that he saw growing and restive all around him in the western Europe of his day.

The same process took place outside Europe. Confucian thought held that China and, indeed, all the earth was united under an emperor who was the Son of Heaven; and the ideal of Chinese unity persisted even, as so often was the case, when China was politically fragmented. The early Indian conception of the state (articulated circa 300 B.C. by Chanakya Kautilya, sometimes likened to Machiavelli) saw the ruler as essentially an executive for Brahmin law (*dharma*) and envisaged realist-style power relations prevailing among local rulers. This conception gave way some years later under the influence of Buddhism to an idea of a peaceful empire under one emperor who was the defender and chief missionary of universalist faith. In the Moslem world, from the outset to the present day, there has been a tension between the secular state in its local manifestations and the state seen as a servant of the universalist religion of Islam and the Islamic Community.

In Europe, Rousseau's vague notion of popular sovereignty as the "general will" formed part of the background of the French Revolution, and Napoleon gave a major thrust to the identification of the state with the nation. Hegel's concept of the state as a moral idea, the realization of self, meshed nicely with later Social Darwinism and found a particularly nasty echo in German extreme glorifiers of the state like Treitschke and finally, of course, Hitler. By contrast, the limited democratic state and national self-determination were the hallmarks of Wilsonian thought and Anglo-American ideology more generally.

Contemporary analyses of the state have been no less infused by normative commitment. "The mark of the modern world," writes the neo-Marxist Immanuel Wallerstein, "is the imagination of its profiteers and the counter-assertiveness of the oppressed. Exploitation and the refusal to accept exploitation as either inevitable or just constitute the continuing antinomy of the modern era. . . ."[19] Nor are such analyses less context-bound, as reflected in Nicos Poulantzas's initial comments on his "theory of the state":

> The urgency behind this book derives above all from the political situation in Europe, since although the question of democratic socialism is far from being everywhere on the agenda, it is being posed in a number of European countries. The urgency also stems from the emergence of the new phenomenon of State authoritarianism, which affects virtually all the so-called developed countries. Finally, it refers to the discussion on the State and power that is developing in France and elsewhere.[20]

For a time, the concept of the state actually fell out of intellectual fashion except for among die-hard realists, only to return in recent years. In the same year (1968) that Wight's essay complaining about the concept's negative impact on international theory appeared, J. P. Nettl was writing, "The concept of the state is not much in vogue in the social sciences right now. Yet it retains a skeletal, ghostly existence largely because, for all the changes in emphasis and interest in research, the thing exists and no amount of conceptual restructuring can dissolve it."[21] Stephen D. Krasner confirmed the trend away from the state concept when he wrote, "From the late 1950s until the mid-1970s, the term state virtually disappeared from the professional academic lexicon. Political scientists wrote about governments, political development, interest groups, voting, legislative behavior, leadership, and bureaucratic politics, almost everything but 'the state.'"[22] Why this trend? For one thing, there was increasing recognition that the realists' world of objective national interests and nonideological behavior is as much a normative conception as the League of Nations. Analysts began asking realists hard questions about "whose national interest?" and "power for what?" and "isn't ideology part of power?"

As Krasner's list suggests, many scholars started to peer within the "black box" or "billiard ball" of the state, explicitly or implicitly questioning its autonomy and stressing the degree to which policy outcomes are shaped by domestic political actors and processes. Some of the same scholars and others emphasized the constraints on state autonomy emanating from the global environment—from the basic structure of the global system to international law, a great variety of international governmental and nongovernmental actors (IGOs and INGOs), regimes, environmental limits, globalized markets, and so on. In these analyses, structure may not be determinant, but it does create opportunities and constraints. Realists, especially neorealists, of course, place great weight on structure, but other theorists were concerned with a richer definition of structure than the distribution of power. In the sense that theirs was an international emphasis, it was reminiscent of the Wilsonian idealism against which realists had harangued. However, that is where the similarity ended. The proponents of what might be called the new internationalism were a disparate group, including Marxist, neo-Marxist, institutionalist, or *dependencia* theorists, as well as theorists who recognized that the receding of Cold War issues allowed other previously neglected global issues to come to the fore. The latter scholars were preoccupied with issues of international political economy such as resource allocation, recession, monetary instability, trade, transnational corporations, and environmental depredation. Temporarily, the state as traditionally conceived was no longer the principal focus of analysis, and the familiar issues of power and peace were no longer seen as necessarily delimiting the boundaries of the discipline. By 1976 Krasner concluded, "In recent years, students of global politics have multinationalized, transnationalized, bureaucratized, and transgovernmentalized the state until it has virtually ceased to exist as an analytic construct."[23]

If this was the situation in the mid-1970s, Krasner and others subsequently succeeded in resurrecting the notion of state autonomy. In their view, the state has significant resources of its own that often allow it to overcome constraints deriving from both domestic and international environments. Krasner's 1984 assessment was that "the agenda is already changing." Reviewing several important works relevant to this subject, he predicted, "'The state[9] will once again become a major concern of scholarly discourse."[24] So it did. Neorealism came into full fashion in the 1980s. The so-called crisis of the state moved beyond discussion among political economists to become a principal concern of behavioral scholars as well. Within yet another decade, however, neorealism itself was besieged both by those who were uncomfortable with its static structural determinism and those who assailed its state-centricity.

Neorealism did little to clarify the essential ambiguity of the concept of the state. For that matter, there is not even full agreement on the meaning of "autonomy" or "sovereignty." Furthermore, while state (however defined) and autonomy (however defined) may have been underrated in the rush to give adequate weight to domestic and systemic constraints, important constraints do continue to derive from other actors and levels. The state's surrogates may well still be the primary actors in global affairs, but this is no longer true by definition. And it is certainly the case that they are not the only significant actors. Recognizing the essential validity of this familiar statement, however, is far from being able to generalize with precision about the relationships involved.

Toward that end, in the early 1990s, Rosenau and others began to differentiate between the government of a state ("activities that are backed by formal authority") and governance ("activities backed by shared goals that may or may not derive from legal and formally prescribed responsibilities").[25] Governance consists of the "numerous patterns that sustain global order" unfolding "at three basic levels of activity"— intersubjective, behavioral, and "the aggregate or political level where . . . rule-oriented institutions and regimes enact and implement the policies" produced at the other levels.[26] It includes an array of authoritative decisions ranging from individual market decisions to "world civic politics"[27] and international regimes and customary law. Governance, in other words, was invented to account for the fact that a considerable degree of "order" exists in global politics even without the decisions of the governments of states. Rosenau currently argues that "the world is not so much a system dominated by states and national governments as a congeries of spheres of authority (SOAs) that are subject to considerable flux and not necessarily coterminous with the division of territorial space." SOAs are . . . "distinguished by the presence of actors who can evoke compliance when exercising authority as they engage in the activities that delineate the sphere."[28]

THE HISTORICAL STATE

Since the absence of a consensual state concept inhibits the development of global-politics theory, it might seem that an analysis of the historical roots of the phenomenon might provide a basis for identifying its essential qualities. In fact, such an analysis offers little solace to the investigator. He or she will discover that, while there have existed since prehistoric times self-conscious political associations able to distinguish themselves from other associations and conduct relations with them, there is little agreement that such entities were states as we understand the concept. On the other hand, those who view the state as the relatively recent outcome of a period of Western political development run the risk of assuming the nonexistence of global politics prior to 1648. "If this is the actual history of the state," declares Sabino Cassese acerbically, "there is no need to disturb Plato and Aristotle in a search for the origin of the concept of the state unless we want to attribute to them, and to other thinkers who followed them, extraordinary abilities to foresee the future."[29]

By contrast, an observer who concludes that the state is historically universal is confronted with a bewildering array of entities with so little in common that he or she is forced to adopt highly abstract and effectively nonoperational definitions of the phenomenon being sought. Thus, the state tends to become, in J. W. Burton's conception, "linked systems and their administrative controls"[30] or some "structural-functional" entity with no clear objective referent. The Greek *polis*, Chou Empire, Hapsburg dynastic territories, and Hanseatic League become simple varieties of a universal phenomenon.

Identifying the origins of the state poses less of historical than a conceptual problem. In other words, whether one conceives of the state as having always existed or having been born in a particular era depends largely on one's definition of the concept. And, as Donald Puchala suggests, "the first questions we must ask about the modern state are: What is it? What are its origins? These questions answer each other."[31] Unfortunately, that is exactly what they do not do, since questions are not answers, and neither question *has* a satisfactory answer (as we shall attempt to explain).

Puchala's questions do, however, help to reveal the circularity of the problem we face. In our own field, the problem is connected with the propensity to universalize an entity that was the product of a particular place and time: Europe from the end of its Middle Ages to roughly the present. Only in doing so can one also universalize the Eurocentric "discipline" of "international politics," which stands or falls entirely on the assumption that there is an autonomous system of states. Ours is a field, then, that uses history selectively while failing to consider that the way in which we organize ourselves for political ends is subject to change. One cannot pinpoint the origins of the state unless one can identify and operationalize the phenomenon one is seeking, and history does not afford an example that one would feel confident of offering as a "state for all seasons." This problem is discernible in the argument of two eminent French scholars, Bertrand Badie and Pierre Birnbaum:

> [T]he writer who wishes to treat the concept of the state faces a dilemma: either he must settle for a broad and therefore useless definition of the state or he must concede that "the state" is not a universal concept but rather the product of a specific historical crisis to which different premodern societies are vulnerable in different degrees. . . . On the other hand, we do not wish to argue that the state is peculiar to a single country or even to a small number of countries. Our point is simply this: in each society, particular historical processes foster state building to a greater or lesser degree. . . .
>
> The sociology of the state should . . . be careful to avoid . . . the conclusion that once the state is established, its nature and form are determined and will never change. In particular, we think it would be useful to study the conditions under which one type of state is transformed into another.[32]

However, if the state is not a "universal concept" but is instead "the product of a specific historical crisis," how are we to assess the "greater or lesser degree" of "state building" in each society, much less construct a useful typology of states and study the dynamics of their transformation?

Anthropologists find themselves on the horns of a similar dilemma in dealing with state formation. In the course of maintaining that the state had its origins in both social conflict (competition over scarce resources) and integration (benefits flowing from centralized authority), Ronald Cohen illustrates the problem:

> It is now becoming clear that there are multiple roads to statehood, that whatever sets off the process tends as well to set off other changes which, no matter how different they are to begin with, all tend to produce similar results. It is this similarity of result, I believe, that has clouded the issue of causality. Similar results—the state—imply common antecedents. Unfortunately, as the data are compared, as more cases appear in the literature, historical sequences support the notion of multiple and varied causes producing similar effects.[33]

The reader who has been following the reasoning thus far may be some-what disconcerted to learn that Cohen's principal focus is on the "early state." He says, "Early states as far removed as Incan Peru, ancient China, Egypt, early Europe, and pre-colonial West Africa exhibit striking similarities. Thus the state as a form of organization is an emergent selective force that has sent humankind along a converging path."[34] Cohen acknowledges that *"Homo sapiens has evolved a number of quite different and distinct political systems; one of these is the state."* Moreover, "[f]rom this baseline of agreement, our notions about what to emphasize in a definition of 'state' begin to diverge sharply." He himself lists three classes of definitions.[35] How, then, can we be confident that the "similar results" of "multiple and varied causes" that he has identified are, in fact, "the state"? Jonathan Haas's analysis of the prehistoric state is worth citing at length because it illustrates just how uncoordinated have been efforts to achieve under-standing of the phenomenon's origins.

> [T]he first problem that needs to be confronted concerns the concept of the "state" itself. The myriad definitions presented in the literature tend to be either idiosyn-cratic or tied to a particular theoretical perspective. . . .
>
> First, "State" is seen as representing the discrete complex of social institutions that operate together to govern a particular, highly evolved society. Under this con-ceptualization, *the* state operates as a concrete entity within the social whole. Lenin, for example, argues that "the state is an organ of class *domination*". . .
>
> The second notion of "state" sees it as referring to a particular kind of society characterized by specific attributes. In an evolutionary sense, this conception uses "state" as a label to classify societies that have reached a particular level of cultural development. . . .
>
> Finally, "state" is used in a way that is somewhat complementary to the second usage. Specifically, it is used to identify individual bounded societies that are char-acterized by a "state" level of organization. In this sense, a "state" is analogous to a "tribe" or a "chiefdom." For example, one might refer to the Aztec *state* or the Zulu *state,* just as one might refer to the Zuni *tribe* or the Kwakuitl *chiefdom.* In contrast to the idea of the state being a part of a society, the third conception sees the state as the entire society.
>
> *These three notions of "state" do refer to different things, and lack of awareness of the dis-tinctions between them has introduced a degree of confusion in the literature. What is one per-son's "state" is another person's "government" and vice versa.*[36]

By inference, we must conclude that a state is *any* form of political organization, and we are left in the dark about the level of organization necessary for an entity to qualify for statehood.

Let us examine how the authors of two other works treat the state as a his-torical and even prehistorical phenomenon, even while failing to denote that which they are seeking to describe. In the view of Ernest Gellner:

> Mankind has passed through three fundamental stages in its history: the pre-agrar-ian, the agrarian, and the industrial. Hunting and gathering bands were and are too small to allow the kind of political division of labour which constitutes the state; and so, for them, the question of the state, of a stable specialized order-enforcing institution, does not really arise. By contrast, most, but by no means all, agrarian societies have been state-endowed. . . . They differ a great deal in their form. The agrarian phase of human history is the period during which, so to speak, the very

existence of the state is an option. . . . During the hunting-gathering stage, the option was not available.

By contrast, in the post-agrarian, industrial age there is, again, no option; but now the *presence*, not the absence of the state is inescapable. Paraphrasing Hegel, once none had the state, then some had it, and finally all have it. The form it takes still remains variable. There are some traditions of social thought—anarchism, Marxism—which hold that even, or especially, in an industrial order the state is dispensable, at least under favourable conditions or under conditions due to be realized in the fullness of time. There are obvious and powerful reasons for doubting this. [37]

Gellner thus admits the appearance of the state at a relatively early, "agrarian" stage of human history. Since the form of the state is said to be variable at any stage, the only apparent requirement is that the entity involved must have been a "stable specialized order-enforcing institution." Yet that is a characteristic of just about any political institution. It is a polity *sui generis!*

For their part, Badie and Birnbaum assert:

To be sure, centralized political systems have been a feature not only of modern but also of many ancient or classical societies. The novelty of modern times is that exceptions to the law of centralization are no longer tolerated, the division of labor in modern society being such that none can escape the need for coordination through a centralized political structure or structures. But this is the only common feature of modern political systems, and as soon as the political sociologist begins to concern himself with history or simply with the empirical data he is forced to admit that political centralization may take many forms and that the particular form that emerges in any given case is largely related to cultural and conjunctural factors: state-building is only one form of political centralization among others, and the models followed in building states vary widely from one society to the next.[38]

According to Badie and Birnbaum, the state is not universal:

Even in the West, however, civil society has at times been able to make do without a state. It has often been able to organize itself and by doing so to prevent the development of a state with some claim to the right to wield absolute power. Wherever a state exists, the entire social system is affected. Civil society invariably organizes around the state once a state has come into existence. . . . Class relations vary widely depending on whether there is a highly institutionalized state or a mere political center whose main function is to coordinate the activities of civil society.[39]

What, then, do Badie and Birnbaum regard as a "true state" as distinct from a "mere political center"? The closest they come to a definition is the following:

[T]he true state (as distinguished from what is merely the center of a centralized political system) is one that has achieved a certain level of differentiation, autonomy, universality, and institutionalization. These features remain characteristic, even if . . . all of the features named may coexist with dedifferentiation and epigenesis.[40]

So a "true state" has "certain" "characteristic features"—or does it? If only selected entities are true states, what does that imply for other entities that behave in state-like ways? In the end, Badie and Birnbaum settle on France as "the ideal type of the state" or "the state model," arguing that the political center of that country carried the "process of differentiation and institutionalization" further than others in Europe because it needed to do so to overcome greater resistance from feudal vestiges in French society.[41] As for the contemporary West:

> It is still possible even today to distinguish between political systems in which there is both a center and a state (France), a state but no center (Italy), a center but no true state (Great Britain and the United States), and neither a center nor a true state (Switzerland). In the first two cases the state dominates civil society and is responsible for its organization albeit in different degrees. In the last two cases civil society organizes itself. It is therefore possible to distinguish between societies in which the state attempts to run the social system through a powerful bureaucracy (of which France is the ideal type, with Prussia, Spain, and Italy exhibiting similar trajectories) and societies in which there is no need for a strong state and governing bureaucracy because civil society is capable of organizing itself (of which Great Britain is the ideal type, with the United States and "consociational democracies" . . . such as Switzerland exhibiting similar trajectories).[42]

Note that, in Badie's and Birnbaum's analysis, less emphasis is laid on the state's autonomy from societal influences than on society's lack of autonomy from organizational influences emanating from the state's "center" (where one exists).

Although it is apparently true, as Morton H. Fried observes, that "the ancients left no self-conscious history of the evolution of their earliest states,"[43] there clearly have been territorial-political entities—some of substantial size and/or authority—in the global system for many thousands of years. "Over the bulk of recorded history, declares Oran Young, "man has organized himself for political purposes on bases other than those now subsumed under the concepts 'state' and 'nation-state.'"[44] Whether one chooses to term them chiefdoms, empires, city-states, principalities, states, or something else seems to us to rest exclusively on the nature of the entity in question and on one's choice of definitions. Nevertheless, although "political entities with exclusive control over a well-defined territory existed well before the Peace [of Westphalia], and feudal and universal institutions . . . continued well after it,"[45] these earlier enterprises in rulership were not the same as the Westphalian state. Indeed, we in our own work on historical polities and the polities model of global politics are careful to classify the Westphalian state as only one form of polity, distinguishable by its sovereign and independent legal status as well as its *claim* to supreme authority within specific territorial bounds.[46]

The important fact remains that early entities evinced several or many of the characteristics customarily associated with the modern state, for example, territory, executives, legislatures, judges, bureaucrats, taxes, an army, interest groups, and social classes; as well as problems of succession, center-periphery relations, alliances, wars, trade, ecology. The list could go on and on.[47]

Second, institutional artifacts from every stage of human political evolution may still be found in the present industrial or postindustrial era, even as the progress of industrialization has varied tremendously from place to place. Just as there are a few remaining pockets of Stone Age culture and many predominantly agrarian societies, so too do there continue to be tribes, city-states, surprisingly autonomous cities, and other political subdivisions (such as states in the

American federal system), monarchs (albeit mostly enfeebled), myriad ethnicities, latent and more substantial nations, complex bureaucracies, classes and masses, a host of interest groups, political parties, transnational corporations, transgovernmental organizations, alliances, ideological empires, and other putative neo-imperialisms. Indeed, many contemporary states have the marks of a prestate past; Saudi Arabia and Iraq, for example, are tribal states with roots in both the pre-and post-Islamic epochs. To borrow a felicitous phrase that Charles Anderson coined for Latin America, the world is indeed a "living museum."

Third and finally, many so-called modern states are sadly lacking in many of the same state-like qualities that characterized the sovereign European states that evolved in the seventeenth and eighteenth centuries. Some old and not-so-old states in the immediate spheres of influence of great powers face grave political constraints. Moreover, it is no secret that many of the states spawned by decolonialization in the twentieth century are shaky enterprises indeed. As Young observes, "If the basic attributes of statehood are taken to be such things as a clearly demarcated territorial base, a relatively stable population, more or less viable central institutions of government and external sovereignty, the contemporary situation immediately begins to appear unclear and confusing."[48]

In sum, the explosion in the number of state-like territorial entities in the world has been striking. There were about fifteen such entities in 1871, twenty-five by the outbreak of World War I, and more than thirty by the 1930s.[49] The vast expansion in numbers took place in the years following World War II. Fifty-one states were charter members of the United Nations, and the number of legally independent units looks to round out at more than two hundred today. By almost any standard—size of territory, size of population, ethnic homogeneity, GNP, degree of industrialization, military force, form of government, ideology, and so on—these units present a wide range of differences. "There is surely at least a *prima facie* case," as David Vital observes, " for asserting that one of the notable characteristics of the modern international scene is the growing disparity in human and material resources to be found where important categories of states are compared—with the result that the only genuine common denominator left is the purely *legal* equality of states that carries with it only such tenuous advantages as membership in the United Nations."[50]

The world is further complicated by the presence of an unspecified number (because there is no precise definition here either) of microstates. Tuvalu, which became the 189th member of the United Nations in 2000, has a population of 10,000, consists of nine coral atolls, and is threatened with submersion by rising seas. The issue of microstates has long troubled international organizations. For example, the League of Nations denied Liechtenstein membership on the grounds that "by reason of her limited area, small population, and her geographical position, she has chosen to depute to others some of the attributes of sovereignty" and having no army, "could not discharge all the international obligations which would be imposed on her by the Covenant." Along with Liechtenstein, the League and the United Nations also refused to admit other microstates including Andorra, Monaco, and San Marino. Like the Vatican, however, these entities have held membership in various technical international organizations. In addition, Liechtenstein and San Marino have participated in the activities of the International Court of Justice, and Liechtenstein was even a party to the 1955 Nottebohm case on dual nationality (Liechtenstein vs. Guatemala).[51] Bruce Russett and Harvey Starr report that when Liechtenstein entered the Council of Europe in 1978, "a British representative warned, 'If we let Liechtenstein join, we may face similar demands from other microstates like Monaco, the Faroe Islands, Guernsey, San Marino and all sorts of others.' More importantly, some members warned that if such microunits were to apply, the Council might have to raise the whole question of what a state *is*!"[52] For theorists, then, these mice continue to roar.

As noted previously, there are also an increasing number of states that are incapable of meeting even the most minimal demands of citizens. Notwithstanding their Westphalian borrowings, states such as Sierra Leone and Congo cannot maintain order at home, let alone manage the large-scale economic and social forces determining their fates. Liberia, a victim of savage intertribal strife, is in the words of one foreign observer, "a demented circus of crooks trying to outdo other crooks."[53] At best "quasi-states," such states embody "a parody of statehood indicated by pervasive incompetence, deflated credibility, and systematized corruption."[54] They are "failed states:"

> From Haiti in the Western Hemisphere to the remnants of Yugoslavia in Europe, from Somalia, Sudan, and Liberia in Africa, to Cambodia in Southeast Asia, a disturbing new phenomenon is emerging: the failed state, utterly incapable of sustaining itself as a member of the international community. Civil strife, government breakdown, and economic privation are creating more and more modern *debellatios*, the term used in describing the destroyed German state after World War II.[55]

As Jeffrey Herbst suggests, we might "formally recognize that some states are simply not exercising formal control over parts of their country and should no longer be considered sovereign."[56]

THE SEARCH FOR AN IDEAL TYPE

The absence of consensus regarding the attributes of a "true" state and the absence of agreement about the historical origins of the state suggest that we are dealing with a condition of *relative* political institutionalization, power, and vulnerability across the millennia. Yet the lack of such agreement may entail regarding virtually all relatively autonomous rulerships as variants of the state; the state then indeed becomes a "conceptual variable" and can no longer be used by scholars of global politics solely as an independent variable.

Under these conditions the problem of constructing generalizable propositions of either a synchronic or diachronic sort becomes exceedingly difficult.[57] Contemporary comparison of state behavior is encumbered by the quite dramatic disparities in the units of analysis. Historical analysis of the sort attempted by projects like the Correlates of War is at least partly undermined also by gross differences—both across time and space—among the units defined as states.[58] If we no longer depend upon states for defining global politics, then war also becomes problematic because it is frequently defined, as in the Correlates of War, as an interstate phenomenon. Indeed, if we restrict ourselves to interstate warfare, we might be tempted to argue that, except for the

Ethiopian-Eritrean conflict, there has been no war since that fought in 1991 in the Persian Gulf. Yet surely no one would be tempted to describe the past decade as peaceful.

Is there an ideal type of state that can be used as a baseline for comparison with other variants of the state phenomenon—an entity that, on the one hand, is largely free from external control and, on the other, is distinct from that of its own society? Such an entity would not be a political subdivision of a larger entity, and it would be based on a different organizational principle from that of its own society as a whole. It would not be a "colony" or "protectorate," or a "local government," or a tribal "chiefdom." Its institutions would represent the political community within its boundaries. Leaders and bureaucratic agents of the state would be readily recognizable as such, however strong or weak their capacity to mobilize human and material resources.[59]

The basic difficulties with such an approach are threefold: First, even in hunter-gatherer and more complex tribal groups, political decisions are made—the "authoritative allocation of values" (in David Easton's terminology) as a process takes place. There are distinct political decisionmaking roles within the group, even though the same individuals simultaneously occupy other social roles. There is usually little doubt about how (in the sense of a process and the individuals involved) it will be decided, for example, whether or not to move the tents to a different pasture, or whether to fight or run from a neighboring group. And in contemporary global politics, values are authoritatively allocated by a variety of institutions such as transnational corporations that are hardly states.

Second, ancient authorities, like states, had a defined (if shifting) territory or at least a "home range," and few of them were unclear about who constituted "we" and who was "they" in relationships with other groups. And in contemporary global politics, nonstate institutions also enjoy political space, which may or may not be territorial in nature. Like the boundaries between states, such institutions also have boundaries that separate those "inside" from those "outside" and that define the extent of identities and probably loyalties as well.[60]

Third, political entities never have been and, one can safely say, never will be, fundamentally distinct or separate from their societies, because political decisionmakers simultaneously do occupy social roles and must be responsive both to their own societies and to external influences. Indeed, as John Hall and others have stressed, the societies in which political entities are enmeshed with regard to matters like defense or trade typically extend far beyond their own "borders."[61] Although this was always the case, it is one of the defining qualities of a world characterized by transnationalism, interdependence, and globalization.

Political leaders interact differentially with *parts* of their own societies and the external world. Decisions of significance and considerable authority with regard to the allocation of values are regularly made at many different levels. Thus, if we are interested in explaining behavior rather than abstractions alone, we have to look both within and without the political entity in question. As we shall argue later, establishing that an entity is widely seen as a state may tell the analyst something relevant to the explanation of behavior, but it is normally far from all that is relevant and may even be the least illuminating, or even a misleading, explanation.

Consider the putative modern state, that "ideal type" that many scholars conveniently date from the Treaties of Augsburg of 1555 and Westphalia in 1648. (Some scholars would suggest an earlier date, which is symptomatic of the problem.) This state is credited, to some extent correctly, with having overcome the universalist pretensions of the church and the Holy Roman Empire, as well as the internal challenge of segmentary feudalism. Monarchs became absolute sovereigns by divine right, viewed as such from both inside and outside their domains, and the state itself took on the attribute—the key one for John H. Herz—of "territoriality" (a "hard shell" of "impenetrability").[62]

How simple it was in the age of *"L 'état, c'est moi."* But perhaps, it was not so very simple after all. The "absolute" monarchs of Europe—those few whose realms were sufficiently integrated for them to claim the title—might beg to disagree. Shakespeare expressed it well when he wrote, "Uneasy lies the head that wears the crown." There always seemed to be a pretender raising an army or dissident nobles to curb or rebellious towns and peasants from whom adequate taxes had to be extracted to pay for a mercenary army to defend the "hard shell."

Nor were things all that much more secure in the "model state" of France.[63] Part of the Sun King's genius was his capacity to make life at the royal court of Versailles more attractive for his nobles than subversive activities back at the chateau. Had Louis XIV been a little less shrewd in adopting flamboyant architecture, dress, and furniture, his sun might soon have set. Moreover, he had to rule in part through his intendants and had to continue to be alert to clientele relations developing between them and various private interests.[64] From *Les Frondeurs* at the outset of Louis's reign to Richelieu's effort at state-building, anchoring popular identities and loyalties in the French state under the Sun King was an arduous undertaking.[65] Badie and Birnbaum comment that "not until the eighteenth century do we find Frenchmen beginning to think of France's borders as 'natural,' as later became commonplace."[66]

In addition, France was considerably less than a unified cultural community. Peter Worsley quotes Eugen Weber on the point that, "As late as 1863, 'French was a foreign language for a substantial number of Frenchmen, including about half the children who would reach adulthood in the last quarter of the century'."[67] Louis XIV ran headlong into the later-celebrated balance of power when he embarked on a campaign of conquest; his eventual defeat, in turn, may be regarded as both a ratification of the hard shells of some of his neighbors and as testimony to the rise of a new external systemic constraint that had replaced the much less formidable Holy Roman Empire. Most significantly, a scant seventy-seven years after Louis XIV's death, the model state dissolved (or was fundamentally transformed) in revolution, and the "sovereign" head of the "absolute" monarchy landed in the basket at the foot of the guillotine.[68]

The American and French revolutions had an impact on the basic units in the international system at least as significant as the emergence of the modern state in Europe. The liberal doctrine of the era held that sovereignty belonged not so much in a personal sense to a divinely appointed monarch but, variously, to the people, the general will, the law, or the nation. The doctrine could justify authoritarianism or even rule by a monarch or self-styled emperor (for example, Napoleon I, as well as republican experiments), but it forever banished the notion that sovereignty was equivalent to a flesh-and-blood sovereign, his lands, or his dynastic pretensions. It was, of course, the concept of nation mutating into nationalism and national self-determination—the idea that each nation should have its own state—that subsequently had the greatest effect on global political boundaries.[69] The wars that swept Europe between the French Revolution and 1815 represented a conflict between what Rodney Bruce Hall calls "territorial-sovereign" and "national-sovereign principles."[70] The resulting "link between people and territory" and the heightened importance of territorial extent were, in the view of Alexander B. Murphy, "to lead to a world war."[71]

With the assistance of Napoleon's campaigns, two world wars in the twentieth century, the League of Nations and the United Nations, and the Cold War rivalry between the United States and the Soviet Union, a multitude of new nation-states emerged. National self-determination reached a crescendo in nineteenth-century Europe, especially with liberal nationalists such as Mazzini in Italy and the members of the abortive Frankfurt Parliament in Germany. It climaxed in Wilson's Fourteen Points. In recent decades, however, growing recognition of the noncontiguity of state and national boundaries especially outside Europe has once more led to increasing conflict between the two ideas. As we shall see, however, this does not mean that issues of culture and identity have become less prominent in recent years. In fact, the opposite has taken place.[72]

Perhaps, as Gellner insists, one should not "conclude, erroneously, that nationalism is a contingent, artificial, ideological invention, which might not have happened, if only those damned busy-body interfering European thinkers, not content to leave well enough alone, had not concocted it and fatefully injected it into the bloodstream of otherwise viable political communities."[73] Nationalism did provide an ideological justification for those who wanted to throw off the yoke of colonial repression and later also for the leaders of the new nation-state to rule. The European idea of nationalism was transmitted to the world, Worsley notes, via the very European imperialism that had the most to lose were it to be taken seriously. Thus, nationalist leaders in the developing world such as Mohandas Gandhi learned the concept from those against whose rule they fought.

One can be charitable, with Gellner, and point out that the achievement of greater political centralization, the maintenance of political order, and the imposition of a high culture were essential if Third World countries were ever to "develop" in a world that was moving inexorably from agrarianism to industrialization. For Gellner, in fact, the imposition of a high culture was critical: "At the base of the modern social order stands not the executioner but the professor. Not the guillotine, but the (aptly named) *doctoral d'état is* the main tool and symbol of state power. The monopoly of legitimate education is now more important, more central than is the monopoly of legitimate violence."[74] Or one can stress, with Worsley, the persecution of dissident groups, ethnic and otherwise; the fact that nationalism has frequently degenerated into "chauvinism, from a pride in Self to a contempt for the Other," resulting in extreme cases in "genocidal brutality."[75]

Most analysts agree, however, that the basic concept of nation itself is little more than an invention and a fiction, that perhaps had some initial substance, especially in a few European contexts[76] (albeit incomplete, for example, Welsh,

Basques, Alsatians) but is truly a "mystification" (Worsley's term) applied to most of the Third World. Gellner observes that:

> It is nationalism which engenders nations, and not the other way round. Admittedly, nationalism uses the pre-existing, historically inherited proliferation of cultures or cultural wealth, though it uses them very selectively, and it most often transforms them radically. Dead languages can be revived, traditions invented, quite fictitious pristine purities restored. . . . The cultural shreds and patches used by nationalism are often arbitrary inventions. Any old shred or patch would have served as well.[77]

Worsley links "nation" and "state" even more tightly, arguing that "it is more heuristically useful to restrict the term 'nation' to that mode of ethnicity which only emerges with the modern centralized State, and which therefore entails not so much continuity with older ethnic identities as their supersession, if necessary, their repression. Nation-building . . . goes hand-in-hand with the formation of the State."[78]

In any event, nationalism is an ideology with proven power to inspire millions to acts of heroism and brutality. The nation may be a legal fiction that defies easy operationalization, but it continues to exercise a powerful grip on the human imagination. An observer's understanding of the concept of nation-state, which has dominated global-politics discourse for two centuries, is basically ideological. This is typical of the concepts that we utilize in global politics. At best, it will be difficult to lend objectivity to concepts that are inherently subjective; at worst, it may be impossible.

THE MANY MEANINGS OF THE STATE

Against this background, then, and with a degree of skepticism, let us briefly summarize and categorize some of the more prominent conceptions of the state. As we shall see, these conceptions repeatedly grow out of normative preferences and ideological predilections. They are fashioned less in an effort to achieve the conceptual consensus necessary for examining the phenomenon scientifically than in order to advance these preferences and predilections.

Although scholars have generally maintained a distinction between "state" and "nation," the past century has witnessed an increasing identification of the two concepts at the popular level. Groups with sufficient ethnic and cultural homogeneity demand the legal autonomy associated with the idea of the sovereign state. In this context, the state is defined as an *ethno-cultural unit*. Commonly, they justify this demand by pointing to a common history or, if necessary, inventing one. By contrast, ethnic heterogeneity has been frequently cited as a source of state weakness and dissension (e.g., Austria-Hungary). Whether one refers to the unifications of Germany and Italy, the spread of the new imperialism, Hitler's campaign for *Lebensraum*, the founding of Israel, the partition of India, the Nigerian civil war, or the violence on the Israeli-occupied West Bank or in Yugoslavia's Kosovo, the potency of this variant of the state is undeniable.

Indeed, it can be argued that it is this definition of the state—widely invoked by political leaders—which is largely responsible for the proliferation of ungovernable and nonviable units in Africa, Asia, and along Russia's southern frontier.[79] As we have noted, young states in particular often reach for "shreds and patches" of past cultures in attempting to build a nation, and some states, through design or historical happenstance, are roughly conterminous with ethnic boundaries. Thus, Uzbekistan is trying to create a national history on the piles of bones left by the late-fourteenth early-fifteenth-century conqueror Timur the Great. But, as Worsley explains:

> The nightmare of the unifiers is . . . the realization that there is no logical limit on the size or number of groups which can legitimately claim to possess a common culture or subculture. The possibility of infinite regress opens up, for any sizable group can always be further decomposed into regional subcultures, each with its own distinctive territory, dialect, history, and so forth, and into further subdivisions within the region.[80]

Some "extinct" "nations" have actually been reborn. Worsley points out, "One of the most horrific cases of genocide known to history is the extermination of the Tasmanian aborigines. Everyone knows they were wiped out. . . . But what 'everybody knows' is wrong, for today there is a militant movement among the thousands who proudly trace their mixed, but nevertheless partly Tasmanian descent to their slaughtered forebears." Some ethnicities, moreover, are much larger than many existing nation-states; Worsley's example is the eighteen million Kurds stretching across Iran, Iraq, Turkey, and Syria—compared to small states like Dominica (pop. 80,000) or Nauru (pop. 8,000).[81]

Nor are the older and more established states immune to the "absent nation" phenomenon. For instance, W. Raymond Duncan emphasizes that in Latin America, where most state boundaries have been in place since the early nineteenth century, Indians "differentiate between highland and lowland Indians in Bolivia or village identities in Guatemala or Peru. Linguistic differentiation between Quechua, Aymara, and Guarani throughout the Andean countries also fragments the Indian community. . . . At least 73 languages are spoken [by Indian groupings in Latin America] and more than 355 separate tribes have been identified."[82] The United States has at least partially "melted" numerous ethnicities, but black, brown, and red underclass tensions remain; ethnic divisions continue to threaten the Soviet successor states; Canada has to contend with its Québecois; Britain has the Scots and Irish as well as the Welsh; France, its Bretons and Corsicans; Spain its Basques; and so on. Mayan self-consciousness in Mexico's Chiapas illustrates the political potency of historical memory and reflects the fact that control of historical interpretation is a powerful source of authority and legitimacy.

A second definition is that of the state as a *normative order*. The state in this conception is a symbol (or cluster of symbols) for a particular society and the laws, norms, and beliefs that bind its people ("the nation") together. In this context, the state and its citizens constitute a moral community bound together by laws and customs. From the vantage point of national *and* international society, such a state has a juridical sovereign identity. Typical of this perspective is the observation of Alessandro Passerin d'Entreves: "The modern state is a legal system. The power it exercises is not mere force, but force applied in the name of, and in accordance with, a body of rules, from which in fact we infer that a state 'exists' . . . the birth of the modern state is no other than . . . the rise and final acceptance of the concept of sovereignty."[83] Clifford Geertz has written persuasively about the symbolic role of the "theatre state" in Bali, which he sees as highlighting a "pomp and ceremony" dimension common even to more complex states.[84] One is also reminded of the glorification of the state under National Socialism or under other regimes, like Getulio Vargas's O Estado Novo in Brazil (1937–45). Virtually all states have their national flag, their national anthem, their leaders' frequent appeals to the mystical national desiny, their ideological banners, usually an Unknown Soldier or other martyrs, and so on.

The definition, however, fails to deal with the fact that many countries, including multicultural ones, are often deeply divided over norms. The civil strife that today rends societies such as Colombia, the Sudan, Afghanistan, and Algeria is merely the most graphic manifestation of these normative schisms. As the example of the United States in the 1860s and 1960s illustrates, severe political turmoil arising from normative cleavages lies closer to the surface almost everywhere than one might think. Aggravating internal divisions are normative identity conflicts sweeping across boundaries: ethnic ties, Sunni versus Shi'ite Islam, and so forth.

Of sovereignty, J. P. Nettl wrote in the late 1960s:

> Nowadays the problem of sovereignty is, for social scientists, a dead duck. More than thirty years ago, Frederick Watkins pushed sovereignty to the margin of political science concerns by insisting that it be regarded as a "limiting concept"—an ideal typical situation that had to be qualified in all sorts of ways. He qualified it with the notion of autonomy, another limiting concept that applied both to the state itself and to all the associations within or below it, and as such eroded the value of sovereignty as a unique political factor. Since then we hear little of sovereignty except in the context of historical and philosophical (and, of course, legal) discussions.[85]

Nettl failed to foresee the situation today. For a "dead duck," sovereignty continues to generate a surprising amount of quackery!

What do we mean by "sovereignty"? Theorists have been contemplating that question for hundreds of years. One can easily see the linkage to the state as a normative order in Hinsley's definition: "the idea that there is a final and absolute authority in the political community,"[86] which legitimizes the decrees of the state. However central this conception may have been to political struggles centuries ago, it seems doubtful that many citizens the world over today ever think about the sovereignty of the state as somehow being the reason they pay taxes, serve in the military, get a marriage license, or whatever. Partly for this reason, the most useful definition for contemporary times, in our view, is a narrower, legal one advanced by Alan James that looks primarily outward from the state—namely, constitutional independence.[87]

Let us not underestimate the importance of a state's possessing constitutional independence. As James points out, it is usually a necessary (although not always sufficient) condition for a state's participation in international organizations and many other formal aspects of international life. Legally independent states can lay claim to various widely recognized rights under international law, including the right to send and receive ambassadors; and with rights come such duties as not allowing the state's territory to be used as a staging base for attack on another state's homeland by its dissident groups.[88]

Also, in a very practical sense, legal sovereignty offers to states a modestly extra dimension of stability and freedom from external interference that they would not otherwise possess. As James notes, for example, there was much more controversy over the Soviet invasion of Hungary, Czechoslovakia, or Afghanistan than there would have been had these areas been formal parts of the USSR. It is not insignificant that the Soviets went to great pains to avoid the embarrassment of sending massive numbers of their own troops into Poland during the Solidarity crisis. For its part, the United States ran into much more criticism of its role in the 1954 overthrow of the Arbenz government in Guatemala, its marine intervention in the Dominican Republic in 1965, and the 1983 Grenada episode than ever would have occurred had any of the target countries been a state in the U.S. federal system.[89] Nevertheless, the global outcry over Russia's war in Chechnya and NATO's intervention in Kosovo, an area legally under Yugoslav sovereignty, suggest the growing limits to this argument.

Robert Jackson has argued that many African states possess "juridical statehood" derived from a right of "self-determination"—what he calls "negative sovereignty"—"without yet possessing much in the way of empirical statehood disclosed by a capacity for effective and civil government"—the latter being what he calls "positive sovereignty."[90] He remarks that "apart from a few qualified exceptions such as Morocco, Zanzibar, Swaziland, Lesotho, Botswana, Rwanda, and Burundi—sovereignty in Africa has never reverted to anything remotely resembling traditional states."[91] Most were "novel European creations" and are today, at best, what James Mayall terms "anachronistic" states or what others term "nascent states," "quasi states" or "pseudo states" states.[92] Why, asks Jackson, are such flimsy states still in existence years after independence? He offers a number of explanations: "Once juridical statehood is acquired . . . diplomatic civilities are set in motion which support it, exaggerate it, and conceal its lack of real substance and value. A new international momentum is inaugurated."[93] Many African states have themselves been too insecure to wish to see boundaries adjusted; the ideology of pan-Africanism has frowned on regional states sitting in judgment on their neighbors, and what Jackson terms "racial sovereignty" forbids the rest of the world from criticizing the affairs of black African countries. Fledgling African states have gained status from participation in regional and world international organizations; and, apart from rivalry over Angola and Ethiopia/Somalia, powerful external states have been reluctant to intervene extensively in African affairs. Most of all, Jackson argues, African ruling elites are doing very well, thank you—their countries are a mansion of great privilege for them, while the masses often starve. Jackson thus takes partial exception to J. D. B. Miller's assertion that sovereignty confers "vitality" on states; often "in Africa" Jackson observes, "it debilitates them and confers luxury on statesmen."[94]

The idea that sovereignty is regularly violated in global politics led Stephen Krasner to argue that there are really several dimensions to the concept, that only some are regularly violated, that some have always been honored in the breech, and that others remain largely intact. "Rulers," he declares "have frequently departed from the principle that external actors should be excluded from authority structures within the territory of their own or other states," and "[t]he norm of equality . . . has been challenged by alternatives including human rights, minority rights, fiscal responsibility, and the maintenance of international stability." All of these facts lead Krasner to conclude, "Organized hypocrisy is the normal state of affairs."[95]

So the legal concept of sovereignty tells us something about the "real" world, but, being "organized hypocrisy," it nevertheless speaks not at all to a great deal that is important about states and global politics. Start with the legal problem of how constitutional independence is, in fact, established, although that is not the most important issue. In fact, there is no mechanism except the consensus—or lack thereof—of the international community. Let us leave aside technical problems regarding associated states and microstates. Consider the Turkish Republic of North Cyprus, or the state of Bosnia or the de facto state of Palestine, or the fallout some years ago from apartheid: the "black homeland" entities like the Transkei that no state but South Africa recognized until those homelands were abolished with the end of apartheid. In contrast, "the former British territory of Lesotho, which is also an enclave within South Africa, but was never ruled by Pretoria and has gained independence from Britain, is a recognized state and enjoys full rights."[96] As these examples confirm, the status question is a highly variable one; an entity's sovereignty is dependent on external recognition (a contradiction in terms?), and some entities are states for some purposes but not for others.

Realists and neorealists tend to ignore or skirt the issue of how sovereignty is conferred and prefer to concentrate on its subsequent effects. Nevertheless, how to describe those effects has caused neorealists no end of trouble. All tend to denigrate empirical tests of state autonomy. John Gerard Ruggie, for example, complains: "The concept of sovereignty is critical. Unfortunately, it has become utterly trivialized by recent usage . . . as a descriptive category expressing unit attributes, roughly synonymous with material autonomy."[97] Turning to what he calls "liberal writings on interdependence," he takes us to task for having spoken some years ago of "the relative irrelevance of sovereignty" in a world wherein all "states are subject to diverse internal and external conditioning factors that induce and constrain their behavior" and some states are apparently "more 'sovereign' than others."[98] Limiting the meaning of sovereignty also troubles Waltz:

> One error lies in identifying the sovereignty of states with their ability to do as they wish. To say that states are sovereign is not to say that they can do as they want. Sovereign states may be hard-pressed all around, constrained to act in ways they would like to avoid, and able to do hardly anything just as they would like to. The sovereignty of states has never entailed their insulation from the effects of other states' actions. To be sovereign and to be dependent are not contradictory conditions. Sovereign states have seldom led free and easy lives. What then is sovereignty? To say that a state is sovereign means that it decides for itself how it will cope with its internal and external problems.[99]

Ruggie is equally disturbed by Waltz's definition: "If sovereignty meant no more than this, then I would agree with Ernst Haas, who once declared categorically: 'I do not use the concept at all and see no need to.'"For Ruggie, in contrast, sovereignty "signifies a form of *legitimation* that pertains to a *system* of relations."[100] It sets up a world of "possessive individualist" states that interact largely on the basis of what Waltz calls an "exchange of considerations." According to Ruggie, domestic private property rights and state sovereignty are analogous. Consequently,

[T]hose who would dispense with the concept of sovereignty . . . must first show why the idea of private property rights should not have been dispensed with long ago in the capitalist societies, where they are continuously invaded and interfered with by actions of the state. Yet we know that, at a minimum, the structure of private property rights will influence *when* the state intervenes; usually it will also affect *how* the state intervenes. If this concept still has utility domestically . . . then its international analogue ought, if anything, to be even more relevant. The reason for the continued significance of the concepts is that they are not simply descriptive categories. Rather, they are components of generative structures: they shape, condition, and constrain social behavior.[101]

Ruggie draws us to a view of sovereignty as "an inherently *social* concept."[102] Thus, European states could deny sovereignty to non-Western peoples who became victims of what David Strang calls "collective delegitimation"[103] or deprivation of what Jackson thinks that sovereignty provides developing countries at the present time.

But, the reader might argue, how effective is that shaping, conditioning, and constraining? In some states like the United States, the concept of private property has greater currency than the concept of sovereignty, and there is a traditional distrust of government, yet government at all levels continues to impose a substantial tax burden, seize property through eminent domain, and the like. The fact is that the concepts of private property and sovereignty both pretend to a degree of autonomy that is often fictitious, and this, indeed, makes the concepts relatively irrelevant.

The fundamental objection to focusing on the state as a sovereign entity is that it tells us little about a state's autonomy from its society and from external influences. Theoretical or legal sovereignty is often small solace to a unit facing severe constraints from within and without; it is by no means the same as having a viable government, economy, society, or unit that is significantly independent from others. Waltz recognizes the dramatic variation in power and capacity among states and, given his assumption about anarchy, recognizes that sovereignty will not protect a careless state from extinction: "Whether units live, prosper or die depends on their own efforts."[104]

All things considered, some actors *do* seem a great deal more sovereign than others, and sovereignty itself appears relatively irrelevant as a guide to understanding actual behavior. Perhaps the concept's principal utility, which has endeared it to realists and neorealists, is that it speaks to the legal framework of state participation in the international system and especially in international organizations and regimes. Politicians can use it in speeches opposing more involvement in transnational schemes. Even they know at heart, however, that participation in interdependence is not nearly as voluntary as the notion of sovereignty suggests, and we must look elsewhere for an explanation of why states do what they do in this regard. It is not enough to wave the tattered banner of "the national interest"; one must be able to specify the source of that interest, why it is—or is perceived—as it is.

The subject of internal constraints brings to mind the very lengthy debate after Bodin and Hobbes about where exactly in the system of government sovereignty resided. In England, was it in the crown, Parliament, or where? In the United States, was it in the people, the Constitution, the law generally, Congress, the president, or where? Theorists debated the question, but what was really happening were struggles over authority. The contest is still going on within countries; for example in the United States, among the president, various bureaucracies, Congress, interest groups, political parties, and voters.

In light of the continued popularity of neorealism, it is worth reiterating something that many of us working in the field used to take almost for granted: Thinking about a world of sovereign states confuses more than it clarifies and certainly does not get us very far in theory building. In explaining behavior in global politics, there is almost always any number of more interesting and important things to say about almost any state than that it is sovereign. States find other states, international regimes, or nonstate actors such as consortia of banks or multinational corporations limiting their options—even as they (states) have an impact on all of them (other state and nonstate actors) in turn. For example, international debt negotiations or international monetary matters generally involve a wide range of intrastate governmental actors, the International Monetary Fund and various international lending institutions, and any number of nonstate private and semiprivate actors. Together, these constitute a global-ized currency market that pays little attention to sovereign boundaries. Again, this is a contest both within and across state boundaries.

A third definition of the state, associated with Max Weber, is that the state is that *entity which has a monopoly of legitimate violence within a society*. Curiously atavistic, Weber's definition is usually associated with his writings on the rise of a "rational" state bureaucracy, of that presumably evolutionary process whereby a society eventually rises above the awarding of offices on the basis of patrimony and as sources of profit for the individuals involved.[105] Echoes of Weber may be found in many quarters, including Eric A. Nordlinger's brief for the relative autonomy of those groups of individuals who occupy decisionmaking roles in the modern democratic state.[106] Weber himself apparently recognized some of the deficiencies in his own generalizations about bureaucracy, acknowledging that not all major states in history had evolved extensive bureaucracies and that even in Germany the bureaucracy had not achieved independence from the landed aristocracy.[107]

Weber's is an ideal type, as Janice Thomson demonstrates. Thomson shows that states actually did not acquire a monopoly on legitimate violence until rather late in the game. This leads her to conclude that "what we commonly take to be a defining characteristic of the state—control over violence within its territory—is actually an expectation of the world polity or of statesmen, an expectation whose realization may vary across time and states." Thus, in contrast to Weber she claims: "It seems prudent to treat sovereignty as a potentially variable institution rather than as a fixed principle."[108]

As for violence, one might well insist that what matters most is not whether a state possesses a monopoly of legitimate violence emanating from within *and* without. Weber's definition speaks not at all to the challenge of military intervention from outside state boundaries. The challenge within is often even more serious. Many leaders of less-developed countries might have found Weber's arguments as to the illegitimacy of military coups singularly unpersuasive. It is also difficult to picture a Latin American or Asian president broadcasting Weber to guerrillas in the hills, convincing them to lay down their arms on the grounds that their violence is illegitimate. In a sense, of course, that is what the government of Colombia does when it insists that it alone acts for all Colombians—for

Colombia as a state.[109] However, if there is no normative order, if there are no accepted ideological ground rules in a society, how can the exercise of violence by the government ever be truly legitimate? If there is no consensus as to whose violence is legitimate in Colombia, does that mean Colombia is not a state?

Insofar as Weber's definition is evolutionary in character, it does provide a bridge to a fourth conception of the state as *a functional unit*. Émile Durkheim, for example, reasoned that "the greater the development of society, the greater the development of the state. The state takes on more and more functions and becomes increasingly involved in all other social functions, thereby centralizing and unifying them. Advances in centralization parallel advances in civilization."[110] In particular, according to Durkheim, the growth of the state goes hand in hand with a pattern of an increasing division of labor in a society. Talcott Parsons's cybernetic model of this process stresses the differentiation of the political system from other social systems, which he sees as influenced by economic factors such as the development of a market economy and cultural events such as the Protestant Reformation. Badie and Birnbaum characterize this model of the state as follows: "[T]he state is one aspect of the rationalizing process that takes place in all societies undergoing modernization. State building therefore plays a part in what functionalists regard as the four central processes of modernization: differentiation, autonomization, universalization, and institutionalization."[111]

Badie and Birnbaum object initially to what they see as a neofunctionalist view of the nation-state as a "perfect functional substitute for vanished community solidarities," an aspect of the theory that shades off into the conception of the state as a normative order. They observe that "once the state becomes an autonomous power center, with access to previously unavailable sources of power, it becomes a target of political action, an objective to be seized by every organized group that wishes to impose its own ends on society as a whole. The state thus tends not to quell conflict but to exacerbate it."[112] In addition, the neofunctionalist model appears to confuse the idea of state with that of a centralized political system. Finally, neofunctionalists seem to imply that "the state" is a "universally valid political form suitable for all societies." In Badie's and Birnbaum's view, the crises experienced by political systems in Latin America, Africa, and Asia stem primarily from an attempt to transfer historical Western models to "radically different cultural traditions."[113]

> [T]he economic, social and political problems faced by third world countries are utterly unlike the problems faced by European countries when states first emerged in Europe. Europe had to deal with a crisis of feudalism involving the private ownership of land by feudal lords. Most third-world societies, particularly in Africa, are currently faced by a quite different sort of crisis, involving the persistence of tribal structures, the crucial importance of kinship, and the limited individualization of property rights in land. Whereas European societies had to find ways to integrate already existing economic elites, the developing countries today need to create a market economy, to say nothing of a full-blown industrial society, from the ground up. Finally, whereas Renaissance Europe had only to contend with a gradual increase in the demand for popular participation, an increase more or less kept in check by organized civil society, today's newly independent societies have to face a much more dramatic rise in the desire for participation, which traditional allegiances by themselves cannot hold back.[114]

We should also recall two of our earlier observations. Contrary to Parsons's view, we have argued that political systems are never fundamentally differentiated from their own societies. Moreover, the societies in which political entities are enmeshed typically extend far beyond domestic borders. Jobs in the United States today may be as much or more a function of the global economic system and the politics of international economic relations than they are of government policy in Washington or of the domestic private sector. The international dimension is even more critical and visible in Europe and certainly throughout the Third World. Neorealists like to picture governments acting jointly as functional managers of these larger societies, but it is far from clear who or what is managing whom, at what level(s), which values are being allocated, and with what degree of authority.

We may discern at least six additional conceptions of the state. There is no need to do more than mention them here, however, because they point directly to the issue of the extent to which the state is autonomous from society. One conception (our fifth) is the Marxist model of the state as *a ruling class*. Marxist analysts differ as to the precise nature of the relationship involved: whether a capitalist economic elite actually occupies governmental roles or only influences decision-makers (or a little of both) and whether government always acts as the ruling class desires or may occasionally act contrary to the immediate demands of the ruling class so as to uphold the best long-range interests of the capitalist system as a whole. (Stephen Krasner distinguishes in this regard between "instrumental" and "structural" Marxists.[115]) Of course, in classical Marxism, once the capitalist class is replaced (as it must inevitably be) by a "dictatorship of the proletariat," the state itself will eventually "wither away." Paradoxically, the ultimate ruling class is thus not expected to be interested in ruling!

Liberal pluralists, on the other hand, have advanced a sixth conception applied at least to democratic political systems—the state as *an arena of interest group competition*, where governmental policies are little more than a reflection of prevailing interest group pressures. As Krasner emphasizes, pluralist analysts and instrumental Marxists both "view formal governmental institutions as relatively passive recipients of societal pressure." The difference is that for "Marxists, power is basically in the hands of a capitalist class; for pluralists, it may be exercised by individuals motivated by any interest that is salient enough to affect behavior."[116]

A seventh definition, which Krasner sees as "the dominant conceptualization in the non-Marxist literature," is that of the state as *"a bureaucratic apparatus and institutionalized legal order in its totality"* As he explains, the "final phrase is critical, for it distinguishes statist orientations from the bureaucratic politics approaches which have parceled the state into little pieces, pieces that can be individually analyzed (where you stand depends on where you sit) and that float in a permissive environment (policies are a product of bargaining and compromise among bureaus)." An eighth definition is, thus, the state as *competing bureaucracies* or *governmental politics* in a somewhat broader sense.[117] Among other things, says Krasner, "statist" analysts view "politics more as a problem of rule and control than . . . of allocation"; it is "not just about 'who gets what, when, how': it is a struggle of us against them." The state, in this interpretation, is "an actor in its own right as either an exogenous or an intervening variable" and "cannot be understood as a reflection of societal characteristics or preferences."[118]

Eric Nordlinger, whom Krasner classifies as a fellow statist, nonetheless cautions that any "definition of the state must refer to individuals rather than to some other kinds of phenomena, such as 'institutional arrangements' or the legal-normative order." In his eyes, "a conception of the state that does not have individuals at its core could lead directly into the anthropomorphic and reification fallacies." Therefore, we have Nordlinger's ninth conception of the state, which he characterizes as being somewhat Weberian: "all those individuals who occupy offices that authorize them, and them alone, to make and apply decisions that are binding upon any and all segments of society. Quite simply, the state is made up of and limited to *those individuals who are endowed with society-wide decisionmaking authority.*"[119] He adds:

> [T]he state should include more than the government and/or the bureaucratic agencies that derive their authority from it. Although the executive and/or the bureaucracy have been said to constitute the "core" of the state, this in itself does not warrant a definition limited to them alone. Since we are concerned with all authoritative actions and all parts of the state as they relate to one another and to societal actors, the definition should include all public officials—elected and appointed, at high and low levels, at the center and the peripheries—who are involved in the making of public policy.[120]

Such a conception of the state invariably poses the problem of defining "autonomy." If the state is a conceptual variable, then it is impossible to say for certain what entity's autonomy we must attempt to weigh. On the other hand, if we cannot define autonomy, how then can we separate the state from other entities and influences that are not states but are said to constrain states? Can autonomy be merely symbolic, or must it mean a real capacity for independent decision and action? If a real capacity, must it be absolute or can it be relative? If relative, relative to what?

Nordlinger asserts, "The autonomy of any social entity refers to the correspondence between its preferences and actions.[121] The social entity of particular interest to him is the "democratic state," which as we have seen, he defines essentially as all individuals (at all levels) who are public officials with the authority to make binding decisions, distinguished from both public employees without that authority and private officials.

Using this definition, he advances a state-centered model, arguing that the autonomy of the democratic state has tended to be underestimated. Part of the reason for this misconception, he believes, is that too much emphasis has been given to cases where state and societal preferences have diverged. Equally significant, in his view, is the frequent convergence of state and societal preferences; and he stresses that in such situations state "preferences have at least as much explanatory importance as societal preferences."[122] (Does it follow, then, that societal preferences have at least as much explanatory importance as state preferences?) Moreover, when state and societal preferences diverge, public officials have significant resources at their command to realign societal preferences with their own or even to act counter to social preferences. Finally, according to Nordlinger:

> Explanations based on societal groups dissuading American officials from making decisions they themselves prefer are undoubtedly valid in some instances, but not necessarily in most. More than likely, there are other important explanations having to do with the officials themselves being unable to agree upon what, if any,

actions to take, what the most desirable and effective policies are thought to be. [In fact, in the United States] the sharing of dispersed power turns public officials into competitors for power, while their distinctive responsibilities help generate incompatible policy preferences. There is also reason to suppose that American officials subscribe to values and beliefs which do *not* place much store upon promptly adopted, coherent, positive, decisive authoritative actions to begin with. On either interpretation the state's preferences are fulfilled; it is acting autonomously.[123]

Nordlinger thus attempts to sidestep a major problem—the extent to which a state finds itself constrained by divisions of authority and policy disputes among its own decisionmakers—by a neat definitional trick: The decisionmakers are inherently unified regardless of their differences because they collectively *are* "the state."[124]

A tenth and (for our purposes here) final conception of the state is as *an executive*. Absolute monarchs of the old school would fit most neatly into this definition. Some traditional dictatorships also would appear to do so. The neon sign that loomed over the Santo Domingo harbor for many years reading "Diós y Trujillo" accurately symbolized (if not that the country was under God) that it was definitely indistinguishable from Trujillo. This definition shades off into the "great man" perspective on history, that is, the impact of particular individuals on state policies. For example, Manfred Wilhelmy describes the foreign policy roles of both Eduardo Frei (democratic president) and August Pinochet (military dictator) in Chile as that of an *animateur* rather than a "referee between contradictory positions."[125]

THE EROSION OF THE WESTPHALIAN STATE FROM ABOVE AND BELOW

Theories of global politics that evolved in a Western context not surprisingly have focused on the specific territorial units that gradually emerged in Europe after the Middle Ages. This Westphalian state has dominated global politics for more than three centuries. Increasingly, its autonomy and capacity are being challenged by two apparently contradictory but actually related tendencies. The first is the growth of regional and global networks of authority that link people physically remote from one another (often denoted as "regionalization" and "globalization," respectively) and that effectively centralize or at least consolidate governance. The second is the fracturing of existing territorial states into smaller and smaller islands of self-identification that localize authority and defy efforts to provide answers to the collective goods dilemma. Rosenau refers to these "centralizing and decentralizing" processes as "fragmegration."[126] Although fragmegration processes have always been present in global politics and reflect a dialectical cycle of expansion and contraction of political communities induced by evolving and clashing human identities and loyalties, international relations theorists have largely ignored them. Realists and neorealists, especially those in the Eurocentric tradition, have, in the words of John Agnew and Stuart Corbridge, "idealized fixed representations of territorial or structural space as appropriate irrespective of historical context."[127]

Some societies are falling apart even as others come together. Both trends have positive and negative features. Integration serves the need for larger political units and market economies of scale but may consign fragmented and less economically competitive parts of the world to far lower living standards. Fragmentation preserves local culture and heightens the psychological efficacy of smaller units, yet may result in marginalization and ethnic strife over pitifully insignificant battlefields like Bosnia and Kosovo.

In some cases, as we have seen, states have failed amidst the collapse of state institutions and civil war. In these countries, "[D]isease, overpopulation, unprovoked crime, scarcity of resources, refugee migrations" interact to explain, according to Robert Kaplan, "the increasing erosion of nation-states and international borders, and the empowerment of private armies, security firms, and international drug cartels."[128]

Yet even as the authority of many states is declining and their boundaries are becoming more porous, transnational authorities and processes, sustained by new means of instantaneous communication and rapid transportation, are proliferating. Nongovernmental organizations with members around the world can mobilize at the drop of an e-mail to campaign for a cause and gather in the hundreds at UN-sponsored conferences; political dissidents with no territorial focus can organize their activities; hedge funds can bring national economies to the brink of catastrophe without ever leaving home through the virtually instantaneous movement of funds from one country and currency to another; and criminal groups can launder and move funds rapidly using computers and electronic cash. Such capabilities further undermine government legitimacy and state authority and lead to the efforts of governments to coordinate state responses to transnational challenges, especially those posed by new technologies. For example, these technologies provide new opportunities for transnational mafias to launder funds and avoid taxes In response, the Clinton administration, along with the British and French governments, unsuccessfully sought to make it possible for law enforcement agencies in the member states of the Organization for Economic Cooperation and Development (OECD) to eavesdrop on computer transactions by restricting the private use of data-scrambling technology to protect the privacy of computer communications, such as e-mail.[129]

Globalization in the economic and cultural realms is reducing state autonomy from above. As economic systems are globalized, hypothesizes Philip Cerny, "the state will lose its structural primacy and autonomy as a unitary actor in the international system. The anarchy of the international system will no longer be one of states competing for power but one of neofeudal rivalries and asymmetric cooperation among a range of interests and collective agents reflecting differentiated economic activities with diverse goods/assets structures."[130]

Cultural globalization entails the spread of modernity and of the secularism associated with it. Two consequences are the politicization of larger segments within societies, especially segments that previously were politically inert, and the erosion of norms that previously had encouraged passivity and on which the authority of traditional elites had been built. To the extent that the masses are loosed from traditional moorings, they become available for mobilization and manipulation by new elites for political and economic ends. Under the banner of religion or nationalism, traditional elites try to prevent or at least stem this process by managing and taming the stream of ideas that flow across national frontiers in the form of television images and information conveyed by satellites, videos, e-mail, and the Internet. Thus, Canada criminalizes illicit reception of American satellite imagery, and China jails individuals for providing e-mail addresses to dissidents in the United States.

This is the world that Rosenau conceives of as "multi-centric;" that is, one where individuals with increased analytic skills no longer unquestioningly comply with authority. He argues that individuals' acquisition of new skills and orientations, which is accompanied by growing self-efficacy, is of fundamental importance. Foreign policy elites in more and more countries are less and less able to navigate global politics without popular approval or knowledge. Hierarchies break down as people develop the "ability to employ, articulate, direct, and implement whatever their attitudes may be" and as they come to "believe they have the skills and orientations to participate in the processes of aggregation."[131] In democratic societies, citizens have always had an indirect impact on foreign affairs through their roles as voters and members of interest groups. Today, however, their role is not merely that of citizen, and their impact is increasingly direct. Whether as consumers, investors, employees, activists, protesters, terrorists, or members of nonstate groups, individuals collectively create global constraints and opportunities.

People's growing sense of political efficacy and their greater capacity to organize for political ends that reflect self-identity and perceived interests are accompanied by a rapid increase in public demands upon existing local, national, transnational, or international institutions, and on the global system more generally. No longer do people meekly accept the status and destiny that come with birth. Modern citizens enjoy advantages that were unavailable to their ancestors, but their expectations have risen even faster. Political institutions must produce or else suffer a loss of legitimacy. Whether reflected in the agitation of Russian and Chinese citizens for a cleaner environment, of Mayans in Central America for a recognition of their cultural heritage, or of indigenous peoples in Canada and the United States for a return of their traditional lands, institutions everywhere must cope with ever greater loads that threaten to outstrip their institutional capacity. In consequence, new institutions—often ad hoc, temporary, and highly specialized—emerge to channel growing demands and seek their satisfaction.

CONCLUSION

Every discipline is defined in terms of a shared set of assumptions and concepts. Those assumptions and concepts at once provide both boundaries that distinguish that field of endeavor from others and a research agenda for the future. Few such assumptions and concepts have evolved in what is variously called "international," "interstate," "global," or "world" politics.

Our account of the multiple connotations accorded the concept of state—surely among the most central ideas in the field—and related concepts like autonomy casts doubt on the present existence of and prospects for a discipline of global politics. It is not simply that there have been multiple meanings from historical perspective, but that there is no greater consensus today than in the past. This is especially startling in light of the professed dedication of two generations of scholars to transforming global politics into a science. Yet, perhaps it should not have been startling at all because, as we have seen, individual scholars have good (sometimes clear) *subjective* reasons for their definitions.

Our concern is not merely that intellectual disturbance characterizes the field, but that as Dina Zinnes notes, "the literature has not been very helpful in identifying the unit of analysis."[132] More importantly, we increasingly suspect that the concepts that bedevil us are inseparable from the norms, ideologies, and political aspirations that animate the practitioners and scholars in our field. If this is so, then concepts like state can never assume the objective and operational qualities that are prerequisites to scientific observation and analysis. To conclude that the phenomena global-politics scholars study change at a more rapid rate than, shall we say, the atoms of a physicist would mean only that social scientists face especially vexatious obstacles that need not dim their faith in the enterprise on which they have embarked. To conclude, as we have, that those phenomena are inherently subjective must sorely try that faith.

CHAPTER 6

The Uncertain Bounds of Bounded Rationality

The sorts of conceptual problems that exist at the level of macroanalysis of global politics also are manifest at lower levels as well. The relationship of rationality and foreign policy illustrates the point. Although rationality can be defined in a variety of ways, it minimally implies acting so as to promote one's interests. It also implies that such action is effective and, therefore, that agents can have significant impact. In its strongest form, it entails the selection of *the* best of *all* alternatives for attaining one's ends. For Kenneth Waltz, rationality "means only that some do better than others—whether through intelligence, skill, hard work, or dumb luck,"[1] and he denies that neorealism needs to make the assumption of rationality. The assumption is often expressed as a principle of expected utility, which is defined by Jack Levy as a claim "that actors try to maximize their expected utility by weighing the utility of each possible outcome of a given course of action by the probability of its occurrence, summing over all possible outcomes for each strategy, and selecting that strategy with the highest expected utility."[2] Work such as this has helped to modify rational-choice and expected-utility approaches, "reducing," in Miles Kahler's words, "the heroic assumptions that provided such an easy target for the psychologists."[3]

The capacity for rational behavior, whether by collectivities or individual decisionmakers, is among the most crucial assumptions that scholars of global politics can make. It is only by making this assumption that an observer can remain confident that objective factors will, in time, be identified that can explain and predict global behavior. It is also crucial if theory is to be parsimonious. The assumption is thus essential for the construction of general theory and its application across time and space. Denial of rationality or disagreement about its meaning, by contrast, must inevitably force us to construct theory out of subjective factors and to reduce dramatically the prospects for fruitful comparison.

Foreign policy analysis is especially dependent upon some assumption of rationality, for without it the concept of interest (national or other) must be distorted beyond recognition.[4] After all, if interest is not recognized and pursued in logical fashion by purposive actors, it is ultimately irrelevant in explaining behavior. And without the sturdy signpost of rationality, scholars must embark on new and highly speculative paths of research. Such paths require skills and insights from fields such as philosophy and psychology, which further reduces the already limited autonomy of the "discipline" of global politics. All of this notwithstanding, it is evident that recent decades have witnessed growing uneasiness about the utility of retaining the rationality assumption, and in the end, probably no other trend is more likely to confound the already elusive quest.

REALISM AND RATIONALITY

A leading critic of power politics models, John Vasquez, summarizes succinctly the major tenets of realism as follows:

> The first major assumption of the realist paradigm is that nation-states or their official decision-makers are the most important actors in global politics. At the core of the realist paradigm, the power politics explanation makes the additional assumption that nation-state behavior can be explained and predicted on the basis of a *rational-actor model.*[5]

The stress on the rational-actor assumption, then, is surely central to realism and other interest-based approaches to understanding politics. Nevertheless, the relationship between realism and rationality is an uneasy one. On the one hand, realists denounce the rationalist assumption implicit in liberalism. "The roots of realism," observes Miles Kahler, "lay in currents of European thought that had undermined the reign of reason. Realism injected an awareness drawn from European social theory and philosophy that the image of a unified and rational self had been overturned."[6] In this vein, Hans Morgenthau argued that "our civilization assumes that the social world is susceptible to rational control conceived after the model of the natural sciences, while the experiences, domestic and international, of the age contradict this assumption."[7] Nowhere is "rational control" more important than in allowing balance of power to function.

Realism's "skepticism toward the power of reason," as Kahler notes, "was soon purged in its new American home."[8] "We put ourselves in the position of a statesman," writes Morgenthau, in one of his most eloquent passages, "who must meet a certain problem of foreign policy under certain circumstances, and we ask ourselves what the *rational alternatives* are . . . (presuming that he acts in a rational manner), and which of these rational alternatives this particular statesman, acting under those circumstances, is likely to choose." He then claims that, without assuming rationality, theorizing becomes banal at best: "It is the testing of this *rational hypothesis* against the actual facts and their consequences that gives meaning to the facts of global politics and makes a theory of politics possible."[9]

But Morgenthau is not talking about rationality exercised by the statesman in an open-ended sense. He condemns the search for a statesman's motives or ideological preferences as not only difficult, but also entirely a waste of time. And, as we shall see, psychobiography is a peculiarly time-consuming exercise the result of which is almost inevitably post hoc insights. The theorist already knows what basic factors will shape the final policy choices: "his [Morgenthau's] *a priori* conception of human nature . . . and . . . his belief in the structural determinance of the international system."[10] Human nature, Morgenthau believes, is essentially imperfect and intensely selfish; and the international system, partly as a consequence, is anarchic and amoral, a struggle for power. The statesman's rational choices are "bounded" or constrained from within (by human nature) and also by external factors, especially the Hobbesian global arena (itself in a sense a collective expression of human nature).

As we stressed earlier, despite Morgenthau's insistence that realism "is governed by objective laws that have their roots in human nature,"[11] the theoretical framework he advances is essentially normative. For Morgenthau and other realists, what is rational is also moral; that which detracts from rationality is fundamentally dysfunctional and immoral. The contradiction between Morgenthau's putative search for objective laws and his own subjective preferences creeps in even as he is waxing about the explanatory and predictive capacity of his assumption "that statesmen think and act in terms of [national] interest defined as power":

> That assumption allows us to retrace and anticipate, as it were, the steps a statesman—past, present, or future—has taken or will take on the political scene. We look over his shoulder when he writes his dispatches; we listen in on his conversation with other statesmen; we read and anticipate his very thoughts. Thinking in terms of interest defined as power, we think as he does, and as disinterested observers *we understand his thoughts and actions perhaps better than he, the actor on the political scene does himself:* [The concept of interest defined as power on] the side of the actor . . . provides for rational discipline in action and creates that astounding continuity in foreign policy which makes American, British, or Russian foreign policy appear as an intelligible, rational continuum, by and large consistent within itself, regardless of the different motives, preferences, and intellectual and moral qualities of successive statesmen.[12]

One might be tempted to ask how rational a statesman is who thinks he or she is doing or wants to do X but ends up doing Y! In fact, Morgenthau, like Machiavelli centuries earlier, acknowledges that policies are actually not always completely rational or predictable: "The contingent demands of personality, prejudice, and subjective preference, and all of the weaknesses of intellect and will which flesh is heir to, are bound to deflect foreign policies from their rational course." But, he continues, "a theory of foreign policy which aims at rationality must for the time being, as it were, abstract from these irrational elements and seek to paint a picture of foreign policy which presents the rational essence to be found in experience, without the contingent deviations from rationality which are also found in experience.[13] Finally, he admits what should already have become evident to his readers:

> Political realism contains not only a theoretical but also a normative element. It knows that political reality is replete with contingencies and systemic irrationalities and points to the typical influences they exert upon foreign policy. . . . Political real-

ism wants the photographic picture of the political world to resemble as much as possible its painted portrait. Aware of the inevitable gap between good—that is, rational—foreign policy and foreign policy as it actually is, political realism maintains not only that theory must focus upon the rational elements of political reality, but also that foreign policy ought to be rational in view of its own moral and practical purposes. Hence, it is no argument against the theory presented here that actual foreign policy does not or cannot live up to it.[14]

Accordingly, Morgenthau probably would not be too unhappy with Vasquez's intended criticism of realism that "reality" is not simply something "out there": "Whenever ideas spread and people believe and act on them, then that part of the world portrayed by these ideas actually comes into being,"thereby constructing realities in a process that makes it impossible for social science to be value free. The power-politics core of realism, then, is less a universal explanation of global politics than a set of "rules and norms" that constructs a particular reality and, like science more generally, reflects "a practice that creates a mode of life that consciously destroys other ways of thinking and living."[15] Rather than explaining some universal truth, realism as a social construction must be explained. From this perspective, Vasquez takes a fresh look at rational-choice analysis[16] (about which more will be said later) and concludes, "Rational choice is seen as a modernist conceit that makes choice pose as Truth." The only way in which such analysis can become "a rigorous science" is if people "accept its rules to guide their behavior. In doing so, they will not only create a reality but people who are 'rationally-calculating individuals.' Such a science succeeds in explaining more and more of the variance not because it is able to uncover the 'causes' of behavior, but *because it produces them.*"[17]

Part of the explanation, as Vasquez suggests, is the fact that realism actually gained such wide acceptance, especially among the post–World War II generation of American policymakers because of their claim that "legalists," "idealists," and "utopians" were responsible for the war by allegedly ignoring the role of power in politics.[18] There was and is something ego-gratifying, macho, and even a little romantic about picturing oneself as advancing the "national interest" in a "struggle for power." Moreover, Morgenthau's emphasis on the putatively amoral nature of global politics allows policymakers to indulge their penchant for pragmatism, thereby hiding from themselves any troubling questions about the values that are actually being advanced by their policies.

In many ways, neorealists' emphasis on the role of system structure in creating incentives for rational egoists reflected a greater dependence on the rationality assumption than was true of the realists before them. Robert Keohane's argument for modifying realism and neorealism entailed accepting their assumption of rationality (thereby protecting himself from charges of idealism) but enlarging the number of structural incentives by including complex interdependence and international regimes to the equation. New incentives would of course alter behavior. "Realists," he argues "are at least clear about their assumptions: states, the principal actors in world politics, are rational egoists." Their "assumption of egoism implies that the preferences of actors in world politics are based on their assessments of their own welfare, not that of others" Neorealists' understanding "of the structure of the situation facing decisionmakers provides the analyst with clues to state action, since leaders, *being rational egoists*, will respond to the incentives provided by the environment in ways calculated to increase the wealth, security, and power of their states."[19]

Neorealists argue that the pursuit of security necessitates rationality, the alternative being elimination. In reality, choices are rarely so stark, and elimination is rarely threatened by the choices confronting foreign-policy elites, especially since it is likely that elites everywhere are equally prone to error, misperception, and stupidity. A more important problem is that we are inevitably led to ask "whose interest" and "whose security"? Neorealist rationality is imposed from above and, unlike earlier realism, the approach is highly deterministic. It assumes a collective wisdom that is usually lacking in the real world and an imaginary unitary state. It also assumes, wrongly, that territorial states monopolize the loyalties of citizens and that citizenship exhausts relevant political identities.

Any leader routinely is asked to choose between internal and external imperatives, and the record is replete with examples in which a leader's domestic political or partisan concerns win the day.[20] Is this rational? Yes, but not in the sense implied by realists or neorealists. Thus, in a recent study of the development of the Direct Broadcast Satellite (DBS), Edward Comor concludes that, even though its development by the United States clearly would have augmented U.S. cultural power, making its development highly predictable according to power theory, the reality was far messier. "In fact," he declares, "the media conglomerates that most proponents of the cultural imperialism paradigm believe were the champions of DBS were, at various times, altogether opposed to its domestic application, indifferent to its international implementation and intimidated by other corporate interests to such an extent that some even conspired against its introduction."[21]

THE RETREAT FROM RATIONALITY

As noted earlier, the rational model, as usually conceived, maintains that an individual decisionmaker reaches a decision via a clearly defined intellectual process: He or she clarifies and ranks values and goals; then weighs all (or at least the leading) alternative courses of action (policies) and the likely consequences (costs/benefits) of each; and ultimately chooses the optimal course(s) of action with regard to the ends pursued. The alternatives or options are given, not constructions, and can be presented in terms of game theory.

In Sidney Verba's classic revision, "Rational models of individual decisionmaking are those in which the individual responding to an international event bases his response upon a cool and clear-headed means-ends calculation. He uses the best information available and chooses from the universe of possible responses that alternative most likely to maximize his goals."[22] This is, however, a demanding version of rationality, one which is essential for game theory and some versions of deterrence theory.[23] As we shall see, there are less demanding versions in which the capacity to impose utilitarian criteria in making decisions is bounded by context, culture, limited information, and a host of other "givens." Bounded it may be, but it is still rationality, and choices still exist independently of the observer.

The rational model of decisionmaking was embedded not only in the dominant realist approach, but also in the movement for a scientific revolution in the study of global politics that reached its zenith in the 1960s. Richard W. Cottam captures the spirit of this "golden age of American academia" when he trumpeted:

> This was the "end of ideology" era. A new and heady positivism had triumphed, and a fierce competition was engaged in to discover what Stanley Hoffmann referred to as the "magic key"—a scientific method which would disclose the essence of man's sociopolitical behavior. . . . Leading figures in each discipline of the social sciences found ready acceptance in Washington. Indeed, formal or informal consultation with leading bureaucrats was as much a mark of achievement in a discipline as membership on boards of the relevant national foundations. Some theorists, especially those focusing on game theory and simulation, had the ultimate satisfaction of seeing their jargon incorporated into the bureaucratic lexicon.[24]

Reading Thomas Schelling on bargaining, bureaucrats played zero-sum and non-zero-sum games, crafted "minimax" strategies, searched for "tacit" agreements, and on dull days perhaps contemplated an exciting round of "chicken" or "prisoner's dilemma." Dulles's earlier "brinkmanship" evolved into a full-blown policy of deterrence, supported by a veritable torrent of scholarly literature that argued for a broad range of weaponry and adequate soldiery to allow for a "flexible response" and "extended deterrence" to enemy challenges anywhere in the world. Herman Kahn thought about various levels of "unthinkable" nuclear war and developed an escalation ladder with precise steps, so that policymakers might apply just the appropriate degree of "compellence" or "coercive diplomacy" to their adversaries at any stage of a conflict.[25] All of this reached its apogee during the Kennedy years with Robert McNamara and the "whiz kids" brandishing new strategic theories and utilizing new technologies in a failed effort to cope with the Vietnam conflict.

As on so many other occasions, academic wizards hastened to reflect the dominant political fads of the moment, a fact implicit in Richard J. Barnet's claim that assumptions of rationality were implicit in the task of social scientists: The social scientist's "job was to tell officials how to do what they wanted to do in the most efficient way and then to help them measure what they had done. Criticizing policy goals or challenging the implicit values behind a policy were considered 'counterproductive' by the managers of university contract teams and by ambitious professors themselves. . . . Built into the contract relationship were profound unspoken assumptions such as: Government is an instrument of problem-solving, not a problem itself."[26]

Theorizing rested upon the stated or unstated premise that policymakers are rational and that they pursue the national interest through Verba's cool and clear-headed means-ends calculations based on adequate information. John Steinbruner speaks of a "heavy investment of the culture in the concept of rationality":

> The theory of deterrence, a direct embodiment of rational assumptions, has become a central element of United States foreign policy, and upon its principles are staked each year billions of dollars in expenditures and the risk of millions of lives. The common-sense mind has been substantially captured, and intuitive

observers who would understand the processes of government have learned to impose rational assumptions on what they see and to work out explanations and expectations along lines required by these assumptions. These developments have all been laborious, consuming many decades and a great many intellectual careers.[27]

And, like other "developments" that consume "a great many intellectual careers," these led to erecting new fortresses to defend the ideas of dominant theorists.

And then, as Cottam reminds us, came the catastrophe in Vietnam, which (together with the continuing civil rights movement and the Watergate scandal) brought the United States to the edge of social upheaval and left a legacy of popular distrust of entanglement in foreign "dirty little wars" that is reflected in public opinion polls even to the present day and in the Pentagon's effort to fight wars without incurring casualties. Government obviously *could be*—and indeed was—*itself* a problem! How could a vast foreign policy "establishment," the "best and the brightest," have been so tragically misguided, seemingly so downright *irrational!* Cottam remarks on shifting perceptions and the consequent dramatic change in the normative climate at the time:

> When the United States took its first steps in Vietnam in 1954, governmental officials, academics, and the interested public overwhelmingly regarded them as necessary to contain [Soviet aggression and ideological appeal]. By 1965 the picture for many . . . had changed drastically. . . . Communism was no longer a great international monolith. . . . The United States was . . . seen fighting North Vietnam, a fourth-class power that was receiving barely enough support to maintain the conflict. . . . For those who persisted in holding the aggressive international communism image, the policy was defensible and as moral as defensive wars ever are. For those who no longer saw the international communist menace, the policy was immoral and possibly racist.[28]

Moreover, the North Vietnamese appeared singularly unmoved by the "compelling" logic of the strategists' escalation ladder. The Johnson administration's "bomb 'em into the Stone Age" campaign was as out of touch with the "real world" as seen from Hanoi as it was with the shifting climate of opinion in the United States.

Against this background, then, it was not coincidental that theorizing about foreign policy decisionmaking beginning in the late 1960s moved increasingly away from reliance upon the assumption of rationality. The spotlight turned to decisionmakers' perceptions and the ways these are shaped by such factors as idiosyncratic variables and the organizational/bureaucratic context in which so many decisions are made. Greater attention to the process by which decisions are made led to prospect theory, which contradicted expected-utility assumptions in its claim that "people tend to evaluate choices with respect to a reference point, overweight losses with respect to comparable gains, engage in risk-averse behavior in choices among losses, and respond to probabilities in a nonlinear manner."[29] There was a new recognition both that policy is made by often fallible human beings and that a veritable "bureaucratic revolution"[30] had taken place in foreign policy decisionmaking processes since World War II, certainly in the United States but also to varying degrees in many governments throughout the world.

As Steinbruner observes, "In common discourse the word 'rational' is drenched with normative connotations."Indeed, the rational model always involved something of a tautology; "rational" decisions were presumed to result from "rational" decisionmaking even when they were as blatantly out of touch with the real world as Lyndon Johnson's bombing campaign of North Vietnam. Accordingly, Steinbruner prefers to substitute the label "analytic" for "rational" as a characterization of this kind of decisionmaking, that is, one "in which the decision problem is broken down into major components, and then a deliberate procedure for aggregation is evoked to achieve a decision."[31]

However the rational model is labeled and purged of normative connotations, as pioneering theorists Richard C. Snyder, H. W. Bruck, and Burton Sapin emphasized, it is still undermined by a fundamental problem: the *dual* objective-subjective nature of reality or, as the Sprouts put it, the need to distinguish between the decisionmaker's "psychological milieu" (the world as that person perceives it) and the "operational milieu" (the real world in which policies have to be implemented). "It is difficult," as Joseph de Rivera argues, "even to intellectually grasp the fact that we *construct* the reality in which we operate. We take our perception of the world for granted. . . . It is precisely in this feeling of certainty that the danger lies."[32]

Unless one adopts the postmodernist contention that everything real is inherently illusion, and even while recalling Plato's simile of the cave, one must grant at least some validity to the concept of objective reality. Exactly how much validity is the hard question. In the words of a familiar maxim: "The real world is only a special case, albeit an important one."[33] Not all perceptions are equally legitimate, for as de Rivera observes, "The stimulus has an *objective structure* that limits the number of possible legitimate interpretations."[34] Although much in political life may be constructed and therefore rests on intersubjective consensus, much of importance—for example, geography and technology—does not. And even that which is constructed is real.

Yet the awkward task for decisionmakers or analysts is how to perceive that objective structure from the vantage point of their own individual subjectivities. Policies that fail miserably surely often *seem* to be running up against a very substantial reality that turned out to be different from that envisaged by the authors of the policy. Our own comment earlier that the Johnson administration's strategy in Vietnam was out of touch with the real world underscores the fact that things did not work out in Southeast Asia or back home in the United States as those who formulated the policy expected. In all fairness, however, the comment also betrays our own prejudices.

Was Johnson's policy wrong because of some objective reality in Southeast Asia? Many American conservatives still insist that the Johnson administration's "punish the enemy" approach was basically correct and that the Vietnam War could have been won if only treasonous left-wing intellectuals in the United States had not created so much domestic dissent that administration decisionmakers lost their nerve. Was it then only domestic objective reality that the Johnson team failed to read properly? Hans Morgenthau and other critics of the Vietnam War, who could hardly be classed as left-wingers, would heartily disagree with that interpretation. In their view, Vietnam was a quagmire into which the

United States could continue to founder deeper and deeper but definitely not a contest of great strategic import or one that could ever be won at acceptable cost.

On the other hand, realist critics like Morgenthau did not share the additional perspective of perhaps the majority of dissenters that, strategic and pragmatic assessments aside, the Johnson administration's policy was plainly immoral. Objective reality, as they saw it, had to include certain bedrock principles regarding abuse of power that the United States should not be violating. If the argument had to turn on strategic and pragmatic grounds, they insisted, it was in the national interest of the United States to make a clear distinction between its own policies and the "aggressive" or revisionist policies of the Soviet camp. Even the cynics should be able to see that morality in this sense could be an ideological weapon in the arsenal of democracy.

The dual objective-subjective nature of reality, of course, is far from the sole problem confronting the rational model. Sidney Verba summarized some of the others in his early path-breaking article. One set of reasons why the rationality model is not an adequate description of decisionmaking," he stated, "lies in human frailty." "There may be too many significant variables, inadequate information, variables that are not easily quantifiable, or decisional methods that are not advanced enough." Yet, according to Verba, human frailty is the "least important reason" why the rational model is insufficient. More important is the fact that a decisionmaker rarely is aware of her or his own values or has them neatly ordered in terms of a personal value hierarchy. Values often conflict and even "depend in part upon the situation one is facing and what is attainable in that situation." Personal preferences may change as the decisionmaking process advances, and means and ends are inextricably interwoven. Yet another objection to the rationality model is that "individuals do not consider all policy alternatives and, what is more important, make no attempt to do so." They look for simple alternatives that are similar to those they have adopted in the past. In fact, fewer decisions are considered at the beginning of the process than toward the end, when other actors have raised their objections to the proposed policy. The rationality model "treats each decision as if it were a separate entity," whereas a decisionmaker cannot. The practitioner is operating not only in a personal context of limited time and energy, but also "within a structure in which there has been previous commitment to policy and organizational vested interest in policy."[35]

Verba approvingly cites early work by Herbert Simon and his associates to the effect that even optimal decisionmaking reflects merely "bounded rationality" and that decisionmakers are almost always "satisficing" rather than maximizing;[36] as well as Charles Lindblom's characterization that most decisionmaking is essentially "incremental" and disjointed, just "muddling through."[37] Verba does concede that, for several reasons, decisionmaking may be somewhat more rational in global politics than in other policy areas: First, foreign policy actors presumably all have a shared loyalty to country that is inherent in citizenship. Second, there do exist groups within government whose primary purpose is to "coordinate and control the bargaining process among the various members of the foreign policy coalition," and "the greater the emergency, the more likely is decisionmaking to be concentrated among high officials whose commitments are to the overall system." Hence "it may be, paradoxically, that the model of means-ends rationality will be more closely approximated in an emergency when the time for careful deliberation is limited." With little time to reach a decision and the small size of the decision unit, interest groups and bureaucracies are likely to be shut out of the process, thereby enhancing the prospects for more coherent decisions. Third, "unattached intellectuals" may be in a much better position to be rational in searching out policy alternatives than are bureaucrats. Nevertheless, cautions Verba, "it may be just because this research approaches the rationality model that it is not often translatable into actual policy." In sum, Verba holds that the rationality model is useful "only if its limitations are appreciated," and he suggests that one of its principal utilities "may be that it facilitates the systematic consideration of deviations from rationality."[38]

Finally, Verba alerts us to the danger of inferring collective rationality from assumptions about individuals. His warning about the relationship between individuals and collectivities anticipated the "agent-structure problem,"[39] that is, the relationship between purposive actors and the social relationships that provide, the context for those actors and their behavior. Most decisions relating to foreign policy are collective, made by ad hoc groups of individuals or by bureaucracies or other organizational units.[40] Can our ideas about how individuals make choices and reach decisions be aggregated and so applied to collectivities? And, if they can, we still confront the problem that there are collectivities within collectivities and that individuals typically are members of a variety of associations, each of which has its own conception of gains and losses.

Inevitably, means-end calculations become much more difficult when various members of a group or different units have different definitions of interest, conflicting goals, or both. In analyzing the limits of rationality in deterrence, Robert Jervis cites five reasons why collectivities are likely to be less consistently rational than individuals: (1) the need for governing coalitions, including factions with different views; (2) disagreements among leaders that preclude decisions; (3) "inconsistencies . . . as first one faction and then another comes to power;" (4) shifting majorities; and (5) "divergent bureaucratic interests and perspectives."[41] What is really at stake here is whether models constructed of unitary actors are useful or usable.

In *Essence of Decision*, his reconstruction of the Cuban missile crisis, Graham Allison, influenced by the earlier work of Snyder, Bruck, and Sapin, took issue with the realist idea that outcomes could be explained satisfactorily by rational analysis of states as unitary actors. As we shall see in the next chapter, Allison offered the organizational process and bureaucratic politics models as two alternatives to the rational actor model (model I)—that is, "[t]he attempt to explain international events by recounting the aims and calculations of nations or governments."[42] Shortly thereafter, John Steinbruner also challenged the rationality assumption in his cybernetic model of organizational behavior.[43]

In sum, what is perhaps most striking about the literature on foreign policy decisionmaking since the mid-1960s is that systematic considerations of deviations from rationality have become the rule rather than the exception. Once enthusiasm for the notion of bounded rationality became unbounded, the theoretical challenge shifted from the task of attacking the rational model to that of establishing precisely what the bounds of bounded rationality were to be. Indeed, some suspect that the entire discussion of rationality is fruitless because in many cases decisions are made and "rational arguments" to explain them are constructed only *afterwards*, as post hoc justifications. This may be especially germane in cases where identities and norms are created or conditioned by institutions and the scope for individual rationality is narrowed. In such cases, utilitarian considerations may come to dominate decisionmaking *after* identities have been formed.[44]

All of this meant that it could no longer be assumed that decisions emanate from purely rational processes. This reopened the central question of what influences were, in fact at work and what weight should be assigned to each of them as explanatory variables? Unfortunately, the move to viewing decisions as somewhat less than rational, or even as nonrational, found its reflection in a substantial measure of theoretical chaos.

The retreat from rationality became a veritable stampede in the 1980s and 1990s with the emergence of constructivist, postpositivist, and postmodern analyses of global politics. Postmodernists, for their part, are less interested in explaining phenomena than in pursuing single-mindedly their normative goal of emancipation. And, as we have noted, constructivists' rejection of utilitarian criteria in decisionmaking and their emphasis on the role of culture and identity in constituting rules of the game leave only limited space for rationality except in its loosest form. For example, the seeming upsurge in ethnic, racial, and national conflict and self-consciousness since the end of the Cold War has generated interest in constructivism generally and in the nonrational sources of behavior, because it appears that "[c]ulture and identity are staging a dramatic comeback in social theory and practice at the end of the twentieth century."[45]

To the extent that culturally derived rules for choice and action constrain or dictate behavior, there may be little room for individual utility maximization. Thus, viewing war as a cultural phenomenon, John Keegan bluntly declares, "War is not the continuation of politics by other means." The contemporary world is no longer like that of Clausewitz or Schelling, with wars that imply "the existence . . . of state interests and of rational calculation about how they may be achieved."[46] Utility maximization becomes especially problematic where culture imposes strong and inflexible ethical perceptions upon decisionmakers. "Strong norms," declares Jon Elster, "have a grip on the mind that is due to the strong emotions their violations can trigger."[47]

Sometimes, of course, cultural rules provide nonrational reinforcement for rational action, so utilitarian considerations may underlie the elaboration over time of cultural or religious norms and mores. Nevertheless, the cultural heterogeneity of global politics means that it is virtually impossible to construct a universal definition of rationality even though culturally determined behavior may be seen as rational in its own context. Thus, in some sense it may be rational for an Islamic activist or a Japanese kamikaze pilot to commit suicide in aid of religion or tradition, but it will be very difficult for those in other cultural contexts to view such actions as rational.

There is virtually no role for rationality in the postmodern exercise.[48] "And the ontological object of this creed [postmodernism]," declares D. S. L. Jarvis, "'Man as a sovereign being,' fully in control of 'his' destiny and, *through the power of rationality*, able to understand fully the existential realm of 'his' existence, is now dismissed by postmodernists as a project in shambles and disrepute."[49] In place of interest-based rationality, postmodernists have substituted power relations and theorists' efforts to use language to shape the world that they prefer.[50]

What place can rationality have if there is no longer a detached observer of political action or if, as advocates of hermeneutics claim, our views of the world are somehow formed before we observe that world? "[H]ow do we know," asks Steve Smith, "what is going on in other minds if we accept that intuitions may differ?"[51] The postmodernist view of the dangers posed by rationality could not be made clearer than it is by Chris Brown: "In the twentieth century the instrumental rationality of the West has so often founded itself at the service of dubious causes that it has become itself politically suspect."[52]

ALTERNATIVES TO TRADITIONAL ASSUMPTIONS ABOUT RATIONALITY

Without rejecting the baby with the bathwater as postmodernists have done, some theorists, looking for alternatives to rational theory, focused on the most basic level of analysis, that of individual decisionmakers and their psychological and intellectual limitations. Following Arnold A. Rogow's pioneering psychobiographical work on James Forrestal, as well as Alexander and Juliette George's work on Woodrow Wilson, the search was on for *idiosyncratic* (although not necessarily aberrant) *behavior* and its origins in such factors as a decisionmaker's personality, family background, education, and life experiences.[53] Robert A. Isaak probed the personality of Henry Kissinger; Joseph de Rivera and others explored the psychological dimension of leadership; and Lloyd Etheridge investigated the "private sources" of policy.[54] Some of these analysts and others have tried to go beyond case studies to develop general propositions about the relevance of personality factors of individual decisionmakers to foreign policy[55]—for example, that personality is most likely to have a significant impact when the political system or particular circumstances (such as perceived crisis) concentrates authority in the hands of an individual decisionmaker; when that individual has the interest, ego, or charisma to impose his or her personal will; and so forth.

Nevertheless, this approach continues to confront several serious obstacles. Not the least of these is the sheer difficulty of gathering reliable data. Despite the path-breaking work of Harold Lasswell, decisionmakers remain understandably reluctant to recline on the foreign policy analyst's couch. Thus much of the evidence has to be gleaned from such questionable sources as speeches, unclassified official documents, letters and diaries, and interviews with friends and associates.[56] And since analysis of individual leaders is for the most part possible only after their careers have reached an end, it is difficult to move beyond postdictive insights. Experimental data may not be applicable to the real world and, as Kahler contends, "the collection and evaluation of data that is aimed at reconstructing very refined, subjective estimates of risk and utility is difficult to accomplish."[57]

Even more vexing is the absence of an acceptable conceptualization of the central variable of personality. Attempts to develop a classification of personality types have not been particularly convincing, partly because the nagging question, "types of what?" remains always in the background. De Rivera asks, "How can we best conceptualize personality; what variables would be most efficient to use?" He concedes that there is no clear answer to his questions "because of our basic ignorance about many of the dynamics of personality." He continues,

"There are so many preferences, abilities, rules, and styles that it is difficult to know how to describe the behavior of a decisionmaker with some economy. Furthermore, it is not clear how to relate these individual differences in behavior to the deeper facets of personality they may reflect."[58] And definitions of "operational code" or "belief system" are hardly more satisfactory.[59]

Furthermore, as has often been pointed out, the individual-as-actor approach is likely to have limited explanatory power because individual leaders are rarely in a position to give their individuality full rein.[60] Their potentially idiosyncratic behavior is usually constrained by the decisionmaking role(s) they occupy and, for that matter, it is usually very hard to distinguish idiosyncratic behavior from that emanating from role or other influences. Did Margaret Thatcher's reaction to the Argentine military's seizure of the Falklands/Malvinas represent yet another manifestation of her "Iron Lady" personality, an action any British prime minister would likely have taken faced with a blatant challenge of that nature, a response to the Conservative Party's declining standing in public opinion polls, or some combination of these factors? Why did such different personalities as John F. Kennedy, Lyndon Johnson, and Richard Nixon continue to wage war in Vietnam?

The operational code offers little more promise. Gunnar Sjoblom writes, "An interesting problem in the study of an individual's OC [operational code] is evidently to what degree it is influenced by personality factors and to what degree it is influenced by role factors."[61] Part of the issue here, as yet unresolved, is how to establish where the operating code of individuals shades off into the standard operating procedures (SOPs) of organizations or into bureaucratic parochialism (discussed later).[62] Finally, whether behavior is idiosyncratic or not, certainly in large countries few individuals are regularly in a position to have a significant impact on the vast institutional network that is involved in making the bulk of foreign policy decisions.

Moving beyond the individual level of analysis, other theoretical approaches to the issue of rationality—somewhat distinct, albeit interrelated and overlapping— have moved to the forefront in recent years. These have explored the sources of perceptions and misperceptions that tend to be common to decisionmakers regardless of their place in the institutional network (cognitive, elites, or shared images), the psychological dynamics of groups and organizations (groupthink or cybernetic), and the particular features of governmental (bureaucratic) politics. As a whole, they produce serious reservations about rational-choice analysis (unless such analysis is regarded as no more than a heuristic device).

"Cognitive psychology," declares Kahler, "overtook psychoanalytic theory as the principal challenger to rational models of behavior."[63] Cognitive theorists emphasized the limitations on rational decisionmaking imposed by information collection and processing and by oversimplification of a complex reality.[64] In efforts to fathom cognitive biases, Alexander George and Ole Holsti advanced and sought to adapt the operational code/belief system concept, and Ole Holsti, in a widely read article, attempted to reconstruct the "operational code" of John Foster Dulles.[65]

In their early path-breaking work on foreign policy, Snyder, Bruck, and Sapin included cognitive variables among the host of factors they believed to condition foreign policy. "It is difficult," they declared, "to see how we can account for specific actions and for continuities of policies without trying to discover how their operating environment is perceived by those responsible for choices, how particular situations are structured, what values and norms are applied to certain kinds of problems, what matters are selected for their attention, and how their past experience conditions present responses." Anticipating what Robert Putnam later termed "two-level games," Snyder, Bruck, and Sapin continue, "the foreign policy machinery mediates among internal and external demands and needs *and* among decisionmakers themselves. Three overlapping environments are implied. Any framework of analysis ought to accommodate the potential effects of these three groups of factors."[66] Subsequent theorists, without providing answers to many of the questions raised by Snyder and colleagues, nevertheless have addressed them with considerable enthusiasm. While enriching the foreign policy literature, these analyses have *not* yet provided anything approaching a coherent general theory, however. They cast doubt on prior theory and tempt us with tantalizing insights but to date have accomplished little more.

Robert Jervis, one of the most persuasive advocates of the cognitive approach, maintains that "it is often impossible to explain crucial decisions and policies without reference to the decisionmakers' beliefs about the world and their images of others. That is to say, these cognitions are part of the proximate cause of the relevant behavior." He is especially interested in "how, when, and why highly intelligent and conscientious statesmen misperceive their environments" and engage in behavior that is "self-defeating . . . or generally lacking in a high degree of rationality."[67] Jervis, de Rivera, Alexander George, Steinbruner, and others have identified a variety of psychological mechanisms which commonly come into play when decisionmakers are forced to confront complex problems involving value conflicts and high uncertainty (what Steinbruner calls "structured uncertainty").[68] For example, decisionmakers tend to avoid recognizing conflicting values and the consequent necessity for value tradeoffs; they abhor cognitive dissonance and thus force the square peg of contrary information into the round hole of preexisting beliefs; they see events in terms of the issues that concern them most (their own "evoked set") and not necessarily in terms of other issues of concern to other decisionmakers; they misuse historical analogies in making sense of events;[69] they engage in wishful thinking; and so on. None of this *necessarily* entails an absence of rationality, but to the degree it produces closure and rigidity, it detracts from the possibility of rational behavior.[70]

The evidence is overwhelming that decisionmakers "differ in their perceptions of the world in general and of other actors in particular"[71] and that this is a matter of major importance. Jervis, for instance, persuasively rebuts Arnold Wolfers's classic argument that external threats (a burning house in Wolfers's analogy) tend to unite decisionmakers regardless of their predispositions (they all head for the exits). "For Churchill," argues Jervis, "the house was burning soon after Hitler took power in Germany; for Chamberlain, this was the case only after March 1939; and for others there was never a fire at all." He continues, "Decisionmakers may even agree that their state's existence is threatened but disagree about the source of the threat. This was true, for example, in the United States around the turn of the nineteenth century, when the Federalists believed France so much a menace that they favored war with her. At the same time, the Republicans believed England an equal menace."[72]

Indeed, a growing body of writing has emerged specifically on the subject of threat perception. Raymond Cohen, for his part, describes threat perception as a dynamic psychological process:

> Within any structure of relations which it is desired to preserve, certain 'rules of the Game' will be developed to regulate permissible behavior between the actors. In a dangerously uncertain world they allow a minimal degree of certainty. But they are like a seamless web. Damaged at one point, the whole fabric begins to disintegrate. Threat, then, is like a tug on this web of rules, its perception an anticipation of a descent into disorder and uncertainty.[73]

Although Cohen believes that even tacit rules of the global game are well understood by the players, he acknowledges that an expectation of occasional "cheating" is built in. Moreover, it does seem obvious that occasional misperceptions of opponents' intentions are unavoidable.

The last observation is central to the spiral model that cognitive theorists propose as a substitute for the theory of deterrence. "Deterrence theorists," writes Jack Snyder, "stress the role of credible threats in deterring potential aggressors," whereas "spiral theorists warn that most conflicts are rooted in mutual security fears, which are aggravated by unyielding 'deterrence' policies but assuaged by concessions."[74] In this perspective, an opponent's acquisition of a new weapons system is more likely to be perceived as an attempt to "get ahead" rather than to "catch up" in the arms race, which, of course, leads to spiraling competition. Jervis comments that in the "Hobbesian state of nature" and "anarchic setting of global politics, . . . we find that decisionmakers, and especially military leaders, worry about the most implausible threats."[75]

All of this to some extent undermines the value of Charles Hermann's older conception of crisis as a situational variable independent of the minds of decisionmakers. According to Hermann, a crisis exists when a situation threatens high-priority goals of the decisionmaking unit, there is limited time for response, and decisionmakers are surprised.[76] Surely, however, decisionmakers have tremendous latitude in perceiving (or not perceiving) varying degrees of threat (if any) to "high-priority goals" ("core values") and the urgency of a response. Thus, an administration other than President Johnson's might have regarded the 1965 revolt in the Dominican Republic as the "pro-Bosch" coup that its supporters declared it to be (and many still believe that it in fact was) welcomed the pending restoration of the legitimate president and political democracy, and simply let the violence run its course. As Richard Ned Lebow declares, "As is true with most important concepts in the social sciences, there is no generally accepted definition of international crisis." Writing more than a decade after Hermann, Lebow includes policymakers' perceptions as a key factor in his own definition.[77] Although much of this debate has reappeared in recent years as part of the agent-structure controversy, the dominant answer— that outcomes are a consequence of the interaction of the two—remains unchanged.

Structural factors as well as other objective explanations of the Cold War are virtually dismissed by Richard Cottam when he declares that "historians will record the Soviet-American Cold War as one that rested predominantly on motivational attribution rather than on conflicting objectives." In addition, he provides some excellent illustrations of perceptions at work in the categorization of "friends" and "enemies." Yugoslavia's Marshal Tito, for instance, appeared in American descriptions "to be two utterly different men": a "simple satellite leader" when he was allied with the Soviets and "an almost liberal democratic leader" when he broke away from the Soviets.[78] According to Cottam (drawing on William Gilmore), the case of Spain's former dictator Francisco Franco "suggests both the limits of ideology as a determinant of foreign policy perceptions and the patterns ideology generates when it is a determinant of perceptions." Prior to World War II, before a threat to the United States was apparent, American Catholics (perceiving a threat to the church in Spain) and American non-Catholic conservatives (responding to their political ideology) viewed Franco favorably, whereas American non-Catholic liberals did not. During World War II, when the United States was clearly threatened, nearly all Americans saw Franco negatively as a fascist who was a virtual ally of Hitler. Immediately after World War II, Franco regained his positive image among American Catholics and non-Catholic conservatives, but it was not until the Soviet threat loomed large with the intensification of the Cold War that American liberals came to view him as an ally.[79] Cottam cites the further cases of Patrice Lumumba and Moise Tshombe in the Belgian Congo as ones that evoked extremely different perceptions among decisionmakers around the world:

> In the United States the right saw Tshombe as one of them, and the far left equally identified with Lumumba. To the right, Lumumba was an instrument of international communism. To the left, Tshombe was an instrument of Western capitalist imperialism. For Egyptians, Lumumba was Nasser and Tshombe was the corrupt Ex-King Farouk. For Indonesians, Lumumba was Sukarno; for Indians he was Jawaharlal Nehru or Mahatma Gandhi.[80]

Still, it seems, to us at least, that structural factors, whether geography, historical memories, or GNP, impose constraints and provide opportunities to actors in *every* situation.

Few cognitive theorists (except Cottam) have themselves perceived, or at least have explicitly acknowledged, the impetus that the shift in the normative climate over the Vietnam issue gave to their approach. On the other hand, they have been candid in admitting their own desire for improved decisionmaking and diligent in teasing out the normative implications of their work toward this end. Unfortunately, in no small part because of the problems of cognitive theory that we will be analyzing, the suggestions they have been able to make have been rather modest in nature. These actually reduce to little more than urging policymakers to make themselves alert to perceptual pitfalls and to try to avoid them by building a measure of "multiple advocacy" into the decisionmaking process, consulting independent academics, and the like.[81] Perhaps cognitive theory's main contribution is, as Steinbruner assesses it, primarily a "negative one" of "challenging the conventional paths to reform." Certainly the theory offers little assurance that "merely" securing better quality leaders and persuading policymakers to pursue the "right" values will greatly improve the performance of government.[82]

Although the cognitive approach holds obvious interest and importance for scholars and practitioners of foreign policy alike, it also has grave weaknesses when considered as a potential basis for general theory. Snyder, Bruck, and

Sapin articulated a central issue early on when the desire to emulate scientists was still an article of faith for many international relations thinkers:

> The fundamental question is whether we can do better than achieve the familiar *Verstehen*—that is, whether we can obtain reliable data concerning the state of mind of actors whose behavior we wish to describe and explain. We are a long way from a hard methodology, but those who take an objectivist position have faith that such a methodology is possible. Can assumptions be replaced by evidence as a basis for inference? If not, we seem destined to remain puzzled about the combinations of determinacy and indeterminacy in the wellsprings of behavior.[83]

Part of the difficulty in obtaining reliable data is similar to that encountered by the individual-as-actor approach: decisionmakers themselves are not normally available for analysis. Consequently, as Christer Jönsson observes, "much of the relevant psychological literature rests on experimental research using subjects who are not—and are likely to differ significantly from—foreign policy decisionmakers." Not only are the subjects of experimental research not the genuine article, they are often observed in a laboratory setting that could hardly contrast more with the Oval Office or a ministry of foreign affairs.[84]

Yet the essential difficulty lies deeper still, in the fact that cognitive behavior varies not only by classes of persons and decisionmakers' institutional setting, but also *decision-by-decision*. Steinbruner, for instance, after outlining three "cognitive syndromes" ("grooved thinking," "uncommitted thinking," and "theoretical thinking"), readily acknowledges that "the three cognitive syndromes identified cannot be assumed to refer to personality types."

> It is reasonably clear that every person at different times and, most critically, *in different decision problems*, is likely to operate according to different syndromes. Many decisionmakers doubtless could be observed fitting all three patterns at one time or another. Second, in any organizational situation the various positions of power are likely to be held by people operating in different modes of thinking. Awareness of this fact is likely to aid analysis when details of the specific context can be supplied, but it is difficult at the moment to provide general propositions of any power.[85]

So one suspects that even if more and better data could be secured, they would far outstrip the capacity of present cognitive theory to explain. Steinbruner himself has doubts about cognitive theory:

> Because the business of establishing the connection between theoretical assumptions and an actual decision is a process of particularization (inevitably a matter of setting up *ad hoc* assumptions), there are few generally applicable rules to follow. The standard rules of scientific method apply, of course, but they, too, need interpretation for any given situation, especially in that the pertinent data are largely non-quantitative. One relies ultimately on the judgment and care of the analysts.[86]

The differences among cases and dependence on the analyst's judgment leave Jervis no more optimistic about the prospects for coherent general theory using psychological insights:

[P]ropositions about both the causes and effects of images can only be probabilistic. There are too many variables to claim more. In the cases in which we are interested, decisionmakers are faced with a large number of competing values, highly complex situations, and very ambiguous information. The possibilities and reasons for misperceptions and disagreements are legion. For these reasons, generalizations in this area are difficult to develop, exceptions are common, and in many instances, the outcomes will be influenced by factors that, from the standpoint of most theories, must be considered accidental. Important perceptual predispositions can be discovered, but they will not be controlling.[87]

In other words, if we turn to cognitive theory to explain foreign policy behavior, we shall be forced to abandon what Hedley Bull called the "scientific approach" in favor of the "classical approach" "that is characterized above all by explicit reliance upon the exercise of judgment."[88] As with so much of psychology, many conditioning factors will no longer be visible; only their consequences will be open to observation. And, like Freudians, we may have to subscribe to theories that are stubbornly nonempirical. When we are forced to consider outcomes "in many instances" to be "accidental," we are almost at the opposite pole from general theory. Indeed, one might wonder whether Jervis's characterization of cognitive-approach propositions as "probabilistic" might not be overstating the case.

STRATEGIC CHOICE AND EXPECTED UTILITY APPROACHES

Notwithstanding the proliferation of doubts about assuming rationality in political life, recent years have witnessed something of a resurgence of the assumption among those called rational-choice analysts. "Rational-choice approaches," in fact, is an umbrella term for a variety of more specific theories and approaches. Ironically, as we shall see, these approaches are almost entirely nonempirical, a fact that aligns them with the antiempiricism of much of postpositivism, which in contrast to rational choice largely abandons any claim of rationality.[89]

As we have seen, enthusiasm for rational or strategic-choice approaches that were built on the rationality assumption was high in the 1960s and 1970s. Many of those who were attracted to this approach were mathematicians (for example, Anatol Rapoport) and economists (for example, Thomas Schelling). Their journal of choice was *Journal of Conflict Resolution*, and they hoped to develop highly parsimonious theory by employing mathematical modeling in their research. In part, enthusiasm for such modeling was fueled by the apparent insights it provided in terms of predicting and dealing with conflict situations, the Cold War generally, and the Vietnam War in particular. Those were the heady days when terms such as "prisoner's dilemma" and "chicken" were frequently to be heard in the halls of departments of political science.

The most visible of these approaches in the earlier period were game and gamelike theories. They, like later versions, sought to explain instances where outcomes were determined by the *joint* decisions of two or more players under conditions of uncertainty. The approaches highlighted the interdependence of agents and the interaction of agents and structure, and they sought an ideal model for describing and prescribing decisions. Of special interest was a formal branch of conflict analysis known as game theory. By the 1950s game theory had entered the study of international politics. It required specifying players, rules, preferences, and outcomes. Through mathematical modeling, game theorists sought to prescribe and predict decisions deductively using only a few axioms and assumptions. Players were assumed to have intransitive preferences that were known to one another and to know the rules governing the interaction, as well as all possible outcomes. Solutions, when they existed, specified the outcome of the game as mathematically deduced from combining preferences and probabilities.

Overall, game theory is deductive because it is based on a priori assumptions about human behavior that are then applied to specific cases. It is nonempirical in that knowledge of preferences, the numerical values attached to different outcomes, or the probabilities associated with different outcomes are not derived from reality. As Raymond Aron was moved to ask, "Can we give a cardinal or ordinal value to the stake of a strategic-diplomatic rivalry?" His answer is that "the mere notion of more and less does not suffice to permit a mathematically valid solution, hence a rational prescription."[90] Overall, game theory achieved little, in part because its assumptions were unrealistic: for example, that players had perfect knowledge either of one another's preferences or of the alternatives available to them. In other words, we could not assume rationality. Thus, by the 1960s it had become clear that most of social and political action could be represented in game analyses only by severely distorting reality and that the mathematical means for "solving" complex games were not available.

With the end of the Cold War, interest in rational-choice analysis declined, but in recent years it has grown again. Among the reasons for its resurgence is that contemporary strategic analysis has confronted and at least partly overcome some of the earlier criticisms. On the one hand, the revised theory has discarded some elements of its predecessor and has benefited from additional theoretical and methodological insights. What remains the same is its focus on explaining actors' choices regardless of whether the actors are states, groups, or individuals. Most also assume, along with Bruce Bueno de Mesquita, that "relations are driven by strategic calculations"[91]; that is that they must take account of the preferences[92] and actions of other actors.

The main elements of the approach are that it focuses on the interactions of purposive actors, it differentiates between actors and their environment (including available information and prior actions), and it claims to overcome the levels-of-analysis problem by focusing on the decisions of individuals at any level.[93] "[E]xplanation must at some point go through the individual." For this reason, "theories of rational choice stand out as a coherent and rigorous potential solution to the problem of the linkage of the micro- and macrolevels of analysis."Individuals, however, are constrained by the "networks, contexts, and institutions" in which they are "embedded."[94]

As a group, strategic-choice analysts continue to applaud the virtues of deductive reasoning and regard mathematics as a highly precise and concise language in which to carry out such reasoning with rigor and internal consistency across a wide variety of cases in very different contexts. They believe that much about decision making can be explained in terms of differences in the preferences of actors and in the information available to them, and that such explanations address interests, which are at the heart of political science. "By analyzing the strategic setting in which individuals must make choices, *rather than in how they process information,*" declare David Lake and Robert Powell, "the strategic-choice approach seeks to account more successfully and parsimoniously for many of the same patterns."[95]

In a succinct description of the strategic-choice approach, Lake and Powell write, "The strategic-choice approach is part of the burgeoning literature on 'rational-choice' theory in political science. Like other rational-choice analyses, the strategic-choice approach assumes that actors make purposive choices, that they survey their environment and, to the best of their ability, choose the strategy that best meets their subjectively defined goals."[96] Unlike earlier game theorists, contemporary strategic-choice analysts no longer require that actors have full information.[97]

> Games of incomplete information . . . now allow strategic-choice theorists to address these same issues in systematic fashion. Rather than assuming that actors know the preferences of others, analysts can now posit that actors possess probability distributions over these variables, and they can examine how actors choose different strategies as their beliefs change.[98]

More importantly, there is far greater room for preferences and probabilities to change in the course of a strategic interaction, a fact evident in the range of investigations undertaken by strategic-choice analysts, especially of cases involving bargaining and negotiation.[99] Such analysts also now accept a bounded version of rationality that merely requires that actors be able to rank order the variety of possible outcomes consistently.[100] They focus on two elements: the strategic environment, which consists of the alternatives and information about those alternatives available to all actors, and the actors themselves, including their own preferences and their beliefs about the preferences of other actors. But modern analysts are better equipped to deal with incomplete information than their predecessors were because, as Lake and Powell observe, they "can now posit probability distributions over . . . variables, and they can examine how actors choose different strategies as their beliefs change."[101]

As a whole, however, such analysis still remains oddly isolated from the reality of global politics. Thus, even a sympathizer with the approach is led to conclude that its weaknesses lie in "excessive simplification, causal incompleteness, and post hoccery."[102] The actors, whatever their level of aggregation, remain essentially unitary with the problems associated with unitary-actor approaches. Indeed, the claim that the approach overcomes levels-of-analysis questions assumes that collective values, preferences, perceptions, and ideas are additive and comparable to individual versions of subjective utility.

The willingness of strategic analysts to accept changing perceptions and preferences has grown, but much still hangs on the meaning we give to very hedged explanations such as that offered by Lake and Powell that from "a longer-term perspective . . . , features of a strategic setting cannot be held constant," "the processes of socialization remain constant over a single 'round' of interaction," and "actors' preferences, their beliefs, and so on—the stuff 'inside' a particular 'box'—remain the same in any given interaction."[103] The two are connected, after all, what is inside and outside the box affect each other, and much hangs on what is meant by a "single 'round' of interaction." But how do we know the nature of preference change except through changes in behavior? This becomes circular, since preferences are inferred from behavior and behavior is said to be the consequence of preferences. Where in all this is the "shadow of the future"? Is there any room for a distinction between rationality based on long-term and short-term interests?

Such central elements as actor preferences, actor beliefs, and probabilities of outcomes are still largely subjective and unavailable empirically. Preferences are critical here because they are the bases of everything else: "Given the focus on subjective utility in a theory of choice," declares Arthur Stein, "it is ironic that scholars typically posit the interests and preferences of actors rather than investigate them empirically."[104] And which preferences should we assume? Jeffry Frieden argues in favor of deducing preferences from behavior,[105] but as we noted earlier, either preferences are needed to explain that behavior, or the theory incorrectly assumes that behavior—which may be taken for tactical reasons, personal whims, or any of a variety of reasons—reflects actual preferences. In any event, this means explanation is necessarily after the fact or post hoc. The alternative is to deduce in some manner from the setting or context that a particular actor "ought to prefer" X or Y, a conclusion that, however logical, relies on no evidence. This allows for mathematical modeling because, once assumptions are accepted, what follows is deductively true by definition without empirical inputs.[106] Some critics even argue that many actors have neither complete nor transitive preferences, or that they determine what they want only *after* their decision is already made (perhaps from passion, fear, or some other deep emotion).

Much of the criticism about identifying preferences in strategic-choice theory implies that what we have, as in the case of postmodernism, is basically a normative rather than an explanatory approach about how we *ought to* approach problems of choice.[107] Few deny the heuristic value of these analyses, but they still remain far from affording empirically grounded explanations and predictions. As Stein observes, "Probability, logic, decision theory, and game theory were all developed to improve human decision making. They were not developed as accurate representations and reconstructions of what people actually do but as tools individuals should apply to achieve more rational decisions than they otherwise might."[108] This observation leads us back to the older question of whether or not individuals are even capable of following those norms in terms of available information, information processing, and cognitive capacity.[109] At this point, all the problems raised earlier about rationality, even bounded rationality, pop up again. Once again, we are embroiled in questions about the role of passions, beliefs, and what Stein calls "political autism."[110]

CONCLUSION

Jervis concludes his analysis of the cognitive approach to the study of foreign policy with what he calls a "simple plea": "let us, as best we can, stop fooling ourselves; let us understand better what we are really about."[111] Although the various approaches described in this chapter cast serious doubt on assumptions of rationality and the models built upon them, none constitutes a coherent alternative.

Certainly, if we reject even modest claims about rationality, it is difficult to imagine constructing a general theory. Ultimately, however, the most vexatious issue confronting assumptions of rationality are related to whether we can usefully theorize about political collectivities, especially states, as though they were unitary actors. It is to this question we turn in the next chapter.

Most of us who labor in the vineyards of global-politics theory have stopped fooling ourselves, at least as far as the usefulness of the rationality assumption is concerned. Few today would accord it more than limited utility, at best, even while mourning its disappearance. Without it, however, little remains that might aid us in reconstructing consensual foreign policy theory from the numerous hypotheses about decisionmaking that have been presented in recent years. If anarchy exists, it is less in the global system than in our theories about it. Stein states this well: "People are crippled rationalists wanting to make rational decisions but constrained and limited by their own psychology; by their emotions and cognitive processes."[112]

CHAPTER 7

Quo Vadis Foreign Policy?

The traditional post-Westphalian picture of global politics is that of a universe of sovereign nation-states, each boasting an exclusive territory and pursuing an autonomous foreign policy. According to realist teachings, the foreign policy each state follows flows from a rational calculation of its national interest defined in terms of power. However, the inadequacy of the state concept and the wholesale retreat from the rationality assumption gravely undermine this traditional model and, more importantly, are devastating to the prospects for general theory about foreign policy. Even more threatening are growing doubts about the barrier between domestic and international politics and, therefore, whether foreign policy really exists as a separate field. Nowhere has the disarray in theorizing about global politics been more painfully evident than in the search for explanations of foreign policy behavior.

Especially in the 1960s and 1970s, the parsimonious realist view (and later the even more parsimonious neorealism[1]) was challenged by approaches to the analysis of foreign policy that emphasized a host of other conditioning and determining factors. Some analysts focused upon variables external to the state such as the essential structure(s) of the global system. (Since realism and neorealism also focus on external factors, especially power distribution, polarity, and the like, in some cases the newer arguments resembled realism clad in new raiment.) Others chose to emphasize basic attributes of states such as size, level of economic development, and the degree to which a political system is open or closed. Here, too, the essential "billiard ball" or "black box" model of the realists was retained, and there remained a tendency to anthropomorphize state entities in order to compare them.[2]

Other scholars chose to open up the black box order to master subtleties and nuances that had eluded realists. In seeking more potent explanations and in combining clusters of different variables into single explanations, such scholars introduced unprecedented complexity into the study of foreign policy. Some studied the supposed linkages (posited by Marxists) between capitalist

140

economies with attendant elite-mass social structures and foreign policy (an interest that has been revived recently in the globalization debates). Others argued for the primacy of ruling elites in determining foreign policy and, in so doing rejected pluralist assumptions about American politics. There was also renewed interest in national cultural factors like ideology, public opinion at large, interest coalitions like the military-industrial complex, and specific interest groups. Internal interactive processes also attracted interest—cybernetics or information/communication factors like the standard operating procedures (SOPS) that characterize organizational process, bargaining among bureaucracies, role formation, and situational variables. An increasing number of scholars (including many who were not trained as political scientists) are investigating particular psychological perspectives on decisionmaking, including personality, cognition, and motivation.

Finally, in recent years, more radical questions have been raised about whether the boundary between "inside" and "outside" a state matters at all, whether the state is any longer an autonomous or dominant actor in global politics, whether governance exists in the absence of government, and whether territoriality has been overcome.[3] Such approaches essentially question whether foreign policy is a field at all.

Owing to the longtime dominance of state-centric analyses of foreign policy, there is a tendency to think of these divergent approaches as more novel than they really are. In fact, virtually all of them have had previous adherents. Arguments regarding the economic bases of foreign policy have been standard fare in Marxist analyses for more than a century, even though many universities only rediscovered political economy in recent decades. Many nineteenth-century theorists regarded ideology as a critical factor, and national character arguments seem almost always to have permeated commentaries on foreign affairs. Concerned observers as diverse as Alexis de Tocqueville, Walter Lippmann, and Harold Nicolson grumbled about what they believed to be the pernicious effects of public opinion, and post-World War I accusations about the culpability of so-called merchants of death were precursors to claims about the military-industrial complex. Long before the current flurry of research into psychological factors, Freud presented a "theory of the instincts which, after much tentative groping and many fluctuations of opinion, has been reached by workers in the field of psychoanalysis" to explain war.[4] Human nature arguments of course permeated the work of classical theorists like Hobbes, Locke, and Rousseau.

The reawakening interest in these and other approaches vastly expanded the checklist of variables with which graduate students interested in foreign policy must become acquainted if they wish to pass their qualifying exams; however, if anything, they vastly complicated the search for general theory. One is reminded of "Moore's law," to wit: "The degree to which a topic is understood is inversely proportional to the amount of literature available on it. *Corollary:* That which seems vague is frequently meaningless."[5] With such a smorgasbord of factors from which to choose, the analyst is hard pressed to decide the relevance of and weight to be attached to each; many factors are so interrelated that they are virtually indistinguishable from one another; several factors bear the hallmark of ethnocentrism; and many are utilized as both independent and dependent variables.

The parsimony of realist theory has disappeared; no theoretical alternative is available to reimpose discipline on the study of foreign policy; and coteries of scholars have ceased communicating with each other. Moreover, as yet no approach has resolved the central ambiguities inherent in the study of foreign policy: What exactly is "foreign" policy when so much of "domestic" policy—for example, interest rates, environmental protection regulations, tax rules, antitrust initiatives, minimum wage legislation, and so forth—has profound international consequences—and vice versa, and when putatively domestic agencies of government have foreign policy departments? Does the foreign domestic dichotomy make sense at all? What, indeed, is policy? Who or what has the authority to make it? Who actually makes it? What, in fact, do we mean by "make"? Is "policy" a statement of goals or the presumed means to - those ends? Is it what policymakers say they intend to do or what they actually do? Or is it merely the behavior (intentional and unintentional) that flows outward from a state? What is a decision, given that most so-called decisions are subject to modification, either by their originators or by others, in the process of policy implementation (or nonimplementation), or that many decisions are made with little consciousness of their having been made?

Finally, foreign policy, at least as usually conceived, is an important topic only as long as we assume that territorial states are the fundamental sources of authority and behavior in global politics. If we abandon that assumption, we must either abandon foreign policy or reconceptualize it to take into account the sources of behavior of a galaxy of diverse polities that authoritatively allocate values, including humanitarian groups, ethnic movements, guerrilla bands, transnational corporations that admit of no home country,[6] or cities that are physically located within national boundaries but that are "transnational urban systems."[7] As we shall see, this raises the issue of governance without government and forces us to rethink David Easton's "authoritative allocation of values." Unfortunately, fundamental questions such as these are rarely addressed; and when they are, they are treated as issues in methodological rather than conceptual debates.

All of the preceding is so murky that we might be tempted to restate the central issue of foreign policy analysis, only partially tongue-in-cheek, as follows: Can we make meaningful *generalizations* about the relative significance of many ill-defined variables in explaining decisions and behavior, often of dubious relevance and impact, made in various state and nonstate contexts by a great number of potentially influential individuals or groups? The outlook for doing so is, to say the least, hardly bright.

REALISM, BLACK BOXES, AND FOREIGN POLICY

It is because realists and neorealists take seriously the state as actor, perceive states as greater than the sum of their parts, and believe them to be endowed with unique interests that flow from their power position in the global arena that they find it unnecessary to peer within states for explanations of behavior. Helen Milner puts it succinctly: "The central paradigms of the field of international relations (IR)—realism and neoliberal institutionalism—have ignored a key aspect of international relations: domestic politics. To understand the major issues in international politics . . . IR theorists must bring a systematic analysis of domestic politics into the field."[8]

Strictly speaking, Morgenthau and earlier realists did distinguish between nation-states and their decisionmakers, but this distinction carried little weight because decisionmakers were conceived to be rational, basically fungible, and guided by a system-determined national interest. Morgenthau does indicate fairly clearly *who acts* on behalf of the nation-state and who inhabits the nation-state box, which is therefore not an entirely black box. In recognizing that supposedly rational statesmen act as surrogates for the nation-state, he avoids the worst excesses of reification. Neorealists essentially do away with decisionmakers. In all events, realists, and even so more neorealists, tend to conceive of foreign policy planning and execution as processes that are coherent and unitary;[9] and, as Steve Smith observes, "one searches in vain through *Politics among Nations* for any linkage between the domestic polity and the international system."[10] For Morgenthau the "most important actor" in *causal* terms is not the decisionmaker either as an individual or as a representative of the nation-state. Rather, the "actor" with the most influence is two key attributes of the interstate arena: the selfish human nature of those who inhabit it and its junglelike character. Finally, as John Vasquez points out, neorealists, especially Waltz, ignore the "interaction level," which, he argues, "has been shown to be much more successful in guiding quantitative research than other levels [of analysis]—looking at the foreign policy of a single state or looking at the system."[11]

Black box and billiard ball explanations rely heavily on acceptance of the rationality assumption. For such approaches to be plausible, it is absolutely crucial to assume that decisionmakers are capable of distinguishing between personal preferences and the dictates of official duty and that they are prepared to sacrifice the former in service of the latter.[12] Moreover, decisionmakers must be able to calculate the national interest of the states for which they are responsible. With this assumption intact, it is perfectly reasonable to identify nation-states with their decisionmakers. Without it, black box explanations begin to fall apart. Sidney Verba early on understood some of these implications of rejecting the rationality assumption when raising questions about that assumption: "Different members [of the foreign policy organization] will prefer different goals, and policy will often be formulated by bargaining among the members of a foreign-policy coalition. . . . Any policy alternative . . . will be considered in relation to a variety of goal systems that may not be consistent."[13] As we shall see, the governmental (bureaucratic) politics perspective, as well as studies of the influence of domestic interest groups and attentive publics, reinforces Verba's contention that nation-states cannot be conceived of as unitary actors.[14] And, as Helen Milner points out, ignoring the domestic dimension of foreign policy does not ensure greater parsimony, even in the study of war.[15]

Realism/neorealism as applied to foreign policy also has been criticized from still other perspectives. For one, its state-centric outlook seems to ignore the impact of nonstate actors.[16] Also, as we have seen, work on cognitive behavior and cybernetics has highlighted the extent to which the actions of individuals and groups vary according to their perceptions. Beliefs also matter.[17] Smith comments:

> [Morgenthau's] key concepts—power, balance of power and national interest—are incapable of objective definition. To accept that these are subjective negates Morgenthau's claim to objectivity that is central to his argument. Once subjectivity enters into the definitions his epistemology collapses, for this is *not* an account of what decisionmakers *think* they are doing, it is an account of what we think we know they are doing.[18]

In addition, as we point out elsewhere, there is a once-and-for-all quality to realism and neorealism that leaves little or no room for change. Finally, realism, as we have argued, tends to seesaw back and forth between empirical and normative analysis, never resolving the contradictions that this poses. Even some realists recognize these problems, as do Buzan, Jones, and Little, who conclude: "Like many realists, we incline toward maintaining the primacy of the state within the political sphere, but have argued . . . that this primacy results from the practical and *wholly contingent* dominance of modern sovereign states." Modern realism, they argue, must allow for change: "Structural Realism is consistent not simply with the reproduction but also with the *transformation* of structures, including the possibility of a displacement of the state system from primacy among other global systems."[19]

Yet the influence of realism persists, not least today in the writings of neo-realist Kenneth Waltz, institutionalist Robert Keohane, and to a much lesser extent the work of neo-Marxists like Immanuel Wallerstein and critical theorists like Robert Cox.[20] What ties these schools together with realism is primarily their emphasis on systemic determinants of state behavior, although neorealists also echo realism in stressing the role of states as the constituent units in world politics. On the other hand, there is nothing approaching a broad consensus as to the most significant attributes of the global system, the nature of the relationships within that system (or subsystems), or the dynamics of change. Everyone agrees that the global system is essentially anarchical, in the very limited sense that no central government exists with a range of authority comparable to that found in strong states. Nearly everyone also admits the existence of at least an element of order arising from the common interests of states and the interdependence of peoples.

At this point, the consensus breaks down. For Waltz, it is the distribution of power, particularly the number of major powers, that is all-important; and the only genuine cooperation possible in the system is a relatively minor "exchange of considerations."[21] As John Ruggie expresses Waltz's argument in this regard: "[T]he management of global problems is governed by 'the tyranny of small decisions,'" and "the international system is not an entity that is capable of acting on its own behalf, for the greater social good. Thus, while a growing number of problems may be found at the global level, solutions continue to depend on national policies."[22] Keohane looks elsewhere, arguing that interstate institutions such as regimes matter: "From a theoretical standpoint," he declares "regimes can be viewed as intermediate factors, or 'intervening variables,' between fundamental characteristics of world politics such as the international distribution of power on the one hand and the behavior of states and nonstate actors such as the multinational corporations on the other." Regime norms and rules can influence behavior "even if they do not embody common ideals but are used by self-interested states and corporations engaging in a process of mutual adjustment.[23]

From Wallerstein's more radical perspective, the global system is virtually synonymous with the "world-economy" and a present "world-system" of capitalist "hegemony," which is slowly but inexorably being transformed by "anti-systemic" forces that will one distant day ensure the triumph of socialism. The system is divided by unequal development patterns into core, periphery, and semiperiphery. Before its collapse, the Soviet Union occupied a somewhat ambivalent position in Wallerstein's framework. A charter anti-systemic, the USSR evolved into a rather "establishment" actor, itself challenged after the 1950s by such new phenomena as national liberation movements in the Third World and Eurocommunism. Wallerstein forecast the disappearance of both the classical liberal economic consensus and "sclerotic" official Marxism.[24]

Wallerstein's approach shares a normative perspective with *dependencia* theory, which in the 1960s and 1970s was a prominent feature of writings about the North-South relationship. Paradoxically, the calculatedly "independent" foreign policies pursued in recent years by the likes of Argentina, Brazil, and Mexico derive much of their support from nationalist resentments created by historical and continued U.S. influence. The *dependencia* perspective also neglects the fact that a sizable percentage of developed-country markets, investments, and sources of supply are in the Third World. When *The Elusive Quest* appeared, we dismissed *dependencia* theory as obsolete, but certainly its normative agenda has been revised in recent years in debates on globalization, especially the activities of the IMF and World Bank and with regard to its impact on peripheral countries and peoples.

There are obviously many forms of interdependence/dependency: economic, political, military, social, cultural, psychological, and so on. The extent of interdependence/dependency thus varies with the issue-areas involved and the linkages among them. Ultimately, however, as we shall see in the next chapter, interdependence/dependence—like power or national interest—are constructions of the actors themselves and do not exist apart from the perceptions of authoritative others.

While elements of realism, then, are alive and well, it is also the case that fewer and fewer scholars of global politics are any longer prepared to accept a black box model of foreign policy. Indeed, this model was always anathema to realism's liberal opponents, many of whom wished to use a domestic analogy in interpreting global politics. As Andrew Moravcsik declares, "The priority of liberalism in multicausal models of state behavior implies . . . that collective state behavior should be analyzed as a *two-stage process* of constrained social choice" in which state preferences are "explained by liberal theories of state-society relations."[25] Our mental maps of the world are probably growing closer to this liberal reality but at the cost of parsimony, generalizability, and objectivity. A host of other approaches have emerged as competitors of realism and neorealism in explaining foreign policy. Unfortunately, none of these appears to have the potential to achieve the same level of universal applicability as realism. This conclusion will emerge more clearly from a brief review of some of these approaches.

ELITES AND SHARED IMAGES

Two closely related approaches—elites and shared images—like cognitive theory, seek the sources of attitudes, perceptions, and misperceptions that are common to decisionmakers across institutional settings. On the other hand, these approaches are less impeded by what we have seen are the decision-specific ultimate implications of cognitive theory.

Elites theory seeks an explanation for foreign policy behavior in society, a different level of analysis from that stressed by students of decisionmaking, who focus on government. The concern is not only with the social origins of elites but also with their ties to powerful institutions and interests in society at large (e.g., the military-industrial complex). The elites approach, with its emphasis on the effects of various economic modes of production, is often—and quite correctly—associated with Marxist theory.[26] The approach also underlies Gramscian hegemonic theory in which "[h]egemony derives from the ways of doing and thinking of the dominant social strata of the dominant state or states insofar as these ways of doing and thinking have inspired emulation or acquired the acquiescence of the dominant social strata of other states."[27] For Robert Cox, a pioneer in this area, culture, which is shaped by dominant elites, is the key to understanding power, and "state actions are constrained by knowledge on the part of the state's agents of what the class structure makes possible and what it precludes."[28]

One need not be a Marxist theoretician, however, to recognize at least the existence of a foreign policy establishment of sorts in most countries. Charles Kegley and Eugene Wittkopf, for example, write of the United States: "In terms of background and experience, the people making up the foreign policy-making elite are strikingly homogeneous. . . . [T]op-level decisionmakers are generally from the upper class and of WASP family origins, have been educated at the country's best schools and trained in law, and have extensive nongovernmental experience in major corporations and financial institutions." In addition, "participation in politics and political aspiration may be functions of personality, with the consequence that those who seek positions of power share psychological traits that make them more like one another and less like 'average' Americans."[29] Of course, even if this description is accurate, it does not necessarily imply or allow the reader to infer any special impact on policy outcomes—though it surely encourages such speculation.

The work of Richard J. Barnet merits special attention because it is characteristic of elites analysis and also because its normative impulse is unusually explicit. Barnet states in *Roots of War* that his "analysis has grown out of a conviction that the United States had committed monumental crimes in Indochina and that these crimes are likely to be repeated unless we gain a much deeper understanding of what we have done as a nation and why we have done it." His "thesis is that war is a social institution, that America's permanent war can be explained primarily by looking at American society, and that America's wars will cease only if that society is changed." Barnet attempts to define "the elusive word 'we' so often invoked in state papers during the past generation."[30] He finds his explanations in a "governing class" composed of individuals with similar backgrounds who control a vast bureaucracy; maintain a "partnership" with business interests; and rule over a public that tolerates and even to some extent supports the kind of global adventurism Barnet deplores. Barnet argues America's definition of national interest has its roots in the economic interests of American elites: "The Vietnam War was certainly a mistake. But it was not an accident. The Vietnam policy arose from the same analysis of the national interest, from the same theories of statecraft and human behavior, from the same technological impetus, and from the same economic pressures that have been the driving forces behind America's successful wars." And, once again, Barnet makes his normative agenda plain: "If we are to recover our sanity as a nation and to earn again the decent opinion of those with whom we share the planet, including our own children, Americans must engage in serious self-examination of those drives within our society that impel us toward destruction."[31]

While elites analysis seeks the wellsprings of foreign policy in society at large, what we have called (for want of a better term) the *shared images* approach looks variously for a national ideology, common national values, or at least shared assumptions among decisionmakers as to the nature of the world and desirability of certain policies (a "foreign policy consensus"). This approach, it is perhaps fair to say, cares less about the exact sources of shared images than the fact that some such images exist and that there is a need to define them more clearly.

Just as one does not have to be a Marxist to focus on elites, one need not adopt the shared images approach to recognize that it has some validity and utility. Robert Jervis, a cognitive theorist who takes strong exception to Wolfers's fire-in-the-building analogy, observes, "When we look at the major decisions of American foreign policy—those that set the terms for future debates and established the general framework within which policy was then conducted . . . what is most striking is the degree of unanimity."[32] Morton Halperin, drawing heavily on the work of Graham Allison—both of them principally identified with the "governmental (bureaucratic) politics" approach (of which more later)—in the mid-1970s some sixteen "shared images" of "American officials." In Halperin's formulation, these included items such as the following: "The surest simple guide to U.S. interests in foreign policy is opposition to Communism;" "The United States has an obligation to aid any Free People resisting Communism at home or abroad;" "Nuclear war would be a great disaster and must be avoided." According to Halperin, there are important reasons why such shared images tend to persist, including societal norms and bureaucratic socialization.[33] Similarly, Robert A. Packenham (following Louis Hartz) places his emphasis on four basic tenets of what he believes to be a "Liberal Tradition" in America's unique political culture ("American exceptionalism"): Change and development are easy; all good things go together; radicalism and revolution are bad; and distributing political power is more important than accumulating it.[34]

The elites and shared images approaches perhaps help explain some of the unity and continuity in foreign policy decisions in particular countries, but they fail miserably to account for what is often more interesting and significant—diversity and change. Presumably, changing elites help explain changes in policy, but two of the perennial problems confronting the elites approach is how "elites" should be identified and the closely related question of the extent to which they should be seen as unified or fragmented. In this spirit, Thomas Dye complains of "ideological disputation"; "endless, unproductive debate"; and a lack of "operational definitions, testable hypotheses, and reliable data" that have long confined this field of study to "the level of speculation, anecdote, or polemics."He concludes his own in-depth study of elites in the United States with an admission that the model does not give rise to entirely coherent answers: "Our findings do not all fit neatly into either an hierarchical, elitist model of power, or a polyarchical, pluralist model of power. We find evidence of both hierarchy and polyarchy in the nation's elite structure."[35] He illustrates the difficulty in achieving consensus in identifying elites in the following manner:

> Approximately 6,000 individuals in 7,000 positions exercise formal authority over institutions that control roughly half of the nation's resources in industry, finance, utilities, insurance, mass media, foundations, education, law, and civic and cultural affairs. This definition of the elite is fairly large numerically, yet these individuals constitute an extremely small percentage of the nation's total population—less than three-thousandths of 1 percent. . . . Perhaps the question of hierarchy or polyarchy depends upon whether one wants to emphasize numbers or percentages. To emphasize hierarchy, one can comment on the tiny *percentage* of the population that possesses such great authority. To emphasize polyarchy, one can comment on the fairly large *number* of individuals at the top of the nation's institutional structure; certainly there is room for competition within so large a group.[36]

There has certainly been competition in identifying elites. Traditional pluralist theory posited overlapping contests between political parties, conservatives and liberals, business and labor, and so on. Elites theory, as Dye sees it, "emphasizes underlying cohesion among elite groups, but still admits of some factionalism." A widely recognized "source of factionalism is the emergence of new sources of wealth and new 'self-made' individuals who do not fully share the prevailing values of established elites." Dye labels these dissenters "the Sunbelt cowboys," and they were major contributors to the Reagan "conservative" (some would say "radical reactionary") tide in the early 1980s.[37] According to Dye:

> The federal law-making process involves bargaining, competition, persuasion, and compromise, as generally set forth in "pluralist" political theory. But this interaction occurs *after* the agenda for policy-making has been established and the major directions of policy changes have already been determined. The decisions of proximate policy-makers are not unimportant, but they tend to center about the *means* rather than the *ends* of national policy.[38]However, terming "decisions of proximate policy-makers" as "not unimportant" may be a serious understatement, not least because (as we have mentioned) in the genuine making of policy, means and ends often become so intertwined as to be virtually indistinguishable.

As in the case of the elites approach, an initial problem facing the shared image approach is the usual—and often fatal—one of definition. It is no accident that beyond a few obvious things like opposition to communism, lists of such images or values almost invariably differ greatly, as do Packenham's and Halperin's. The irresistible temptation is to ask questions such as: If during the Cold War most United States officials held it as an article of faith that "the

United States has an obligation to aid any Free People resisting communism at home or abroad," why was there not a more potent response to the Hungarian uprising in 1956 or the 1968 Soviet intervention in Czechoslovakia? Was the shared image that only rhetorical "aid" need be given, didn't the Hungarians or Czechs qualify as "Free People," or was the obligation to be waived in the event that a superpower confrontation loomed?

Nor is this approach capable of explaining (let alone predicting) changes in shared images,[39] like the apparent rise, fall, and rise of U.S. commitment to the global advancement of human rights that took place between the Carter, Reagan/Bush, and Clinton administrations. Halperin speaks of the effect of changes in government personnel especially on regional policies, of the fact that "events in the outside world may bring about fundamental changes in the way American society looks at the world" (the sixties and Vietnam are his example), and of the phenomenon that "changes in national mood lead to changes in the images of the world held by the population at large" and "these changes come to be reflected in the bureaucracy."[40] Richard Cottam posits a "presidential decisionmaking level," with a "worldview" that becomes increasingly relevant in times of crisis and is more capable of change than the bureaucratic level.[41] Claims such as these, however, are remarkably vague and unsatisfying for purposes of theory building.

A final, and perhaps the most injurious criticism of the shared images approach gets back to the matter of ends versus means that has already been raised. Even if we could agree on what the relevant shared images/values are, decisionmakers still must wrestle with value tradeoffs and translate objectives into specific policies. For instance, a shared images defender might insist, possibly quite correctly in the most general sense, that the Carter, Reagan, Bush, and Clinton administrations *all* recognized a U.S. obligation to support human rights abroad. Nevertheless, how does one then explain the relative priority attached to this goal in two administrations, the different weights Carter and Reagan/Bush assigned to Soviet human rights abuses versus abuses in countries friendly to the United States, the contrast between Carter's pressure on South Africa and Reagan's "constructive engagement," and so on? What accounted for the willingness of the Clinton administration to engage in humanitarian intervention like NATO's involvement in Kosovo or the turnaround of George W. Bush's administration regarding U.S. policy toward the Middle East after the terrorist bombing of the World Trade Center in New York?

Leading up to his own personal interest in bureaucratic politics, Halperin admits the muddiness of shared images: "A proposed course of action that can be shown to be unambiguously necessary to preserve a shared objective will be agreed to by all. However, this is a very rare event." In his view, shared images are more useful in predicting what decisionmakers will *not* do than what they will do: "Widely shared images often do lead to agreement on basic objectives and therefore to the exclusion of certain conceivable courses of action."[42] This might help to explain why the Truman administration refused to consider a preventive nuclear attack against the Soviet Union when it enjoyed a nuclear monopoly or why Robert Kennedy allegedly opposed launching surprise air strikes against Cuba during the 1962 missile crisis. To be sure, Washington officials will be exceedingly unlikely to pop champagne corks and raise their glasses in celebration of a victory for Saddam Hussein or Iran's mullahs anywhere in the world. The shared values approach allows us that much of an "insight," but not much more.

GROUP DYNAMICS

We turn next to two additional approaches, *groupthink* and *cybernetics*, that focus on the psychological dynamics of particular decisionmaking groups. "Groupthink" is identified primarily with the work of Irving Janis,[43] which found its inspiration in the Vietnam experience and then was extended to other case studies. The thrust of the groupthink perspective is that decisionmaking groups, especially but not exclusively small groups, develop similar mindsets (attitudinal conformity). The cybernetic approach, according to John Steinbruner, involves a search for the "routine behavior of men in organizational settings." Steinbruner sees an organization as essentially a "servomechanism," that is, "a very simple decision mechanism but one with considerable logical power."[44] Organizations develop their own views of the world and SOPs, which are designed to minimize uncertainty, cope with repetitive behavior, and ensure institutional survival; hence, organizations respond to their environment in a remarkably stable, predictable, and unimaginative fashion. Joseph de Rivera discusses several related "constraints" affecting "organizational perception": There are always competing interests in an organization; officials are usually pressed for time; "the conflict of interests often prevents any action that is not absolutely necessary"; and "there are often legitimate differences of opinion as to what a situation is really like." Therefore, "the organization will 'view' as reality whatever will help to establish a consensus" and allow it to act; and the path of least resistance is normally "the policy they currently believe in."[45]

The cybernetic approach is distinguishable from other approaches, though barely so in several instances. Insofar as it highlights attitudinal conformity—at least as expressed in an organization's traditional worldview, procedures, and policies (albeit masking internal divisions)—cybernetic theory might be regarded as groupthink writ large. Steinbruner, as we have seen, speaks of studying "the routine behavior of men in organizational settings," but his emphasis is mainly on organizations as actors because they develop their own identity into which decisionmakers *to a significant extent* submerge theirs. The separate identities of organizations quickly lead one into the realm of the "governmental (bureaucratic) politics" approach. Lastly, to the extent that decisionmakers *do not* submerge their own identities into the organizational whole, we must either refer to the individual as actor or return to the cognitive approaches.

As theories, both groupthink and the cybernetic approach are significantly constrained. Despite what we have said, it is difficult to extend the concept of groupthink much beyond cases where a relatively small group of persons is involved in making important decisions and then only when a clear consensus emerges that appears to be based on shared misperceptions. On the other hand, as Steinbruner is the first to acknowledge, the cybernetic approach "still resides largely in the laboratories of basic research." In his opinion, it is not only insufficiently developed, but also "there are two critical problems with cybernetic logic." These are ignorance about "how cybernetic decision processes might work for the complex environments of public policy, which are highly interactive and not rigidly or simply structured," and "a view of the human mind (clearly the ultimate locus of decisionmaking), which does not account for one of its most critical faculties—the ability to make inductive inferences on its own initiative. Both problems indicate the need to supplement simple cybernetic theories in building a paradigm of the decision process competitive with that operating in rational decision theory." Steinbruner finds the required supplement in cognitive theory: "In essence," he says, "it is cognitive operations of the human mind working in interaction with the organizational structure of the government which set workable limits on highly diffuse decision problems, and it is cybernetic theory, thus supplemented, which offers a base paradigm for political analysis competitive with the rational position."[46]

Yet it is precisely what is meant by the "working in interaction" with the cognitive approach—not to mention groupthink and governmental (bureaucratic) politics—that is not adequately spelled out in cybernetic theory. De Rivera states the key problem succinctly: "Our current language and thinking are not precise enough to indicate exactly what an organization is and how it behaves; we are forced to rely on terms . . . which really apply to the behavior of individuals or machines." He argues the need to exercise great care in the use of such terminology and that we should not "speak of an organization as though it were either an individual or a machine." An organization has no motivation "in the sense that a person feels himself to be motivated, nor is it determined by the constraints that govern the behavior of even the most complicated machine." Nor does an organization perceive the world or make decisions; "individuals in the organization do that. On the other hand, an organization does exist in its own right—it is not simply the sum total of the individuals in it—and it does act."[47]

"PLAYERS IN POSITIONS"

A final approach we will consider, *governmental (bureaucratic) politics*, conceives of policymaking as an elaborate bargaining game among decisionmakers who are "players in positions." According to Graham Allison, "The governmental actor is neither a unitary agent nor a conglomerate of organizations, but rather is a number of individual players. . . . Players are men in jobs."In a bargaining game, "where you sit influences what you see as well as where you stand (on any issue)";[48] and the policy outcome is the result of competition and compromise, "pulling and hauling"—often an outcome that none of the individual players exactly wanted or anticipated.

Assessing the normative implications of this perspective, Stephen Krasner complains that it appears to relieve decisionmakers of any ultimate responsibility for their actions:

> The failure of the American government to take decisive action in a number of critical areas reflects not so much the inertia of a large bureaucratic machine as a confusion over values which afflicts the society in general and its leaders in particular. It is, in such circumstances, too comforting to attribute failure to organizational inertia, although nothing could be more convenient for political leaders who have either not formulated any policy or advocated bad policies [than to] blame their failures on the governmental structure.[49]

The governmental (bureaucratic) politics approach suffered at its inception from some confusion regarding its label. Kim Richard Nossal argues that:

> Because Allison chose to term it a "governmental (bureaucratic) politics" paradigm (and subsequently used, with Halperin, the term "bureaucratic politics"), the model is invariably interpreted as focusing on bureaucracies and bureaucrats alone. However, Allison makes it clear in *Essence of Decision* that the proper focus of the model should be on "players in positions," which includes players in bureaucracies, in the legislative branch, or in the political executive."[50]

Nossal points out a failure to distinguish "between 'Indians and Chiefs'": a "player in position" can be a desk officer in the foreign ministry or the head of government. A careful reading of Allison does clarify his intentions as to the relevant players, but this, if anything, only compounds the problems inherent in the governmental (bureaucratic) approach.

One major problem with the approach is that it appears to rest on our old friend, the dubious assumption that bureaucratic actors behave in a rational fashion (though not in this case according to some abstract criterion of national interest). To allow some of the insights of cognitive theory to creep in would completely change the nature and flavor of the "game." As Steinbruner points out, cognitive actors "will by-pass bargains which under analytic assumptions would appear to be obvious."[51] Yet the precise nature of this rationality is unclear. It is not the ideal rationality described by Verba, and it grows from more parochial roots than the rationality that realists derive from the national interest. At best, it reflects personal or group interests. Second, to the extent that the actions of individual players in the game reflect their institutional role and loyalty—that is, insofar as their primary goal in the competition is to preserve their organization's health and mission—would it not be better to conceive of them just as extensions of the "organizational process"? This, of course, is the province of the cybernetic approach.

Third, it is decidedly unclear where the boundary exists (if it does at all) between institutional role performance and idiosyncratic or uniquely personal behavior. Robert Art observes, "Organizational role (or institutional responsibility) is a component of a participant's outlook, but often only a component and often not even the overriding one."[52] Leading theorists of the governmental (bureaucratic) politics school only muddy the waters on this score. Halperin, for example, can tell us little more than, "The way an individual copes with . . . uncertainty is *affected* by his background—the personal experiences, intellectual baggage, and psychological needs he brings with him—as well as by his position in the bureaucracy."[53] Affected, surely, but how? And Allison throws everything into his kitchen but the proverbial sink:

> The hard core of the bureaucratic politics mix is personality. How each man manages to stand the heat in *his* kitchen, each player's operating style, and the complementarily or contradiction among personalities and styles in the inner circle are irreducible pieces of the policy blend. Then, too, each person comes to his position with baggage in tow. His bags include sensitivities to certain issues, commitments to various projects, and personal standing with and debts to groups in the society.[54]

Notice that the relative weight of the variables identified by Halperin and Allison and the relationship among them are not specified.

A fourth criticism is that it is extremely hard to determine the degree to which institutions like the U.S. Congress or particular executive departments are actors in their own right versus merely conduits for the demands of their clienteles. If the latter is the case, the analytical emphasis should be on interest groups or pluralism rather than on governmental (bureaucratic) entities. Krasner, for example, classifies the United States as basically "a weak political system" in which "central decisionmakers may find it difficult to overcome the resistance of specific societal interest groups, because political power in the United States is fragmented and decentralized." He emphasizes that it is interest groups that really matter: "There are many points of entry to the political system, especially in Congress and some executive bureaus. Once an issue falls into these decisionmaking arenas state preferences can be blocked. The American polity resembles a black ball system. Any major actor, public or private, can often prevent the adoption of a policy."[55]

A fifth problem is how to establish the precise identity of the governmental/bureaucratic players involved in the decisionmaking process. Policy is often made by a shifting set of ad hoc committees. Moreover, in most countries, bureaucratic roles tend to overlap. In the United States, for example, the president's political appointments to top-level bureaucratic posts ensure at least a modicum of presidential control, even as the individuals concerned find themselves immediately counterpressured to represent their agency's interests to the president and to cultivate close working relationships with key committees and committee chairmen in Congress. Role perceptions and definitions vary widely; some bureaucratic leaders (for example, William Casey at the CIA) have seemed to press their agency to follow presidential leads, others (for example, William Cohen at Defense) have tended to press their agency's interests upward, and still others (for example, Colin Powell at State) have reflected an independent, more personal position.

Bureaucratic divisions are further blurred by the fact that policy differences exist not only among various agencies but also within them (and within clientele interest groups like "business" or "farmers," as well), setting up the possibility (indeed, the probability) of interagency and inter-clientele factional alliances. Congress, in particular, is so fragmented that it has no true spokesperson and rarely expresses through its votes anything approaching a genuine consensus. "There is no single theory of behavior," argues Stephen Cohen, "that can explain all of the attitudes and actions of the two houses of the U.S. Congress." He is probably correct when he argues that, since members of Congress wish to be reelected and are, therefore, responsive to local concerns, "congressional members are responsive to outside stimuli, mainly the constituents." Presidential preferences and interest groups are too broad to allow us to predict or interpret their influences on congressional behavior. Cohen concludes, "The U.S. Congress, while frequently adhering to general theories of organizational behavior and specific behavioral models, is often a mystifying institution with a number of important idiosyncrasies. It has been suggested that no one who has not served or worked in the legislative branch for many years can fully comprehend the techniques and vicissitudes of the Congress's pattern of operation."[56] It is for such reasons that the United States may have its *black ball* dimension (Krasner's term), but that is not to say that its governmental/bureaucratic entities (any more than the state itself) should be treated as *black boxes*.

Putting aside the difficulty of identifying the players, yet a sixth problem is the task of establishing their relative influence in the policymaking process. Allison's answer is hopelessly tautological: "Power (i.e., effective influence on government decisions and actions) is an elusive blend of at least three elements: bargaining advantages [Allison "explains" that these are such things as formal authority and control over information], skill and will in using bargaining advantages, and other players' perceptions of the first two ingredients."[57] "Elusive blend" it certainly is! Krasner insists that Allison gives inadequate attention to the role of the president as a "king" standing above all the bureaucratic "chiefs."[58] Or, is it the perception that a crisis exists that brings the president to the fore?

Is a more important variable the nature of the issues and their attributes? James Rosenau, for example, points to what he calls "interdependence issues" (food, seabed mining, pollution, and the like) that are highly technical in nature, encompass many nongovernmental actors, and appear to require additional multilateral cooperation. Such issues, he argues, tend to "fragment the governmental decision-making process" and therefore to give additional "authority and clout" to bureaucratic agencies with appropriate technical expertise and links to specialized clientele.[59] Rosenau argues that many issues of foreign and military policy "are founded on nation-wide constituencies and can be managed by heads of state and prime ministers through their foreign offices and military establishments." In contrast, "interdependence issues render the politically responsible leadership much more subject to the advice, direction, contradictions and compromises that emanate from a fragmented bureaucratic structure. They normally do not have the time or expertise to master the knowledge necessary to grasp fully such issues and ordinarily they lack the political fortitude to resist, much less reject, the pressures from the special clienteles that seek to be served.[60]

A seventh problem raised by Glenn H. Snyder and Paul Diesing is that the governmental (bureaucratic) politics approach pays too little attention to the constraints on policy emanating from the external environment.[61] Finally, an eighth problem with the approach is that its relevance depends upon the nature of the particular political systems or societies in which players are enmeshed. This leads us to the subject of the comparative study of foreign policy.

THE COMPARATIVE STUDY OF FOREIGN POLICY: APPLES, ORANGES, BUT VERY LITTLE FRUIT

At the height of the scientific project in global politics during the 1960s and 1970s, significant empirical breakthroughs were thought to be just around the corner in a field labeled "the comparative study of foreign policy." With great enthusiasm James Rosenau declared, "All the signs are pointing in the same direction: as a television commercial might describe it, 'Comparative Foreign Policy is coming on strong for the 1970s!"[62]

Rosenau's seminal essay published in 1966, "Pre-Theories and Theories of Foreign Policy," speaks volumes in its very title about the expectations that characterized the era, even as the number of categories (five variables, eight types of societies) he advanced and the difficulty of operationalizing such dichotomized concepts as "small" versus "large" country and "developed" versus "underdeveloped" society offered more than a hint of grave problems lurking over the horizon.[63] Christer Jönsson hit the nail on the head when he concluded, "Whereas the early calls for nomothetic rather than idiographic orientation, scientific rigour and statistical treatment of data met with considerable enthusiasm, the subdiscipline is now accused of using deterministic logic for indeterminate phenomena, of confusing correlation with causation, of selecting variables in terms of their quantifiability, and of using simple indicators of multidimensional concepts."[64]

In the end, Rosenau concluded that the pre-theory was "a static product of a static era" and "that to aspire to theoretical breakthroughs we need to return to fundamentals."[65] As it transpired, the theories to which his categories were to be "pre" never materialized and, without theoretical guidelines, the veritable flood of quantitative induction that ensued ultimately contributed little to the task of comparison and generalization. Thus, Patrick McGowan and Howard Shapiro, two leading proponents of the scientific approach to the comparative study of foreign policy, surveyed some two hundred research studies in 1973 and candidly admitted, "Recognizably empirical theory is so limited in what it purports to explain and predict that it is uninteresting except to a few specialists."[66] Unfortunately, there has been little improvement in this regard. By 1982, Linda Brady was suggesting that "some subsets of the implicitly conceptualized properties [describing foreign policy] scattered throughout the literature need to be developed into *rigorous concepts.*"[67]

McGowan and Shapiro viewed the failure to construct powerful empirical theory as due to a regrettable division of labor between "theorists" and "empirical researchers." In their view, "Much of the technically sophisticated work in comparative foreign policy studies has been theoretical ex post facto"; that is, "quantitatively oriented scholars have tended to collect data prior to theorizing and then they have proceeded to analyze these data in a bivariate fashion." On the other hand, "theorists" had erred by concentrating on individual case studies rather than comparisons and by paying inadequate "attention to formal theory as embodied in mathematical models and computer simulations." Despite these problems and still other shortcomings that they identified, McGowan and Shapiro were confident that good empirical theory could yet be developed and that it would even serve as the basis for policy evaluation and prescription.[68]

Expressions of faith along these lines now seem as dated as the assumptions about the capacity to engineer economic and political development by means of the 1960s foreign aid programs. Much more common today are expressions of despair, like that of Bahgot Korany, the editor of a collection of essays on foreign policy in the Third World: "If the study of the foreign policies of underdeveloped countries is underdeveloped, the systematic analysis of their foreign policy decisions is not. It is simply nonexistent." Korany acknowledges that there are difficulties in securing (and creating) data (most of which do exist), but he believes that the fundamental issue is "the relevance of foreign policy theory": "Not only is this 'theory's' applicability to the Third World situation still to be demonstrated, but the field is still dominated by debates over the best approach and even over basics such as the definition of foreign policy itself."[69] In the end, it is improbable that the comparative study of foreign policy will make much headway until this and other basic questions that we raised earlier in this chapter are answered, and at present, the subfield is receiving little attention.

The fragmentation of the foreign policy field after the collapse of the rational model has greatly complicated not only the task of "explaining" the foreign policy of particular countries but also the search for valid bases for comparison. Indeed, even if we retain the rationality assumption, the concept is likely to have many definitions that vary depending upon cultural setting. Idiosyncratic behavior as an approach might seem to have special relevance to the few countries dominated by old-style dictators, charismatic leaders, unusually strong elected chief executives, or powerful foreign ministers. However, the approach is, by definition, so tied to the idiosyncrasies of particular individuals that it is obviously limited as a tool for comparison. In addition, such leaders are rarely as dominant as they appear to outsiders.

Nor do we know the extent to which the patterns of perceptions or misperceptions highlighted by cognitive theory, groupthink, and cybernetics are applicable to decisionmakers in all countries versus being significantly modified by different cultures or types of government. In any event, it is hard to imagine how perceptions or motivations can really be compared across national boundaries unless decisionmakers are treated—contrary to the most interesting insights of cognitive theory—as unified, rational actors. For this reason, Kalevi Holsti, for example, investigated what he called "national roles" through content analysis of the speeches of high-level policymakers of seventy-one countries.[70] In addition to the rational-actor issue, questions arise regarding the reliability of the data (speeches as indicators of perceived roles) and the extent to which "role" is defined by self or others.[71] Moreover, the results of Holsti's study, although thought provoking, are at such a high level of generalization that it is difficult to link them to specific policies.

The last problem is also characteristic of the elites and shared values approaches. Consider, for instance, Henry Kissinger's tripartite classification of "leadership" as "bureaucratic-pragmatic," "ideological," and "charismatic-revolutionary."[72] The scheme appears to leave little room, say, for the pursuit of pragmatic initiatives by leaders like Fidel Castro or for such ideological policies on the part of American leaders as Ronald Reagan's crusade against the "Evil Empire" or George W. Bush's denunciation of the "Axis of Evil." Not surprisingly, the classifications were of little value in predicting the end of the Cold War or the later War on Terrorism

The perils of ethnocentrism are especially evident with regard to the governmental (bureaucratic) politics approach. This approach appears to be unusually applicable to the United States because of the sheer size and diversity of the U.S. bureaucracy, as well as for three other important reasons. First, the constitutional separation of powers gives the president and the executive branch, major responsibility in the field of foreign policy while allowing competition in the exercise thereof from an independent legislature (power over budget, treaties, appointments, and so on) and an independent judiciary (which can even entertain civil suits against alleged foreign human rights abusers). Power is thus, paradoxically, concentrated in the president and yet still remarkably fragmented. Second, bureaucracies within the executive branch are expected to build close working relationships with both clientele interest groups and relevant congressional committees, which greatly increases bureaucratic autonomy from the White House. Third, the "rules of the game" of American politics allow for spirited and often public competition among bureaucratic agencies in the shaping of public policy.[73]

The foreign policy role of a U.S president is hardly identical with, for example, that of the British prime minister, a charismatic leader like Castro, a military junta, or a Russian president. Moreover, the U.S. Congress has far more direct and indirect influence over foreign policy than any other national legislature, and since Vietnam, Congress has had a greater propensity to exercise that influence. This influence was apparent especially during the Clinton years, when there was a Democratic president in the White House and Republican majorities in Congress. In contrast, with regard to external affairs, most national legislatures are little more than cheering sections or rubber stamps for an executive or, at best, debating societies that air a few key issues. With a more active contest between the U.S. president and Congress underway since the late 1960s, combined with the growing importance of global economic and human rights issues, the courts in the United States have also become more visible in affecting foreign policy; this, too, is a development unparalleled elsewhere in the world.[74]

When it comes to bureaucracies per se, the distinction between the U.S. pattern and that of other countries is somewhat more subtle but nevertheless substantial. In the sense that the governments even of many developing countries have become increasingly bureaucratized, rivalry among agencies is much more of a global phenomenon than it used to be. For instance, in Brazil the traditional dominance of the foreign ministry (Itamaraty) was severely challenged by a host of entities—ministries of planning, finance, industry, commerce, mines and energy, along with the Bank of Brazil and the Central Bank—brought to the fore by international economic issues.[75]

The character of bureaucratic competition varies tremendously in different political systems, however, and the model may lack general applicability. Nossal concludes a case study of Canada with the observation that "in parliamentary systems the concentration of political authority in the cabinet allows the political executive to impose constraints on legitimate conflict between policy-makers at lower levels in the decision process." He continues, "This is not to suggest that there will not be divergences of interest between players in the foreign policy game in parliamentary systems, but rather that their propensities to engage in conflict to ensure that their preferences will be transformed into policy may be sharply reduced by the imposition of central authority."[76] Stephen Cohen's careful analysis of policymaking for global economic relations in a number of Western countries tends to bear out Nossal's generalization: The style in Britain's Whitehall is to mute policy differences so as to give every possible appearance of a common front to the public. In Germany, the ministries seem almost to coordinate themselves, insofar as top-level decisions rarely have to be made in order to resolve which bureaucracies will prevail over particular issues. Japanese decisionmaking proceeds in glacial fashion while bureaucrats engage in polite negotiations leading to mutual accommodation, and so on.[77]

Differences from country to country are also pronounced with regard to bureaucratic relations with their interest-group clienteles. A striking and unique example was the intimate relationship between the powerful Ministry of

International Trade and Industry (MITI) and big business in Japan that lasted until the 1990s, with MITI essentially identifying and providing support for research and development in a few promising export industries. Unlike the situation in Japan, in so-called corporatist systems, many groups are initially organized by the government, but only a few are officially recognized as legitimate. Those that are recognized tend to enjoy a symbiotic relationship with government bureaucracies that is considerably more dependent than the MITI example or any notion of a clientele in the United States. Comparative politics specialists originally developed the corporatist model, from Iberian and Italian precedents, mainly in an attempt to characterize the "new" military regimes that emerged in Latin America in the 1960s and 1970s.[78] "Corporatist" may also be about as good a label as any for the Getulio Vargas and Juan Perón regimes, as well as for the Mexican one-party system, which survived until 2000. On the other hand, the current trend toward redemocratization suggests that what transpires today in most Latin American countries, including Mexico, is an uneasy balance between corporatism and liberal democracy, both of which have roots in the past. Meanwhile, a so-called neocorporatist approach has been applied by some scholars to the analysis of collaboration between government and interest groups in the making and implementing of public policies in western Europe, especially in Scandinavia.[79]

There are other relationships of potential significance to policymakers as well, including those with political parties and public opinion at large. In one-party systems, of course, the line between government and party is at best poorly delineated. Where more than one political party exists and there is any semblance of election campaigns (even when one party is clearly dominant and the system is thus not competitive in the fullest sense), parties can help to articulate foreign policy and other issues. Occasionally, however, party competition can be downright paralyzing.

Presumably, even leaders in authoritarian regimes have some concern about maintaining at least a minimum level of popular support for their policies. The Argentine military, for instance, found that initiating and then bungling the Falklands/Malvinas war made it impossible for them to go on ruling, and the botched campaign to "liberate" Kashmir of Pakistan's civilian leaders in 1999 led to a military takeover. In reasonably democratic systems, on the other hand, it is usually said that the public mood sets broad constraints on policies, if only because many policymakers must face the voters at election time. To be sure, voters rarely have clear views on foreign policy issues, nor are they often offered a clear choice as to policies during an election. However, Bernard Cohen writes of the United States that "while officials routinely deny any *obligation* to pay attention to public opinion, in practice they admit—sometimes readily, sometimes reluctantly—to *responsive* behavior;"[80] and they often devote considerable time and effort to trying to manipulate public opinion. Cohen argues that

> We have to ask whether those efforts do not themselves constitute a significant *direct* opinion input into the policy process. The mechanism involved is a feedback loop, in the sense that foreign policy officials dominate the public discussion of a policy, which they (and Congressmen also) then monitor and on the basis of which they draw conclusions about their freedom to take next steps. The loop may not even go any further or deeper than the media of communication.[81]

Cohen's observation points up yet another influence, the role of the media, whose impact, too, obviously varies greatly from country to country. It is hard to imagine any other country than the United States where the media is less constrained in what it does and more influential in councils of state. Richard Merritt goes so far as to conclude with regard to the role and impact of public opinion and foreign policy in West Germany versus the United States: "The striking differences between the structures of the West German and American political systems suggest that findings generated for one may not be directly applicable to the other. Moreover, neither set of findings may apply to France, Belgium, or any of the other industrialized countries of Western Europe not to speak of the rest of the world."[82] The changing nature of the media, especially the spread of the Internet, may require us to take a fresh look at this issue.

Finally, no meaningful comparison can fail to consider either the effect of the relative autonomy on certain issues granted to regional and local components of various federal and decentralized unitary systems or the impact of those "outlaw" groups that refuse to play by the political system's rules of the game.[83] American states and cities set the normative agenda in debates over South African apartheid. For its part, the Belgian government must pay careful attention to the relative impact that *any* policy decision (foreign or domestic) will have on the Flemish and French-speaking regions of the country.

As for "outlaws," particularly in Latin America and Africa, to what extent should the military be regarded as just another bureaucratic actor? The military is certainly not like other bureaucracies in that it has a special capacity, regularly exercised, to wield force to impose its policy preferences and to protect its institutional interests. Would any Turkish government, for example, risk the wrath of the military and dare alter the secular basis of the country's Kemalist constitution? And what of large restive ethnic groups, multinational corporations, terrorist groups, or guerrilla movements—and their external allies?[84] What of the Latin American *narcotraficantes* or other criminal cartels that Susan Strange argues add "a new problematic to the ever-growing agenda of world politics."[85] Military involvement in drugs led to the 1980 "cocaine coup" of General García Meza in Bolivia. Local drug peddlers have declared open warfare upon Colombian and U.S. enforcement officials, and Mexican cooperation in antidrug campaigns has been severely undercut by government and military corruption.

THE DECLINE OF SOVEREIGN BOUNDARIES, GOVERNANCE, AND THE END OF TERRITORIALITY

Ultimately, traditional analysis of foreign policy is most endangered by growing suspicion that the boundary that separates "domestic" from "international" politics is much less significant, that the territoriality on which sovereign states were constructed is being undermined, and that states themselves are no longer the only—sometimes not even the principal—actors in global politics. Repeatedly, the long arm of intersocietal, transnational, or civic relations dominates the state-to-state relations that were the main focus of foreign policy scholars, and much of the research on these topics is a linear descendent of the "discovery" of transnational relations in the 1970s, which itself in fact echoed earlier integration and liberal theory.

It is, for example, extraordinary to realize that the foreign policy issues that most bedevil U.S.–Mexican relations—capital flows and trade, immigration, and drugs—are all managed largely by nonsovereign authorities and cannot be managed by either government alone or even the two together. Consider, too, the relationship among Europeans themselves or between Americans and Europeans. John Gerard Ruggie cites the integration of Europe, especially its "transnational microeconomic links," to question the conceptual adequacy of state boundaries and territoriality:

> Perhaps the best way to describe it is that these links have created a nonterritorial "region" in the world economy—a decentered yet integrated space-of-flows, operating in real time, which exists alongside the space-of-places that we call national economies. . . . In the nonterritorial global region . . . the conventional distinctions between internal and external. . . are exceedingly problematic, and any given state is but one constraint in corporate global strategic calculations.[86]

States, as we have seen, are not the only actors to carry out foreign policy. A vast galaxy of actors—many nonterritorial in a conventional sense and a few existing largely in cyberspace—calculate their interests and pursue objectives and goals sometimes in alliance and sometimes in conflict with states. As with an increasing number of powerful transnational corporations, such actors are located neither exclusively within or outside states, but rather are elements in *both* a state's domestic and foreign calculations. Indeed, concepts like "national trade surplus" or "deficit" have lost their meaning in a world where most trade is within or among firms. And far from lining up behind "their" state in pursuit of some national interest defined in terms of power, firms may do all they can to undermine and oppose it because their interests diverge. We need only look at the often-acerbic relations between putatively American oil companies and the U.S. government over issues such as investment in Iran and Iraq or petroleum prices.

Edward Comor highlights such corporate-government tensions in his narrative of the evolution of American telesatellite technology. Comor documents the efforts of "AT&T, Comsat, and American broadcast interests" to sabotage the development of direct broadcast satellite technology because it threatened their terrestrial investments, despite the fact that such technology offered an inexpensive means of countering Soviet propaganda efforts. Similarly, he argues that during the 1970s and 1980s, conflict between the United States and the less developed countries over the latter's demands for a New World Information and Communications Order was driven by "domestic vested interests and related American state structures" more than any interstate factor. Indeed, according to Comor, far from acting in a unitary manner in regard to this issue, official policymakers discerned little in the way of national interest apart from the preferences of competing private interest groups, thereby producing a "fragmented" and "at times, conflictual" process,[87] until the Office of the United States Trade Representative (USTR) gained the upper hand in the mid-1980s. Until then, apparently "no one" in the U.S. government was "in charge."[88] Even then, U.S. policy aimed at opening up the global market for telecommunications was less a conscious effort to increase national power than a response to a powerful coalition of corporate interests.

Since the end of the Cold War, American-European relations, like inter-European relations, are increasingly characterized by issues—especially moral questions that reflect social and cultural linkages—that are more domestic than international (or "intermestic") as traditionally conceived,. Karsten Voight, a German foreign ministry official captures this duality when he declares, "What we have now with the United States is a relationship so close that it is quasi-domestic. The distinction between foreign and domestic policy has blurred as our societies have interwoven. That is why emotional issues like genetically altered food or the way we treat the children of international divorces rise to the surface. In a way, foreign policy was easier when it dealt with interests rather than emotions and morals."[89]

To understand current American-European relations, it is necessary to take account of the "frequent and dense exchange among individuals, groups, and organizations" that constitutes global civil society and that limits governments by "aggregating and expressing the wishes of the public" and "safeguards public freedom by limiting the government's ability to impose arbitrary rule by force."[90] Popular movements ranging from human rights, environmental, and gender networks to epistemic and racist communities, often taking advantage of advances in global communications technologies, organize and mobilize in cyberspace, interact frequently with governments and international organizations, and compete with governments for the loyalties of citizens.[91]

The "water's edge" between domestic and foreign politics and territoriality is a defining feature of foreign policy. How can foreign policy be foreign if state frontiers no longer differentiate "us" from "them"? Some of the research aimed at answering that question is plotting an escape from what John Agnew and Stuart Corbridge call "the territorial trap": "The merging of the state with a clearly bounded territory is the geographic essence of the field of international relations. The centrality of the association ranges from realist and neorealist positions where it is vital, to liberalism and idealism where it appears relatively less important."[92] It is not merely that the frontier between domestic and foreign is breaking down,[93] but that in addition nonsovereign and often nonterritorial polities are emerging, capable of authoritatively allocating values. They are autonomous and exist across, above, or below states. They occupy political space without being strictly territorial and participate in governing, sometimes with and sometimes without the cooperation of state governments.

It is, therefore, as Rosenau argues, "possible to conceive of governance without government,"[94] "Governance" has emerged in recent years as a hot topic of inquiry in global politics among those who emphasize "the diminished competence of states, the globalization of national economies, the fragmentation of societies into ethnic, religious, nationality, linguistic, and political subgroups, the advent of transnational issues that foster the creation of transnational authorities, and the greater readiness of citizenries to coalesce in public squares." The latter recognize that we live "in a world where authority is undergoing continuous relocation."[95] Nevertheless, "governance" is a vague concept the attraction of which lies largely in the fact that it connotes that "things get done" and authoritative decisions are made, sometimes by ordinary people voting with their feet or their pocketbooks, even in the absence of and often contrary to the preferences of states.

This takes us to the nub of the matter. One cannot thumb through the essays published by the Commission on Global Governance in *Issues of Global Governance* without recognizing the shift from thinking about global politics as a world of territorial states to contemplating a world of individuals . . . [96]"citizenship and individual loyalty," "political self-consciousness," "massive new movements," "simultaneous tendencies towards globalization and localization," and "relocation of authority."[97] *Global governance, then, is the new liberalism.*

Underlying and necessary for all of these claims is another dynamic, that of the diminishing importance of territory in global politics.[98] Jessica Matthews captures what is happening when she writes, "The absolutes of the Westphalian system—territorially fixed states where everything of value lies within some state's borders; a single secular authority governing each territory and representing it outside its borders; and no authority above states—are all dissolving."[99] In other words, various forms of "private authority" are challenging the once unquestioned "public" authority of sovereign states.[100]

The idea of deterritorialized authority has important normative consequences. Democracy, as it evolved in the West, is a state-level system. Effective state sovereignty has been a necessary though not sufficient condition for the exercise of democracy. In the absence of effective sovereignty, states and their citizens are no longer autonomous and, therefore, no longer capable of self-determination. Hence, the "democratic deficit." As David Held argues, "theorists of democracy have tended to assume a 'symmetrical' and 'congruent' relationship between political decision-makers and the recipients of political decisions. In fact, symmetry and congruence have often been taken for granted at two crucial points: first, between citizen-voters and the decision-makers whom they are, in principle, able to hold to account; and secondly, between the 'output' (decisions, policies, and so on) of decision-makers and their constituents–ultimately, 'the people' in a delimited territory."[101]

Political democracy and self-determination are largely irrelevant to the relationship between individuals and authorities associated with polities ranging from transnational corporations and international organizations such as the IMF all the way to the global market itself, yet those nonsovereign authorities have, for example, wrested considerable authority over economic matters from the state and its economic ministries. In doing so, they have also wrested control over economic matters from the citizens of states. Their decisions determine the economic well-being of citizens, just as the decisions of states, especially powerful ones such as the United States, affect the lives of people around the world. "Territorial boundaries," as Held poses the issue, "demarcate the basis on which individuals are included in and excluded from participation in decisions affecting their lives . . . , but the outcomes of these decisions often 'stretch' beyond national frontiers."[102]

CONCLUSION: A CONTINUING SEARCH
FOR THE SOURCE(S) OF FOREIGN POLICY

Perhaps we should begin to contemplate the possibility that foreign policy as we have studied it for many years, is no long a stand-alone subject. The erosion of state capacity and uniqueness have produced doubts about the utility of distinguishing domestic from foreign affairs and have raised questions about the subject's autonomy. Nevertheless, as long as sovereign states exist, the search for the sources of foreign policy will doubtlessly continue.

Although proponents of the comparative method looked to it for an answer to the persistent problem of ethnocentricity, it has proven more of a nostrum than a genuine cure. In part, this is because certain phenomena are genuinely unique to individual societies and sufficiently important so that masking them in an effort to highlight similarities effectively hides key conditioning factors. In addition, the effort at comparison has necessitated casting other phenomena at such a level of abstraction or vagueness that resulting research has virtually no conceivable applicability to the real world. While the birth of the comparative foreign policy approach effectively focused attention on the need for precision in the study of foreign policy, many of the early hopes that the approach raised have been dashed.

The opening of the traditional black box model left us with an acute case of theoretical overload and, in this respect, to paraphrase Robert Jervis, we decidedly *do not* understand better what we are really about. Opening the black box was rather like opening Pandora's box. To be fair, scholars such as Allison, Jervis, Steinbruner, and Rosenau never suggested that their particular models should be relied on to the exclusion of others. Quite the contrary, they stressed that their contributions merely illuminated one or another of the significant dimensions of the complex reality that is the foreign policymaking process, rather like a cubist painting depicts an object from various points of view. However, the effect of adding to the complexity—except insofar as complexity itself is indeed the central message—has been to leave us even more profoundly confused.

The cubist simile takes us to some of the more recent literature about transnationalism, global civic society, governance, and deterritorialization. Like cubist paintings, these have shown us still other ways the world might look. No longer does the globe appear simply divided into territorial units, but instead it is covered by layered, overlapping, and interacting authorities and networks. However much conceptualizing complexity in this fashion does bring us closer to the probable reality of a postinternational world, parsimony and operationalization are victims of this transformation in our thinking.

The essential difficulty is not the definitional and other weaknesses of each individual theoretical approach, although as we have seen, these are serious enough. Rather, the main problem is that we have too many choices of approaches, a host of "new" variables, and less-discrete levels of analysis that we have no effective means of ordering and integrating. We have an expanded checklist of factors that may influence foreign policy but no sure way of assessing their importance in particular cases, let alone comparing or generalizing across cases. To exacerbate matters, old ideas have been recycled with new terms, and graduate students are repeatedly forced to reinvent the wheel. As a consequence, genuine empirical theory as convincing and useful, say, as that which students of American politics have in the field of voting behavior, seems ever further beyond our grasp.

Our vase or bowl of fruit has now been left to each individual artist to paint as he or she wills. Theoretical cubism has been carried to such an extreme that the object under scrutiny has almost disappeared from view. In sum, despite our increasing theoretical sophistication and the accumulation of much more data since the heyday of realism, we still are far from *knowing* who or what makes foreign policy—or even how to go about finding out.

CHAPTER 8

The Challenge of Anarchy and the Search for Order

The development of theory regarding any phenomenon presupposes predictability, yet for many observers the defining characteristic of global politics remains anarchy. The effort to reconcile these *apparently* paradoxical assumptions has been a recurrent challenge to theorists for generations.[1] There were even significant differences among classical scholars in the emphasis placed upon anarchy. Rousseau and Hobbes, for example, stressed the absence of bonds among international actors and the consequent propensity for conflict among them. In contrast, Hugo Grotius pointed to the presence of common interests and solidarity that constrain the autonomy of actors and limit conflict.[2] There is also a British liberal tradition associated with the likes of John Stuart Mill and David Cobden that assumes a global harmony of interests and focuses on normative questions, individualism, and limited government.[3]

ANARCHY: THE DEFINING CHARACTERISTIC OF THE FIELD?

Complete unpredictability is, of course, an extreme version of anarchy, and few scholars or statesmen have perceived global politics as equivalent to utter chaos. Although authors usually try to limit their use of "anarchy" to the narrow sense of lacking central authority, the tone conveyed, especially by realists, is one of a dangerous world in which states must be prepared for almost any contingency. In this sense, anarchy almost always assumes a broader meaning. Nevertheless, scholars are forced to assume at a minimum that behavior is to some degree patterned, that prediction is possible (at least in principle), and that the phenomena they are studying, although constantly changing in some respects, do so sufficiently slowly that most descriptions and explanations provided one day will be valid the next. The weaker definition of anarchy as the absence of supranational authority is used as a contrast to the (mythical) well-ordered domesticity of internal politics. Even this weaker definition implies problems of prediction, at least according to Waltz, who argues that under anarchy "patterns emerge and endure without anyone arranging the parts or striving to maintain them."[4]

The conventional definition of the field revolves around the interactions of sovereign nation-states, each of which enjoys a monopoly of the means of coercion within its frontiers but above which there is no higher authority. This simple "sovereignty" dichotomy between the international and domestic spheres—for centuries the basis for assuming that global politics was a distinct field—appears, as we have seen, an increasingly dubious proposition. Minimally, linkages among issues in both arenas are apparent so that it is impossible to assess either sphere in isolation from the other. Maximally, the distinction between the two arenas has virtually ceased to exist. Certainly, the distinction between the two spheres based on the assumption of centralized authority in the one and its absence in the other (the correlative of which is the assumption of relative peace and order in the former and disorder and violence in the latter) is empirically nonsensical.[5] And if there is nothing distinctive about behavior in the international sphere, then it is necessary to ask whether the traditional subfield boundaries between, for instance, international and comparative politics serve any purpose. Going further, it leads us to ask why so little effort has been made toward developing an integrated theory of politics *sui generis,* the answer to which surely lies in academic vested interests and the bureaucratic inertia of universities rather than a persuasive intellectual position. Such a theory would doubtless reveal that there is far more order and predictability than the opposite in global politics, but that most authority/effective control is radically decentralized among a host of polities.

In practice, the conventional definition of global politics as an anarchical arena, although utilized by countless textbooks as a defining characteristic of the field, serves more of a metaphorical than an analytic purpose. It signifies little more than the obvious absence of central authority in world politics, the corollary of which is that actors are free to and, indeed, have no choice but to rely on their own devices ("self-help"). This corollary is by no means a logical necessity, but it has had an immense impact on the field. Despite its limited analytic value, we cannot dismiss the anarchy concept lightly because, as a metaphor, it has exercised and continues to exercise a powerful hold on the imagination of observers and participants. Most importantly, it is used to explain and legitimize the resort to coercion and the repeated occurrence of discord and conflict in global politics. It is widely accepted that the absence of authority, as Waltz declares, "is a *permissive* or underlying cause of war" in the sense that "wars occur because there is nothing to prevent them."[6]

There are both strong and weak variants of the claim that anarchy produces war, but, whichever form it takes, it serves as the premise for many analyses of global politics, especially in the realist/neorealist tradition. In international law, anarchy is the basis of legitimizing self-help and self-defense; in international organization, it lies behind Article 51 of the UN Charter; in game theory, it is the logic of "prisoner's dilemmas" and, by extension, the nonmathematical application of "maximin" strategies; and it has been a pillar of foreign and defense policy even in a nuclear era of mutual assured destruction (MAD).

One of the consequences has been to focus scholarly and policy analyses on conflict—how to prevent it, minimize it, or engage in it effectively.

Unfortunately, this central metaphor of anarchy turns attention away not only from the fact that the threat of violence is probably greater within many societies than among them, but also from what are truly the *dominant* patterns in global politics of order, cooperation, and peace. While no one would deny the critical importance of conflict and the threat of war (though apparently declining) in global politics, a preoccupation with disorder has precluded concerted efforts to understand the more normal situation that transpires state-to-state and in the global marketplace. The equivalent in microeconomics would be to study corporate failures rather than corporate successes when starting up a business enterprise. Security-minded scholars began to move in a somewhat more positive direction in the late 1980s and 1990s with their successive interest in studying what had been a "long peace" among the great powers and then a possible relationship between democracy and peace. But those for whom interstate violence is both mother's milk and a paycheck have been reluctant to cheer up.

Even the fundamental assumption that anarchy exists in any meaningful sense, beyond the obvious lack of an all-encompassing world government, is questionable. A strong case can be made, for example, that the world arena is actually to a very substantial degree hierarchical and that powerful norms and institutions also exist that make global politics into something of a society. The hierarchy that prevails, however, is among leaders and followers in countless polities of many different types, and thus the society that results is much more like Rosenau's complex relationships among spheres of authority (SOAs)—or Bull's prospective new medievalism—than the latter's state-centric conception of international society.

INTERDEPENDENCE: A HIDDEN CONSTRAINT

Although the assumption of anarchy pervades analyses of conflict, there is widespread recognition that even state actors are not free to do as they please, that the interests of actors in sustaining some global patterns of cooperation reduce conflict, that self-sustaining institutions exist to facilitate cooperation, and that interdependence attenuates anarchy. Maximin strategies are actually viable only in zero-sum games of which there are virtually none in global politics, and perceptions of zero-sum relationships are often transformed during repeated plays of such games.

Increasingly disillusioned by the bankruptcy of seeking a military solution to the Vietnam conflict, and attracted by the possibly revolutionary implications of East-West détente and continuing movement toward European economic integration, some scholars in the 1960s and 1970s began to turn their attention to those aspects of world politics that seemed to contradict the assumption of anarchy or at least to modify it. The simple idea that one could modify a structural attribute was then an important challenge to the realist tradition, and no one was more important in making this challenge than Ernst Haas, who celebrated the capacity of "pragmatic interests" to overcome anarchic conflict.[7] New factors, generally lumped under the heading of interdependence, were viewed as providing the intellectual wherewithal for opening up new theoretical vistas in global politics and for escaping the sterility of analyses based on unchanging power politics.

The disutility of force in Vietnam reinforced existing frustrations with the East-West arms race and the nuclear stalemate. In addition, there emerged a new generation of scholars who were persuaded that the critical issues of the future were increasingly economic and environmental in nature and that the distinction between "high politics" (security issues) and "low politics" (everything else) was an illusion. Some of these scholars also believed that the emphasis on power politics had involved their predecessors too closely with government, thereby limiting the independence of the academic community and precluding its addressing and starting to overcome these serious intellectual problems.

In addition to Vietnam and détente, other events and factors that had influenced these scholars included the OPEC oil embargo of 1973 and predictions of energy and other resource shortfalls, the plight of the Palestinians and the growth in ethnic discontent globally, the increasing frequency of incidents of international terrorism, the report of the Club of Rome regarding environmental limits, the growing demands of developing societies for a greater share of the global economic pie, and high rates of inflation in the West.

Influenced by the dramatic growth in the flow of transactions across national boundaries, many theorists in the 1970s and 1980s concluded that interdependence was intensifying.[8] This conclusion was reinforced by the progress of the European adventure in integration that had started in 1950 and had survived the nationalist challenge posed by French President Charles de Gaulle in the 1960s. But theorists disagreed about what the concept meant. For example, Richard Rosecrance and his colleagues observed, "In a very loose and general sense, one can say that interdependence is a state of affairs where what one nation does impinges directly upon other nations. In this most general sense, higher foreign trade, the ability to threaten atomic war, the development of worldwide inflation or recession all mean higher interdependence among states." They claimed that this broad but vague conceptualization "is quite unsatisfactory for analytic purposes," embracing as it does everything from "fully cooperative" to "fully conflictful" relations among states—with the highest level of interdependence perhaps existing between "opponents in war," where "any improvement in one state's position would directly and adversely affect the other." Instead, for Rosecrance and his colleagues "'interdependence' [should be seen as] the direct and positive linkage of the interests of states such that when one state changes, the position of others is affected, *and in the same direction.*" These lead them to conclude that an interdependent system is one in "which states tend to go up or down the ladder of international position (economic strength, power, welfare, access to information and/or technology) together . . . Wherever interdependence is high, there should be high cooperation."[9]

Should interdependence be limited to situations of "mutual benefit"? Robert Keohane and Joseph Nye Jr. argued vigorously that this conception was far too limiting, because reciprocal transactions may have mutual costs as well. "[I]nterdependent relationships will always involve costs, since interdependence restricts autonomy; but it is impossible to specify *a priori* whether the benefits of a relationship will exceed the costs. This will depend on the values of the actors as well as on the nature of the relationship." They go on to build their definition of interdependence around two dimensions: "sensitivity," or the responsiveness of one actor to events occurring in another, and "vulnerability," or the ability of an actor to insulate itself from events occurring elsewhere.[10]

The work of Keohane and Nye formed the core of an approach that has been variously labeled "neoliberalism," "neoliberal institutionalism," or simply "institutionalism." Using assumptions not unlike those of neorealists, Keohane and others sought to show that cooperation was possible even under anarchy owing to the role of institutions and information. The economically advanced world, in particular, according to Keohane, is the site of complex interdependence among states and societies, which produces interests that foster cooperation. Keohane distinguishes between his approach and that of Waltzian neorealists by arguing that the latter can be modeled as a single-play prisoners' dilemma in which the "assumption of rational egoism creates an abstract, unreal world for analysis." In this world, actors that could jointly gain from cooperation are unable to do so owing to the absence of trust under anarchy. For Keohane, reality is better captured as an iterated prisoners' dilemma, a world in which "bargaining typically occurs not only in one bargaining episode, but in several, over a period of time." Anarchy remains, but experience and information are added. Why is cooperation the outcome? "The essential reason for this difference is that, in a multiple-play or iterated prisoners' dilemma, defection is in the long run unrewarding, since the short-run gains thereby obtained normally will be outweighed by the mutual punishment that will ensue over the long run." The only condition is that "future rewards must be valued,"[11] or, as Robert Axelrod puts it, "the future must have a sufficiently large shadow,"[12] and actors must be concerned about far more than immediate interests.

For Keohane and Axelrod, cooperation results from mutual interests that are revealed in the course of interaction:

> [W]hat is most interesting is how little had to be assumed about the individuals or the social setting to establish these results . . . . The individuals do not have to be rational: the evolutionary strategies allow the successful strategies to thrive, even if the players do not know why or how. Nor do the players have to exchange messages or commitments: they do not need words, because their deeds speak for them.[13]

The key is a strategy of reciprocity, that is, "tit for tat." "[T]here is no need to assume trust between the players," continues Axelrod; "the use of reciprocity can be enough to make strategy unproductive."[14] Under these conditions, according to Keohane and Axelrod, neither altruism nor central authority is necessary to produce cooperation.

To some extent, discussions of interdependence are, as Waltz puts it, "confused by the use of dissimilar definitions."[15] Indeed, owing to disagreement and confusion about the definition of interdependence, theorists differ in their operationalization of the concept and, therefore, reach different conclusions regarding the degree of interdependence in global politics. Rosecrance and his colleagues argued that in the contemporary world industrialized societies no longer stand to profit—as they did prior to 1914—from the operation of free-market forces; American hegemony has in some respects been declining; the response of one economy to another has become less predictable; and the advantages that might be derived from greater multilateral cooperation have not been fully explored.[16] Stephen Cohen, for his part, views the situation as one of "mutual dependency" arising from "the growing obsolescence of the nation-state as an entity capable of serving its people's economic needs."[17] Keohane reaches the stronger conclusion that international cooperation among advanced industrial countries "has probably been more extensive than international cooperation among major states during any period of comparable length in history," yet "cooperation remains scarce relative to discord because the rapid growth of international economic interdependence since 1945, and the increasing involvement of governments in the operation of modern capitalist economies, have created more points of potential friction."[18]

By contrast, Waltz—preoccupied as always with great-power politics and striving to maintain a "pure" system-level perspective—concludes that interdependence is less now than in the past. But he is not simply defining interdependence in terms of interstate transactions:

> When I say that interdependence is tighter or looser I am saying something about the international system, with system-level characteristics defined by the situation of the great powers. In any international-political system, some of the major and minor states are closely interdependent; others are heavily dependent. The system, however, is tightly or loosely interdependent according to the relatively high or low dependence of the great powers. Interdependence is therefore looser now than it was before and between the two world wars of this century.[19]

As long as there are disagreements over the level of interdependence in global society, there will also be disagreements over asymmetrical interdependence or dependency relationships.[20] There is, for example, little consensus as to the actual degree of "dependency" in North-South relations.[21] Alberto van Klaveren, for instance, argued in 1884:

> Latin American countries are now adopting foreign policies that are increasingly autonomous from the hegemonic power in the region. Those societies continue to be characterized by a general situation of structural dependency, but the new realities of the international system and the relative autonomy of the state and its bureaucracy vis-á-vis the dominant classes allow for considerable independence in the field of foreign policy.[22]

As we noted in the preceding chapter, it is paradoxical that the "independent" foreign policies pursued in recent years by the likes of Argentina, Brazil, Peru, and Mexico derive much of their support from nationalist resentments created by historical and continued U.S. influence. In addition, the *dependencia* perspective always did fail to explore all the implications of the fact that the developing world accounts for a sizable percentage of developed-country markets, investments, and sources of supply, thereby providing some leverage. For example, former U.S. Trade Representative William E. Brock estimated that the 1982 Mexican debt crisis alone resulted in the loss of roughly 240,000 jobs for U.S. workers.[23] The Alfonsín government in Argentina recognized the leverage provided by strength through weakness and was a hard bargainer in international debt negotiations,[24] well aware that "if a country owes one billion, it's in trouble; if it owes 50 billion, the banks are in trouble."[25] Furthermore, according to David Leyton-Brown, the "pendulum" has swung, and "the initial incursions of multinational enterprises have been responded to with a reassertion of state prerogatives."[26] Multinational corporations found themselves occasionally "at bay" in host countries and nearly everywhere had to contend with at least some restrictions on their investment strategies and day-to-day operations.

Many of these claims, as we shall see, foreshadowed current globalization debates. Since interdependence is a defining assumption of globalization, differences in that term's usage have resurfaced in the variety of definitions of globalization. However, few current observers would agree with a contention that today's oligopolistic transnational corporations(TNCs) play second fiddle to governments, especially in the developing world. Indeed, the ascendancy of neoliberal principles and the failure of the demands of the New International Economic Order (NIEO), coupled with the replacement of import-substitution policies by export-generated growth and services have made most of the developing world eager for TNCs and the direct investment and access to world markets they bring.

CONTINUITY IN THE DEBATE

The idea of interdependence in the basic sense that the behavior of actors affects others or that changes in one part of the world usher in changes elsewhere is, of course, not new. What was different about the 1970s was that some scholars began to emphasize the constraints that interdependence putatively placed on self-help. Not only did they de-emphasize the effects of anarchy, but they also tended to perceive interdependence as a force for cooperation—a claim the truth of which is by no means certain. *More than anything else this shift signified a change in normative commitment among scholars and some statesmen.* The apparent loss of American dominance and autonomy and the limits of military power signaled by Vietnam, as well as the rise of OPEC, produced echoes in the literature of a contention that Norman Angell originally made shortly before World War I: Economic interdependence made war a losing proposition for victors and vanquished alike.[27] Increasingly, economic factors came to be seen as part of national security.

Interdependence theorists were also heirs to the regional integration theorists of the 1950s, especially communications, functionalist and neofunctionalist thinkers, such as Karl Deutsch and Ernst Haas, [28] who believed that the growth of a dense web of transnational transactions reduced the probability of conflict as a whole and paid little attention to Rousseau's contention that such transactions might actually provoke conflict. John Burton was especially influential in this regard, as he contemplated a map of the world that "would appear like millions of cobwebs superimposed one upon another, covering the whole globe, some with stronger strands than others representing more numerous transactions, some concentrated in small areas, and some thinly stretched over extensive areas." Such a map would reflect "a world society" which would "have no administrative boundaries."[29] It is important to appreciate that scholars like Angell, Deutsch, and Burton were passionately committed to the processes they were describing and explaining.

In a more recent expression of Angell-like confidence in the power of economic cooperation to eliminate conflict, Rosecrance argues that "as factors of labor, capital, and information triumph over the old factor of land, nations no longer need and in time will not covet additional territory." As services and knowledge industries replace manufacturing and agriculture as sources of wealth, there are emerging what Rosecrance calls "a new and productive partnership between 'head' nations, which design products, and 'body' nations, which manufacture them."[30] In good liberal fashion, Rosecrance's model depends heavily on the role of education. As in the case of Rosenau, proliferating individual skills play a critical role in changing global politics.[31] Like other liberals, Rosecrance focuses on the role of individuals in global politics and, in vivid contrast to neorealism and its advocates of balance of power or power transition, he emphasizes the dynamic side of global politics. Indeed, had *The Virtual State* been published fifty years ago, realist critics would doubtlessly have labeled Rosecrance an "idealist."

Rosecrance's debt to nineteenth-century liberalism reminds us that similar differences in the relative emphasis placed on anarchy versus interdependence also existed among classical scholars. For a time, such differences were masked by realists who emphasized anarchy and national interest at the expense of interdependence and community interest, and who polemically called those who optimistically believed in the pacific consequences of interdependence "idealists," "utopians," and the like. For example, classical scholars who sought to institutionalize and legitimize the independence and autonomy of city-states and territorial states stressed the sovereign independence and equality of the new units and wrote at length on "reason of state." In contrast, focusing on the balance of power entailed recognition of the limits of anarchy even in a system that lacked central authority.

Balance-of-power theorists understood that states constrained one another's independence and that such constraints reflected the normative bases of eighteenth- century Europe. Such theorists included both optimists and pessimists, who drew very different conclusions about the consequences of such ties. Representative of the pessimists was Rousseau, who viewed the ties among states as making war inevitable. They "touch each other at so many points that no one of them can move without giving a jar to all the rest; their variances are all the more deadly, as their ties are more closely woven."[32] For Rousseau, interdependence among states generated quarrels, and the absence of a central authority above them produced an environment conducive to mistrust and obedience to short-term calculations of self-interest: "All the Powers of Europe have rights, or claims, as against each other. These rights are from the nature of the case, incapable of ever being finally adjusted, because there is no common and unvarying standard for judging of their merits"[33] It was this version of a permissive environment, metaphorically depicted in Rousseau's stag-hare parable that was largely adopted by the postwar generation of realists writing in the United States and Great Britain.[34] Thus, Waltz concludes that balance-of-power theory "depicts international politics as a competitive realm,"[35] and this balance is the essential institution under anarchy.

Extending Rousseau, Edmund Burke saw the interdependence that flowed from the balance of power as enlarging and spreading conflict. Rousseau had, of course, shared this concern and had viewed the creation of relatively small and isolated communities like his own Geneva as one means of establishing and institutionalizing peace. In Burke's view, the balance "has been the original of innumerable and fruitless wars. . . . The foreign ambassadors constantly residing in all courts, the negotiations incessantly carrying on, spread both confederacies and quarrels so wide, that whenever hostilities commence, the theater of war is always of a prodigious extent."[36] The pessimism of Rousseau and Burke concerning the balance of power, especially their belief that it fostered parochial perceptions of interest, was echoed in George Washington's Farewell Address and in Woodrow Wilson's reformist zeal.[37]

In contrast to Rousseau, thinkers such as Tomassio Campanella, Emeric Cruné, and William Penn believed that the balance of power contained the seeds of a greater European unity that would largely eliminate the opportunities for conflict that grew out of anarchy.[38] Still others, notably the international law theorists Hugo Grotius and Emmerich de Vattel, saw in the balance the interplay between the forces of anarchy and interdependence. Vattel, for instance, believed that the balance was sufficiently institutionalized to be considered part of the law of Europe and as constituting the basis for a moral community. "Europe," he argued "forms a political system in which the Nations inhabiting this part of the world are bound together by their relations and various interests into a single body. It is no longer, as in former times, a confused heap of detached parts, each of which had but little concern for the lot of the others." And in a memorable passage equating balance of power to the foundation of Europe society, Vattel argued, "The constant attention of sovereigns to all that goes on, the custom of resident ministers, the continual negotiations that take place, make of modern Europe a sort of Republic, whose members— each independent, but all bound together by a common interest—unite for the maintenance of order and the preservation of liberty. This is what has given rise to the well-known principle of the balance of power."[39]

In the view of learned Europeans, then, balance of power was more than a principle that could be deduced from and could limit anarchy, it was a norm that at once defined the legitimate players in the game (territorial states, especially the great powers) and defined how the game should be played. The balance was an international regime in the sense that term is used by Friedrich Kratochwil, a reflection of "deference to *authoritative decisions* that establishes what 'the law' is, or from the acceptance of norm-regulated practices." And as norms change, as they did during the French Revolution, so too does the essential nature of global politics. As Kratochwil argues from a constructivist perspective, "one of the most important sources of change . . . is the *practice of the actors* themselves and its concomitant process of interstitial law-making in the international arena."[40] Adherence to balance-of-power principles reflected a willingness to subordinate national interests to system interests, or at least to equate the two.[41]

Debates over the relationship between the balance of power and global order have as contemporary corollaries efforts to discern the relationship (if any) between polarity and conflict. Does concentration of power or its diffusion lead to peace?[42] Or, is the *change* in such concentration, rather than either condition, the key factor?[43] Many of participants in these debates were realists who sought to relate different power structures to the question of war and peace. In recent years, some of these scholars have challenged the balance-of-power assumption that war erupts when an imbalance arises. Instead, they tend to argue that major war is most likely when the system's leading power or hegemon is being passed by a challenger.[44] Overall, such analyses adopted what was termed the systems approach.

THE SYSTEMS APPROACH

Scholars have a remarkable capacity for reinventing the wheel, and so it was that in the 1950s students of political science in general and global politics in particular were smitten with the idea of "system." Although they had used different terminology, classical scholars like Rousseau and Grotius had, of course, viewed the relations of actors from a systemic perspective, appreciating keenly the implications of variables interacting with each other to produce patterned relationships among actors. As we have seen, they understood that because actors "touch each other at so many points" their behavior could be understood as a complex pattern of action and reaction in which individual acts served as feedback for targets. The balance of-power metaphor was an expression of the consequence of patterned relationships out of which various forms and levels of dependency emerged.[45]

That metaphor, which continued to play a central role in realist theory, was rediscovered by scholars who sought to transform it into a scientific concept as part of their quest for parsimonious grand theory based on macroanalysis.[46] In their eagerness to construct deductive models based on structural variables, they failed to heed those who argued that balance of power was either a value-laden, prescriptive concept or a vanished historical reality.[47] It was not surprising, therefore, that efforts to extend the balance-of-power model beyond its original milieu were unsuccessful.[48]

In its most general sense—interdependence of variables and patterned interaction among parts—the idea of a system has heuristic and descriptive value for global politics, because it de-emphasizes randomness as a consequence of anarchy. But its actual theoretical contribution, in the sense of explanation or prediction, is minimal. The systems approach is, as Robert Lieber argues "really a set of techniques for systematic analysis that facilitates the organizing of data, but which possesses no ideal theoretical goals."[49] For the most part, scholars—who seemed oblivious to the fact that they were still talking about the same old things—introduced a whole new vocabulary into the analysis of global politics. Thus, the "international system" was for a majority of scholars merely the old post-Westphalian state system; and "subsystems," "parts," and "units of analysis" were still largely understood to be sovereign nation-states or regions. Morton Kaplan, for instance, was simply reiterating that there is an absence of central authority in world politics when he characterized the contemporary system as "subsystem-dominant" in which "essential rules" are not treated as "givers" by the subsystems (i.e., territorial states).[50] One is compelled to ask with Harold and Margaret Sprout "whether one derives clearer and richer insight into the operations of political organizations by endowing them even metaphorically with pseudo-biological structures and pseudo-psychological functions."[51] Nevertheless, young scholars in the 1950s and 1960s soon recognized that one road to promotion was to invent one's own system.

If the systems approach entailed little more than a restatement of classical observations about the relations among European states, why did the discipline so eagerly adopt the new jargon and regard the approach as so promising? Perhaps the most important reason was the currency of the systems concept in the natural sciences, especially biology and cybernetics, at a time of growing enthusiasm among political scientists for adopting the techniques of the natural sciences into their own disciplines.[52] General Systems Theory, in particular, was attractive because it sought to cut across existing disciplinary boundaries; it seemed a "useful tool *providing*, on the one hand, models that can be used in, and transferred to, different fields, and *safeguarding*, on the other hand, from vague analogies which have often marred progress in these fields."[53] Even before political scientists took up the systems idea, it had attracted scholars in other social sciences like economics (e.g., Kenneth Boulding) and sociology (e.g., Talcott Parsons), who were also committed to breaking down the walls separating disciplines.

A second reason for the acceptance of the idea, especially in global politics, was a realization that the scope and domain of global politics had become global. This is not actually a tautology. To some degree, global politics had always been global, but for American scholars in particular, this fact was made more salient by a series of events and processes—the end of American isolationism, the relative decline of western Europe in the scheme of things, the global nature of the 1939–45 war, the globalizing of the Cold War as it spread outward from Europe after 1950, and the process of decolonization and emergence of a multitude of newly independent societies in the developing world. Previously, American scholars, heirs to the classical European approach, had viewed the world through a largely European lens. Historical examples and cases were almost entirely drawn from European history between 1648 and 1914, and theoretical approaches like realism were based largely on assumptions inherited from Europe's classical tradition.

Typically, textbooks began to emphasize something called an "international system," which was said to encompass all independent actors and their interactions. Such a system was contrasted with earlier systems of limited scope and domain that functioned in relative isolation.[54] While it is true that in some sense the behavior of every actor affects all others either directly or indirectly, it is not at all clear that the conventional wisdom was correct in asserting a relatively abrupt evolution from historically local systems to an all-encompassing global one. Imperial powers had for centuries enjoyed global interests, and transnational activities like trade, immigration, disease, and tourism had periodically waxed and waned, as they continue to do. Indeed, recognition of the lack of explanatory power in positing a single global system was implicit in the proliferation of ideas about regional subsystems and issue-based systems, and in the propensity of many scholars to invoke the international system metaphor but then routinely to focus analysis on the behavior of only a very large states.[55] In reality, most actors matter little for key problems and issues that preoccupy observers of global politics, and there are variations in level of activity and in role by issue.

Almost inevitably the aspirations of systems enthusiasts were largely disappointed because, in the words of Jerome Stephens: "In global politics, as well as in political science, no isomorphisms have been established, and the changes that have been made in GST [general systems theory] since its inception have not been any more beneficial in helping us find isomorphic relations than the original formulation was."[56] This disappointment notwithstanding, global-politics theory has remained littered with the debris of systems. We are left with largely vacuous formulations like that of John Spanier: "The term 'system' is used for two reasons. First, it encompasses all the sovereign states and therefore possesses the virtue of being comprehensive. . . . Second, it helps us to focus on the relations or interactions among the component units."[57] The formulation is almost entirely nontheoretical, but, so we are told, at least it reminds us that we are dealing with the world as a whole and that states' behavior affects one another.

Ultimately, the concept of an international system is revealed to be as muddy as are so many of our other key concepts. There is nothing approaching a consensus among students of global politics as to what constitutes the fundamental structure of that system or its subsystems, or what lies behind change within it.

For general systems theorists what transpires in the international system is little more than a reflection of the nature of the whole, although there is hardly agreement as to the essential nature of that whole. For neo-Marxists like Immanuel Wallerstein, the key is the dominance of international capitalism within the system and, therefore, hierarchy rather than anarchy.[58] By contrast, structural or neorealists like Waltz view the global distribution of power, especially the number of major powers, as the all-important system attribute, using an analysis taken from microeconomics. "Market structure," he writes, "is defined by counting firms; international political structure by counting states. In the counting, distinctions are made only according to capabilities." The fact that "[i]nternational systems are decentralized and anarchic" (in contrast to centralized and hierarchical) is one of three "ordering principles" of international structure, the others being the character of the units and the distribution of capabilities. Structure "acts as a selector," eliminating states that fail to yield to its imperatives.[59]

In striking contrast to Waltz, whose model of the international system he believes lacks a "determinant of change," John Gerard Ruggie argues that anarchy is not a constant but varies according to "the quantity, velocity, and diversity of transactions that go on within society."[60] In fact, what *really* underlies the gap between Waltz and Wallerstein in conceptualizing the international system is a profound difference in normative commitment: Waltz sees a fundamental need for order; Wallerstein believes in the necessity of redistribution and change to bring about equity. Waltz wishes to tame anarchy; Wallerstein is prepared to encourage it if it would help to realize his preferred world.

Although a systems approach has not enriched our theoretical understanding of global politics to any great extent, the language has remained with us because of its association with natural science, especially its apparent divorce from normative claims.[61] In fact, scholars who employed the language of systems had normative predispositions that were every bit as strong, though not as clearly drawn, as those of their classical predecessors, the balance-of-power theorists.

Above all else, most of the latter valued the independence of those sovereignties that emerged from the Treaties of Augsburg and Westphalia and the political and social status quo within the states of Europe. "[P]eace," declared Edward Vose Gulick, "was no more essential to equilibrist theory than the barnacle to the boat."[62] War was of concern only if it threatened the independence of states, the "liberties of Europe." "In war," wrote Edward Gibbon, "the European forces are exercised by temperate and undecisive contests," but such wars were only "partial events" that "cannot injure our general state of happiness."[63]

The degree to which balance-of-power theorists were committed to domestic stability or the "legitimacy principle," as well as international stability, became apparent after the collapse of the balance of power under the weight of the Napoleonic expansion. Meeting in Vienna after the defeat of Napoleon, European statesmen quarreled about many matters but agreed fully on "the condemnation of the revolutionary principle"[64] and, in general, on domestic factors that system analysis usually ignores. And the Concert of Europe structure was explicitly intended to enforce a domestic stability that the eighteenth-century balance had been unable to ensure.[65] Even among recent balance-of-power partisans, notably Henry Kissinger, domestic and international stability has been regarded as a cardinal virtue. Thus, Kissinger's "grand design" (a variant of the balance of power) and his interpretation of the meaning of détente were infused by the aim of achieving global stability.

A similar preference for stability is evident in the work of systems theorists who do not invoke the balance. Although there is considerable variation among systems theorists regarding the degree to which the structural elements of global systems determine actor behavior, such theorists generally ascribe considerable importance to the impact of structure upon behavior.[66] In other words, global distributions of resources (especially power) and attitudes are generally perceived to govern what is possible and probable in the global realm, a view that follows logically from the original premise concerning the relative anarchy of global politics. For this reason, these theorists tend to agree that it is difficult to change substantially basic patterns of relations except at the margins. What is more, many of these theorists are openly pleased at the relative stability that they believe is the consequence of structural dominance and caution against efforts to alter things except at the margin.[67]

INTEGRATION AND DEVELOPMENT THEORY

The systems approach, though it highlighted the limiting conditions on anarchy in global politics, has been largely sterile and static. Heretics who sought to develop theory that might explain change were correctly seen as overt or closet advocates of such change and were summarily dismissed by realists as utopians or moralists (much as opponents of Ronald Reagan were dismissed as liberals.) However, two popular (closet liberal) schools of thought in the 1950s and 1960s—political development and regional integration theory—were able to employ a systems approach, address themselves to change, and still be regarded as mainstream.

Interestingly, the development theorists, while concerned with the process of change toward modernization, shared the realist bias toward stability and implicitly regarded stability or status quo as normatively desirable. In the first place, political development theorists were profoundly ethnocentric; that is, modernization was seen as entailing change of the sort that western Europe and the United States had passed through on the road to modernity. The term then implied becoming more like "us." "'Modern" means being Western,"[68] and modernization is "all those social and political changes that accompanied industrialization in . . . Western civilization."[69] In the second place, such theorists placed a high value on order. The study of politics itself was seen, in Leonard Binder's felicitous phrase, as "the study of the legitimation of social power."[70]

In fairness, some development theorists were less Eurocentric than others. For example, Barrington Moore in his broad comparative historical analysis of the transition from agricultural to industrial society and the implications of this transition for the nature of authority carefully avoided equating democracy with modernization. Indeed, his core question regards the factors in that transition that produced democratic versus authoritarian styles of rule.[71]

Regional integration theorists also sought to use variants of the systems approach to explain and predict change in global politics. Their normative agenda was, however, significantly different than that of modernization theorists. Unlike the latter—many of whom believed that the nation-state as it had evolved in the West represented the highest level of political, economic, and social organization—the former concluded, for the most part, that the nation-state was and ought to be only a way station on the road to higher and more encompassing forms of organization.

Heirs to the utopian tradition of Kant and the Abbé de St. Pierre, early integration theorists like David Mitrany were functionalists who argued that supplies of valued human goods such as food, shelter, and security *must* keep pace with the growing demand for such goods.[72] Functionalists believed that growing exchanges of goods and people had increased the problem of satisfying demands, which in turn increased the probability of war. Viewing history in teleological terms, they saw a progressive growth in the size and scope of political institutions as necessary to handle the ever-greater problems confronting humankind. Like later World Order Models' Project (WOMP) theorists,[73] functionalists saw a close connection between security and nonsecurity issues and were openly committed to encouraging trends which they believed would ensure peace. In Sewell's words; "Is peace the aim? Its foundations must be laid by piecemeal international efforts in commonly recognized transnational problem areas that are readily acceptable to the procedures shaped and accepted by modern man."[74] Functionalists pinned their hopes on the specialized agencies of the United Nations, which they foresaw gradually assuming specialized burdens previously assumed by nation-states, and they believed that, as these agencies showed they could perform "nonpolitical" tasks, politicians would be willing to surrender greater authority to them in more overtly political areas. In this manner peace would spread through the gradual erosion of the nation-state.

Functionalists did recognize the anarchic aspects of global politics, especially with regard to the sovereign nation-state, which they sought to transcend by taking advantage of countervailing tendencies toward interdependence. Unfortunately, it became clear that there was no inevitability to the process they had identified; there is no "necessary" reason that human wants must be satisfied.[75] Nor was it easily possible to differentiate between political and nonpolitical issues in global politics. International agencies and even their parent organizations have proved quite expendable, and governments have generally been loath to surrender authority (a point to which we will return shortly). Nevertheless, functionalists did share with later integration theorists the idea that the nation-state was increasingly unequal to the burdens placed upon it and that its existence, as the main element of anarchy in global politics, was closely connected to war. Long before globalization or constructivism entered our vocabulary, Karl Deutsch was warning about the "cognitive trap" created by the nation-state: "All the nation-state can do now is to risk or spend the lives of its soldiers and its cities as gambling stakes on the gaming tables of power, strategy or ideology, in games which none of the players control or fully understand. The nation-state is thus in danger of becoming for its people a cognitive trap in times of peace and a death trap in the event of war."[76]

Although elaborating the several strands of integration theory is beyond the scope of this work, what is important here is to note that such theorists tended to highlight processes and factors that were revived by interdependence theorists in the 1970s. One important group, closely associated with Deutsch in his years at Yale, derived insights from cybernetic systems and theorized that high levels of communication and transactions among groups were linked to the formation of integrated societies. For Deutsch, integration did not require the disappearance of states, but rather a degree of trust sufficient to create "security communities" in which war would be inconceivable.[77]

Whether levels of communications and transactions were causally connected to integration or whether they were merely indicators of the process remained an unanswered question. Restated, the question can be asked whether high levels of communication and transactions generate interdependence or are the result of it. Do they predict greater interdependence, or do they result from interdependence? The answer is unclear in part because of different definitions of the concept.[78] In any event, this group of theorists saw a relationship between the level of information exchange and other transactions, especially trade, that heighten common perceptions and create material interdependencies.[79] Such exchanges were believed to increase mutual sensitivity and responsiveness to the needs and problems of the actors involved.[80] Richard Meier explained the logic of this claim as follows: "A large continuous flow of information makes it possible to mobilize the requisite experience and data . . . to bring the anticipated crisis to the attention of decisionmakers sooner than would otherwise occur. Large flows of information . . . make it possible to reduce the chances of blundering into international conflicts."[81] Rising communication and transactions, then, were seen to encourage learning; learning, in turn, supposedly would generate the knowledge necessary for mutual responsiveness.

Insights from functionalist and communications theory were combined by a second important group into what became known as neofunctionalist theory.[82] Basically, neofunctionalism postulated that interstate agencies produced by agreements among nation-states, though initially based on common interests, could generate pressures for broadening or intensifying their own authority as learning and socialization took place among participants. Elements of neofunctionalism were later to reappear in regime, institutionalist, and constructivist theory. In addition, neofunctionalism moved decisively away from system-level analysis, exploiting instead insights into interest-group behavior and putting forward ideas that Putnam would later use in his discussion of two-level games.[83]

Much of the initial enthusiasm for integration theory was, however, based on the limited experience of postwar western Europe, and the several theories of regional integration suffered from the same kind of parochialism as had modernization theory. Efforts to apply insights derived from a European context proved largely disappointing, suggesting that the European experience was historically unique.[84] In addition, it appeared that even in western Europe the movement toward political integration had begun to lose its momentum after achieving the Treaty of Rome (1957) that created the European Common Market. Latin American variants like the Central American Common Market and the Andean Common Market also soon collapsed. Instead of greater supranational integration, the 1970s and 1980s witnessed significant subnational movements revolving around ethnicity, language, and culture. As a result research into regional integration at least temporarily began to flag.

Like so many of their predecessors, integration theorists knew what they wanted to happen, but the world failed to oblige. Not surprisingly, integration research flourished, especially in the United States, at a time when American leaders were enthusiastic about the prospect of a united Europe as a buttress against the Soviet Union and as a reliable and prosperous trading partner. Its decline occurred as frictions grew between the United States and western Europe, the European experiment seemed to flag, and interest in U.S.–Soviet détente increased.[85] In the same way, modernization theory was partly a response to official American interest in the developing world during the era of decolonization and was associated with efforts to identify policies that could assure stability in the developing world and thereby noncommunist solutions to socioeconomic problems.[86] Despite the revival of European integration in the 1990s, the Maastricht Treaty, the emergence of a common currency, the Euro, and the expansion of the EU to the east, there was little renewed interest in integration theory. Scholars who continued to focus on Europe tended to regard the regional situation there as unique or as generating insights about multilevel governance rather than integration. Meanwhile, other analysts had shifted their attention to regime theory.

REGIME THEORY

Theorizing about the relative impact of anarchy and interdependence on global politics did not cease with declining interest in regional integration. As we have observed, the 1970s witnessed an upsurge in concern over environmental and economic issues, especially after the several oil "shocks" and major changes in international monetary and trade practices. Governments, publics, and scholars alike shared these concerns, though in different ways and to different degrees. "Interdependence" became the symbol for those who argued the existence of a "spaceship earth," the collective ecological and economic well-being of which was threatened by narrow nationalism and egoistic behavior. Interest in the implications of interdependence was also intensified by the political agenda of the Carter administration, which was quite different from that of its predecessor in emphasizing energy, human rights, environmentalism, and problems of developing societies. Consciousness was further raised by the varied demands associated with the New International Economic Order (NIEO) and the New International Information Order (NIIO).

The interdependence concept was at the heart of a revitalized interest in international organization among theorists who were less concerned with formal institutional mechanisms like the United Nations or regional integration than with more amorphous practices and institutions labeled variously "transnational actors and behavior" and "international regimes." The growing interest in transnationalism was reflected in the publication of a special issue of the journal *International Organization* (vol. 25, no. 3) in 1971 entitled "Transnational Relations and World Politics."[87] Its editors, Robert Keohane and Joseph Nye Jr. argued that the traditional model of global politics—the state-centric model—ignored a vast web of interactions occurring directly between and among societies while attending exclusively to relations among governments or between governments and international organizations. "We can distinguish," they declared, "four major types of global interaction: (1) communication, the movement of information, including the transmission of beliefs, ideas, and doctrines; (2) transportation, the movement of physical objects . . . (3) finance, the movement of money and instruments of credit; (4) travel, the movement of persons." Echoing proponents of regional integration, Keohane and Nye argued that one key effect of transnational interactions and organization was "increases in constraints on states through dependence and interdependence."[88]

Keohane and Nye admitted that the phenomena on which they were focusing were not of recent origin.[89] Why then was the publication of their volume followed by an upsurge in research and theory on transnationalism, and why was there such renewed interest in the interdependent, as opposed to the anarchic, elements of global politics? As we noted earlier, the key reasons were to be found in the realm of real politics rather than scholarship. Thus, a large number of contributions to the volume dealing with transnational economic processes and institutions focused on issues like the collapse of the Bretton Woods arrangements, the prominence of transnational corporations in the world of international trade and finance, and the impact of subnational revolutionary groups on interstate politics highlighted by the behavior of the Viet Cong and Palestine Liberation Organization. Perhaps the most important influence on this trend in scholarship, however, was the declining preoccupation with East-West security issues that accompanied the flourishing of détente.

As the implications of these developments became clearer and additional events seemed to confirm their importance,[90] the initial insights about transnationalism were elaborated into theoretically tantalizing ideas about "complex interdependence" and "international regimes." The idea of complex interdependence as elaborated by Keohane and Nye included but went beyond the earlier transnational model to capture the features of a world dominated by interdependence rather than anarchy. In such a world, societies enjoy interstate, transgovernmental, and transnational ties across a wide variety of distinct, though often linked issues.[91]

Keohane and Nye explicitly contrasted their model of complex interdependence with realist and neorealist models of world politics which placed greater emphasis on the threat and use of military force and relative gains and losses. Keohane and Nye believed that their model was applicable to certain issues, notably those of an economic nature, but that realist and neorealist explanations still suited traditional security issues. Nevertheless, they argued that the world was becoming increasingly characterized by complex interdependence and that this was a good thing because it implied less frequent resort to military force. While applauding the growing constraints on state autonomy, they carefully hedged their bets, cautioning readers, "So long as complex interdependence does not encompass all issue areas and relationships among all major states, the remaining role of military force will require sovereign states to maintain military capabilities. Moreover, so long as the world is characterized by enormous inequality of incomes among states . . . citizens are likely to resist the dismantling of national sovereignty."[92]

In sidestepping the teleology of their functionalist predecessors and in developing a model of world politics that encompassed state bureaucracies as well as nonstate groups and international organizations, they avoided being branded utopians, which would probably have happened twenty years earlier during the era of realist dominance of scholarly discourse.

At heart, however, Keohane and Nye in those days remained semirealists, realists with liberal leanings, or something along those lines. They did not envision a major change in the decentralized character of world politics. Indeed, they appreciated that among the key trends in global politics in the 1970s were a decline in the control that could be exercised by the superpowers, a dispersion of resources, and growing difficulty in effectively using the conventional levers of power, especially coercion. How then did things get done in a world of complex interdependence lacking central authority? The answer, they contended, lay in the existence of "networks of rules, norms, and procedures that regularize behavior and control its effects."[93] These they termed "international regimes," and if the definition, resembles that of "global governance" that is because it embodies at least some similar assumptions and comes from much the same tradition. Although regimes may involve explicit rules for behavior, they are viewed as being less formal and more elastic than, for instance, international law. A strong or effective regime, then, does not require that the rules be explicit, but it does require that rules and norms be understood consensually and intersubjectively so that "predictable, orderly behavior takes place."[94] This requirement for intersubjective norms would, as we shall see, also become a key element in constructivism.

Like earlier integration theorists, regime theorists emphasized the central role of information exchange and learning. Keohane argued that regimes encouraged cooperation by easing transaction costs in negotiating agreements and by providing information and institutional memory that could reduce uncertainties and reinforce cooperative expectations.[95] More information reduced the prospects for deception, thereby providing reassurance of participants' compliance. According to Keohane, these assets allowed regimes to flourish even after the decline in American hegemony that had been instrumental in their creation: "Once an international regime has been established . . . it begins to benefit from the relatively high and asymmetrical level of information that it generates. . . . Viewing international regimes as information-providing and transaction cost-reducing entities rather than as quasi-governmental rule-makers helps us to understand such persistence."[96] The emphasis placed by regime theorists on information exchange places them squarely in the rationality camp.[97]

Despite retaining an assumption of rationality, regime theory was perhaps the most explicit challenge to date to the dominance of the classical view of the role of anarchy in global politics since idealists had been forced into hiding by the rhetorical wounds inflicted upon them by Morgenthau and his followers. For the most part, regime theorists were able to avoid this fate by accepting, in Krasner's words, "the basic analytic assumptions of structural realist approaches, which posit an international system of functionally symmetrical, power-maximizing states in an anarchic environment."[98] In other words, most regime theorists followed Keohane's view that international regimes could function effectively only under specified conditions. Nevertheless, they all were grappling, as Arthur Stein puts it, "with the problem of trying to describe and explain patterns of order in the anarchic world of global politics" starting from an assumption of "the existence of interdependence."[99] Some like Donald Puchala and Raymond Hopkins, however, were prepared to go further, challenging frontally the classic assumption of anarchy by arguing the existence of regimes in virtually all aspects of global politics such that order exists even in the absence of centralized authority: "[A] regime exists in *every* substantive issue-area in global politics where there is discernibly patterned behavior. Wherever there is regularity in behavior some kinds of principles, norms or rules must exist to account for it."[100] This claim almost precisely anticipated what came to be called "governance."

Although there are significant differences in emphasis among regime theorists, they are all part of that strand of thinking in global politics that places great weight on the constraints on actors and the limits of sovereignty imposed by the existence of interdependence. Interestingly, those among them who accept the broadest conceptualization of regimes have been characterized by their own colleagues in the English School as heirs to the "Grotian tradition;"[101] yet in a very real sense all regime theorists owe something to this tradition that posits, in Hedley Bull's words, "the solidarity, or potential solidarity, of the states comprising international society, with respect to the enforcement of the law."[102]

Indeed, one repeatedly hears echoes of international law in descriptions of regime theory. Stephen Krasner, for instance, notes that since "regimes encompass principles and norms, the utility function that is being maximized must embody some sense of general obligation."[103] And Keohane himself admits that "the norms and rules of regimes can exert an effect on behavior even if they do not embody common ideals but are used by self-interested states and corporations engaging in a process of mutual adjustment."[104] No better reason could be proffered for claiming the existence of law or for explaining its origin! Certainly, regimes, like international law, have, as Bull argues, "helped to maintain, in a period of inevitably contracting consensus, some elements of a common framework."[105] Could not "international law" be substituted for "regime" in Krasner's observation that "[t]he use of diplomatic cover by spies, the bugging of embassies, the assassination of diplomats by terrorists, and the failure to provide adequate local police are all indications that the classic regime protecting foreign envoys has weakened"? Moreover, the sense that regime is a rehabilitated version of law is heightened by Krasner's assertion that a major source of regimes is "usage and custom."[106] These are, of course, offered as key sources of positivist law. Ultimately, much of the disagreement among regime theorists regarding definition and applicability replicates in new guise the debate over definition and sources of international law between positivists and Grotians.

The divergence in definitions of international regime reflects not only the absence of sharp and consensual concepts in the discipline, but also the lack of novelty in the idea itself. Stein, for instance, points out that broad definitions of regimes signify no more than "a disaggregated issue-area approach to the study of global politics" whereas narrower definitions that equate regimes with international institutions merely entail "an attempt to redress a tired and moribund field."[107] The broader definitions, that identify regimes with enduring patterns of behavior in specific issue-areas reveal a clear debt to the original systems approach described earlier. The narrower definitions not only recall earlier studies of international organization, as Stein suggests, but also functionalist and neofunctionalist formulations. And, like functionalists and neofunctionalists, regime theorists do not distinguish what they analyze empirically from what they ardently desire. Regime theory, as Susan Strange caustically observed, "takes for granted that what everyone wants is more and better regimes, that greater order and managed interdependence should be the collective goal." Again, order is the implicitly or explicitly preferred value. Again we confront a body of theory generated in response to policy preferences, in this case the maintenance of stability in an era of what then appeared to be declining American hegemony, a preference which Strange contrasts to the earlier interest in integration theory that "started with the perceived U.S. need for a reliable junior partner in Europe."[108] Again, the theory is parochial, derived largely from the experience of the developed West and ignoring anomalies revealed by analysis of the developing world.

Ultimately, regime theory of whatever coloration reflects another instance in the enduring debate between those who see interdependence as severely limiting the impact of a decentralized world and those who believe it only marginally lessens anarchy. Thus, as Strange suggests, regime theory "tends to exaggerate the static quality of arrangements for managing the international system and introducing some confidence in the future of anarchy, some order out of uncertainty," and it "gives the false impression (always argued by the neofunctionalists) that international regimes are indeed advancing against the forces of disorder and anarchy."[109]

INTERDEPENDENCE: A NONTHEORETICAL CONCEPT?

As we have emphasized, however, global politics has never been anarchic in the sense of chaos. Nor have actors ever enjoyed unbridled autonomy. Policymakers have always sought to reduce the prospect of surprise and to routinize their tasks to the greatest extent, even while resisting constraints on their autonomy. As a result, global politics is characterized today, as in the past, both by decentralization of power and purpose and a by tremendous variety of allocation mechanisms and more or less institutionalized (though often tacit) norms and rules that provide interaction with coherence.[110] Theorists who have argued the dominance of either anarchic or integrative features are driven largely by their own normative and policy predilections (e.g., for order or change), failing to appreciate the variability in such dominance by place, issue, and time.

International theory in the 1950s and 1960s tended to emphasize the role of anarchy in political life, even while the United States and Soviet Union, like "scorpions in a bottle," were tightly linked in a potentially deadly relationship of negative interdependence. International theory in the 1970s and 1980s accorded interdependence a more central role, even while global politics remained fundamentally decentralized, subject to the parochial decisions of independent (and occasionally maladjusted) leaders. Interdependence and regime theorists did, for the most part, recognize this duality. Perhaps that is why neither they nor their predecessors were able to give theoretical meaning to the impact of interdependence beyond pointing to a world of greater complexity. Similarly, realists and others who stressed anarchy could do little more than advise prudence. Were we to admit that growing webs of transnational economic, informational, and technological flows were linking the fates of actors ever more tightly—what would this tell us? Despite the best efforts of generations of theorists, we really do not know whether interdependence is related in any way to cooperation or conflict.[111] Those like Norman Angell who believed the former have been repeatedly disappointed, even while the ideas of Rousseau and other pessimists have not been confirmed. Whose "iron logic" are we to accept?

Neither liberals nor constructivists accept the structural "iron logic" of realism and neorealism. Social structures, like anarchy, argues Alexander Wendt, have no necessity or logic apart from the meaning attached to them by "agents" or actors:

> While it may make sense to say that a natural structure has an existence apart from the behavior of its elements, social structures are only instantiated by the practices of agents. The deep structure of the state system, for example, exists in virtue of the recognition of certain rules and the performance of certain practices by states; if states ceased such recognition of performances, the state system as presently constituted would automatically disappear . . . . [T]he existence and operation of social structures are dependent upon human self-understandings . . . social structures acquire their causal efficacy only through the medium of practical consciousness and action.[112]

Returning to Waltz's idea of anarchy as a permissive rather than efficient cause of war (as articulated in *Man, the State, and War*), Wendt declares that there "is no 'logic' of anarchy" apart from the behavior of actors derived from their self-perception of identity and interest. Just as Margaret Mead declared war to be an invention, Wendt argued persuasively, "Self-help and power politics are institutions, not essential features of anarchy. *Anarchy is what states make of it.*"[113] Anarchy may or may not produce power politics, and power politics may itself produce anarchy. But one additional thing is certain (which Wendt seriously underplays): a host of other actors and polities are at least as significant as states in shaping order and governance (or the lack thereof).

Interdependence is thus what actors of many sorts make of it, but the concept remains essentially nonpredictive. Power theory implies that the high costs potentially involved in escaping interdependence (or dependence) *should* endow selected actors with new forms of leverage and *should* allow us to predict that those who are at once sensitive and vulnerable to commodity, financial, and other pressures will succumb to influence attempts. The fact that this is not the case would not surprise anyone acquainted with the "puzzle of power." If the British retreat from Suez in 1956 under the threat of U.S. veto of an IMF loan to London tends to confirm the thesis, the OPEC oil boycott of 1973 tends to disconfirm it. "On balance," observes Roy Licklider, "the short-term impact of the oil weapon on the foreign policies of the target countries toward the Arab-Israeli issue was small or negligible. . . . In the long run not much changed."[114]

A number of reasons account for the nonpredictive nature of analyses of interdependence. In the first place, the proliferation of transnational economic, political, military, social, cultural, and psychological ties on which much of the discussion of interdependence is based entails both potential benefits and costs. This is true even under conditions of asymmetrical interdependence; the relatively dependent actor inevitably will contain groups that could reap benefits from efforts to change the *status quo* even while leaders may judge the overall impact of such an effort as harmful to the national interest. In the case of the soaring energy prices that followed the oil boycott, for instance, Western banks stood to gain from the investment of recycled petrodollars; export industries acquired new markets for their products; and firms engaged in developing petroleum substitutes were suddenly provided with new economic incentives. At the same time, consumers and groups vulnerable to the inflationary effects of oil price rises were harmed. Thus, Licklider suggests that "the contribution of the oil weapon to Middle East policy change was at best indirect"; whatever change took place in policy he ascribes to "the increase in wealth rather than the fear of future oil supplies which the supply theory of economic sanctions would predict."[115] Ultimately, judgments regarding relative costs and benefits will be based on incomplete or murky information, and the final balance sheet will be at best crude, heavily influenced by subjective factors.

That balance sheet is, moreover, significantly affected by countervailing currents in global politics. Rising global interdependence produces external pressures on governments in the form of new potential costs and opportunities, while rising rates of participation at home create additional, often contradictory, pressures on leaders of states from within. The increasingly participatory nature of political cultures in both democratic and nondemocratic societies places severe constraints on formal decisionmakers' ability to act autonomously. The stability and even the survival of governments increasingly depend on their ability to satisfy a diversity of economic, ethnic, linguistic, ideological, and other interests; and many of these groups perceive their interests as contrary to the external pressures imposed by the logic of interdependence. Thus, recent protests in Seattle and in Prague against globalization are really protests against the fact of interdependence itself. We must be careful, however, not to confuse interdependence with authority. Although the protests are directed against interdependence, the protests themselves illustrate how globalization entails the erosion of state authority and the accelerating fragmentation of authority to smaller and more specialized polities and even individuals. The result is a further breakdown in global hierarchy and still greater "anarchy" as the concept has been used by realists and neorealists.

In the developing world, the growth in political consciousness and localist militancy has created powerful countercurrents to external pressures, making it extremely difficult and dangerous for elites to capitulate (or be seen to capitulate) to these pressures. Popular antipathy toward the IMF and the "banks," for instance, in a number of major debtor countries such as Indonesia, Brazil, Russia, and South Africa threaten the international monetary system. The intensification of local and sublocal "nationalisms" produces resistance to rising interdependence, repeatedly forcing local elites to act contrary to the logic of national or global interests produced by that interdependence. And it is less possible than ever to coerce apparently dependent societies to obey the norms of international regimes. Military intervention will produce massive local resistance; other forms of coercion will likely topple governments.

Developed societies have not escaped the consequences of this participation explosion. Its tremors were felt in the United States during the Vietnam War and are again felt as intense pressures build in favor of protectionist policies that could erode global trading norms and strategic policies (e.g., construction of an antiballistic missile system) that could threaten the fragile arms control regime. In Europe, too, the formerly protected character of policy-making in foreign and defense affairs is being challenged by social forces which threaten an Atlantic relationship that "serves the interests of so many states."[116] Until the late 1960s, the mutually profitable web of economic, political, and military arrangements was largely protected from attack by an elite consensus regarding the necessity of maintaining cooperative relations. Thereafter, the relative passivity of publics toward foreign and defense issues began to disappear, as greater access to higher education and the increasing impact of the mass media familiarized and sensitized people, especially youth, to controversial issues such as Vietnam, nuclear power, environmental degradation, nuclear arms, and more recently, globalization, immigration, and gasoline taxes.[117] Thus, during the debate over intermediate nuclear forces (INF) in the late 1970s and early 1980s European leaders came to appreciate the difficulty of steering a safe course between the Scylla of American pressure and the Charybdis of domestic protest.

In developed societies the ability to respond effectively to the logic of interdependence has also been complicated by the proliferation of giant bureaucracies with close ties to specific constituencies. In the ebb and flow of bureaucratic conflict and competition that often accompany political decisions (or nondecisions) in developed societies, individual bureaucrats and organizations are apt to represent the interests of their constituencies as well as their own organizational interests. To the extent this dual representation takes place, internal pressures as opposed to external exigencies further condition decisions.[118]

Internal pressures, including bureaucracies, that push decisionmakers in several directions must be factored into any cost-benefit equation. As we have suggested, they may well outweigh pressures imposed by the apparent logic of global interdependence. In the case of the 1973 oil embargo, the Arab effort to force developed societies to change their policies toward Israel enjoyed only modest success. A principal reason such pressure did not succeed, according to Licklider, was the existence of "unwritten but real limits on the kinds of concessions which were 'politically possible.'"[119] When internal pressures make it impossible for governments to respond "rationally" to the costs liable to be imposed by violating the norms of an international regime or by severing ties, it may almost seem as though behavior is autistic.

Levels of interdependence, then, do not predict much, nor is interdependence adequate to explain behavior. Indeed, the fact of growing interdependence tells us little more than that life is increasingly complex for decisional elites. Like other structural factors, it constrains and affords opportunities but does not determine decisions (either rational or irrational). Ultimately elites must determine the relative balance of the potential costs and benefits they are confronting on the basis of very incomplete information. Additionally, their evaluations of the impact of interdependence likely will vary by issue-area, often with only a rudimentary appreciation of possible linkages among issues. On some occasions, they will fail to see important linkages where they exist, as did Lyndon Johnson regarding the relationship between the Vietnam War and global inflation. On others, they may construct linkages that previously did not exist in order to justify their decisions after the fact. Many factors are likely to contribute to shaping the perceptions of decisionmakers about the nature of linkages and the relative costs and benefits imposed by interdependence or dependence. Among these are subjective definitions, political obligations, interest-group pressure, ideology, memories (individual and organizational), and personality attributes. Objective indicators like transaction flows and the availability of alternatives may encourage the theorist to advise decisionmakers that they *ought* to feel interdependent or dependent or run the risk of dire consequences for themselves and those for whom they are a surrogate. In the end, however, the latter's perceptions will be formed on the basis of both objective and subjective factors.

And even if there is consensus as to the probable costs associated with severing ties or the availability of substitute partners, actors will vary dramatically in terms of the price they are willing to pay for principle. Whereas Neville Chamberlain was willing to go to great lengths in 1938 to avoid the terrible price of war, Hungary (1956) and Czechoslovakia (1968) were prepared to risk terrible costs to assert their independence from the Soviet Union. Similarly, Cuba was objectively "dependent" on the United States in 1960 (and Washington was confident it could tighten the screws sufficiently to keep Havana in line), but Fidel Castro (unlike his predecessor, Fulgencio Batista) chose to seek political and economic substitutes at great "objective" cost (though perhaps great "subjective" gain).[120]

GLOBALIZATION

Just as economic and environmental crises in the 1970s focused academic attention on interdependence and regime theory, major developments in the last decade of the twentieth century put the spotlight on globalization.[121] Significantly, Keohane and Nye elected to add a new chapter on the subject in the latest revision of their book on interdependence.[122] These developments include the end of the Cold War and its companions—authority crises, civil conflicts, failed states, increased migration and refugees; a renewed interest in UN peacekeeping, punishing war crimes, and advancing human rights and democracy; impressive strides in computer technology and telecommunications, notably the Internet and e-mail; a consequent information revolution; a vast surge in corporate mergers, alliances, and networks; the increasing denationalization of production, services, and markets generally; the near-instantaneous movement of unprecedented amounts of money, attendant currency speculation, and recurrent monetary crises;[123] intensified concern about such environmental issues as global warming, ocean degradation, and vanishing species and ecosystems; the rapid spread of diseases like AIDS and other bioinvasions;[124] the transnational organization of terrorism, the illegal drug trade, human smuggling, and other criminal activities; the spread of Western popular culture; the fusion of cuisines; and so on. More and more observers began to write of the sheer pace of change; the increasing density and complexity of institutions, relationships, and transactions that transcend states; and of two closely related and linked currents: globalization and its antithesis, localization (Barber's Jihad vs. McWorld, Friedman's Lexus and olive tree, and Rosenau's "fragmegration").[125] Declares James Rosenau:

> What distinguishes globalizing processes, is that they are not hindered or prevented by territorial or jurisdictional barriers. They can spread rapidly across national boundaries and are capable of reaching into any community everywhere in the world. . . . [T]hey consist of all those forces that impel individuals, groups, societies, governments, institutions, and transnational organizations toward engaging in similar forms of behavior or participating in more encompassing and coherent processes, organizations, or systems. Contrariwise, localization derives from all those pressures that lead people, groups, societies, governments, institutions, and transnational organizations to narrow their horizons and withdraw to less encompassing processes, organizations, or systems.[126]

Globalization in the realm of theory is another step away from realism and neorealism, especially with regard to the central role of sovereign states. Globalization—perhaps even more than earlier approaches of international integration, transnationalism, interdependence, and regimes—felicitously highlights the significance of nonstate actors, multiple identities, and the multidimensional changes that appear to be affecting contemporary global politics. Globalization remains merely a "perspective" rather than a full-fledged theory, however, and a rather unsatisfactory one at that—in several respects. There is a grave problem of definition, which makes it extremely difficult to resolve arguments over how different the present era is from others that evinced substantial interdependence, like the late nineteenth and early twentieth centuries. Not only does globalization obviously have many different facets—economic, cultural, environmental, military, and so on—but also there are different dimensions even within those usual categories. For instance, the degree of "economic" globalization will surely appear very different if one's focus is on the ratio of internal to external trade in manufactured goods, capital investment, services, currency flows, or business organization and management styles. Moreover, globalizing trends continue to coexist with intensive bilateral and regional relationships. "Global cities" tend to be more engaged than national economies generally; the Northern Hemisphere in the global economy, rather than the Southern; elites rather than the masses. Yet there are significant exceptions to all of the foregoing generalizations.

There are other difficulties as well. Globalization suffers somewhat from the same sort of determinism—"the velocity of history" that "seems beyond our mortal capacity"[127]—or, at least, the rationality assumption, as some of its intellectual predecessors. Multidimensional changes seem to be altering the playing field of global politics dramatically, but they have not eliminated human choice and perception. Normative considerations, as always, remain central. Defenders of globalization (so called "globalists") point to its supposedly inexorable nature, the growth and increased efficiency of the world economy, and the degree to which cultural homogenization undermines dangerous national and ethnic parochialisms. Skeptics point to growing disparities in wealth, sweatshops in the developing world, environmental destruction, and the issue of a "democratic deficit."

At the end of the day, somewhat contradicting what we said at the outset of this section about globalization's being a step away from realism and neorealism, debates continue to rage about what effect it will actually have on the centrality of states in global politics.[128] Some analysts insist that the role of states is only changing rather than diminishing. This line of reasoning holds that states still will need to provide a stable legal environment, infrastructure improvements, police protection, and a variety of human services like better education and health care if they are to remain competitive in the global economy. Furthermore, they will be called upon by firms and citizens alike to craft legislation curbing market abuses and instability. To the extent that opening markets and fashioning new rules of the game require cooperation among states, they can in effect regain many of their "lost" prerogatives and stature through participation in international regimes. By contrast, we and others maintain that states are losing substantial control to other actors within and transcending their boundaries; that multidimensional changes are too sweeping and coming too rapidly for often gridlocked or otherwise incapacitated governments either adequately to understand or counter, whether individually or through regimes; that movements to a more facilitative role for states in the interest of competitiveness and towards more engagement in regimes cannot be disguised as anything but an effective loss of traditional state authority; and that over the longer run the implications for shifts in human identity and loyalties to other actors are bound to be profound.

CONCLUSION

Theoretical debate regarding the degree to which global politics is characterized by anarchy or solidarity is an enduring one. There is no greater consensus today regarding this key assumption than there was in classical antiquity.[129] Nor is there theoretical consensus as to the impact of these features on behavior in world politics. Like other debates in global politics, the theoretical controversy over anarchy is colored by hidden normative and policy preferences, an absence of conceptual clarity, and the repeated intrusion of policymakers' concerns and slogans into intellectual discourse.

Nevertheless, the field has come some distance since it was dominated by realism in the 1950s and 1960s. There has been a reawakening of interest in the cooperative side of global politics as opposed to conflict and, more generally, in liberal views that were dismissed as "idealism" and "utopianism" by early realists. A series of approaches including regional integration, systems, transnationalism and interdependence, international regimes, and globalization have focused on the links among actors and peoples and have tended to reduce the earlier emphasis on the sovereign prerogatives of states. Most of these perspectives also emphasize the dynamic elements in global politics, and several no longer maintain the pretense that facts and values are separable.

Where, then, does this leave us? In the following chapter, we shall try answer that question, suggesting some of the ways changing premises and methods make us less gloomy about the field than when *The Elusive Quest* appeared, while others are extremely disheartening, notably the flight from empiricism on the part of some theorists.

CHAPTER 9

The End
of the Elusive Quest?

By the late 1980s, when *The Elusive Quest* appeared, the quest for theory in global politics was becoming, if anything, increasingly elusive. Those embarked on that quest stood as in the midst of a maze, with the paths they had elected to pursue leading nowhere. There was no longer widespread confidence that the maze even had an entry or an exit, certainly no consensus as to what the objective was, and growing doubt as to whether what might be found would be worth the effort of continuing to look for it. Disappointed by the failure of science to realize its promise, political practitioners, some of whom (perhaps mistakenly) in the 1950s and 1960s had looked to the academic world for guidance in matters like deterrence, found little of interest or relevance in international relations theory and made little attempt to read it.

DEAD ENDS

The 1980s witnessed a decline in academic interest in the subject of theory. Many graduate students and professionals seemed to conclude that it was hardly worth trying to penetrate the turgid prose and jargon of many theoretically inclined books and journal articles because they had little of use to say. More and more academics turned to policy questions in journals like *Foreign Affairs* and *Foreign Policy* or to purely descriptive analyses of current events and issues, without attempting to explore the theoretical implications of their work. The resulting analyses were often journalistic or at least were soon overtaken by events. Without a coherent body of theory, the field of global politics existed but was not by any stretch of imagination a genuine discipline.

The absence of theory has serious consequences across all our concerns. McGowan and Shapiro, for example, acknowledged in 1973 with regard to the study of foreign policy:

Without theory we cannot explain the relationships we 'discover' and we can only make predictions of the crudest sorts based upon projections from empirical trends, not upon a profound understanding of foreign policy behavior. Without theory to guide our research we must depend upon luck and educated guesses to come up with worthwhile research hypotheses. Without theory research becomes ad hoc in the extreme, with no justification provided for the selection of cases, with no system to the definition and measurement of concepts, and with no consistency in the use of research techniques and data-processing routines. In brief, a field without theory is hardly an area of disciplined scientific inquiry. Since the comparative study of foreign policy lacks both middle-range and general theories of foreign policy behavior it fails to meet the basic objective of any science: a body of theoretically organized knowledge that is based on cumulative empirical research.[1]

When the 1980s came to a close, we were far from meeting even the less ambitious vision advanced in 1961 by Morton A. Kaplan before the idea of science had captured the field's imagination. Gloomily Kaplan predicted:

[O]ur explanations or theories can never have the authority of theory in physics, or its explanatory or predictive power. The important problem is whether they can be stated in ways that permit additional analysis and investigation. Whether they are tautological dead ends or fruitful aids to historical and scientific imagination, whether the statements in them permit at least reasonable analysis and investigation or whether they are dogmatic fiats, the science of the discipline does not lie in absolute certainty but in reasonable belief, in definite canons of procedure and investigation, and in the attempt to permit confirmation or falsification even though of an imprecise order. The object is not to seek a certainty or precision that the subject matter does not allow, but to reject a dogmatism that the subject matter does not make necessary. The very difficulties of theory building and confirmation in global politics demand sincere dedication to scientific canons of procedure.[2]

Why were we so far short of our goals? Kaplan was right up to a point, that the factors inhibiting the development of a powerful, predictive, theoretical social science are fundamental and . . . it is not merely a matter of waiting for a Galilean breakthrough."[3] First, global politics deals with matters that are exceedingly complex. The distinguished physicist Sir Brian Pippard remarks:

In olden days a prince of the church would employ a chaplain to remind him of his mortality. It would be no bad custom if at prize-giving ceremonies it was whispered in the ears of mathematicians and scientists, in their hour of triumph, that they had succeeded because they had chosen to tackle relatively straightforward problems, and that if politicians and social reformers [surely we might add persons studying global politics] are not so obviously successful it is because they have challenged problems of enormously greater complexity.[4]

In Pippard's view, the latter problems, "when represented by physical models, seem to belong to that class of problems that physicists find most difficult to reduce to order—problems of instability and chaos."[5]

The physical scientist, by contrast, normally focuses on problems in which only a relatively few number of major variables are relevant. Moreover, as Kaplan

stressed four decades ago, the physical scientist "carries on his studies and experiments in a laboratory that is closed to outer-world or historical forces." On the
other hand, "each science gets less theoretical as we move from laboratory generalizations to engineering applications and to the complexities and uncertainties of the real world."[6] Advocates of science did not ignore this, but they did
underestimate the problems it posed.

Theorists of global politics not only have a staggering number of potentially relevant and often linked variables with which to wrestle outside of a
closed laboratory setting; but also, unlike the physical scientists, they must
proceed with little agreement as to how variables should be labeled and
defined. One would be hard-pressed to find very many physical science terms
as vague as social science concepts like personality, power, state, anarchy, identity, interdependence, democracy, globalization, and so on. When concepts
such as these require separate definition by theorists, it seriously undercuts
the persuasiveness of generalizations resulting from their application. Any
agreement regarding definitions would be illusory at best because, as we have
seen, meanings shift in time and place in reaction to changing human norms
and commitments.

Another difficulty arises from the fact that in our effort to comprehend the
world around us there is no alternative but to build theories or models that
inevitably oversimplify whatever reality they model. "Pure empiricism," as Robert
Jervis argues, "is impossible: facts do not speak for themselves."[7] Adopting a theory or model, then, has the effect of channeling perceptions so as to filter out
contradictory evidence in the name of parsimony, which in turn leaves the theory or model open to the charge that it has neglected an important part of the
picture:

> The world is not so cleanly constructed that all the evidence supports only one the-
> ory. There are so many variables, accidents, and errors in observations that [in
> Thomas Kuhn's words] 'There is no such thing as research with counter-instances.'
> No parsimonious explanation for any actor's behavior in a complex set of cases will
> be completely satisfying. Some aspects of the truth simply do not make
> sense. . . . Because it is rare that all the facts are consistent with the same conclu-
> sion, the closer one looks at the details of a case the greater the chance that some
> of them will contradict the accepted explanation.[8]

For Kaplan, an advocate of system-level explanations, "as we come closer to
reality . . . we lose generality." Parsimony, then, becomes very important but
involves costs:

> If we want to apply our models to concrete cases, we must choose just those factors
> and just those factor values that we have some reason to believe operate in the par-
> ticular instance we wish to understand and explain. In the endeavor, as our analy-
> sis gains in richness of relevant detail, we face a continuing loss of generality and a
> growing vagueness and lack of specification concerning the weight that each factor
> contributes to the total event or situation. This is the price we must pay when we
> deal with actual history.[9]

   An optimist might note that fragmentation in theory building is a reflection of the fragmentation of world politics itself and that a proliferation of perspectives is a necessary prelude to later coherence. But one must not hide behind complexity alone, in the sense of numbers of variables. Marion Levy is probably correct in asserting that "the level of complexity that faces one varies as an inverse function of the state of one's theory."[10] We have no way of knowing in advance just how many variables are relevant to our concerns. But there is a more important sort of complexity that becomes apparent in efforts to isolate and study specific variables: Such reductionism isolates selected factors from their context when it is the context itself in which we are interested. Thus, empirical elements are sifted and viewed apart from the normative yeast that animates them and lends them meaning.

   Were we advancing along the path outlined by Thomas Kuhn, the general-versus-specific dilemma and other issues would be resolved through a gradual refinement of models in the progress of normal science. When a model proves inadequate, the usual and proper reaction is not to abandon it entirely but, as Pippard puts it, to "modify it if we can or, at least, recognize its limitations—'I don't really understand so-and-so,' we say."[11] On the other hand, the replacement of even a dominant paradigm with another is possible and may be necessary if too many anomalies are observed and problems of major importance, remain unsolved as a result.

   Kuhn's analysis of the process of scientific progress, as we have seen, greatly encouraged a post-World War II generation of scholars who were determined to make the study of global politics more scientific. Many still hold that the theoretical fragmentation and ferment which ensued offer substantial evidence of real progress in Kuhnian terms. Such an interpretation is a misreading of Kuhn, however, because it obscures the reasons for the field's plight at the time. Kuhn insisted, in the first instance, that scientific progress must start with a genuinely dominant paradigm. Retrospectively, realism seemed the nearest thing to such a paradigm in global politics, but it was far from a genuine one. In fact, it was less a theory than a set of normative emphases that shape theory, a self-contained syllogism that closes off further analysis and sustains a particular theology. Second, Kuhn stressed that an existing paradigm is discarded only when an alternative is available and that, meanwhile, progress is achieved through the process of normal science within the accepted framework.

   In contrast to Kuhn's description, the self-styled scientific revolution in global politics was mainly methodological, and there was little agreement from the outset on a common research agenda. Theorists started off in any number of different directions, with no consensus as to the basic puzzles to be addressed or the concepts and methodologies to be employed. Hence, lines of research were essentially idiosyncratic, without the kind of convergence that seems to make for cumulative knowledge in the Kuhnian sense. Knorr and Verba recognized in 1961 that "in the long run, progress will be made in theories of the international system only if various approaches begin to converge and move in the same direction. Only in that way will our work, both theoretical and empirical, begin to be cumulative."[12] Unfortunately, after a fairly long run, theory in the field appears more divergent and consequently less cumulative than before. Perhaps we have seriously misunderstood the enterprise itself.

THE FLIGHT FROM EMPIRICISM

By the 1990s, the pessimism that permeated *The Elusive Quest* book had spread throughout the field. Others had concluded, as we had, that part of the problem was the failed effort to separate facts and values, with the latter *largely being ignored*. Unfortunately, in some circles what followed was a wholesale flight from empiricism, an aesthetic and intellectual relativism, and on the whole, a further retreat from reality. Some scholars abandoned facts and focused only on values.

In an article published in 1989, a year after *The Elusive Quest* first appeared, Yosef Lapid announced "the demise of the empiricist-positivist promise for a cumulative behavioral science." In consequence, declared Lapid, "some of the most highly prized premises of Western academic discourse concerning the nature of our social knowledge, its acquisition, and its utility—including shibboleths such as 'truth,' 'rationality,' 'objectivity,' 'reality,' and 'consensus,'—have come under renewed critical reflection."[13] Whereas we bemoaned the breakup of the field into a multitude of quarreling coteries, Lapid welcomed such pluralism as a way of opening "thinking space" and reducing the dominance of the field by American academics.

Lapid saw the field of international relations as engaged in a third debate—the first two having been "idealism versus realism" and "history versus science." Just as "history versus science" marked "the ascendance of positivism in Western social science," so the third debate was connected "to the confluence of diverse anti-positivistic philosophical and sociological trends."[14] Lapid believed there was reason to "celebrate" this new debate in contrast to the despairing words of others he cites, such as Waltz, who grumbled, "Among the depressing features of international-political studies is the small gain in explanatory power that has come from the large amount of work done in recent decades. Nothing seems to accumulate, not even criticism."[15]

Having identified the debate as taking place between positivists and postpositivists, Lapid admitted that postpositivism "is not a unitary philosophical platform" but rather "a rather loosely patched-up umbrella for a confusing array of only remotely related philosophical articulations."Three themes seemed to him to underlie the debate: "the preoccupation with meta-scientific units (paradigmatism), the concern with underlying premises and assumptions (perspectivism), and the drift towards methodological pluralism (relativism)."The first referred to a shift away from "the positivist choice of the empirically corroborated law or generalization as the fundamental unit of scientific achievement" to the "relatively long-lived, and multi-tiered constructs—such as 'paradigms' (Kuhn, 1962), 'research-programmes' (Lakatos, 1970), 'research traditions' (Laudan, 1984), 'global theories' (Hooker, 1987), and 'Weltanschauungen' (Wisdom, 1987)—[as] knowledge-producing, knowledge-accumulating, and knowledge-conserving units."[16]

The rethinking of assumptions or "perspectivism" was most "audible" "among a small but vocal group of 'postpositivist,' 'post-structuralist,' and 'postmodernist' critics of mainstream international relations."These had in common the claim that "meaning and understanding are not intrinsic to the world but, on the contrary, are continuously constructed, defended, and challenged. Their main purpose is to 'problemize' answers, make 'strange' what has become familiar, and reverse the process of construction in order to reveal how problematic are the taken-for-granted structures ('anarchy' for instance) of our social and political world."[17] Many of those most interested in questioning assumptions also, according to Lapid, offered an epistemology steeped in "relativism." Such relativism not only questions individual truth claims, but also "implied and embedded standards, criteria, norms, and principles that *make judgments possible and give them privileged status.*"[18] Refusing to accept any criteria for regulating science makes it difficult to legitimate knowledge. Accepting "a multitude of potentially fruitful research strategies," and undermining scientific consensus, declares Lapid, indicated "a collapse of the highly influential Kuhnian equation of an inability to achieve paradigmatic consensus with an inability to achieve significant theoretical growth."[19]

Lapid wrote optimistically about "postpositivist messages." First, "preoccupation with meta-scientific constructs," he viewed as preferable to "the positivist choice of the empirically corroborated law or generalization as the fundamental unit of scientific achievement" because of the absence of the "cumulative progress" promised by empiricists. By contrast, the proliferation of "paradigms" or "research programs" was indicative of a maturing discipline. Second, a return to first principles and a rethinking of long-accepted premises promised "vigorous theoretical growth through available substitutions or revisions of 'defective' thematic premises." In other words, facts were coming less and less to dominate theory, and the purportedly scientific methodology that had dominated the discipline had to confront rivals. Positivist science had been "the tragedy of international relations scholars," and positivism had "locked" the discipline "in a sterile and frustrating worshipful relationship to the natural sciences."[20]

Lapid's enthusiasm for the new currents of postpositivist thinking was tempered by recognition that "paradigmatism" might be used for polemical ends. Dilution of positivist criteria of evidence might create "tempting opportunities for instant scientific redemption of vast bodies of theoretical literature by simple shifts of epistemic standards of appraisal." For its part, "perspectivism" ran the risk of confusing rather than clarifying the debate. Finally, and most dangerous, was the relativism implied by postpositivism that might produce "epistemological anarchy" under which "almost any position can legitimately claim equal hearing."[21]

More than a decade later, Lapid's optimism about the third debate seems only partly merited. Acquaintance with Nietzsche, Wittgenstein, Derrida, and Foucault provided fodder for relativist ideas. Language, the relativists and "dissidents" concluded, reflects normative and political biases, which enter into the problems we seek to study, the ways we address them, and the conclusions we reach. This argument was a seductive challenge to both empiricists and conventional normative theorists. Initially, the argument found favor in Europe, where many scholars had never accepted the premises of the scientists and were searching for a genuine European "voice."

For empirical theorists like Peter Katzenstein Robert Keohane, and Stephen Krasner postpositivism and self-styled postmodernists were regarded as dangerous and seditious. Anger was evident in neorealist Robert Gilpin's attack on Richard Ashley's 1984 demolition of neorealism that appeared in *International Organization*:

> Speaking of philosophy and the clarity that its ancient Greek inventors hoped it would bring to our thinking, what is an accused to make of the following: "For eschatological discourse . . . the objective truth of the discourse lies within and is

produced by the discourse itself." (section 2c). Unfortunately, *International Organization* failed to send an English translation with the original text. Therefore, although I am sure that this statement and many like it throughout the article are meaningful to Ashley, I have no idea what it means. It is this needless jargon, this assault on the language that gives us social scientists a bad name.[22]

For their part, Katzenstein, Keohane, and Krasner conclude that "postmodernism falls clearly outside of the social science enterprise, and in international relations research it risks becoming self-referential and disengaged from the world, protests to the contrary notwithstanding."[23]

What the empiricists did no grasp was that the relativists were engaged in games of another sort: language games with double entendres and other clever word play.[24] "All interpretations," as Martin Hollis declares, "become defensible but at the price that none is more justifiable than the rest. If this is indeed the upshot, the circle turns vicious and the hermeneutic imperative to understand from within leads to disaster."[25] Language was indeed a casualty of the third debate. Charles Hostovsky was wickedly close to the mark when he argued that, for postmodernists, "plainly expressed language is out of the question" because it is "too realist, modernist and obvious." "Postmodern language required that one use play, parody and indeterminacy as critical techniques to point this out. Often this is quite a difficult requirement, so obscurity is a well-acknowledged substitute." Sometimes a writer did not have time to "muster even the minimum number of postmodern synonyms and neologisms to avoid public disgrace," hence one strategy was "to use as many suffixes, prefixes, hyphens, slashes, underlinings and anything else your computer . . . can dish out." Top it all off by inserting "a few names [e.g., Continental European theorists] whose work everyone will agree is important and hardly anyone has had the time or inclination to read [as in de/gendered-Baudrillardian discourse]."[26] Then hope that someone does not ask what you are talking about, in which case you could always reply with more postmodern-speak.

Disappointment with the fruits of science prepared the ground for a variety of postpositivist projects that rejected strict science and emphasized the subjective dimensions of knowledge.[27] Such projects were also partly a consequence of the rapidly changing nature of global reality, skepticism about the power tradition and grand theory more generally, and the ensuing anarchy that characterized theory in the field. Postmodernists "deconstructed" and helped to undermine traditional theories, which in some respects has been for the good, and reemphasized the normative dimension in global politics. Unfortunately, postmodernism in none of its guises has yet provided a serious foundation upon which to reconstruct a theory of global politics, which indeed was eschewed by postmodernists from the outset as an impossible and even undesirable goal. Thus, Richard Ashley, as interpreted by Darryl Jarvis, does not seek "a theory of world politics as a tool of analysis to foster greater understanding, but . . . a means to transformation and ideological insurrection, a strategy to overturn, destroy, and then make anew the discipline and its theory in forms that few would recognize."[28]

A number of variants of postmodernism emerged. At one pole were extreme relativists or poststructuralists, including James Der Derian, Richard Ashley, Jim George, David Campbell, and Michael J. Shapiro.[29] They were intellectual heirs of Jacques Derrida, Michel Foucault, Ludwig Wittgenstein, and others who insisted that language made sense only in particular contexts.[30] For Derrida, context is individuals; for Foucault, social (power relations); and for Wittgenstein, the rules of a particular "game" in which language is engaged. In the view of poststructuralists, language has no dependable meaning, but, since the world can be described only through language, our views of it are undependable and fundamentally incommunicable to others. Language must, therefore, be continually "deconstructed" and its "genealogies" explored to reveal the different versions of reality ("discourses") reflected therein. There is no such thing as a better epistemology, only hermeneutics, or the philosophical concern with understanding and interpretation. New language must be invented and used, both to shock readers out of their complacency and to describe new understandings, however ephemeral they may be.

Postmodernists conclude that there is no hope for genuine human progress, only the inevitable alienation and exile encountered in an essentially meaningless universe. Critical theory is often loosely classified as one fairly wide branch of postmodernism. Writing of critical theory, Kubálková, Onuf, and Kowert declare:

> Philosophers have used the term in a specialized sense that goes back to Immanuel Kant. In the hands of Marxist theorists, it acquired a different, though still specialized, meaning. Other scholars had always used the term to refer to the "ability to find defects and faults," once regarded as a critical faculty of every scholar. Thanks to the diffusion of a specifically neo-Marxist dialect, scholars in several disciplines now use the term in ways that neither Kant nor any ordinary person would understand. . . . Not being critical might mean that a scholar is positivist or interested only in proposing policies to solve narrowly defined problems.[31]

Some versions of feminist theory overlap with postmodernism, especially its emphases on language as power and on identity. Feminists argue that what is missing from much of global politics is the dimension of gender.[32] According to J. Ann Tickner, feminists regard gender as characteristics associated with masculinity (e.g., "power, autonomy, rationality, and public") and the opposite characteristics with femininity (e.g., "weakness, dependence, emotion, and private"). Both men and women assign "a more positive value to masculine characteristics," and gender relations "affect every aspect of human experience," including global politics. How did this come to be? "While many feminists do see structural regularities, such as gender and patriarchy, they define them as socially constructed and variable across time, place, and cultures, rather than as universal and natural." Although not all feminist theorists are postmodern or even postpositivist, most, according to Tickner, are properly classified as "critical" theorists and have "a preference for hermeneutic, historically based, humanistic and philosophical traditions of knowledge cumulation, rather than those based on the natural sciences." In her view, "feminists cannot be anything but skeptical of universal truth claims and explanations associated with a body of knowledge from which women have frequently been excluded as knowers and subjects." "While feminist perspectives do not claim to tell us everything we need to know about the behavior of states or the workings of the global economy, they are telling us things that have too often remained invisible."[33] Much the same, of course, could be said about literature on indigenous peoples[34] and gays, whose "nation" has been regarded as "alien" far beyond the condition of "straight" humans in the current age.

The broader condition of alienation was central to another strain of critical theory, typified by the work of Jürgen Habermas and the Frankfurt School. Habermas argued that, whereas class divisions were the main source of conflict and change in Karl Marx's day, these had lessened in modern society to the point where business, government, and labor had compromised on welfare capitalism. To the extent that that compromise was threatened, it could either aggravate what Habermas called "crises of legitimation" or open more opportunities for constructive dissonance. Such crises arose, he believed, from the technocratic character of the political order in which ordinary individuals have little role or direct stake. Hope for the future in his view lay in social movements—ranging from environmental groups to religious revivals—that try to reinject values into political debate. What Habermas presented, argues Giddens, was nothing less than "a radical defense of human freedom," although he offers just the vaguest outline of how the reforms he earnestly desires might be achieved.[35]

Habermas was not a relativist, as Felipe Fernández-Armesto explains:

> Repelled by nihilism, [Habermas] has tried to rebuild the fragments of the 'deconstructed' world. His greatest enemy is the self; so he directs [us toward] truth [as] a collective enterprise, in which we learn from each other. As a truth-finding strategy, this is objectionable on the grounds that is vague and slow; as a political prescription, it can be criticized for endorsing woolly minded 'community politics.' But it has merits [in that] it is humane, undogmatic, solidly rooted in tradition, optimistic and, in effect, good for the individual who practices it and the society which benefits from it."[36]

In fact, postmodernism is one of a cluster of approaches that share a belief that knowledge is less a consequence of impartial inquiry than an expression of power relations in social and cultural contexts. Far from being a neutral seeker after truth, the scholar, in Steve Smith's words, "is always caught up in a language and mode of thinking which, far from interpreting a world, instead constructs it."[37] "[P]ostmodernism is essentially a 'contrast concept,'" declares Krishan Kumar. "It takes its meaning as much from what it excludes or claims to supersede as from what it includes or affirms in any positive sense. The primary, or at least initial, meaning of post-modernism must be that it is not modernism, not modernity. Modernity is over." Well, yes, except that there remains some debate about in what sense postmodernism is "post"? "The 'post' of postmodernity," as Kumar admits, is ambiguous. "It can mean what comes after, the movement to a new state of thing, however difficult it might be to characterize that state in these early days. Or it can be more like the post of *post-mortem*: obsequies performed over the dead body of modernity, a dissection of the corpse. The end of modernity is in this view the occasion for reflecting on the experience of modernity; post-modernity is that condition of reflectiveness. In this case there is no necessary sense of a new beginning, merely a somewhat melancholy state of an ending."[38]

But what was "modernism"? As Kumar points out, "modernity" and "modernism" are often used interchangeably and also might be different. He prefers to use "modernity" to mean "all of the changes . . . that brought into being the modern world" and to reserve "modernism" for the late-nineteenth-century cultural movement in the West that was partly a reaction against modernity. The first meaning is the one that most postmodernists adopt, although the second reminds us that postmodernism, like most "isms," has antecedents. Even before the modern era, as Fernández-Armesto observes, Protagoras's "guiding maxim" was that man "is the measure of all things that are and the non-existence of the things that are not." Socrates found such relativism profoundly disturbing. "Is this not roughly what [Protagoras] means," he said, "that things are for me such as they appear to me, and for you such as they appear to you?" Socrates, reports Fernández-Armesto, "confessed to 'vexation and actual fear. . . . After whirling all day in a vortex of circular arguments, Socrates dismissed them all as 'wind' and postponed the discussion to a morning which, in surviving texts, never comes."[39]

Rebellion against aspects of modernity has been going on for a long time. "The early revolts in Rousseau, Romanticism and other developments of the early nineteenth century," declares Kumar, "yield nothing to later examples in their force and clarity." Unlike later revolts, the earlier movements retained a sense that the world could still be redeemed, not altogether unlike some versions of contemporary postmodernist thought of a "critical" variety. Kierkegaard and Nietzsche were more pessimistic about the prospects for "civilization," as were Baudelaire and Rimbaud. Authors from Eliot, Proust, Woolf, and Joyce to Strindberg, Brecht, and Faulkner also broke dramatically with traditional forms, playing with ideas and language through such techniques as stream of consciousness and free verse. Stravinsky and Berg assaulted established tonal music. Artists like Picasso and Braque, philosophers like Sorel and William James, architects like Wright and Le Corbusier, and psychiatrists like Freud and Jung were equally "antimodernist" from time to time. Dadaists during and after World War I "attacked all the official ideas and institutions that had conspired to produce the mess," even art itself, "the sacred cow of the establishment." Surrealists like "Dali and Buñuel aimed to show that the fantastic was as real as the reality revealed by modern science."[40]

Arguments and visions of apocalypse or cries for reform have also been around for a long time. Marx was an alien thinker in his day and still inspires some postmodernists. But the political system and industrial economy built by Stalin was modernity at its most monolithic and oppressive. As David Ashley reports:

> By the 1950s, the work of abstract expressionists such as Jackson Pollock was being funded by the Central Intelligence Agency as part of an official state effort to demonstrate that American artists were more 'advanced,' more imaginative, and more 'progressive' than their Soviet counterparts. This propaganda effort . . . was additionally intended to win the hearts and minds of avant-garde intellectuals, many of whom stubbornly continued to insist that Marxism had more to offer the world than Dwight Eisenhower's America.[41]

The Great Satan for nearly all postmodernists was strict empiricism or positivism. According to Jim George, there is "no logical basis, even in positivism's own terms, for the proposition that knowledge of reality is directly derived from an independent world 'out there,'"[42] and, adds David Campbell, "nothing exists outside of discourse."[43] To be sure, in the 1960s the prophets of science oversold their particular brand of salvation, and postmodernists were rebelling against those like J. David Singer and other modernists who had been "quite alert to the epistemological concerns of philosophy but often indifferent to its normative concerns."[44] Data and method, rather than the normative concerns raised by threats of nuclear war, environmental overload, human rights abuses, a globalized economic system, and so forth, too often seemed to drive empirical analyses. Ultimately, according to postmodernists, cumulating insights based on induction contributed little to understanding the world.

Thus, a major casualty of criticisms of the (non)accomplishments of the field's scientists and the anarchy that engulfed theory building was empiricism itself, as postpositivist scholarship—hermeneutics, critical theory, and postmodernism—rejected the assumptions underpinning empirical research. Some of this reaction, as we have suggested, was a healthy corrective to the unalloyed positivism adopted by many of the field's mainstream scholars and its refusal to acknowledge the field's normative and subjective dimensions. Theory and the information and interpretation it conveys *do* reflect and reinforce power relations among and within societies and cultures; and scholars (and practitioners), while seeking to explain the world around them, *do*—wittingly or unwittingly— help to construct it by what they say and do.

Even though undermining traditional theories and opening up "thinking space" were contributions of postmodernism, the movement did *not* formulate a basis for reconstructing theory in global politics; and, in throwing empiricism out the window with positivism or strict science, it threatened to make theory irrelevant. In asserting that knowledge and understanding are constructed from language and that "reality" is, therefore, open to a possibly infinite number of interpretations, none of which can claim precedence, postmodernists rejected the possibility of truth claims and even undermined their own fervently expressed desire to restore the ethical foundations of political life. If we accept their argument that no clear distinction can be made between ourselves as observers of reality and reality itself, then truth and judgment are no longer accessible beyond individual understanding and reflection. In the end, it may prove at best dangerous and at worst impossible to reform the world without trusting our observations of it.

For the field's "dissidents," knowledge and understanding are less important than smashing the crockery, creating conceptual chaos, and manipulating language to twit those who traditionally dominated the pages of leading professional journals. Postmodernism's "central tenet," according to Steve Smith, "is one which seeks nothing less than the overthrow of virtually all preceding positions on epistemology."[45] Whether we accept Fred Halliday's harsh conclusion that "'scientific' and 'professional' forms of analysis and theorisation" are a "feckless cult" that "has been an almost wholly unmitigated catastrophe for the study of international relations," we can sympathize with his characterization of "its apparent opposite, the more recent flight into various forms of relativism and post-modernism." He writes, "Beyond a set of suggestive, but by no means original, claims about meaning, discourse and the position of the speaker, this trend is remarkable above all for claims to rational analysis, and for an affectation of language and reference."[46]

But is everything we "know," including the puzzles we choose to address as, subjective as postmodernists claim? *Is it all agent, and no structure?* The answer is yes and no. Consider an example from literary criticism (which, after all, was a major inspiration for postmodernism): the works of Ernest Hemingway. Hemingway's most famous persona is the macho writer who chronicled heroism in the Spanish Civil War or matadors defying death in the bullring. Then there is the existential Hemingway familiar to college students who read "A Clean Well-Lighted Place" and experience the anguish of its key characters, who are deeply suspicious that there is *nada* at the root of all. Most surprising is the androgynous Hemingway of the posthumous novel, *The Garden of Evil*, in which the main protagonists of both sexes continually switch roles. Other readers might mention his *verismo* journalism and travel accounts, or his political activism including his actual participation in the Spanish Civil War and intelligence boat runs in the Caribbean during World War II. There are thus "several" Hemingways and perhaps more than have yet been "discovered," either by way of interpretation or because more manuscripts are still waiting in a vault somewhere. But there are only a limited number of the author's views that can reasonably serve as a basis for fruitful discussion. It would be difficult to convince anyone that Hemingway was a master of science fiction or a crusader for anticolonialism in Africa. Indeed, theory guides us toward some interpretations and away from others.

It is much the same with historical interpretation. What caused the collapse of classical Mayan civilization? Was it land exhaustion from overcropping? Lack of water compounded by drought? Other natural disasters such as pestilence or plagues of locusts? A revolt of peasants against their oppressors? Constant warfare among Mayan cities? There is some evidence for each of these interpretations or, most probably, more than one of them operating together. We can discuss these things and literally dig for further evidence. But there are not an infinite number of possibilities, and all explanations are not equally plausible. Although some sensationalists have suggested that extraterrestials visited and helped inspire Mayan civilization, no one has maintained that aliens took them all away in spaceships.

Likewise there are multiple interpretations of the causes of the Cold War and its eventual demise?[47] Was the Cold War a realist struggle for power or a clash of two superpowers in a neorealist bipolar contest? Was it a war between two incompatible political and economic ideologies, that is, democracy and capitalism versus totalitarian socialism? How much was misperception on both sides? How much was the struggle a product of personalities like the paranoid Stalin? How much was dictated by history and national character: Russians acting like Russians, Americans in one of their "periodic fits" of morality? Once again, there are convincing arguments for these and other factors affecting outcomes either alone or in various combinations. It is an interesting and useful debate with manageable parameters. But no one is seriously suggesting that bears and eagles are natural enemies.

Is everything of importance subjective? Is language no more than a means of exerting power? Can we discuss and debate ideas despite personal biases, weasel language, and imperfect information? Whether or not the readers of this book accept our arguments, we assume they understand what we are saying—and that there are only a limited number of counterarguments that are admissible. Although deconstructionists properly highlight the ambiguities of language that make it difficult for truth-seekers to communicate, not least the ambiguity of social science concepts, it does not mean that the "stories" advanced by social scientists are tales told by idiots. Although there may be no such thing as absolute truth—at least none that is ever fully discernible to us in a changing universe—there is often a sufficient amount of intersubjective consensus to make for a useful conversation arising out of common identity, norms, and culture, which produce common expectations about legitimate behavior.[48] That conversation may not lead to proofs that satisfy metaphysicians or strict scientists, but it can be illuminating.

And what is to replace empiricism? "Dissidents" freely admit that they want to shatter the little theoretical consensus that existed in the name of "an ethics of freedom" but deny any responsibility for providing a serious alternative: "[D]issident scholars," wrote Ashley and Walker, "have persistently refused to do what many insist they are obliged to do. . . . They have not offered a new paradigm. . . . Indeed, to read almost any dissident text is to find not only a formal refusal or paradigmatic conceit but also a series of textual moves that function to disrupt any attempt to conduct a memorializing reading and turn a text into a paradigm of any sort."[49]

There is nothing here to go on, except a sort of self-righteous purity of noncommitment, and it does not justify abandoning empiricism. Unlike postmodernists, we have little wish to throw the baby out with the bathwater. At the end of the day, we remain empiricists and have no inherent objection to science, only skepticism (based on past nonperformance) that positivism or strict science can produce much in the way of convincing results. Yes, empirically oriented theorists of global politics often ignored the subjective and normative dimensions of what they did,[50] but this does not mean that we are unable to acquire useful knowledge about global politics independent of the language we use or that we cannot distinguish between an observer and that which is observed. With no standards for evidence, why should an observer accept the postmodernist perspective more than any other? Or as Roger Scruton puts it, "The man who tells you truth doesn't exist is asking you not to believe him. So don't."[51] Ah yes, but why then should we believe Roger Scruton?

CONSTRUCTIVISM: A PROMISING COMPROMISE?

For those of us who had been arguing for years about the need to take account of the subjective dimension of global politics, the popularity of constructivism in the 1990s was a welcome development. In a real sense, this popularity owed much to the fact that the perspective, while not offering a full-blown theory of global politics or even a research program (what else is new?), seemed a compromise between the "brute facts" of scientists and the antiempiricism of postpositivists, and between the claims of those who assumed rationality and those who denied it.[52] Contrary to Marion Levy's prophecy, the scientific approach has not generated "a set of generalized propositions containing variables . . . with deductive interdependencies among the members of the set,"[53] yet postmodernism seems extremely remote from the reality of global politics. Constructivists do not abandon facts, but they distinguish among different classes of facts. The fact that we are cultural beings, argues John Ruggie,

> gives rise to a class of facts that do not exist in the physical object world: social facts, or facts that . . . depend on human agreement that they exist and typically require human institutions for their existence. Social facts include money, property rights,

sovereignty, marriage, football, and Valentine's Day, in contrast to such brute observational facts as rivers, mountains, population size, bombs, bullets, and gravity,
which exist whether or not there is agreement that they do.[54]

Realists and neorealists reject constructivist subjectivism. Krasner, borrowing from James March and Johan Olsen, distinguishes between constructivist
"logics of appropriateness"—which sees action as a result of rules, roles, and
identities—and realist "logics of consequence"—which sees action "as the product of rational calculating behavior designed to maximize a given set of unex-
plained preferences." He argues that, owing to the relative obscurity of roles and
rules in global politics in contrast to domestic politics, "the international system
is an environment in which the logics of consequences dominate the logics of
appropriateness."[55] As we have seen, however, the boundary between domestic
and international is coming down and was always seriously overestimated. In
addition, though sometimes murky, there are many discernible rules and features of the game in global politics (or at least most actors discern them). In the
end, action in global politics is probably the result of some combination of both
of Krasner's logics.[56]

Social facts acquire meaning through the dynamic interaction of "agents"
and "structures," or actors and the environment in which they act. Collective
understanding and agreement about social facts, then, is the product of practice
within particular social contexts. But what is the relationship between agents and
structures in global politics?

Decades earlier, the levels-of-analysis "problem" had been a hot theoretical
issue, not least because it reflected differences among theoretical perspectives in
a young discipline. Realists saw a world of individual states as actors; others
focused on individuals, especially decisionmakers; and still others, like Waltz,
attributed the course of events to what they saw as the basic structure of the global
system. In fact, the "problem" was probably exaggerated then as now, because it
was more properly a logical problem of parts and wholes than an empirical question. Nearly everybody knew that decisionmakers reflected influences from their
environment, that leaders' behavior could sometimes be erratic (even Hans
Morgenthau lamented that some decisionmakers, blinded by morality or ideology, often failed to act like realists), and that they could misperceive the "objective national interest" of their countries or identify it with parochial interests. In
fact, causal chains seemed to differ issue by issue and case by case. In one case,
structure might seem the most powerful influence; in another, personality; in yet
another, a widely shared consensus about national interest, and so on.

Oddly enough, theorists did not start to accommodate deviations from
dominant state-centric and neorealist modes until the 1980s, when the lessons of
political psychologists like Robert Jervis finally began to take hold.
Postmodernism made subjectivity downright normal, and British sociologist
Anthony Giddens's structuration theory and his sociological approach had an
impact in certain intellectual circles that were unwilling to embrace relativism
with open arms.[57] Giddens argued that structural properties constrained behavior but also were reinforced by that behavior, thereby producing what Frank
Ninkovich described as "an active process of interpretation and construction of
reality."[58] Thus, the "agent/structure problem" was born, a mutation of the old
levels-of-analysis problem.[59] It represented a rebellion against what Hall calls the

"[f]ailure to recognize that the functioning of a system is dependent on the variable 'needs,' motivation, interests, and agency of social actors" which is "the greatest error of structural realist teleologies."[60]

Individual agents' perceptions of their environment, including its structures, condition their actions, which in turn affect the environment/structures in which they are engaged, and then returns in a giant feedback loop to influence the perceptions and behavior of individual agents. In fact, it is difficult to see how "agent" and "structure" can be separated, in that each conditions and "constitutes" the other in a continuous process. All actions and decisions take place within some context, and actors (along with their perceptual and normative baggage) and structures necessarily are part of that context. Behavior, then, reflects a mix of voluntarism and determinism.

Constructivist thought nevertheless has focused on the agent/structure issue. "Since the mid-1980s," write Katzenstein, Keohane, and Krasner, "a new debate between constructivism and rationalism (including both realism and liberalism) has become prominent" in which "constructivists, influenced by new trends in the humanities, put forward sociological perspectives that emphasized shared norms and values but which were in epistemological terms sharply differentiated from postmodernism."[61] "[S]tudents of international politics," adds Alexander Wendt, "have increasingly accepted two basic tenets of 'constructivism': (1) that the structures of human association are determined primarily by shared ideas rather than material forces, and (2) that the identities and interests of purposive actors are constructed by these shared ideas rather than given by nature."[62] Thus, facts mean little until observers give them meaning, and such meanings are themselves facts that we construct. In this way, norms and values are facts.

Since conventional constructivists emphasize how ideas and norms "constitute agents and their interests," they "differ sharply from rationalists on questions of ontology."[63] Rationalists, argue Katzenstein, Keohane, and Krasner, emphasize "preferences, information, strategies and common knowledge," whereas constructivists emphasize "identities, norms, knowledge, and interests." Thus, whereas rationalists like regime theorists emphasize the role of positive and negative incentives in achieving preferred outcomes, constructivists "insist on the importance of social processes that generate changes in normative beliefs, such as those prompted by the antislavery movement of the nineteenth century, the contemporary campaign for women's rights as human rights, or nationalist propaganda."[64] Identities and interests are not exogenous, constructivists argue, they are "constituted" by practices and intersubjective agreement.

Constructivism, it is important to recognize, has at least two distinct branches. One, lately popularized by Wendt, focuses on the way decisionmakers of states perceive their environments. The environment is supposedly objective, but decisionmakers' understanding of it and their own policy priorities reflect the subjective side of global politics. Of course, the Sprouts, who never heard of constructivism, made a similar distinction between objective and subjective environments decades ago. Wendt groups his brand of constructivism with postmodernists, feminists, and others into a "family of theories" loosely classified as "critical IR theory." He writes, "All observation is theory-*laden* in the sense that what we see is mediated by our existing theories, and to that extent knowledge is problematic. But this does not mean that observation, let alone reality, is theory-*determined*. The world is still out there constraining our beliefs, and may punish us for incorrect ones." Wendt offers the example of Aztec Emperor Montezuma who thought the Spanish were gods and paid dearly for that misperception.

Note well, however, as we also stressed previously, that in Wendt's constructivism, "anarchy" in the modern world is still what "states make of it"[65] and he admits to sharing most of the other central assumptions of realism.[66] When all is said and done, reified states are the actors whose perceptions matter most to Wendt. Perhaps the fact that one can be almost a realist in the Bull tradition[67] and just a little bit postmodern too helps account for the wide appeal of his state-centric constructivism.

There is another broad stream of constructivism that is far less tied to realism than to Durkheim and the legal realism of Myres McDougal and others of the Yale school of international law, which in global politics evolved through the work of Giddens, Nicholas Onuf, Friedrich Kratochwil, and John Ruggie.[68] Ruggie's definition of episteme, which he acknowledges owes much to Foucault, was an early effort to emphasize the importance of the intersubjective construction of meaning. Epistemes, he wrote, "refer to a dominant way of looking at social reality, a set of shared symbols and references, mutual expectations and a mutual predictability of intention. Epistemic communities may be said to consist of interrelated roles which grow up around an *episteme;* they delimit, for their members, *the* proper construction of social reality."[69] For his part, Onuf dislikes the term "structure" and prefers to address the continuous and reciprocal relationship between people and society, mediated by rules that include but are not limited to legal rules. As he, Kratochwil, and others discuss it, rules shape the relationships of a wide range of actors in global politics. Constructivists of this stripe are particularly interested in formal and less-formal international regimes, which they see as necessary and natural, rather than directly traceable to calculated (what Ruggie calls "neo-utilitarian"[70]) state interests as in Keohane's neoinstitutionalist version[71] or even the slightly more venturesome vision of international society propounded by Bull (echoed in Wendt). As Onuf expresses it, rules form institutions, institutions form societies, and rules yield rule (what others might describe as patterns of governance).

This second broad stream of constructivist thought, as well as the work of R. B. J. Walker—whom it is hard to classify because he incorporates currents from postmodernism, constructivism, and critical theory—has been especially insightful with regard to the traditional organizing concept of sovereignty. Walker sees sovereignty as a constructed concept that defines "outside" and "inside" but is not an objective "given" in global politics:

> The patterns of inclusion and exclusion we now take for granted are historical innovations. The principle of state sovereignty is the classic expression of those patterns, an expression that encourages us to believe that either those patterns are permanent or that they must be erased in favour of some kind of global cosmopolis. It is possible to understand how this claim to resolve all contradictions works. It, most of all, is not simply there. Its fixing of unity and diversity, or inside and outside, or space and time is not natural. Nor is it inevitable. It is a crucial part of the practices of all modern states, but they are not natural or inevitable either.[72]

Onuf argues in the same vein that sovereignty "is not a condition," rather "an ideal that is never reached, in a world where each step toward the ideal takes effort and costs resources, possibly in increasing increments, to prevent even smaller amounts of unwanted behavior."[73] Finally, for Biersteker and Weber, state sovereignty is a "social construct" whose "meaning is negotiated out of interactions within intersubjectively identifiable communities." In their view, "practices construct, reproduce, reconstruct, and deconstruct both state and sovereignty."[74] This is paralleled by Ruggie when he declares that sovereignty, "like money or property rights, exists only within a framework of shared meaning that recognizes it to be valid—that is, by virtue of collective intentionality."[75] In this way, constructivists restore a dynamic dimension to global politics. Key concepts like sovereignty acquire meaning that evolves through action and belief. For constructivists, sovereignty is an important constitutive rule that decrees who may play the game of international politics. Declares Robert Jackson; "Who can play the game? One must be legally entitled: the players, or teams, are sovereign states and only sovereign states. Obviously, there are always many more spectators than players, and there is consequently a high value on sovereignty. The title 'player' or 'team' is governed by rules of recognition which acknowledge who can play."[76] But if sovereignty is merely a constructed concept, then its meaning and role in global politics may change as the preferences and perceptions of actors evolve.

When all is said and done, it seems to us that agent/structure is a nonissue, not because asking who are the agents and what are the structures is not an important question, but because it either gives us the wrong answer—that is, states and the state system—or not much of an answer at all. Asserting that agents "read" their environment and act accordingly, from which there are consequences, is obvious. But *specifically* who or what *are* those agents and structures, and what patterns in global politics result?

Once again, as in the question of parts and wholes, the situation changes from issue to issue and even from case to case. An agent in one issue or case may be part of the structure in the next, or even largely irrelevant. For example, whether a particular group of banks (agent) extends loans to Russia may have an impact on both the Russian economy (structure) and global financial markets (structure); at the same time, the volatility of global financial markets (agent) may discourage depositors and investors (agents) from putting their money in banks with high percentages of foreign loans (structure). Of course, banks and financial markets have little or no impact upon the development of regime rules to protect the whales or to distribute food. In the end, it is fair to ask not only what the major issues and trends in global politics are, but also what types of actors/agents seem to be gaining and losing in the contests for influence and in the processes observed. Constructivists have yet to offer much enlightenment on subjects like these. Indeed, like postmodernists, constructivism, as Ruggie admits, "is not itself a theory of international relations . . . but a theoretically informed approach to the study of international relations."[77] Unlike postmodernists, however, constructivists see themselves as obliged to make empirical statements about the perceptions and norms that shape actual behavior in global politics.

CONCLUSION

The future for theory in global politics is modestly less gloomy than we thought in 1988, when—in the absence of anything better—realism and neorealism appeared to be staging something of a revival. At that time the scientific enterprise that had been launched with such hope some decades earlier was experiencing seriously diminishing returns. The scientific enterprise has continued, even grown, in some quarters, but our understanding still has not significantly improved. The postpositivist movement of the 1990s and beyond was something of a declaration of surrender. Empiricism had not worked and could only be scrapped in favor of "dissidence." To what end was unclear, if indeed that was a valid question. The field was still fragmenting, and the resulting cliques and subcliques set up their own sections in professional associations, organized and attended their own panels, and wrote papers which were mainly read and footnoted by like-minded scholars and coteries of gushing graduate students. As before, journals developed reputations that tended to place them in one or another camp. For example, *International Studies Quarterly* and *Journal of Conflict Resolution* were the journals of choice for scientists and rational-choice theorists[78]; *International Organization* remained the preferred journal for neo-institutionalists and regime theorists; and *Millennium* and the *European Journal of International Relations* were favored by postpositivists.

Still, a number of positive results have flowed from postpositivism. The subjective dimension of global politics is no longer excluded or marginalized, and postpositivist efforts correctly recognize that theory and knowledge are potential sources of political power and prestige in the academy. Antiempiricists remain in a minority, even while they stir sometimes-useful controversy over the limits of empiricism, its relationship to norms, and the importance of ideas and identity in political reality. Constructivism, through both of its divergent streams, has provided something of a middle ground and at least serves to maintain a semblance of "softer" empiricism.

In a variety of ways, modesty aside and with all due respect, the "new thinking" is compatible with some of the claims that we have been making for years. Although we are not constructivists and are more attuned than most scholars to a world of different types of polities, we are especially comfortable with the idea of building dynamic theory from the conceptual base of multiple identities. It is to some of these ideas and their implications that we turn our attention in the final chapter.

CHAPTER 10

The Quest Continues

The postmodern challenge adds to the urgency of making a decision about what sort of theory we want. To the extent that this challenge reveals growing frustration over using new jargon to (re)discover old ideas and adding bells and whistles to simple principles in order to appeal to policymakers, university deans, grant referees, and naive students, it should act as a wakeup call to reduce publishing and take time to think about how and why we theorize.

The scientific revolution in global politics was based on faulty premises about science, started without a reliable theoretical foundation, and counted what it could without much result. It failed to achieve "a thoroughgoing jail-break"[1] from the habit-driven thought patterns in our field. Both the universal pretensions of the field's scientists and the insistence of naive inductivists that "facts speak for themselves" are misleading. As both constructivists and extreme relativists remind us, our understanding of facts is conditioned by context and norms and is, therefore, constantly changing.[2] The selection of facts and their arrangement—the most important tasks for a theorist—is a dangerous business, and postmodernists correctly point out that the selection process has political consequences. Both tasks are conditioned by inevitable though not always conscious prejudices arising from normative claims. We perceive what we look for, and as in Poe's "Purloined Letter," we sometimes miss what is in front of our noses. Since meaning is attached to facts as a result of normative and political commitments, it is important to study them from a variety of perspectives and to remain aware of what is *not* included in resulting theory.

Still, despite the ambiguity of central concepts, there are "facts" (including values, norms, and rules) independent of the observer about which consensus is possible even though meaning is attached to them by the observers themselves. Those facts, along with reason, provide the elements for what Michael Nicholson calls "moderate positivism."[3] Reliable data can buttress persuasive theory, and often it is helpful to know how much of X or some other variable we have. Having something useful to count partly depends on conceptual clarity, which has been difficult to achieve, and the wish to count must *never* determine fact selection. However, and this is critical, the sort of empiricism we need must recognize that our most important "facts" are "invented" by us and are complex constructs with no little or no meaning independent of us. Whether or not one agrees with Donald Puchala that such facts are "unobservables which we nevertheless hope are knowables," it is difficult to deny his contention that "none of these are observable as wholes, and they never will be observable as wholes."[4]

The difficulties encountered by theorists in recent decades suggest that, rather than abandoning empiricism lock, stock, and barrel, we need a less demanding empiricism of the sort Rosenau has in mind when he speaks of "potential observability." "In this procedure," he declares, "each step in the construction of a model is taken only after a determination of whether its components are at least theoretically susceptible to being observed, even if some innovation in observational techniques must first be made."[5] This version of empiricism requires the sacrifice of some of the high level of parsimony (ratio of inferences to assumptions in a given theory) and abstraction demanded by Waltz and other neorealists. The way in which Martha Finnemore and Kathryn Sikkink approach research on norms is an example reflecting this less demanding empiricism.[6] As we shall see shortly, historical analysis sensitizes the theorist to the costs of parsimony, yet historical analysis is critical to any theory that is sensitive to the dynamics of global politics. Parsimony may be desirable, but it is hardly an end in itself, and it is downright dysfunctional when it exaggerates similarities at the cost of critical contextual differences.

Rosenau and Nicholson's version of empiricism would allow for the reunification of facts and values in a manner that recalls John Dewey's less-demanding and more philosophical version of empiricism as problem-solving pragmatism infused by socially conditioned norms.[7] For Dewey, universal truth is suspect; instead, he views knowledge as contextual, contingent, and subject to change depending on time and place. Social scientists may have to put both natural-science and social-science models (that have had ample time to prove of limited worth) aside for a spell and "just" start describing what we perceive is *actually happening* in the world of politics. To be sure, such an approach threatens "barefoot empiricism," and postmodernists would properly caution that however hard we try, we cannot avoid "seeing" through "the glasses inside our heads" whenever we look out at the world. Nonetheless, we will not make theoretical progress until we do some ruthless ground clearing of failed approaches and try—and try again—as best we can.

HISTORICAL SENSITIVITY

Throughout this book and elsewhere, we have argued that much of what we know about contextual global politics is historical and that many of the illusions and errors perpetuated by international relations theorists—for example, the centrality of the territorial state and of anarchy—arise from a particular Westphalian mindset. There is also a widespread failure to account for change or seek the sources of change. Such theory is historically myopic in failing to see before the Westphalian era and, indeed, as Krasner reminds us (albeit for his own realist purposes), even caricatures and distorts practically everything that has happened since.[8]

New theory will have to account for the past rather than ransacking it as realists and neorealists did, but the cost will surely be the loss of parsimony. "I cheerfully and consciously surrender parsimony," declares Rodney Hall, "for richer and more nuanced characterization of the societies and systems I wish to study. Social reality is complex. It always has been. Thus we cannot expect to apprehend the evolution of social reality without a serious foray into history."[9] Hall is right.

Too often realists try to transform messy historical reality into a story of how the sovereign state climbed out of the segmented ooze of the Middle Ages and then, wedded with nationalism, conquered religious fanatics, exploitative nobles, and so on until history could come to an end (in the fashion of *1066 and All That*). In the United States, the triumph of the scientists precluded serious historical analysis. "The millennial belief in American exceptionalism," argues Ole Waever, "exempted the United States from qualitative change, and the historicist threat to this ideology was kept at bay with the assistance of a naturalistic social science containing change within the categories of progress, law, and reason. This historical consciousness adapted and survived dramatic challenges and thus sustained . . . a more abstract and 'scientific' social science, divorced from history."[10]

The past is part of any present context because the latter has been at least partly shaped by the former and is the basis of whatever perceptual lenses theorists and decisionmakers use to make sense of what is happening. Although ours is a turbulent world and much that catches our attention seems unprecedented, it is an error to think only in the present. Certainly, the present is different in some respects from anything that came before, and it can be studied on its own terms, but the ebb and flow of political communities and their fission and fusion have been characteristic of global politics for more than five thousand years.[11] Some patterns have not changed all that much, and the past is a rich source of clues about what to look for in the present—and even to help us predict the future. The sheer pace of change has accelerated, but we should not make too much of this: The mighty Assyrian Empire collapsed in only thirty years, and the Aztecs Empire (with help from the Spanish), about as fast as the Soviet Union did. Chaos and complexity have been with us since the big bang, and there have been many eras of extreme instability. Some of the sources of instability are also strikingly different today from what they were, say, in ancient Egypt or the Roman Empire at its height, but many such sources—for example, nested polities and multiple identities—are not different.

The bottom line is that one is obliged to specify the extent to which the *present is not only different from the past but also similar to it*. In addition, where there are differences one should trace the roots and rates of change to avoid concluding that the world has suddenly been remade. The past, broadly defined, is more relevant to our understanding of the present and future than the limited state-centric Westphalian world of international relations. It was the "Westphalian moment" (however extended) in global politics that was exceptional. Global politics today retains aspects of the state system even as it in many ways increasingly resembles politics as it was before the onset of the

European-dominated era of sovereign states. That era was a moment in historical time of only a few hundred years—itself punctuated by major changes and always involving many local variations—against the long train of human history. What Bull called "the new medievalism," though the label is a little too Eurocentric for our taste, captures the idea of the overlapping political authorities and loyalties that apologists for sovereignty thought had been legislated out of existence.

Virtually no contemporary state is like those that Metternich knew and about which Henry Kissinger wrote his doctoral dissertation. And all contemporary states reflect the peculiarities of their unique pasts. For Arab states, that past combines tribal traditions with the effects of achieving imperial unity based on Islam. The Shi'ite-Sunni schism of the seventh century A.D. continues to divide countries as well as communities within and across countries. The Chinese state bears the imprint of the Middle Kingdom and the cultural continuity of millennia. Mexico (as events in Chiapas remind us) and Central America still bear the scars of the collision between European Spain and the Aztecs, Mayas, and other indigenous tribal peoples. And Africa's states are witnessing the violent revival and reconstruction of old tribal and ethnic identities. And so it continues. Nor should we assume that such fragmentation is a permanent condition. History offers a variety of possibilities, including a new authoritarianism, the growing authority of specialized, nonsovereign institutions, the transformation of many states into servants of global markets, or some combination of these.

International relations theorists nonetheless often remain unaware of the historical sources of what they are examining. Alternatively, they may select what they need from history and mythologize events, thereby *appearing* to acknowledge those historical sources. The contingent nature of knowledge, along with the suspicion that timeless and universal concepts like territorial state are neither timeless nor universal make it urgent to make research historical and cross-cultural. How else can we recognize the contingent and contextual nature of what we take for granted?

A historical perspective also assures that we recognize the dynamic nature of our enterprise, making us skeptical of any claim "that the fundamental nature of international relations has not changed over the millennia."[12] The limited historical horizons of neorealists are apparent when Waltz proudly proclaims that states-as-territorial-actors "are" and " will long remain" "the units whose interactions form the structure of international-political systems." So convinced was he that his key dimensions would not change that he rhetorically (and unfortunately, as it turned out) asked in 1979 whether the Soviet Union or Ford and IBM were more likely to be "around 100 years from now."[13] Well might Robert Cox conclude that Waltz and other realists adopt a "fixed ahistorical view,"[14] and well might Ruggie claim that "a dimension of change is missing from Waltz's model."[15]

There are, of course, some even in the realist tradition who recognize the need for greater historical sensitivity in order to allow for system transformation. Although E. H. Carr thought it difficult "even to imagine a world in which political power would be organised on a basis not of territory," he recognized that "[f]ew things are permanent in history; and it would be rash to assume that the territorial unit of power is one of them."[16] More recently, Buzan, Jones, and Little, self-styled structural realists, declared that:

> Neorealists do not deny the relevance of history or the potential for change in international politics. *But they do assert that there are important features of international politics . . . that have occurred throughout the history of the international system and that need to be accounted for in terms of an unchanging systemic structure.* It is this claim that analysts imbued with historicism wish to deny. . . . [T]he historicists insist that distortion will inevitably occur if it is presupposed that these practices always play an identical role in the international system or that they always carry the same subjective meaning simply because they are identified by a common label.[17]

To the extent that social scientists try to emulate natural scientists, there is little room for historical variation and little sympathy for analyses that deny universally valid concepts that might limit a theory's capacity to generalize. Instead of demanding parsimony, by contrast, we admire historical sociologists like Michael Mann, who describes a rich political universe in which the role of key social forces and institutions in shaping global politics varies by time and place.[18] For Mann, "real human societies" constitute a "mess" strewn with "many mistakes, apparent accidents, and unintended consequences."[19] This description allows Mann a degree of causal and descriptive complexity that violates parsimony but emphasizes the impact of context on, and the dynamic nature of, global politics. It is not simply that the Westphalian state was historically contingent,[20] but that its functions and capacity also evolved historically and flowered under a specific set of conditions that, to a greater or lesser extent, no longer exist. We ourselves are somewhat less sanguine about the current situation for states than is Mann,[21] but both of our judgments as to whether the state's glass is half-full or half-empty (this being about the degree of our disagreement) are historically informed.

Before leaving this topic, it is important to recognize that historical analysis has its own perils. Objectivity is no easier for a historian than a social scientist. As historian Felipe Fernández-Armesto readily acknowledges, "Historians like me know, at least as well as practitioners of any other discipline, how elusive objectivity is. Even if we perform miracles of self-immolation, we are left with sources which derive from other hands and bear the imprint of other subjects— witnesses, reporters, compilers of data and hearsay."[22] To stand paralyzed and ignore history because historical research is partly theory-dependent and subjective is absurd, however. One must be conscious of this and recognize that the result is few givens—only probabilities and sometimes only possibilities. We have to live with ambiguity and proceed as best we can. If our investigations seem to provide a more useful or convincing view of political reality than other constructions, that may be the most we can hope for.

Finally, we must avoid the liberal fallacy of believing that history is going somewhere. There is no grand historical plan and no fated destination. History, far from "ending," is forever being revived and at least partially relived. Contemporary political patterns reflect history's revenge. As Stephen Kobrin reminds us, we should avoid "the very modern assumption that time's arrow is unidirectional and that progress is linear."[23] Any analysis should make every attempt to establish what remains the same, what is changing, and the approximate rate of change.

FOCUSING ON IDENTITIES

One important and productive focus of postmodernists has been on human identities, as the idea of "the self" and "the other" suggested. As R. B. J. Walker declared: "The usual categories and valorizations—of cultures and nations, of passions and Balkanizations—remain with us. Even so, a sense of novelties and accelerations is also pervasive. . . . [A] common identity is precisely what we do not have. . . . Modern political identities are fractured and dispersed among a multiplicity of sites, a condition sometimes attributed to a specifically postmodern experience but one that has been a familiar, though selectively forgotten, characteristic of modern political life for several centuries." Sovereignty, he contends, remains a key concept partly because of the absence of an effective substitute: "Whatever avenues are now being opened up in the exploration of contemporary political identities, whether in the name of nations, humanities, classes races, cultures, genders or movements, they remain largely constrained by ontological and discursive options expressed most elegantly, and to the modern imagination most persuasively, by claims about the formal sovereignty of states. The Cartesian coordinates may be cracked, identities may be leaking, and the rituals of inclusion and exclusion sanctified by the dense textures of sovereign virtu(e) may have become more transparent. But if not state sovereignty . . . what then?"[24] What, indeed?

Renewed interest in the subjective dimension of global politics and in the normative roots and consequences of global behavior auger well for the field. The emergence, repression, transformation, reemergence, and manipulation of human identities lie at the heart of our own effort to unify facts and values and to get beyond the barriers to insight erected by science and postmodernism. Individuals have multiple identities that provide them with cues about how to respond to particular issues and in specific contexts. In any context, dominant identities define the bases of authority and political organization and, therefore, constitute boundaries between moral communities, between "self" and "other."[25]

Identity is not primordial, although it is often reconstructed from bits and pieces of the past. Whatever the individual characteristics associated with it (e.g., skin color, sexual characteristics, blood lineage, membership, professional, and so forth), the meaning of those characteristics is acquired in the course of political interaction.[26] Gender becomes a significant identity category because women discover they are treated *as a group* differently than (and often less well than) men; Bosnian Muslim and Albanian Kosovar become important collective self-identities when individuals with those labels are *as groups* targeted for ethnic cleansing; and German Jews could no longer be German *and* Jewish when forced to wear yellow stars that isolated them from other Germans. Authorities from within the group or from other groups can undertake the symbolic manipulation necessary for creating, sustaining, or revitalizing identities. Wherever this manipulation originates, its result is to draw a line or a boundary separating those within what we refer to as polities from those outside.[27]

The clash of identities is an engine of historical change, and outcomes include the repression of some identities, and the merger of some with others, the triumph of new identities, and the revival of old ones. The idea that citizenship defined one's highest loyalties evolved with the merging of state and nation in the late eighteenth century in Europe. The emergence of this identity had consequences for all the realms of global politics. As Rodney Hall observes, "the enfranchisement of the citizen *qua* co-national implies closure against non-nationals and creates noncitizens, and thus disenfranchises others." The wall between "inside" and "outside" was reinforced by the territorial basis of the state: "Territorial sovereignty," continues Hall, "permitted closure against [citizens of other states] through the physical control of a contiguous territory, and of its borders, by a centralized political administration."[28]

The new identity of citizenship revolutionized warfare. Citizen-soldiers infused war making with unprecedented energy, and Napoleon "personified, and profited from, the unique fusion of social, political, and military elements brought about by the overthrow of the Old Regime in France."[29] The impact was no less in other realms, transforming global politics by strengthening the vertical barriers dividing territorially based groups and attenuating the horizontal bonds of common culture and class that had formerly linked political and diplomatic elites across Europe and that had placed limits on political and ideological cleavages.

By contrast, recent decades have witnessed a divorce of nation from state and the growing vitality of new or revived identities the emergence of which had formerly been impeded by the nation-state. "Culture and identity," declares Yosef Lapid, "are staging a dramatic comeback in social theory and practice."[30] As we noted in chapter 5, the territorial state is being eroded from above and below, and the essential meaning of territory and territoriality is undergoing change. Under these conditions, the cultural roots of states are exerting more and more influence on political behavior, especially in those states outside of Europe. Thus, the role of religion as a mode of identity, a badge of loyalty, and a source of norms is spreading not only in the Muslim world, but among Hindus, Christians, and Jews as well. The groups and movements that have adopted religion as their source of collective self-identity, *many of which threaten the autonomy and integrity of territorial states,* can trace their origins to a much older world, a world that seemed finally to disappear with the end of the European wars of religion.

National identities are eroded and muddled as the revival of older identities and the creation of new ones produce cleavages within or across societies that had formerly prevented or repressed them in the name of national unity. In Guatemala, for example, ancient Mayan identities are challenging the primacy of the Westphalian state. "It is not that someone is speaking on our behalf, defending us," declares a Maya social scientist, "but that we ourselves are developing visions of our own identity, from a colonialist church to our relationship with the state."[31] Such identity shifts require freeing local history from the control of dominant elites. To do so entails conflicts for control of historical meaning in order to legitimate policies for and interpretations of the present. As everyone in Northern Ireland and Serbia recognizes, acts of remembering, such as national pageants, ceremonies, or parades are part of the contest over the meaning of history. Once again, historical analysis is critical to understanding contemporary conditions, but so is the accelerating rate of technological change.

Technological change is facilitating the eroding dominance of citizenship as the principal collective political identity because it is weakening the state itself, depreciating the importance of territoriality,[32] and making it possible for political identities and organizations to overcome the once-insurmountable impediment of physical distance. Perhaps the most dramatic technological changes in this sense are in the speed and scope of communication. The "printing press, telephone, radio, television, and personal computer," declares Rosenau, "have created conditions for skill development among citizenries that governments could not totally control and that have helped make citizenries more effective in relation to the centers of authority."[33] More information is available to more people than ever before. "Modern" images and homogenized ethics and aesthetics swamp local and national identities, structures, and institutions. "Foreign" norms, habits, and practices overwhelm existing identities, as nothing remains to buffer and regulate excessive individualism and heightened anomie.

Among the beneficiaries of information economies are managerial and technocratic elites, money launderers and drug smugglers, currency traders, fund managers, and others in the private sphere with few responsibilities to citizens of states. Such nonsovereign institutions are certainly not democratic. Comparing corporate elites to Renaissance princes, Susan Strange declared, "They can usually divide and rule. No single elected institution holds them accountable. The cartels and oligopolists that practise private protectionism and manage markets for their own comfort and convenience are even less accountable. Neither are the insurance businesses or the big-time accountancy partnerships. And the mafias least of all."[34]

Information and, more importantly, the capacity to act upon it are unevenly distributed globally and within societies. Cities such as New York, London, Tokyo, and Singapore are information hubs and the centers of information economies, and the process of cultural homogenization is most visible among those who are integrated in the global economy and whose tastes and norms are the same. These cites are "geographies of centrality" that are economically far ahead of their hinterlands, "the geographies of marginalization," even while the cities themselves are divided into core and peripheral populations.[35] The new knowledge elites have been substantially "denationalized," are surrogates of globalization, and have little interest in or time for those from whom they are separated by barriers of class, knowledge, wealth, or taste. Thus, the psychological distance between these new urban elites and the much larger and poorer underclass in their own country grows, even as geographic distance between these classes has narrowed owing to massive urbanization.

New globe-girdling communication technologies also tend to erode national cultures and practices that reinforce state legitimacy. Even democratic societies fear the corrosive effects of cultural homogenization. Thus, in democratic Israel, the Knesset voted to require that half the songs on national radio stations be in Hebrew. The nationalist reasoning behind this requirement was evident in the comments of one of its advocates, who declared, "We are putting up a protective wall against the flood of foreign culture. The country is 50 years old. Its culture has yet to be formed, and we thought it should be protected."

"Part of the essence of setting up an independent state," he added, "was to establish our own culture here. The bill is a cultural statement."[36]

In the process of cultural homogenization, new elites are created, and the authority of old ones is eroded. Instead of a world of distinctive local cultures and traditional values reinforced by religion and custom, there is a secular globalized culture, that places a premium on individual choice and market forces. It is less important that urban elites dress the same, eat the same foods, and listen to the same music than that people substitute the mainly secular norms of the post-modern West, especially possessive individualism, for stabilizing customs and norms on which traditional authority structures rest. In some cases, social conflict explodes between advanced and traditional sectors, As new local elites are empowered and integrated into the globalized culture, traditional social groups, fearful of losing authority, are mobilized to resist the "strange," "secular," or "sensual" that flows from outside their identity boundaries. The corrosive effect of homogenization on local cultures and norms may trigger a backlash such as that which brought down the Shah of Iran or brought Afghanistan's Taliban to power.

The speed and reach of the new technologies have altered the meaning of time and physical distance and, in consequence, have opened new possibilities for regional and global authority structures. Ideas, people, and things can be moved at unprecedented speeds over vast distances. According to a recent UN report, the "Internet is an easy vehicle for trafficking in drugs, arms and women through nearly untraceable networks."[37] Whether through television, radio or, increasingly, the Internet, people learn that there are others "like themselves" whom they had never known about before and with whom they can now communicate. New categories of "us" are made available for political mobilization and action. As the new micro-electronic technologies provide knowledge about noncitizen identities, facilitate communication among those who share these identities regardless of physical distance, and permit group mobilization at a distance, loyalties to states are placed under greater and greater stress. In sum, what Jonathan Boyarin calls the "close genealogical links between the 'Cartesian coordinates' of space and time and the discrete, sovereign state" are in the process of being severed, and technology has redefined "our possible experiences of 'proximity' and 'simultaneity.'"[38]

The impact of technology, identity, and authority is increasingly evident in the economic sphere. Whereas the frontiers of markets and states were once congruent, markets today are increasingly deterritorialized, leading Strange to conclude that we are witnessing a "retreat of the state."[39] The revolution in microelectronics enables instantaneous transmission of information and money from anywhere to anywhere. Thus, in 1990 the Emir of Kuwait spirited the national treasury out of the country by clicking a few computer keys, thereby placing it beyond the reach of Saddam Hussein. More importantly, as Miles Kahler argues, "Cross-border economic integration and national political sovereignty have increasingly come into conflict, leading to a growing mismatch between the economic and political structures of the world. The effective domains of economic markets have come to coincide less and less with national governmental jurisdictions."[40]

Availing themselves of the new technologies, oligarchic transnational corporations and banks utilize global production and marketing strategies that can take advantage of globalized capital markets and financial flows. Globalized capital flows, currency speculation and investment decisions, markets, and flows dramatically complicate (and sometimes even dissolve) state capacity to set macroeconomic policies for citizens. National trade policies are routinely undermined by intra-and inter-firm trade, as is monetary policy by investment flows, corporate investment decisions, and offshore and joint ventures. "[B]y the 1990s," declared Strange, "communication by fax and telephone was . . . becoming obsolete as electronic mail and the Internet became the preferred and habitual systems by which markets, financial and other, were integrated into a single system."[41] Financial institutions and markets, she argued, have been revolutionized and globalized by computers, chips, and earth-orbiting satellites. Not only do ever-accelerating technological changes afford opportunities for global reach, in some respects they make it imperative for firms to globalize operations. Strange suggests:

> [I]n manufacturing—and indeed in mining and agriculture—the nature of innovatory technology is such that both the products and the processes of their production are becoming more capital intensive and less labour intensive than those they replace. The combination of added costs of investment and diminished time for the realisation of profits from the product or process has effectively pushed firms into seeking larger markets from which to extract the income necessary to amortise the debts incurred for capital investment in time to be ready for the next wave of technological innovation.[42]

The conventional capabilities of states are of little use in halting capital flight, currency speculation, or yawning trade deficits. Nor are territorial states well suited for managing nonterritorial economic entities.

The declining role of territory and its relationship to technology are also evident in warfare. The territorial state was the principal beneficiary of military and commercial innovations in Europe at the end of the Middle Ages.[43] Firearms and fortress construction and the growing size of armies increased "the minimum size necessary to make political units militarily viable."[44] Currently, the link between territory and warfare is cracking. Thus, in the 1999 Kosovo conflict, the United States dispatched B-2 stealth bombers from Missouri to strike targets deep in the Yugoslav Republic. In a round trip taking nearly thirty hours the bombers were able to attack the most dangerous and highly valued targets in Yugoslavia, then return to their own bases safe within the American hinterland. Advances in information processing, telecommunications, remote sensing, and precision-guided munitions are producing "a vast improvement in the quality and quantity of information made available to military commanders by improvements in computers and other devices for collecting, analyzing, storing, and transmitting data."[45] The same advances in microelectronics are also responsible for the creation of pilotless drones and "smart" weapons such as cruise missiles that can destroy targets such as a factory in the Sudan or a terrorist camp in Afghanistan from vast distances. And we may yet struggle over cyberspace in "cyberwars" much as we did over territory in earlier centuries.

SHIFTING NORMS

The central thesis of this book remains that ideas and theories emerge and compete in global-politics scholarship in a decidedly non-Kuhnian pattern—that is, in response to the normative temper of the times. Schools of thought in global politics reflect the *Zeitgeist* of their age fully as much as do ideas in art and literature. Different normative commitments lie behind debates regarding which actors should be studied, which levels of analysis are most fruitful, which variables are critical, which issues are most important, and so forth. This should not be at all surprising, considering that the very problems which scholars choose to study and the data they amass derive initially from a set of value-based concerns.

These concerns always are to some extent personal, but they also typically reflect the current anxieties of political leaders and society at large, as well as intellectual fashions in the halls of academe. Further, what is a value priority today may run a distant second or third tomorrow. Psychological and material rewards go to those individuals and institutions working on the problems that governments and fellow citizens are worried about today. Moreover, academics who want to get grants and to advance their careers are aware that their analyses had better be wearing this year's theoretical fashion. In sum, scholarship is inevitably influenced not only by major historical trends, but also by more ephemeral considerations.

Value hierarchies and the global agenda of issues change in response to contextual or situational factors that heighten perceptions of deprivation of some values and reduce anxieties about others. The focus is on arms control when technological advances in weapon systems appear likely to escalate the arms race, on the environment when there are severe famines or dying rivers and lakes, on the international monetary system when currency fluctuations grow intolerable and market collapse looms, on capital flows when debtor countries are on the verge of bankruptcy, and so on. Sometimes the changes to which theorists respond have been slow and evolutionary in nature; perhaps more often, theoretical shifts have reflected the impact of cataclysmic or at least profoundly disillusioning events. Wars have often been the catalyst: the Peloponnesian War that influenced Thucydides, the fall of Rome, the French invasion of Italy in 1498, the religious wars of the sixteenth and seventeenth centuries, the French Revolution and its Napoleonic aftermath, the two world wars, Vietnam, and the Cold War. Each ushered in a period of introspection, a general questioning of existing norms and ideas, leading eventually to the emergence of "new" norms and theories.

The quotation marks around the word "new" in the previous sentence are required because our second main assertion is that what is remarkable about debates among theorists in global politics—and what distinguishes them from debates among natural scientists—is that essentially the same (often stale) arguments and emphases tend to recur over and over through time despite superficial changes in concepts and language. There are enduring normative themes like realism versus idealism or anarchy versus order. Each draws its inspiration from partial views of a world that, despite genuine evolution and critical events, is not changing nearly as much as shifting theoretical fashions and the rhetoric of scholarly contests might appear to suggest. Moreover, theoretical shifts occur, often at the same time, along several fairly constant dimensions, including those we have identified as being the most important: mutability/immutability, optimism/pessimism, competitiveness/community, and elitism/nonelitism.

We began our historical survey with the period from medieval Europe to the Renaissance, or the Middle Ages to Machiavelli, an epoch—like all other epochs—in which theories of global politics were products of a prevailing social and cultural milieu. The medieval era is a millennium that has usually been overlooked by scholars, no doubt because its pattern of complex overlapping jurisdictions seems to make it difficult to comprehend in "modern" terms. As we pointed out, however, the medieval era did have autonomous actors, violence and war, system solidarity and culture, and supranational organization. This period is also interesting and significant, in part, because the very lack of a clear domestic arena created a purer interstate arena than was the case either before or after. Medieval theory of a universal imperium, an overarching Roman Church and the ultimate perfectibility of humanity as a spiritual collectivity mirrored an economically and socially stratified real world. Political and military power was local and limited, and it was hardly possible to demarcate individual and collective interests, or domestic and global politics.

In our own era, the erosion of the boundary between the domestic and international realms and the spreading recognition of a multitude of shifting political boundaries have served to undermine traditional realist theories. The effect on theory has been no less profound than when the Middle Ages waned and the domestic/international distinction was rediscovered. The hardening of boundaries, growth of state power, shifts in the bases of economic and military power, breakdown of feudal society, increasing secularization, and progress in science paved the way for Marsilio and Machiavelli. Machiavelli's political realism was an eloquent statement of the belief in the immutability of the security dilemma, basic pessimism, intense competition, and elitism that characterized his Renaissance age. But it was *not* a statement of basic and permanent truths any more than are the liberal visions of global order that reappeared and intensified after the Cold War ended.

For centuries after the Renaissance, until World War I, conditions were conducive to the advance of one or another version of realism. Religious strife in France gave birth to Bodin's articulation of the doctrine of state sovereignty; Louis XIV consolidated a model centralized state resting on a monarchy having divine right; and the 1648 Peace of Westphalia ushered in what is usually termed the modern state system. The eighteenth century was a veritable age of realism and rationalism, featuring absolute monarchies, intense competition among states, shifting alliances, and limited wars, as well as cosmopolitan diplomacy, consensus around the idea of war as an extension of politics, and relative political stability. The French Revolution and the rise of Napoleon presented serious domestic and international threats to the rest of Europe, but fusion of the ideas of state and nation revitalized both the state as an institution and as an idea. After the mid-nineteenth century, glorification of state and nation as organic and primordial associations began a march toward pathological nationalism, especially in Germany, with disastrous results.

The disillusionment with realism after World War I set the stage for a period of what realists characterized as idealism or utopianism, which was itself supplanted after World War II by resurgent realism and an attendant emphasis on the scientific method. Idealists blamed the useless bloodletting primarily on selfish and unbridled nationalism, authoritarian governments, manipulative professional diplomats, and greedy arms merchants. In contrast to the old realism, the new idealist phase emphasized optimism, social and political mutability, cooperation through international law and organization, and broader political participation. The latter was to be accomplished both by giving greater weight to the views of an educated public opinion at home and by allowing national self-determination for previously subjugated peoples throughout the world.

The failure of the League of Nations and Western governments to satisfy German, Japanese, and Italian dissatisfaction or curb their expansionism, the calamity of World War II, and the onset of the Cold War ushered in another period of realism. If the eighteenth century had been the age of realism among foreign policy practitioners, the years following World War II saw a realist perspective capture the imagination of foreign-office professionals and academics alike. First and foremost, Hans Morgenthau, but also E. H. Carr, Kenneth Thompson, Reinhold Niebuhr, and others gave realism a rich new literature and intellectual respectability. Realism's claim to offer a science, its stress on the unitary state as actor, its amoralism (except, as we have noted, its own normative bias), and its rational model of foreign policy decisionmaking also meshed nicely with the aims of a later generation of American theorists who were determined to engineer a scientific revolution in the study of global politics. The behavioralists, while retaining much of the normative baggage of realism, promised a value-free approach, precise concepts, hard data, and relentless falsification of propositions in accordance with the scientific method. The magic key that would unlock all-important secrets, it appeared, might well soon be in hand.

By the 1970s, not only was the magic key still missing but also both realism and the scientific approach came under increasing attack—but not because they were less promising than they had been the decade before. Again, the reason was a shift in normative emphases occasioned by widespread disillusionment, this time over Vietnam and such other challenges as the energy crisis, endemic stagflation, environmental degradation, and North-South tensions. Theorists gave renewed attention to the nonrational roots of decisionmakers' actions, to bureaucratic politics and organizational behavior, to transnationalism and interdependence, to nonstate actors, and to the impact of issues. With considerable justification, advocates of the scientific approach were accused of ignoring the inevitable influence of values in all inquiry, of generating useless jargon, of confusing methodology with theory, of gathering data and "number crunching" without clear purpose, and (most damning of all) of simply having precious few hard results to show for decades of work and countless research dollars spent. Faced with the normative demands of the period, both realists and aspiring scientists looked increasingly irrelevant.

As global conditions evolved in the 1980s, both the world and theory about it—perhaps symbolized by the "compromise" of neorealism—became more complex and confused than at any time before. If the upsurge in U.S.-Soviet tensions in the early 1980s had revived the attraction of realist/neorealist "lessons," so realism's failure to predict or explain the end of the Cold War and the surge in optimism accompanying that event encouraged a movement away from realist norms.[46] As the pessimism and fear of the early 1980s—mirrored in nuclear freeze and peace movements—evaporated, both IR theory as epitomized by constructivism and the daily headlines reflected growing faith that opportunities for change were unlimited. Environmental challenges, failed states, globalized capital and investment markets, and identity conflicts produced renewed calls for

cooperative institutions—international and transnational—and cooperative policies. These "facts" reverberated in the realm of theory via the challenge posed by
neoliberal institutionalism to neorealism. Finally, the growing focus among both
practitioners and academics on democracy, human rights, and economic liberalism and associated norms reflected a shift from realism's statist elitism toward
a spirit of individualist equality. In theory, the relativism of postmodernism and
the vigorous assertion of feminist norms recalled the rejection of elitism,
whether in the name of sovereign states or of males.

As this summary suggests, there is always a correspondence between theory
and reality, but it is far from perfect. While change in political reality is constant,
it may be quite different from the changes identified by theorists. The latter may
be responding less to those changes than to a changing normative atmosphere.
*Often it is not even that the world has changed so much as it is that theorists have noticed
something that had always been there or have rediscovered something that is not new at all.*

What, then, will be the future course of theory and global politics? A few
guesses can be offered. First, the search for theory will continue, although with
no grand synthesis or true paradigm and hence certainly nothing like a Kuhnian
progression. The scientific revolution, which never really got under way despite
the best efforts of its advocates, has now been all but abandoned as a goal.
Method without theory is no solution, and, regrettably, theory that could provide
an adequate base for the extensive application of genuine scientific canons of
procedure is likely to remain well beyond our grasp. Statistical ingenuity will
resolve little; data collection without a consensual theoretical framework to
guide it is senseless; and rational-choice games are mere games. So are language
games and a grand rejection of objectivity. The recent willingness to combine
elements of subjectivity and objectivity, of rationality and nonrationality, and of
agent and structural causality are positive signs, especially if they lead to an end
of calls by one side for surrender by the other.

We can and must continue to use concepts heuristically, as aids to thinking,
research, and most importantly, teaching. Unfortunately, since there is still no
consensus as to the meaning of the key concepts, we will have to go on defining
them each time we use them. Partly for this reason, whether we undertake case
studies, investigate particular issue-areas, or look for properties of the general
global system—whatever we attempt—research will probably remain substantially idiosyncratic and noncumulative. As it has always done, the study of global
politics will also continue to reflect the normative temper of its time and place,
and will alternate between familiar themes along the dimensions we have
described.

A FUTURE ONLY DIMLY SEEN

What will the global milieu that shapes norms be like in years to come? The
record of the tumultuous past three decades—from détente to renewed superpower rivalry to the end of the Cold War and the proliferation of ethnic strife,
from energy shortage to oil glut, from global monetary system controls to global
capital markets, from petrodollar recycling to "Asian contagion," from stagflation to boom in America, from New International Economic Order demands to
competition for foreign investment, from a decline in interstate wars to apoca-

lyptic terrorism—holds ample warning for those bold or foolish enough to try to read the future. To be sure, our crystal ball is no less cloudy than everyone else's is. In some ways, the future seems more opaque today than it did when *The Elusive Quest* was published.

The world in 1988 was vastly different than the world in 1945, but the outlines and consequences of 1945 were still visible. Changes since 1988 are qualitatively so extensive that they threaten the outlines and consequences of 1648. The implications for theory are immense. Consider the question of power. Among the criticisms of realism and neorealism voiced by other theorists and us for decades have been its obscure nature and the difficulty in measuring it. Nevertheless, just as the end of the Cold War made conclusions drawn from a generation of research about U.S.–Soviet relations instantly obsolete, so the changing nature of global politics in recent years threatens to make obsolete, even irrelevant, both analyses and criticisms of power and power theory. What is "polarity," for example, in a world of multiple identities and overlapping polities? How useful is GNP as an indicator of wealth in a world of TNCS? How relevant or useful is a generation of research on the relationship between polarity (and a host of other variables) and interstate war in a world in which both states and interstate war are less and less the most important or interesting things of theoretical concern? Yet how difficult for many and traumatic for some to conclude that all that research, all the funds that made it possible, and all the careers that were built on it are merely of historical curiosity. Next to this the doctoral dissertations that were not completed or published owing to the sudden end of the Cold War seem but a minor tragedy.

At least theorists can be certain that a complex world will continue to be sufficiently ambiguous to offer theorists plenty of room to maneuver. There will continue to be grounds for both optimism and pessimism, opportunities for change and apparently immutable factors, competition (chaos) and cooperation (order), and a large measure of elitism as well as equality. Which emphases will move to the forefront of theoretical fashion, and when, will depend entirely upon the vicissitudes of the normative climate, itself influenced by the surfacing of long-term trends and traumatic events.

In sum, the search for theory in the field of global politics will go on, despite the existence of doubts about its accomplishments to date and its long-range prospects. As T. S. Eliot stated in another context, "we shall not cease from exploration," largely because there is not any acceptable alternative. Our field is too important to abandon, and confining ourselves to policy prescription and descriptive analyses of current events—which persons closer to the policymaking process and journalists, respectively, are often better equipped to do than are we—is not the answer. Nor can we solemnly announce our own irrelevance. We obviously must move ahead as systematically as possible, and that means that we cannot escape the task of theory building. If we are to proceed without illusion and with greater tolerance for diversity than did the prophets of the scientific revolution (and some traditionalists) in the past, and postmodernists more recently, then we have to recognize that the quest for theory will likely continue to be as elusive and to understand the reasons why.

Recent developments in the study of identity politics, a world of various types of polities, and processes of (patterned) chaos and complexity provide some signposts for the future. Some theorists of global politics are also abandoning their explicit and implicit analogies to the natural sciences and, instead, are trying to make sense of the way in which humanists approach their materials. (Ironically, the humanities, too, are trying to develop "scientific" methods and become "disciplines" and, in doing so, are embarking upon a fruitless path.) We, too, retain a strong preference for "historically based, humanistic and philosophical traditions of knowledge" because it fits the nature of the beast so much better than the scientific method, which assumes a clear distinction between that which is internal versus external to ourselves. We ourselves construct and give meaning to so much of the political world that it makes sense to focus increasingly on humanistic approaches to those processes. Obviously what we construct becomes part of the external world with which we wrestle and therefore part of an empirical universe. But to assume, as do scientists, a clean break between subjective and objective and between who we are and our beliefs and what we study is a road to nowhere.

We must confront squarely the political and normative environments that shape our consciousness and infuse our theories about the world around us. Only when our concepts, like Freud's, are "vibrant with special humanistic resonances" will integrated explanations of global politics have a chance to emerge. Indeed, Bruno Bettelheim's description of the effects of translating Freud into English might also refer to what has happened to much of global politics scholarship—"abstract, depersonalized, highly theoretical, erudite, and mechanized–in short, 'scientific!'"[47] Theorists must retreat from reductionism, correlative analysis, and abstract games. Causal theory that aims at understanding the shifting *Gestalten* of societies should be their object. Above all, students of global politics should recall what Aristotle recognized—that politics is an architectonic subject, so efforts to build disciplinary walls around it cannot and should not succeed.

Notes

CHAPTER ONE: PARADIGMS AND THEORETICAL GROWTH IN GLOBAL POLITICS

An early version of this chapter appeared in Margaret P. Karns (ed.), *Persistent Patterns and Emergent Structures in a Waxing Century* (New York: Praeger, 1986), 11–34.

1. Michael Brecher, "International Studies in the Twentieth Century and Beyond: Flawed Dichotomies, Synthesis, Cumulation," *International Studies Association* 43, no. 2 (1999), 214.
2. Ibid. For what is meant by "science," see Carl G. Hempel, *Aspects of Scientific Explanation* (New York: Free Press, 1965).
3. There is no single and universally accepted definition of "theory." Minimally, however, theory is a statement that explains or sheds light on a "why" question regarding some aspect of reality. By contrast, we eschew any more formal definition such as that requiring a set of interdependent propositions.
4. It is increasingly clear that few of those areas we have traditionally called disciplines are any more so than global politics itself. Combined names ranging from political economy and historical sociology to political psychology and political sociology only begin to indicate the degree to which disciplinary boundaries are collapsing and have come to intellectual ends less than administrative purposes.
5. Donald J. Puchala, "Woe to the Orphans of the Scientific Revolution," in Robert L. Rothstein (ed.), *The Evolution of Theory in International Relations* (Columbia, SC: University of South Carolina Press, 1991), 44–45.
6. David Dessler, "What's at Stake in the Agent-Structure Debate?" *International Organization* 43, no. 3 (1989), 445.
7. Imre Lakatos, "Falsification and the Methodology of Scientific Research Programmes," in Imre Lakatos and Alan Musgrave (eds.), *Criticism and the Growth of Knowledge* (Cambridge: Cambridge University Press, 1970), 91–196. Lakatos provides no criteria for determining when this point is reached. Some efforts have been made to apply Lakatos's notion of a research program to evaluating progress in international relations. See, for example, Brian Ripley, "A Lakatosian Appraisal of Foreign Policy Decision-Making" (paper delivered at the 1990 meeting of the International Studies Association, Washington, DC); Jonathan M. DiCicco and Jack S. Levy, "Power Shifts and Problem Shifts: The Evolution of the Power Transition Research Program," *Journal of Conflict Research* 43, no. 4, (1999), 675-704.
8. Thomas S. Kuhn, *The Structure of Scientific Revolutions*, expanded ed. (Chicago: University of Chicago Press, 1970).
9. We are grateful to Alex Tuckness for pointing this out to us.

10. Some of the issues that are addressed here echo concerns expressed by Stanley Hoffmann more than four decades ago. Hoffmann, "International Relations: The Long Road to Theory," *World Politics* 11, no. 3 (1959), 346–77.

11. James N. Rosenau, "Before Cooperation: Hegemons, Regimes, and Habit-Driven Actors in World Politics," *International Organization* 40, no.4 (1986), 853.

12. Friedrich V. Kratochwil and John Gerard Ruggie, "International Organization: A State of the Art on an Art of the State," *International Organization* 40, no. (1986), 754.

13. Thomas S. Kuhn, *The Structure of Scientific Revolutions*, 175.

14. Mario Bunge, *Finding Philosophy in Social Science* (New Haven, CT: Yale University Press, 1996), 97.

15. Little attention has been paid to boundary problems in recent years, even though they have never been addressed adequately.

16. This movement was part of the behavioral revolution that was taking place throughout political science. See, for example, Heinz Eulau, *The Behavioral Persuasion in Politics* (New York: Random House, 1963). Actually, the behavioral movement has roots in the 1920s. See Bernard Crick, *The American Science of Politics* (Berkeley and Los Angeles: University of California Press, 1960).

17. Herbert Butterfield, *The Origins of Modern Science* (New York: Free Press, 1957), 7, 28. See also Robert K. Merton, "Priorities in Scientific Discovery: A Chapter in the Sociology of Science," *American Sociological Review* 22, no. 6 (1957), 635–59.

18. See, for example, David Bloor, "Two Paradigms for Scientific Knowledge?" *Science Studies* 1, no. 1 (1971), 101–15. For his part, Popper argued that a theory required advance specification of what evidence would be sufficient to *disprove* it. Induction, he believed, could never prove a theory, although it could falsify one. Karl Popper, *Logik der Forschung: The Logic of Scientific Discovery* (London: Hutchinson, 1935). Lakatos carried on the tradition of falsification established by Popper for testing hypotheses in his argument that scientific progress occurs through successively superior scientific research programs. Lakatos, "Falsification and the Methodology of Scientific Research Programmes," and, *The Methodology of Scientific Research Programmes*, vol. 1 (Cambridge: Cambridge University Press, 1978), 32. Also see Thomas Nickles, "Lakatosian Heuristics and Epistemic Support," *British Journal for the Philosophy of Science* 38, no. 1 (1987), 181. Both Popper and Lakatos believed that falsification progressively reduced error. For a discussion of falsification in an international relations context, see Bruce Bueno de Mesquita, "Toward a Scientific Understanding in International Relations," *International Studies Quarterly* 29, no. 2 (1985), 121–36.

19. M. D. King, "Reason, Tradition, and the Progressiveness of Science:" in Gary Gutting (ed.), *Paradigms and Revolutions: Appraisals and Applications of Thomas Kuhn's Philosophy of Science* (Notre Dame, IN: University of Notre Dame Press, 1980), 104, 105.

20. Kuhn himself admitted that he had failed to stipulate consistently and clearly what a paradigm is. He therefore added a postscript to the second edition of *The Structure of Scientific Revolutions* in which he sought to identify the two central meanings of paradigm: "On the one hand, it stands for the entire constellation of beliefs, values, techniques, and so on shared by members of a given community. On the other, it denotes one sort of element in that constellation, the concrete puzzle-solutions which, employed as models or examples, can replace explicit rules as the basis for the solution of the remaining puzzles of normal science" (175). Perhaps the most useful and succinct definition of a paradigm is "the fundamental assumptions that scholars make about the world they are studying." John A. Vasquez, *The Power of Power Politics: From Classical Realism to Neotraditionalism* (Cambridge: Cambridge University Press, 1998), 23.

21. Kuhn, *Structure of Scientific Revolutions*, 10.

22. Alan Ryan, *The Philosophy of the Social Sciences* (New York: Pantheon Books, 1970), 72.

23. Kuhn, *Structure of Scientific Revolutions*, 24.

24. Puzzles, according to Kuhn, are discrete, often esoteric, problems for which there are assured solutions that are sought according to rules "that limit both the nature of acceptable solutions and the steps by which they are to be obtained." Kuhn, *Structure of Scientific Revolutions*, 38.

25. Ibid., 52, 52–53.

26. J. W. N. Watkins, "Against Normal Science," in Lakatos and Musgrave (eds.), *Criticism and the Growth of Knowledge*, 26.

27. Kuhn, *Structure of Scientific Revolutions*, 84.

28. Lakatos, "Falsification and the Methodology of Scientific Research Programmes," 91–196.

29. See King, "Reason, Tradition, and the Progressiveness of Science," 112.

30. Kuhn, *Structure of Scientific Revolutions*, 165.

31. Ibid., 163.

32. Ibid., 150.

33. See, for example, John D. Heyl, "Paradigms in Social Science," *Society* 12, no. 5 (1975), 61.

34. Kuhn, *Structure of Scientific Revolutions,* 19.

35. Larry Laudan, *Progress and Its Problems: Towards a Theory of Scientific Growth* (London: Routledge & Kegan Paul, 1977), 81. Laudan advocates using "research traditions" rather than "paradigms" or "research programs" to evaluate scientific progress. Theory, he believes, must be evaluated according to its contribution in solving real problems.

36. Brecher, "International Studies in the Twentieth Century and Beyond," 235.

37. Harold Guetzkow, "Sizing Up a Study in Simulated International Processes," in James N. Rosenau (ed.), *In Search of Global Patterns* (New York: Free Press, 1976), 91. See also Guetzkow, "Long-Range Research in International Relations," *American Perspective* 4, no. 4 (1950), 421–40.

38. Thomas S. Kuhn, "Reflections on My Critics," in Lakatos and Musgrave (eds.), *Criticism and the Growth of Knowledge,* 256.

39. In contrast, subspecialties in the natural sciences do not exist to gainsay one another's achievements. Rather, they tend to represent efforts to solve different puzzles that are posed by the paradigms within which they exist.

40. Douglas Lee Eckberg and Lester Hill Jr., "The Paradigm Concept and Sociology: A Critical Review," in Gutting, *Paradigms and Revolutions,* 122, 132.

41. See, for example, Henrika Kuklick, "A 'Scientific Revolution': Sociological Theory in the United States," *Sociological Inquiry* 43, no. 1 (1972), 2–22. The ascendance of structural-functionalism in sociology in the late 1950s was paralleled by its entry into political science, and the debate between structural-functionalists and operationalists in some respects resembled that between scientists and traditionalists in international relations.

42. George Ritzer, *Sociology: A Multiple Paradigm Science* (Boston: Allyn & Bacon, 1975).

43. See, respectively, C. G. A. Bryant, "Kuhn, Paradigms, and Sociology," *British Journal of Sociology* 26, no. 3 (1975), 354–59; versus, R. Serge Denisoff, Orel Callahan, and Mark H. Levine, *Theories and Paradigms in Contemporary Sociology* (Itasca, IL: F. E. Peacock, 1974); and Andrew Effrat, "Power to the Paradigms: An Editorial Introduction," *Sociological Inquiry,* 42, nos. 3–4 (1972), 3–34.

44. Eckberg and Hill, "Paradigm Concept and Sociology," 131.

45. Mark Blaug, "Kuhn versus Lakatos, or Paradigms versus Research Programmes in the History of Economics," in Gutting (ed.), *Paradigms and Revolutions,* 137.

46. David A. Hollinger, "T. S. Kuhn's Theory of Science and Its Implications for History," in ibid., 195.

47. See, for example, Jorg Baumberger, "No Kuhnian Revolution in Economics," *Journal of Economic Issues* 11, no. 1 (1977), 1–20; Martin Bronfenbrenner, "The 'Structure of Revolutions' in Economic Thought," *History of Political Economy* 3, no.1 (1971), 136–51; A. W. Coates, "Is There a 'Structure of Scientific Revolutions' in Economics?" *Kyklos* 22, no. 2 (1969), 289–95; and L. Kunin and F. S. Weaver, "On the Structure of Scientific Revolutions in Economics," *History of Political Economy* 3, no. 2 (1971), 391–97.

48. Blaug, "Kuhn versus Lakatos," 137.

49. Hollinger, "T. S. Kuhn's Theory of Science," 203.

50. Sheldon S. Wolin, "Paradigms and Political Theories," in Gutting, *Paradigms and Revolutions,* 174.

51. Ibid., 182, 183, 184. See also Hollinger, "T. S. Kuhn's Theory of Science," 198.

52. Gutting, *Paradigms and Revolutions,* 13.

53. Kuhn, "Reflections on My Critics," 245.

54. James N. Rosenau, *The Scientific Study of Foreign Policy* (New York: Free Press, 1971), vii.

55. P. Terrence Hopmann, Dina A. Zinnes, and J. David Singer (eds.), *Cumulation in International Relations Research* University of Denver Monograph Series in World Affairs, (Denver: Graduate School of International Studies, 1981), 4.

56. Little agreement exists regarding the degree of progress in the field. See, for example, Raymond E. Platig, *International Relations Research: Problems of Evaluation and Advancement* (Santa Barbara, CA: Clio Press, 1967); Robert Pfaltzgraff Jr., "International Studies in the 1970s," *International Studies Quarterly* 15, no. 1 (1971), 104–28; and Kalevi J. Holsti, "Along the Road to International Theory," *International Journal* 39, no. 2 (1984), 337–65. For a more general analysis of the state of political science, see Dag Anckar and Erkki Berndtson (eds.), *The Evolution of Political Science,* special edition of *International Political Science Review* 8, no. 1 (1987).

57. Richard K. Ashley, "Noticing Pre-paradigmatic Progress," in Rosenau, *In Search of Global Patterns,* 150–51.

58. As in other social sciences, taxonomies are regularly imposed upon international relations scholarship in efforts to identify paradigms (e.g., realism/idealism, state-centric-multi-centric/global-centric, and so forth). See, for example, R. Maghroori and B. Ramberg (eds.), *Globalism versus*

Realism: International Relations' Third Debate (Boulder, CO: Westview Press, 1982); R. Meyers, "International Paradigms, Concepts of Peace, and the Policy of Appeasement," *War and Society* 1, no. 1 (1983), 43–65.

59. P. Terrence Hopmann, "Identifying, Formulating, and Solving Puzzles in International Relations Research," in Rosenau, *In Search of Global Patterns,* 192. See also Ashley, "Noticing Pre-paradigmatic Progress," 151.
60. Robert Jervis, "Cumulation, Correlations, and Woozles," in ibid., 183.
61. Kuhn, *Structure of Scientific Revolutions,* 24.
62. Ashley, "Noticing Pre-paradigmatic Progress," 151.
63. G. R. Boynton, "Cumulativeness in International Relations," in Rosenau, *In Search of Global Patterns,* 145.
64. Introduction to Hopmann, Zinnes, and Singer, *Cumulation in International Relations Research,* 5.
65. Michael P. Sullivan and Randolph M. Siverson, "Theories of War: Problems and Prospects," in ibid., 10.
66. Brian L. Job, "Grins without Cats: In Pursuit of Knowledge of International Alliances," in ibid., 55.
67. Introduction to Hopmann, Zinnes, and Singer, *Cumulation in International Relations Research,* 7.
68. Richard Smith Beal, "A Contra-Kuhnian View of the Discipline's Growth," in Rosenau, *In Search of Global Patterns,* 159.
69. Wolin, "Paradigms and Political Theories," 166.
70. King, "Reason, Tradition, and the Progressiveness of Science," 104, 105, 173–73.
71. Kuhn, *Structure of Scientific Revolutions,* 35.
72. Boynton, "Cumulativeness in International Relations," 146. Emphasis in original.
73. Ashley, "Noticing Pre-paradigmatic Progress," 152, 153. Emphasis in original.
74. Dina A. Zinnes, "The Problem of Cumulation," in Rosenau, *In Search of Global Patterns,* 162. Emphasis in original. Zinnes sees additive cumulation as an "ingredient" of integrative cumulation.
75. Kenneth N. Waltz, *Theory of International Politics* (Reading, MA: Addison-Wesley, 1979), 9. The appearance of this book and what some call "neorealism" and others "structural realism" seemed to many to reflect the sort of progressive research program described by Lakatos. See Martin Hollis and Steve Smith, *Explaining and Understanding International Relations* (Oxford: Oxford University Press, 1990), 60.
76. Zinnes, "Problem of Cumulation," 163. Emphasis in original.
77. Puchala, "Woe to the Orphans of the Scientific Revolution," 50.
78. Behavioralism is actually a misleading term because political analysts have been observing human behavior since at least biblical times. What distinguished the so-called behavioralists was their determination to introduce the methods common to the natural sciences into the study of politics.
79. J. David Singer, "The Incompleat Theorist: Insight without Evidence," in Klaus Knorr and James N. Rosenau (eds.), *Contending Approaches to International Politics* (Princeton: Princeton University Press, 1969), 83–84.
80. Puchala, "Woe to the Orphans of the Scientific Revolution," 59.
81. Wolin, "Paradigms and Political Theories," 181.
82. Arend Lijphart, "The Structure of the Theoretical Revolution in International Relations," *International Studies Quarterly* 18, no. 1 (1974), 41–74.
83. See, for example, G. D. Wagner and J. Berger, "Do Sociological Theories Grow?" *American Journal of Sociology* 90, no. 4 (1985), 702–04.
84. Hopmann, "Identifying, Formulating, and Solving Puzzles in International Relations Research," 196. Emphasis in original.
85. Ibid., 20.
86. Vasquez, *Power of Power Politics,* chap. 4, p. 37. We disagree with Vasquez's contention that realism itself constitutes an overarching paradigm. See chapter 4 in this volume. Vasquez' list of realist assumptions is compatible with that of Keohane who adds state "rationality," omits the bifurcation of domestic and global politics, and restates the struggle for power and peace as interests calculated in terms of relative rank in global hierarchy. Robert O. Keohane *International Institutions and State Power: Essays in International Relations Theory* (Boulder, Co.: Westview Press, 1989), 38–39.
87. Boynton, "Cumulativeness in International Relations," 147. Vasquez in ingenious fashion reviewed and tested hypotheses that were guided by realist assumptions between 1956 and 1970 and concluded that there is a connection between "the dominance of the realist paradigm in the

field and the failure of the field to produce much new knowledge." Vasquez, *Power of Power Politics,* 152.
88. Vasquez, *Power of Power Politics,* 369.
89. Zinnes, "Problem of Cumulation," 164.
90. See, for example, Richard N. Rosecrance, "The Failures of Quantitative Analysis: Possible Causes and Cures," in Rosenau (ed.), *In Search of Global Patterns,* 177.
91. Zinnes, "Problem of Cumulation," 164.
92. See, for example, Harold D. Lasswell and Abraham Kaplan, *Power and Society* (New Haven, CT: Yale University Press, 1950), xxiv.
93. Richard W. Mansbach, Yale H. Ferguson, and Donald E. Lampert, *The Web of World Politics: Nonstate Actors in the Global System* (Englewood Cliffs, N.J.: Prentice-Hall, 1976), 30.
94. Hopmann, "Identifying, Formulating, and Solving Puzzles in International Relations Research," 193.
95. Annette Freyberg-Inan, "Human Nature in International Relations Theory: An Analysis and Critique of Realist Assumptions about Motivation," (paper delivered at the meeting of the International Studies Association, Washington, DC, 1999), 50.
96. P. Braillard, "The Social Sciences and the Study of International Relations," *International Social Science Journal* 102, no. 4 (1984), 634.
97. J. David Singer, "Tribal Sins on the QIP Reservation," in Rosenau, *In Search of Global Patterns,* 171.

CHAPTER TWO: VALUES AND PARADIGM CHANGE IN GLOBAL POLITICS

1. See Klaus Knorr and James N. Rosenau (eds.), *Contending Approaches to International Politics* (Princeton, NJ: Princeton University Press, 1969).
2. Thomas S. Kuhn, *The Structure of Scientific Revolutions,* expanded ed. (Chicago: University of Chicago Press, 1970), 164.
3. Patrick J. McGowan and Howard B. Shapiro, *The Comparative Study of Foreign Policy: A Survey of Scientific Findings* (Beverly Hills, CA: Sage Publications, 1973), 223.
4. Ibid., 224.
5. E. H. Carr, *The Twenty Years' Crisis 1919–1939* (New York: St. Martin's Press, 1962), 2.
6. By norms, we refer to considerations that are viewed as ethically compelling.
7. Carr, *Twenty Years' Crisis,* 4.
8. R. J. Rummel, "The Roots of Faith," in James N. Rosenau (ed.), *In Search of Global Patterns* (New York: Free Press, 1976), 11. For an interesting apologia entailing value change, see Glenn D. Paige, "On Values and Science: *The Korean Decision* Reconsidered," *American Political Science Review* 71, no. 4 (December 1977), 1603–9.
9. Jacob Bronowski, *The Origins of Knowledge and Imagination* (New Haven, CT: Yale University Press, 1978), 127–29. Quotation on p. 129. Natural scientists are no more consensual as regards normative commitment than are social scientists. Such commitments are often revealed when scientists are called upon to give advice about controversial public issues like the SALT II Treaty or the Strategic Defense Initiative. For analysis of scientists as advocates, see Robert Gilpin, *American Scientists and Nuclear Weapons Policy* (Princeton: Princeton University Press, 1962); Harold K. Jacobson and Eric Stein, *Diplomats, Scientists, and Politicians* (Ann Arbor, MI: University of Michigan Press, 1966); Eugene B. Skolnikoff, *Science, Technology, and American Foreign Policy* (Cambridge, MA: MIT Press, 1967); and C. R Snow, *Science and Government* (Cambridge, MA: Harvard University Press, 1961).
10. For an excellent discussion of the role of levels of analysis in global politics, see Nicholas Onuf, "Levels," *European Journal of International Relations,* 1, no. 1 (1995), 35–58.
11. For a similar approach, see F. Parkinson, *The Philosophy of International Relations: A Study in the History of Thought* (Beverly Hills, CA: Sage Publications, 1977). The varied normative cleavages in classical Greece are discussed in E. R. Dodds's *The Greeks and the Irrational* (Berkeley, CA: University of California Press, 1964).
12. See Friedrich Meinecke, *Machiavellism: The Doctrine of Raison d'Etat and Its Place in Modern History,* trans. Douglas Scott (New Haven, CT: Yale University Press, 1957). Significant idealists in the European tradition might include Dante, Emeric Crucé, the Duc de Sully, William Penn, the Abbé de Saint Pierre, Rousseau, and Kant.

13. See José Ortega y Gasset, *The Dehumanization of Art and Other Essays on Art, Culture and Literature* (Princeton: Princeton University Press, 1948), 4.
14. See Lionel Trilling, *Beyond Culture* (New York: Harcourt, Brace, Jovanovich, 1965), 81.
15. Pierre Bourdieu, *Distinction: A Social Critique of the Judgement of Taste*, trans. Richard Nice (Cambridge, MA: Harvard University Press, 1984), 6.
16. The following discussion is partly based on Richard W. Mansbach and John A. Vasquez, *In Search of Theory: A New Paradigm for Global Politics* (New York: Columbia University Press, 1981), 57–60.
17. Among the key values that have been identified as universal are wealth, security, order, freedom, peace, status, health, equality, justice, knowledge, beauty, honesty, and love. See Harold J. Lasswell and Abraham Kaplan, *Power and Society* (New Haven, CT: Yale University Press, 1950), 55–56; and Ted Robert Gurr, *Why Men Rebel* (Princeton: Princeton University Press, 1970), 24–26. All are subjective constructs that express human aspirations for self-improvement.
18. Efforts to identify relatively permanent value hierarchies are at best elusive and, at worst, probably wrongheaded. See, for example, A. H. Maslow, "A Theory of Human Motivation," *Psychological Review* 50, no. 4 (1943), 37–396; and Vernon Venable, *Human Nature: The Marxist View* (Cleveland, OH: Meridian, 1966), 74–97. Strict Freudians would in all likelihood disagree with this claim.
19. Barbara W. Tuchman, *A Distant Mirror: The Calamitous Fourteenth Century* (New York: Knopf, 1978), 104–5.
20. Hugh Thomas, *A History of the World* (New York: Harper & Row, 1979), 61.
21. See, for example, Jacob Bronowski and Bruce Mazlish, *The Western Intellectual Tradition: From Leonardo to Hegel* (New York: HarperCollins, 1986).
22. Hans J. Morgenthau, *Scientific Man and Power Politics* (Chicago: University of Chicago Press, 1946), 201.
23. James N. Rosenau, "Before Cooperation: Hegemons, Regimes, and Habit-Driven Actors in World Politics," *International Organization* 40, no. 4 (Autumn 1986), 861.
24. See, for example, Peter Dombrowski and Richard W. Mansbach, "From Sovereign States to Sovereign Markets?" *International Politics* 36 (March 1999), 1–23.
25. James N. Rosenau, *Turbulence in World Politics: A Theory of Change and Continuity* (Princeton: Princeton University Press, 1990), 128.
26. Ibid., 190. Emphasis added.
27. James N. Rosenau, *Along the Domestic-Foreign Frontier: Exploring Governance in a Turbulent World* (Cambridge: Cambridge University Press, 1997), 27.
28. Rodney Bruce Hall, *National Collective Identity: Social Constructs and International Systems* (New York: Columbia University Press, 1999), 86.
29. Michael Mann, *The Sources of Social Power*, vol. 2, *The Rise of Classes and Nation-States, 1760–1914* (Cambridge: Cambridge University Press, 1993), 193.
30. Hall, *National Collective Identity*, 135–72.
31. Yale H. Ferguson and Richard W. Mansbach, *Polities: Authorities, Identities, and Change* (Columbia, SC: University of South Carolina Press, 1996), 276–300.
32. For a discussion of these variables and the manner in which they function, see Mansbach and Vasquez, *In Search of Theory*, 59–63, 87–124.
33. "Actor" in this context should not be equated with state or government. Rather the concept refers to any purposive group that behaves in a collective and autonomous fashion.
34. See, for example, the work of Ronald Inglehart, especially *Culture Shift in Advanced Industrial Society* (Princeton: Princeton University Press, 1990) and *Modernization and Postmodernization: Cultural, Economic, and Political Change in 43 Countries* (Princeton: Princeton University Press, 1997).
35. Cited in Carr, *Twenty Years' Crisis*, 11. Carr argues that the realism-idealism dichotomy reflects the contrast between a belief in determinism versus free will (11–12), yet the Marxian tour de force was precisely turning Hegel on his head and enrolling determinism in the service of idealism. Carr also sees realism as the philosophy of the hardheaded practitioner in contrast to the utopian intellectual (12–19). This, too, seems superficial. There are practitioners and theorists of both stripes, and great leaders—Napoleon, Hitler, Lincoln, Franklin Roosevelt, and others— tend to portray themselves as devotees of first one and then the other school. And a "realist" leader like Ronald Reagan has little difficulty in rejecting his predecessor's devotion to human rights as quixotic while embracing a technological fix such as the Strategic Defense Initiative as the solution to the threat of nuclear war.
36. Robert Gilpin, *War and Change in World Politics* (Cambridge: Cambridge University Press, 1981), 5. Like Gilpin, others with realist sympathies acknowledge the static bias in much of realism and

neorealism. See, for example, Barry Buzan, Charles Jones, and Richard Little, *The Logic of Anarchy: Neorealism to Structural Realism* (New York: Columbia University Press, 1993), 85.

37. Hans J. Morgenthau, *Politics among Nations: The Struggle for Power and Peace*, 5th ed., revised (New York: Knopf, 1978), 4.

38. Kenneth N. Waltz, "Reflections on *Theory of International Politics: A Response to My Critics*," in Robert O. Keohane (ed.), *Neorealism and Its Critics* (New York: Columbia University Press, 1986), 341-43.

39. John Gerard Ruggie, "Continuity and Transformation in the World Polity: Toward a Neorealist Synthesis," in Keohane (ed.), *Neorealism and Its Critics*, 152. Waltz disagrees, declaring that "structure is a generative notion, and the structure of a system is generated by the interactions of its principal parts." Waltz, *Theory of International Politics* (Reading, MA: Addison-Wesley, 1979), 72.

40. Robert W. Cox, "Social Forces, States and World Orders: Beyond International Relations Theory," in Keohane (ed.), *Neorealism and Its Critics*, 211.

41. Morgenthau, *Politics among Nations*, 4.

42. Ibid., 3.

43. Alexander Wendt, *Social Theory of International Politics* (Cambridge: Cambridge University Press, 1999), 164–65, 367.

44. Andrew Moravcsik, "Taking Preferences Seriously: A Liberal Theory of International Politics," *International Organization*, 51, no. 4 (1997), 513.

45. Robert Jervis, *System Effects: Complexity in Social and Political Life* (Princeton: Princeton University Press, 1997), 146.

46. Moravcsik, "Taking Preferences Seriously," 535.

47. Ibid., 540.

48. Wade L. Huntley, "Kant's Third Image: Systemic Sources of the Liberal Peace," *International Studies Quarterly*, 40, no. 1 (1996), 67, 67–68.

49. Kenneth N. Waltz, *Man, the State, and War* (New York: Columbia University Press, 1959), 18ff.

50. Among natural scientists, Freudian psychologists may be viewed as relative pessimists, owing to the dark forces that they see as inherent in the human psyche and the putative intractability of these forces. Nevertheless, Bruno Bettelheim has eloquently challenged even this relative pessimism. See Bruno Bettelheim, *Freud and Man's Soul* (New York: Knopf, 1983), esp. 103ff. See also Erich Fromm, *Beyond the Chains of Illusion* (New York: Simon & Schuster, 1962), 174ff.

51. See Waltz, *Man, the State, and War*. Richard K. Ashley characterizes "neorealist" theory as lending "itself wonderfully well to becoming an apologia for the status quo, an excuse for domination." "The Poverty of Neorealism," *International Organization* 38, no. 2 (1984), 257.

52. See Carr, *Twenty Years' Crisis*, 22–27.

53. A similar logic had governed the views of Rousseau and Kant in the eighteenth century.

54. George Soule, *The Coming American Revolution* (New York: Macmillan, 1935), 20. See also Crane Brinton, *The Anatomy of Revolution* (New York: Norton, 1938).

55. By contrast, Edmund Burke in his *Reflections on the Revolution in France* (Garden City, NY: Doubleday, 1961) represented the views of a pessimist whose conservatism would not allow him to accept unbridled change.

56. See Kenneth N. Waltz, "The Stability of a Bipolar World," *Daedalus* 93 (summer 1964), 881–909, and *Theory of International Politics*. The arguments of neorealism and its opponents are summarized in Keohane, *Neorealism and Its Critics*.

57. It is, thus, a paradox that so many scientists employed realist assumptions. Whether this was due to cognitive reconciliation of opposite or simple unconsciousness is not clear.

58. Robert Heilbroner, *An Inquiry into the Human Prospect* (New York: Norton, 1975), 136–37. Ronald Reagan's rejection of the pessimism of the Carter years was an important factor in his 1980 electoral victory.

59. Waltz, *Theory of International Politics*, 192.

60. This view underlies the realist claim that perceptions of relative rather than absolute gain dominate policy. See Robert O. Keohane, "Institutional Theory and the Realist Challenge after the Cold War," and Joseph M. Grieco, "Anarchy and the Limits of Cooperation: A Realist Critique of the Newest Liberal Institutionalism," both in David A. Baldwin (ed.), *Neorealism and Neoliberalism: The Contemporary Debate* (New York: Columbia University Press, 1993), 269–300 and 116–42.

61. Sheldon S. Wolin, *Politics and Vision: Continuity and Innovation in Western Political Thought* (Boston: Little, Brown, 1960), 218.

62. Morgenthau, *Politics among Nations*, 231.

63. George F. Kennan, *American Diplomacy 1900–1950* (Chicago: University of Chicago Press, 1951), 82.

64. James Burnham, *The Machiavellians: Defenders of Freedom* (Chicago: Henry Regnery, 1943), 34.
65. For an effort to find a middle path, see Hedley Bull, *The Anarchical Society: A Study of Order in World Politics* (New York: Columbia University Press, 1977). For his part, Robert O. Keohane seeks to provide a less stringent and abstract definition of self-interest based on "a less egotistical formulation of the concept." Keohane, *After Hegemony: Cooperation and Discord in the World Political Economy* (Princeton: Princeton University Press, 1984), 110; see also 111–32.
66. Kenneth W. Thompson, "The Study of International Politics: A Survey of Trends and Developments," *Review of Politics* 11, no. 4 (October 1952), 443.
67. Waltz, *Theory of International Politics*, 74.
68. Research on the "democratic peace" has become something of a growth industry in "scientific" international relations. See, for example, Kristian S. Gleditsch and Michael D. Ward, "War and Peace in Space and Time: The Role of Democratization," *International Studies Quarterly*, 44, no. 1 (March 2000), 1–29; John R. Oneal and Bruce M. Russett, "The Classical Liberals Were Right: Democracy, Interdependence, and Conflict, 1950–1985," *International Studies Quarterly*, 41, no. 2 (1997), 267–93; Paul D. Senese, "Democracy and Maturity: Deciphering Conditional Effects on Levels of Dispute Intensity," *International Studies Quarterly*, 43, no.3 (1999), 483–502.
69. The distinction between these two emphases reflects the problem of private versus collective benefits. See Mancur Olson Jr. *The Logic of Collective Action* (Cambridge, MA: Harvard University Press, 1965).
70. Arnold Wolfers, "The Role of Power and the Pole of Indifference," in Wolfers, *Discord and Collaboration: Essays on International Politics* (Baltimore: Johns Hopkins Press, 1962), 86.
71. Kenneth N. Waltz, "International Structure, National Force, and the Balance of World Power," *Journal of International Affairs* 21, no. 2 (1967), 215–31, and Waltz, "Stability of a Bipolar World."
72. The relationship between status and conflict has become an important and unresolved issue in international relations research. The work of scholars such as Johan Galtung, R. J. Rummel, Manus Midlarsky, and Michael Wallace is especially relevant. Their conclusions largely deny the validity of the elitist assumptions of realists.
73. Walter Lippmann, *The Public Philosophy* (New York: Mentor, 1955), 29.
74. Alexis de Tocqueville, *Democracy in America*, vol. 1 (New York: Knopf, 1945), 234.
75. Kennan, *American Diplomacy*, 81.
76. Morgenthau, *Politics among Nations*, 591.
77. Training in the discipline will, therefore, continue to be characterized by diversity, and this in turn will tend to perpetuate competition among theories.

CHAPTER THREE: CHANGING NORMS AND THEORY

1. Hedley Bull, *The Anarchical Society: A Study of Order in World Politics* (New York: Columbia University Press, 1977), 264–76.
2. Hendrik Spruyt, *The Sovereign State and Its Competitors* (Princeton: Princeton University Press, 1994), 35.
3. Martin van Creveld, *The Rise and Decline of the State* (Cambridge: Cambridge University Press, 1999), 59.
4. H. G. Koenigsberger, *Medieval Europe, 400–1500* (London: Longman, 1987), 324.
5. George Holmes, *Europe: Hierarchy and Revolt, 1320–1450* (London: Fontana, 1975), 90.
6. Michael Mann, *The Sources of Social Power: A History of Power from the Beginning to A.D. 1760*, vol. 1, *A History of Power from the Beginning to A.D. 1760* (Cambridge: Cambridge University Press, 1986), 301.
7. Harold Nicolson, *The Evolution of Diplomatic Method* (London: Cassell, 1954), 41.
8. Ibid., 380, 381.
9. Spruyt, *Sovereign State and Its Competitors*, 35.
10. The chapter focuses upon the evolution of ideas in a Western context. Our perspective is applicable outside that context, however, and may well arouse less controversy in non-Western contexts where the tradition of science described here is less deeply embedded. It is important to note that ethnocentrism remains a significant problem in global-politics theory.
11. Philippe Contamine, *War in the Middle Ages*, trans. Michael Jones (Oxford: Basil Blackwell, 1984), 15. This description conforms to John H. Herz's idea of the "impenetrable" territorial nation-state successfully affording a protective "hard shell" for its inhabitants. Herz, *International Politics in the Atomic Age* (New York: Columbia University Press, 1959), 96–108.

12. Contamine, *War in the Middle Ages,* 15.
13. Ibid., 31.
14. Ibid., 43.
15. Van Creveld, *Rise and Decline of the State,* 53.
16. Clive Perry, "The Function of Law in the International Community," in Max Sorensen (ed.), *Manual of Public International Law* (New York: St. Martin's Press, 1968), 11.
17. Although the practice of electing the Holy Roman Emperor continued until 1713, when it was abolished by the Pragmatic Sanction, the selection of a Habsburg became almost automatic by the middle of the sixteenth century.
18. Adda B. Bozeman, *Politics and Culture in International History* (Princeton: Princeton University Press, 1960), 264.
19. Feudalism achieved its highest form in the eleventh and twelfth centuries after the decline of the Frankish Empire.
20. Van Creveld, *Rise and Decline of the State* 143–47.
21. Janice E. Thomson, *Mercenaries, Pirates, and Sovereigns* (Princeton: Princeton University Press, 1994), 143.
22. Van Creveld, *Rise and Decline of the State,* 159–60.
23. Rodney Bruce Hall, *National Collective Identity: Social Constructs and International Systems* (New York: Columbia University Press, 1999), 52.
24. Spruyt, *Sovereign State and Its Competitors,* 35.
25. See Marc Bloch, *Feudal Society,* vol. 2, trans. L. A. Manyon (Chicago: University of Chicago Press, 1961).
26. Ibid., 1:295.
27. Ibid., 296, 297.
28. Bozeman, *Politics and Culture in International History,* 273.
29. Bloch, *Feudal Society,* 1:296.
30. For additional information on the evolution of papal doctrine and the position of individual popes on this question, see Nicholas Cheetham, *Keepers of the Keys: A History of the Popes from St. Peter to John Paul II* (New York: Charles Scribner's Sons, 1983).
31. Cited in Van Creveld, *Rise and Decline of the State,* 61.
32. Bozeman, *Politics and Culture in International History,* 243.
33. Van Creveld, *Rise and Decline of the State,* 60.
34. John of Salisbury, "The Statesman's Book," in William Ebenstein (ed.), *Great Political Thinkers,* 4th ed. (New York: Holt, Rinehart & Winston, 1969), 203.
35. Bozeman, *Politics and Culture in International History,* 255.
36. Ibid., 256.
37. Ibid.
38. Van Creveld, *Rise and Decline of the State,* 65.
39. Dante Alighieri, "De Monarchia," in Ebenstein, *Great Political Thinkers,* 250–60.
40. George H. Sabine, *A History of Political Theory,* 3rd ed. (New York: Holt, Rinehart & Winston, 1961), 261.
41. Pierre Dubois, cited in Bozeman, *Politics and Culture in International History,* 247.
42. The Franciscans were under attack from Rome for insisting that the church follow Christ's example of poverty, and other Franciscans, including William of Ockham, were critical of papal power.
43. Marsilio of Padua, "The Defender of Peace," in Ebenstein, *Great Political Thinkers,* 281.
44. Cited in James Burnham, *The Machiavellians: Defenders of Freedom* (Chicago: Henry Regnery Co., 1943), 84–85.
45. For example, Hans Morgenthau in *Politics among Nations,* 5th ed., revised (New York: Knopf, 1978) cites Machiavelli on alliances, conceptions of politics, limited war, and revolutions in warfare. Raymond Aron in *Peace and War: A Theory of International Relations* (New York: Praeger, 1968) refers to him or his ideas on fourteen occasions; Arnold Wolfers in *Discord and Collaboration: Essays on International Politics* (Baltimore: Johns Hopkins Press, 1962) refers to Machiavelli on nine occasions; he is cited on seven occasions in Herbert Butterfield and Martin Wight (eds.), *Diplomatic Investigations: Essays in the Theory of International Politics* (London: Allen & Unwin, 1966); and E. H. Carr cites him even more often in *The Twenty Years' Crisis, 1919–1939: An Introduction to the Study of International Relations.* (New York: St. Martin's Press, 1962).
46. Kenneth N. Waltz, *Theory of International Politics* (Reading, MA: Addison-Wesley, 1979), 117; Carr, *Twenty Years' Crisis,* 63; J. L. Brierly, *The Law of Nations: An Introduction to the International Law of Peace,* 5th ed. (New York: Oxford University Press, 1955), 6.

47. *The Prince,* chap. XV. We have used the Modern Library edition, *The Prince and The Discourses,* introduction by Max Lerner (New York: Random House, 1950).
48. For an analysis of the development of Italy's city-states as a unique political form, see Spruyt, *Sovereign State and Its Competitors,* 131–50.
49. Winfried Franke, "The Italian City-State System as an International System," in Morton A. Kaplan (ed.), *New Approaches to International Relations* (New York: St. Martin's Press, 1968), 426. See also Bozeman, *Politics and Culture in International History,* 485–89, 464–77.
50. Ibid., 477.
51. Ibid., 479.
52. Francesco Guicciardini, *The History of Italy,* trans. Sidney Alexander (London: Collier-Macmillan Ltd., 1969), 48–49.
53. *The Prince,* XXVI.
54. In *The Discourses* (Book 3, XXXI), Machiavelli reiterated this theme. Indeed, he wrote *The Art of War* explicitly to instruct his countrymen in how to wage war successfully against countries such as France and Spain.
55. Felix Gilbert, "Machiavelli: The Renaissance of the Art of War," in Edward Mead Earle (ed.), *Makers of Modern Strategy: Military Thought from Machiavelli to Hitler* (New York: Atheneum, 1967), 5.
56. Francesco Guicciardini, cited in Felix Gilbert, "Machiavelli," 8.
57. *The Prince,* XII. Emphasis added.
58. *The Discourses,* Book 3, XL.
59. See, for example, Sheldon S. Wolin, *Politics and Vision: Continuity and Innovation in Western Political Thought* (Boston: Little, Brown, 1960), 195–203.
60. Ibid., 201.
61. Carr, *Twenty Years' Crisis,* 64.
62. See *The Prince,* XI.
63. *The Discourses,* introduction to Book 2. As for the common man, Machiavelli stated: "For it may be said of men in general that they are ungrateful, voluble, dissemblers, anxious to avoid danger, and covetous of gain." *The Prince,* XVII.
64. Wolin, *Politics and Vision,* 209.
65. Friedrich Meinecke, *Machiavellism: The Doctrine of Raison d'Etat and Its Place in Modern History,* trans. Douglas Scott (New Haven, CT: Yale University Press, 1957), 33.
66. See *The Prince,* XXV, and *The Discourses,* Book 2, XXIX. Machiavelli's "fortune" is not unlike what Clausewitz later called "friction" in his discussion of war. Carl Maria von Clausewitz, *On War,* edited and translated by Michael Howard and Peter Paret (Princeton: Princeton University Press, 1976), Book 1, VII.
67. Meinecke, *Machiavellism,* 37.
68. *The Discourses,* Book 1, 1.
69. *The Prince,* XV; *see also* ibid, XVIII, and *The Discourses,* Book 2, XIII.
70. Meinecke, *Machiavellism,* 42.
71. *The Prince,* XXI.
72. *The Discourses,* Book 3, XLI.

CHAPTER 4: THE VICISSITUDES OF NORMS AND THEORY

1. From time to time, realists themselves are prepared to see their ideas as part of more general worldviews that come to dominate particular periods of history. See Kenneth W. Thompson, *Political Realism and the Crisis of World Politics* (Princeton: Princeton University Press, 1960), 71.
2. See John A. Vasquez, *The Power of Power Politics: From Classical Realism to Neotraditionalism* (Cambridge: Cambridge University Press, 1998). Ironically, behavioral research—even while retaining realist assumptions—contributed mightily to provoking doubts about the adequacy of its ideas by falsification of its propositions. Such research has been an important factor in producing theoretical fragmentation in the field even while encouraging new methodological orthodoxies.
3. In the case of ancient China, for instance, the competition among Legalism, Confucianism, and Taoism reflect these several strains. See Yale H. Ferguson and Richard W. Mansbach, *Polities: Authority, Identities, and Change* (Columbia, SC: University of South Carolina Press, 1996), 201–13.
4. John H. Herz, *The Nation-State and the Crisis of World Politics* (New York: David McKay, 1976), 74.

5. See, for example, Robert E. Osgood, *Ideals and Self-Interest in America's Foreign Relations* (Chicago: University of Chicago Press, 1953); George F. Kennan, *American Diplomacy 1900–1950* (Chicago: University of Chicago Press, 1951); Norman A. Graebner, *Ideas and Diplomacy: Readings in the Intellectual Tradition of American Foreign Policy* (New York: Oxford University Press, 1964).
6. David Dessler, "What's at Stake in the Agent-Structure Debate?" *International Organization* 43, no. 3 (1989), 441–73.
7. Richard Rosecrance, *The Rise of the Virtual State: Wealth and Power in the Coming Century* (New York: Basic Books, 1999), xi.
8. As Inis Claude observed, "I have noted . . . a series of charges that Woodrow Wilson, being a critic of the balance of power and an advocate of collective security, thereby stamped himself as a man unable to stomach the reality of power. This conclusion can be sustained only by indulging in the following process of deduction: Everybody who is realistic about power in international relations believes in the balance of power; anybody who attacks the idea of the balance of power is *ipso facto*, unrealistic about power; Wilson attacked the balance of power, thereby showing himself as one possessed by the illusion that the power problem is unreal and that power is unimportant in international relations. It is *not* a conclusion which can withstand careful consideration of the evidence about Wilson." *Power and International Relations* (New York: Random House, 1962), 95. Emphasis in original.
9. Alfred Zimmern, *The Greek Commonwealth: Politics and Economics in Fifth-Century Athens* (New York: Oxford University Press, 1961), 199.
10. Friedrich Meinecke, *Machiavellism* (New Haven, CT: Yale University Press, 1957), 208.
11. Arnold Wolfers and Laurence W. Martin (eds.), *The Anglo-American Tradition in Foreign Affairs* (New Haven, CT: Yale University Press, 1956), xxv.
12. Ibid., xviii. It is probably not coincidental that a number of leading postwar American realists, such as Morgenthau and Reinhold Niebuhr, reached maturity in Europe.
13. See Kenneth N. Waltz, *Theory of International Politics* (Reading, MA: Addison-Wesley, 1979), 18–37.
14. Luther's expedient endorsement of state power as necessary to achieve heavenly paradise resembles Lenin's later compromise recognizing state power as necessary for the achievement of an earthly paradise and the withering of the state itself.
15. See, for example, the Huguenot tract *Vindiciae contra tyrannos* published in 1579 under the pseudonym of Stephen Junius Brutus.
16. See Martin van Creveld, *The Rise and Decline of the State* (Cambridge: Cambridge University Press, 1999), 176–78.
17. For an excellent analysis of Bodin's ideas and their context, see Julian H. Franklin, *Jean Bodin and the Rise of Absolutist Theory* (Cambridge: Cambridge University Press, 1973).
18. Richard N. Rosecrance, *Action and Reaction in World Politics: International Systems in Perspective* (Boston: Little, Brown, 1963), 25.
19. W. Edward Vose Gulick, *Europe's Classical Balance of Power: A Case History of the Theory and Practice of One of the Great Concepts of European Statecraft* (Ithaca, NY: Cornell University Press, 1955), 4. Emphasis in original.
20. Stephen D. Krasner defines these as "domestic" and "international legal" sovereignty respectively, and he argues that their violation, which he calls "organized hypocrisy," "is the normal state of affairs." *Sovereignty: Organized Hypocrisy* (Princeton: Princeton University Press, 1999), 9.
21. See J. D. B. Miller, "Sovereignty as a Source of Vitality for the State," *Review of International Studies* 12, no. 2 (1986), 79–91. See also Robert H. Jackson, *Quasi-States: Sovereignty, International Relations and the Third World* (Cambridge: Cambridge University Press, 1990). In contemporary global politics, recognition of the sovereign independence of a political entity is less a source of vitality than it is a post hoc acknowledgment by other states (or some group within them) that the entity already is playing a significant international role. Or, in the case of many new states, recognition of sovereignty is merely an honorific appellation that only marginally alters their impotence and dependence.
22. Harold Nicolson, *Diplomacy*, 3rd ed. (New York: Oxford University Press, 1963), 24.
23. Cited in Kenneth N. Waltz, *Man, the State and War* (New York: Columbia University Press, 1959), 101.
24. Cited in Paul H. Beik and Laurence Lafore, *Modern Europe: A History Since 1500* (New York: Henry Holt, 1959), 335.
25. The hypothesis that revolution is an expression of frustrated optimism is articulated by James C. Davies, "Toward a Theory of Revolution," *American Sociological Review* 27, no. 1 (1962), 6.
26. Rodney Bruce Hall, *National Collective Identity: Social Constructs and International Systems* (New York: Columbia University Press, 1999), 169.

27. René Albrecht-Carrié, *The Concert of Europe* (New York: Harper & Row, 1968), 4.
28. Rosecrance, *Action and Reaction in World Politics*, 55–56.
29. John Bowle, *Politics and Opinion in the Nineteenth Century* (New York: Oxford University Press, 1964), 27.
30. Hegel, for one, enthusiastically greeted the invading French armies as harbingers of cultural advance. See Shlomo Avinieri, "Hegel and Nationalism" in Walter Kaufmann (ed.), *Hegel's Political Philosophy* (New York: Atherton Press, 1970), 110.
31. Liah Greenfeld, *Nationalism: Five Roads to Modernity* (Cambridge, MA: Harvard University Press, 1992), 330–33.
32. Bowle, *Politics and Opinion in the Nineteenth Century*, 30.
33. Greenfeld, *Nationalism*, 363.
34. Bowle, *Politics and Opinion in the Nineteenth Century*, 37. For a persuasive argument that Hegel was actually antinationalist but was misunderstood by his followers, see Avinieri, "Hegel and Nationalism," 109–36.
35. Greenfeld, *Nationalism*, 348.
36. Ibid., 42. Bowle, *Politics and Opinion in the Nineteenth Century*.
37. Steven B. Smith, "Hegel's Views on War, the State, and International Relations," *American Political Science Review*, 77, no. 3 (1983), 628.
38. Compare the ebullient and optimistic nationalism of *Fidelio* with the dark Volk mythology of *The Ring*.
39. The French attitude is perhaps best summarized in Leon Gambetta's advice regarding the lost provinces: "Think of it always, speak of it never." Cited in René Albrecht-Carrié, *A Diplomatic History of Europe since the Congress of Vienna* (New York: Harper & Row, 1958), 167. In Russia, the individual who perhaps best reflected prevailing currents of Pan-Slavist nationalism was Mikhail Nikoforovich Katkov, editor of *Moskovskie Vyedomosti*. See George F. Kennan, *The Decline of Bismarck's European Order: Franco-Russian Relations, 1875–1890* (Princeton: Princeton University Press, 1979), 33, 94–95.
40. Hall, *National Collective Identity*, 225.
41. Heinrich von Treitschke, "The State Idea," in M. G. Forsyth, H. M. A. Keens-Soper, P. Savigear (eds.), *The Theory of International Relations: Selected Texts from Gentili to Treitschke* (New York: Atherton Press, 1970), 326.
42. Heinrich von Treitschke, "International Law and International Intercourse," in ibid., 338, 339.
43. Treitschke, "The State Idea," 327.
44. Michael Mann, *The Sources of Social Power*, vol. 2, *The Rise of Classes and Nation-States, 1760–1914* (Cambridge: Cambridge University Press, 1993), 733, 734; Hall, *National Collective Identity*, 227.
45. For an excellent critical analysis of Marx's historicism, see Mann, *Sources of Social Power* 2: 23–34.
46. Bowle, *Politics and Opinion in the Nineteenth Century*, 299.
47. Alfred Zimmern, *The League of Nations and the Rule of Law, 1935–1938* (London: Macmillan, 1939), 2.
48. See Edward Hallett Carr, *The Twenty Years' Crisis 1919–1939* (New York: St. Martin's Press, 1962), 2.
49. See Kenneth W. Thompson, "The Study of International Politics: A Survey of Trends and Developments," *Review of Politics* 14, no. 4 (October 1952), 437–39.
50. David Wilkinson, *Deadly Quarrels: Lewis F. Richardson and the Statistical Study of War* (Berkeley, CA: University of California Press, 1980), 7.
51. Vasquez, *Power of Power Politics*, 33.
52. Thompson, "Study of International Politics," 434.
53. Ibid., 438, 437.
54. The functional approach pioneered by David Mitrany reflected this strain of thought. See Mitrany, *A Working Peace System* (London: Royal Institute of International Affairs, 1943).
55. Cited in William T. R. Fox, "Interwar International Relations Research: The American Experience," *World Politics* 2, no. 1 (October 1949), 68.
56. Hedley Bull, "The Theory of International Politics 1919–1969," in B. Porter (ed.), *The Aberystwyth Papers: International Politics 1919–1969* (London: Oxford University Press, 1972), 34.
57. Waltz, *Man, the State and War*, 111.
58. Woodrow Wilson, "The World Must Be Made Safe for Democracy," from an address to Congress, April 2, 1917, in John A. Vasquez (ed.), *Classics of International Relations* (Englewood Cliffs, NJ: Prentice Hall, 1986), 16.
59. Woodrow Wilson, "The Fourteen Points," from an address to Congress, January 8, 1918, in ibid., 18. This passage reflects the influence that Immanual Kant had on Wilson.

60. Such analogies were sharply denounced by realists as false and misleading. In Hans Morgenthau's words: "All history shows that nations active in international politics are continuously preparing for, actively involved in, or recovering from organized violence in the form of war. In the domestic politics of Western democracies, on the other hand, organized violence as an instrument of political action on an extensive scale has become a rare exception." *Politics among Nations: The Struggle for Power and Peace*, 5th ed., rev. (New York: Knopf, 1978), 42.
61. Woodrow Wilson, cited in Waltz, *Man, the State and War*, 118. See also Arnold Wolfers, "The Pole of Power and the Pole of Indifference" in Wolfers, *Discord and Collaboration: Essays on International Politics* (Baltimore: Johns Hopkins Press, 1962), 101.
62. Vasquez, *Power of Power Politics*, 34.
63. Niccolò Machiavelli, *The Prince and the Discourses* (New York: Random House, 1950), xv.
64. See, for example, Hans J. Morgenthau, "Another Great Debate: The National Interest of the United States," *American Political Science Review* 46, no. 4 (1952), 961–88. See also Morgenthau, *In Defense of the National Interest* (New York: Knopf, 1951).
65. Ole Waever, "The Rise and Fall of the Inter-Paradigm Debate," in Steve Smith, Ken Booth, and Marysia Zalewski (eds), *International Theory: Positivism and Beyond* (Cambridge: Cambridge University Press, 1996), 169. Waever argues that the English school is easily linked to postmodernist ideas.
66. See James E. Dougherty and Robert L. Pfaltzgraff, Jr., *Contending Theories of International Relations: A Comprehensive Survey*, 2nd ed. (New York: Harper & Row, 1981), 10, 45 n. 38. International relations courses in the 1950s consisted largely of realist texts and analyses of U.S.–Soviet relations.
67. Vasquez, *Power of Power Politics*, 36.
68. In recent years, heated disputes arising from shifting normative emphases have been clearly reflected in analyses of the causes of the onset and ending of the Cold War, but they were equally characteristic of analyses of earlier wars as well. Revisionist history is an almost inevitable companion of changing social norms.
69. Morgenthau, *Politics among Nations*, 134–55, 158.
70. Relatively little has been written regarding the utility of Kuhn's framework to international relations. For contrasting views, see Richard Smith Beal, "A Contra-Kuhnian View of the Discipline's Growth," in James N. Rosenau (ed.), *In Search of Global Patterns* (New York: Free Press, 1976), 158-61, and Arend Lijphart, "The Structure of the Theoretical Revolution in International Relations," *International Studies Quarterly* 18, no. 1 (1974), 41–74. The "paradigm" concept is finding increasing acceptance in the discipline, though often in a largely metaphorical sense. Of special interest in this regard is the work of Hayward R. Alker, Jr. See Alker and Thomas J. Biersteker, "The Dialectics of World Order: Notes for a Future Archeologist of International Savoir Faire," *International Studies Quarterly* 28, no. 2 (1984), 121–42.
71. Thomas S. Kuhn, *The Structure of Scientific Revolutions*, expanded ed. (Chicago: University of Chicago Press, 1970), 52–53.
72. See, for example, Morgenthau, *Politics among Nations*, 193. Realists were enamored of European balance-of-power practice, frequently arguing that Americans had been able to ignore this practice—at their peril—because of the fortunate circumstances of geography. See Osgood, *Ideals and Self-Interest in America's Foreign Relations*.
73. Morgenthau, *Politics among Nations*, 3, 16.
74. Realists have astutely pointed out that a nation-state's self-image is not always compatible with the realities of power. This insight has provided a basis for theories of status equilibrium and disequilibrium.
75. Morgenthau, *Politics among Nations*, 12.
76. See Robert A. Packenham, *Liberal America and the Third World: Political Development Ideas in Foreign Aid and Social Science* (Princeton: Princeton University Press, 1973), 245.
77. Bernard Brodie, *War and Politics* (New York: Macmillan, 1973), 368, 365.
78. Richard J. Barnet, *The Roots of War: The Men and Institutions behind U.S. Foreign Policy* (Baltimore: Penguin, 1973), 65.
79. David Halberstam, *The Best and the Brightest* (New York: Random House, 1972), 69.
80. Steve Smith, "Positivism and Beyond," in Steve Smith, Ken Booth and Marysia Zalewski (eds.), *International Theory: Positivism and Beyond* (Cambridge: Cambridge University Press, 1996), 23.
81. Arnold Wolfers, "National Security as an Ambiguous Symbol," in Wolfers, *Discord and Collaboration*, 147.
82. Barnet, *Roots of War*, 109ff.
83. Morgenthau, *Politics among Nations*, 7.

84. Kuhn, *Structure of Scientific Revolutions*, 34. Perhaps the best analysis of the work of behavioral and quantitative scholars in this context remains Vasquez, *Power of Power Politics*.

85. On nonrational decisiomaking, see Robert Jervis, *Perception and Misperception in International Politics*. Princeton: (Princeton University Press, 1976). On situational effects on decisonmaking, see Charles F. Herman *Crises in Foreign Policy* (Indianapolis: Bobbs-Merrill, 1969). On organizational behavior, see Graham T. Allision, *Essence of Decision: Explaining the Cuban Missile Crisis* (Boston: Little, Brown, 1971), and Morton H. Halperin, *Bureaucratic Politics and Foreign Policy* (Washington, DC: Bookings Instition, 1974. On transnationalism, see Robert O. Keohane and Joseph Nye Jr. (eds.), *Transnational Relations and World Politics* (Cambridge, MA: Harvard University Press, 1972), and Keohane and Nye, *Power and Interpendence: World Politics in Transition* (Boston: Little, Brown, 177). On nonstate actors, seeRichard W. Mansbach, Yale H. Ferguson, and Donald E. Lampert, *The Web of World Politics: Nonstate Actors in the Global System* (Englewood Cliffs, NJ: Prentice-Hall, 1976). Finally, for issue influences, see Edward L. Morse, *Modernization and the Transformation of International Relations* (New York: Free Press, 1976), and Richard W. Mansbach and John A. Vasquez, *In Search of Theory: A New Paradigm for Global Politics* (New York: Columbia University Press, 1981).

86. Kuhn, *Structure of Scientific Revolutions*, 182. See also Kuhn, "Second Thoughts on Paradigms," in F. Suppe (ed.), *The Structure of Scientific Theories* (Urbana, IL: University of Illinois Press, 1971), 462–63 and Kuhn, *The Essential Tension* (Chicago: University of Chicago Press, 1977), xvi–xxiii.

87. See, for example, Harold D. Lasswell, *World Politics and Personal Insecurity* (New York: McGraw-Hill, 1935); and Alexander L. George and Juliette George, *Woodrow Wilson and Colonel House: A Personality Study* (New York: Day, 1956).

88. See, for example, Samuel P. Huntington, *The Common Defense* (New York: Columbia University Press, 1961); and Warner P. Schilling, Paul Hammond, and Glenn Snyder (eds.), *Strategy, Politics, and Defense Budgets* (New York: Columbia University Press, 1962).

89. See, for example, Ernst B. Haas, *The Uniting of Europe: Political, Social and Economic Forces, 1950–1957* (Stanford: Stanford University Press, 1958).

90. See, for example, Bruce M. Russett, *Trends in World Politics* (New York: Macmillan, 1965); and Raymond Vernon, *Sovereignty at Bay: The Multinational Spread of U.S. Enterprises* (New York: Basic Books, 1971).

91. Joseph S. Nye Jr. *Bound to Lead: The Changing Nature of American Power* (New York: Basic Books, 1990).

92. The postwar explosion of scholarly publications in international relations theory was dominantly American. Consequently, perceived changes in American status have had a fundamental impact on theory. See Kalevi J. Holsti, *The Dividing Discipline: Hegemony and Diversity in International Theory* (Boston: Allen & Unwin, 1985), 102–28.

93. See, for example, Michael Howard, "Reassurance and Deterrence: Western Defense in the 1980s," *Foreign Affairs* 61, no. 2 (1982–83), 309–24.

94. See Mansbach and Vasquez, *In Search of Theory*, 110–13. The concept of 'critical issue' has been analyzed largely in the context of American politics and has to date received little attention in international relations. At present, the process in which a single, all-encompassing issue arrives at the apex of the global agenda is only poorly understood.

95. See Richard K. Ashley, "The Poverty of Neorealism," *International Organization* 38, no. 2 (1984), 232.

96. See, for example, Keohane and Nye, *Transnational Relations and World Politics;* Ole R. Holsti, Randolph M. Siverson, and Alexander L. George (eds.), *Change in the International System* (Boulder, CO: Westview Press, 1980); Stephen D. Krasner (ed.), *International Regimes* (Ithaca, NY: Cornell University Press, 1983); and John Gerard Ruggie (ed.), *The Antinomies of Interdependence: National Welfare and the International Division of Labor* (New York: Columbia University Press, 1983).

97. See Robert O. Keohane, *After Hegemony: Cooperation and Discord in the World Political Economy* (Princeton: Princeton University Press, 1984), esp. 5–17. See also Keohane, "Theory of World Politics: Structural Realism and Beyond," in Keohane (ed.), *Neorealism and Its Critics* (New York: Columbia University Press, 1986), 158–203.

98. Keohane, *After Hegemony*, 105.

99. See, for example, John J. Mearsheimer, "Maneuver, Mobile Defense, and the NATO Central Fronts," *International Security* no. 3 (1981), 104–23, and Mearsheimer, "Why the Soviets Can't Win Quickly in Central Europe," *International Security* 7, no. 4 (1982), 3–40.

100. In "The Poverty of Neorealism," Ashley argues that a new synthesis—neorealism—has already emerged to replace classical realism, and he declares, "In the United States of the 1980s, neo-

realism and its structural theory of hegemony frames the measured discourse and ritual of a generation of graduate students in international politics" (227). In addition, Ashley provides something of a *Weltgeist* interpretation for this development by viewing it as paralleling "structuralist triumphs in such fields as linguistics, sociology, anthropology, and philosophy" (234). While some of his criticisms of neorealism are telling (e.g., reliance on economic logic and revival of state-centricity), his argument is diluted by a self-conscious polemicism. See Robert G. Gilpin's response, "The Richness of the Tradition of Political Realism," *International Organization* 38, no. 2 (1984), esp. 289. Nevertheless, Ashley correctly sees a renewed emphasis upon immutability (structural dominance), pessimism, competitiveness, and elitism (hegemony). These and several other arresting critiques of neorealism are reproduced in Keohane, (ed.), *Neorealism and Its Critics*.

101. Waltz, *Man, the State and War*, 167–71.
102. For an excellent comparison of realism and neorealism, see Randall L. Schweller and David Priess, "A Tale of Two Realisms: Expanding the Institutions Debate," *Mershon International Studies Review* 41, no. 1 (1997), 1–32.
103. David Dessler, "What's at Stake in the Agent-Structure Debate?" *International Organization* 43, no. 3 (1989), 448.
104. John J. Mearsheimer, "Back to the Future: Instability in Europe after the Cold War," *International Security*, 15, no. 1 (1990), 5–56; Mearsheimer, "The Case for Ukrainian Nuclear Deterrent," *Foreign Affairs*, 72, no. 3 (1993), 50-66; and Mearsheimer, "The False Promise of International Institutions," *International Security*, 19, no. 3 (1994), 5–49. See also Kenneth N. Waltz, "Structural Realism after the Cold War," *International Security* 25, no. 1 (2000), 5–41.
105. Rey Koslowski and Friedrich V. Kratochwil, "Understanding Change in International Politics: The Soviet Empire's Demise and the International System," *International Organization*, 48, no. 2 (1994), 218.
106. See, for example, ibid., 222–27, for a "constructivist approach" to the issue of change.
107. Vasquez, *Power of Power Politics*, 373.
108. Wade L. Huntley, "Kant's Third Image: Systemic Sources of the Liberal Peace," *International Studies Quarterly*, 40, no. 1 (1996), 67.
109. Robert O. Keohane and Lisa Martin, "The Promise of Institutionalist Theory," *International Security* 20, no. 1 (1995), 39.
110. Alexander Wendt, "Constructing International Politics," *International Security* 20, no. 1 (1995), 72.
111. Charles E. Lindblom and David Cohen, *Usable Knowledge: Social Science and Social Problem Solving* (New Haven: Yale University Press, 1979), 79. See also Oran R. Young, "The Perils of Odysseus: On Constructing Theories of International Relations," *World Politics* 24 suppl. (Spring 1972), 179–203.
112. See, for example, Michael Useem, "Government Influence on the Social Science Paradigm," *Sociological Quarterly* 17, no. 2 (1976), 159–60.
113. Bernard Barber, *Science and the Social Order* (London: Allen & Unwin, 1953), 4. See also Duncan J. Macrae, *The Social Function of Social Science* (New Haven: Yale University Press, 1976), passim.

CHAPTER 5: THE STATE AS AN OBSTACLE TO UNDERSTANDING GLOBAL POLITICS

1. Martin Wight, "Why Is There No International Theory?" in Herbert Butterfield and Martin Wight (eds.), *Diplomatic Investigations: Essays in the Theory of International Politics* (London: Allen & Unwin, 1966), 17. For a more positive evaluation of the state of global-politics theory, see Warren R. Phillips, "Where Have All the Theories Gone?" *World Politics* 26, no. 2 (1974), 155–88.
2. Even so, purportedly cosmopolitan thinkers like Thomas Paine thought in terms of a world of states, albeit democracies.
3. Wight, "Why Is There No International Theory?" 18.
4. Ibid., 21.
5. James N. Rosenau, *Along the Domestic-Foreign Frontier: Exploring Governance in a Turbulent World* (Cambridge: Cambridge University Press, 1997).
6. See R. B. J. Walker, *Inside/Outside: International Relations as Political Theory* (Cambridge: Cambridge University Press, 1993).

7. Hans J. Morgenthau, *Politics among Nations: The Struggle for Power and Peace*, 5th ed. rev. (New York: Knopf, 1978), esp. chap. 1 and part 3.
8. Inis L. Claude Jr., "Myths about the State," *Review of International Studies*, 12, no. 1 (1986), 1.
9. Claude discusses seven myths that he sees as having grown up in specialized contexts and eras. Ibid., 1–10.
10. Benjamin N. Cardozo, *The Nature of the Judicial Process* (New Haven: Yale University Press, 1921), 13.
11. William J. Brennan, Jr., "The Constitution of the United States: Contemporary Ratification," Text and Teaching Symposium, Georgetown University, Washington, DC, October 12, 1985, 9.
12. Oliver Wendell Holmes, *The Common Law* (1881), cited in Jack Greenberg, "Litigation for Social Change: Methods, Limits and Role in Democracy" *Record of the Association of the Bar of the City of New York* 29 (1974), 347.
13. Cardozo, *Nature of the Judicial Process*, 76–77, 81–82, 82–83.
14. This is a proposition we first explored at length in Yale H. Ferguson and Richard W. Mansbach, *The State, Conceptual Chaos, and the Future of International Relations Theory* (Boulder, CO: Lynne Rienner, 1989).
15. Kalevi J. Holsti, *The State, War, and the State of War* (Cambridge: Cambridge University Press, 1996), 83
16. It was this concern that prompted us to examine the concept of international actor over twenty-five years ago. See Richard W. Mansbach, Yale H. Ferguson, and Donald E. Lampert, *The Web of World Politics: Nonstate Actors in the Global System* (Englewood Cliffs, NJ: Prentice-Hall, 1976). At that time, we argued that among the factors accounting for the longevity of the concept were the relatively easy availability of aggregate data regarding states, the desire of scholars to work with readily comparable data, and their preference for units of analysis that did not overlap (30). We have no reason to revise that assessment but have concluded that the problem has significantly deeper sources than we then suspected.
17. F. H. Hinsley, *Sovereignty*, 2nd ed. (Cambridge: Cambridge University Press, 1986), 120.
18. Martin van Creveld, *The Rise and Decline of the State* (Cambridge: Cambridge University Press, 1999), 126.
19. Immanuel Wallerstein, *The Modern World-System: Capitalist Agriculture and the Origins of the European World-Economy in the Sixteenth Century* (New York: Academic Press, 1974), 357.
20. Nicos Poulantzas, *State, Power, Socialism*, trans. Patrick Camiller (London: NLB, 1978), 7.
21. J. P. Nettl, "The State as a Conceptual Variable," *World Politics* 20, no. 4 (July 1968), 559.
22. Stephen D. Krasner, "Approaches to the State: Alternative Conceptions and Historical Dynamics," *Comparative Politics* 16, no. 2 (1984), 223.
23. Stephen D. Krasner, "State Power and the Structure of International Trade," *World Politics* 28, no. 3 (1976), 317.
24. Krasner, "Approaches to the State," 244.
25. James N. Rosenau, "Governance, Order, and Change in World Politics," in Rosenau and Ernst-Otto Czempiel, eds., *Governance without Government: Order and Change in World Politics* (Cambridge: Cambridge University Press, 1992), 4.
26. Ibid., 14.
27. See Paul Wapner, "Politics beyond the State: Environmental Activism and World Civic Politics," *World Politics* 47, no. 3 (1995), 311–40.
28. Rosenau, *Along the Domestic-Foreign Frontier*, 39; see also chap. 8, "Governance."
29. Sabino Cassese, "The Rise and Decline of the Notion of State," *International Political Science Review* 7, no. 2 (1986), 121.
30. J. W. Burton, *Systems, States, Diplomacy and Rules* (New York: Cambridge University Press, 1968), 9.
31. Donald J. Puchala, *International Politics Today* (New York: Harper & Row, 1971), 28.
32. Bertrand Badie and Pierre Birnbaum, *The Sociology of the State*, trans. Arthur Goldhammer (Chicago: University of Chicago Press, 1983), 139–40.
33. Ronald Cohen, introduction, in Ronald Cohen and Elman R. Service (eds.), *Origins of the State: The Anthropology of Political Evolution* (Philadelphia: ISHI, 1978), 8. For intriguing support from the perspective of natural selection theory that the state emerged from processes of both cooperation and conflict, see Roger D. Masters, "The Biological Nature of the State," *World Politics* 35, no. 2 (1983), 161–93.
34. Cohen, introduction to Cohen and Service, *Origins of the State*, 8.
35. Ibid., 2. As we suggest elsewhere in this book, Cohen's personal definition is essentially Weberian. See also Ronald Cohen, "State Origins: A Reappraisal" in Henri J. M. Claessen and

Peter Skalnik (eds.), *The Early State* (The Hague: Mouton, 1978), 31–75. Two additional essays in part 1 of this collection are particularly useful: the editors' "The Early State: Theories and Hypotheses," 3–29; and Anatoli M. Khazanov, "Some Theoretical Problems of the Study of the Early State," 77–92.

36. Jonathan Haas, *The Evolution of the Prehistoric State* (New York: Columbia University Press, 1982), 2–3. Emphasis added.

37. Ernest Gellner, *Nations and Nationalism* (Ithaca, NY: Cornell University Press, 1983), 5. Emphasis in original. See also, George Modelski, "Agraria and Industria: Two Models of the International System," in Klaus Knorr and Sidney Verba (eds.), *The International System* (Princeton: Princeton University Press, 1961), 125 ff.; and Roger D. Masters, "World Politics as a Primitive Political System," *World Politics* 16, no. 4 (1964), 595–619.

38. Badie and Birnbaum, *Sociology of the State*, 65.

39. Ibid., 103.

40. Ibid., 60.

41. Ibid., 105–15; quotation on 105.

42. Ibid., 103–4.

43. Morton H. Fried, "The State, the Chicken, and the Egg: Or What Came First?" in Cohen and Service *Origins of the State*, 37.

44. Oran R. Young, "The Actors in World Politics," in James N. Rosenau, Vincent Davis, and Maurice A. East (eds.), *The Analysis of International Politics* (New York: Free Press, 1972), 127.

45. Stephen D. Krasner, "Westphalia and All That," in Judith Goldstein and Robert O. Keohane (eds.), *Ideas and Foreign Policy: Beliefs, Institutions, and Political Change* (Ithaca, NY: Cornell University Press, 1993), 235.

46. See Yale H. Ferguson and Richard W. Mansbach, *Polities: Authority, Identities, and Change* (Columbia, SC: University of South Carolina Press, 1996).

47. For example, see Adda B. Bozeman, *Politics and Culture in International History* (Princeton: Princeton University Press, 1960); Robert G. Wesson, *State Systems: International Pluralism, Politics, and Culture* (New York: Free Press, 1978); Allen W. Johnson and Timothy Earle, *The Evolution of Human Societies: From Foraging Group to Agrarian State* (Stanford, CA: Stanford University Press, 1987); S. N. Eisenstadt, *The Political Systems of Empires* (New York: Free Press, 1963); John H. Kautsky, *The Politics of Aristocratic Empires* (Chapel Hill, NC: University of North Carolina Press, 1982); M. I. Finley, *Politics in the Ancient World* (Cambridge: Cambridge University Press, 1983); John A. Armstrong, *Nations before Nationalism* (Chapel Hill, NC: University of North Carolina Press, 1982); Anthony D. Smith, *The Ethnic Origins of Nations* (Oxford: Basil Blackwell, 1986); and John H. Hall (ed.), *States in History* (Oxford: Oxford University Press, 1986).

48. Young, "Actors in World Politics," 131. See also Mansbach, Ferguson, and Lampert, *Web of World Politic*, 22–25.

49. Charles W. Kegley, Jr., and Eugene R. Wittkopf, *World Politics: Trends and Transformation*, 2nd ed. (New York: St. Martin's Press, 1985), fn. 78–79.

50. David Vital, "Back to Machiavelli," in Klaus Knorr and James N. Rosenau (eds.), *Contending Approaches to International Politics* (Princeton: Princeton University Press, 1969), 155–56.

51. William W. Bishop Jr., *International Law: Cases and Materials*, 3rd ed. (Boston: Little, Brown, 1971), 306–7.

52. Bruce M. Russett and Harvey Starr, *World Politics: The Menu for Choice* (San Francisco: W. H. Freeman, 1981), 68. Emphasis in original.

53. Cited in "Unreformable?" *The Economist*, January 8–14, 2000, 44.

54. Robert H. Jackson, "Quasi-States, Dual Regimes, and Neoclassical Theory: International Jurisprudence and the Third World," *International Organization* 41, no. 4 (1987), 526, 527.

55. Gerald B. Helman and Steven R. Ratner, "Saving Failed States," *Foreign Policy* 89 (Winter 1992–93), 3.

56. Jeffrey Herbst, "Responding to State Failure in Africa," *International Security* 21, no. 3 (1996–97), 142.

57. See Johan Galtung, "The Social Sciences: An Essay on Polarization and Integration" in Knorr and Rosenau, *Contending Approaches to International Politics*, 243–85.

58. See, for example, J. David Singer, *The Wages of War, 1816-1965: A Statistical Handbook* (New York: Wiley, 1972). Efforts by Correlates of War scholars to test hypotheses about the onset of war using status ordering, alliance aggregation, and so forth, as intervening variables are complicated by uncertainty as to the comparability of the units that constitute the global system during different historical eras.

59. This is the thrust of the model advanced in Hinsley, *Sovereignty*.

60. Yale H. Ferguson and Richard W. Mansbach, "Global Politics at the Turn of the Millennium: Changing Bases of 'Us' and 'Them,'" *International Studies Review*, Special Issue 1, no. 2 (1999), 77–107.
61. Hall, *States in History*, 16–17.
62. John H. Herz, *International Politics in the Atomic Age* (New York: Columbia University Press, 1959), chaps. 2–4. See also John H. Herz, *The Nation-State and the Crisis of World Politics* (New York: David McKay, 1976), chaps. 3, 8. In addition, see especially on this period, Charles Tilly (ed.), *The Formation of National States in Western Europe* (Princeton: Princeton University Press, 1975).
63. J. P. Nettl observes, "It is significant that the word *l'Etat* in French should be the only one normally beginning with a capital letter." "The State as a Conceptual Variable," 567.
64. Badie and Birnbaum, *Sociology of the State*, 114.
65. See Liah Greenfeld, *Nationalism: Five Roads to Modernity* (Cambridg, MA: Harvard University Press, 1992), 112–33.
66. Badie and Birnbaum, *Sociology of the State*, 105.
67. Peter Worsley, *The Three Worlds: Culture and World Development* (Chicago: University of Chicago Press, 1984), 273.
68. Wesson describes the process of decay in the later stages of Louis XIV's long reign: "The model monarchy of Louis XIV decayed in its last decades, and some began calling for security of property and an end to religious persecution and arbitrary government. . . . Personal monarchy decayed into bureaucratic as government became professionalized. Roads, communications, and postal services that governments fostered for ease of administration and improvement of national economies, made for greater political awareness. New middle classes deriving wealth from nonofficial sources acquired more importance . . . and there was a revolutionary increase of foreign trade . . . Growing knowledge of far-off lands broadened horizons and assisted criticisms of domestic foibles. The idea that the wealth of the people made the greatness of the sovereign . . . grew into the thesis of "benevolent despotism" by which it became fashionable to think of princes ruling not by divine mandate, which lost intellectual respectability, but because enlightened, therefore benevolent despots were responsible for the progress and happiness of their people—a doctrine dangerous for monarchy. Although the philosophers saw no alternative to monarchy, recollection of medieval natural law gave a basis for new ideas of rights; and several thinkers derived sovereignty directly from the people. Power became a trust rather than a God-given privilege, a mandate to be exercised by reason. Contract theories of the state, a reflection of the importance of commercial relations, gained in importance (Wesson, *State Systems*, 142).
69. Among the extensive literature on nationalism see, Benedict Anderson, *Imagined Communities: Reflections on the Origin and Spread of Nationalism* (London: Verso, 1983); Gellner, *Nations and Nationalism;* Greenfeld, *Nationalism;* Hans Kohn, *The Idea of Nationalism* (New York: Macmillan, 1944); Frederick Hertz, *Nationality in History and Politics* (New York: Humanities Press, 1944); E. J. Hobsbawm, *Nations and Nationalism since 1780: Programme, Myth, Reality* (Cambridge: Cambridge University Press, 1990); and Hugh Seton-Watson, *Nations and States* (Boulder, CO: Westview Press, 1977).
70. Rodney Bruce Hall, *National Collective Identity: Social Constructs and International Systems* (New York: Columbia University Press, 1999), 140–45.
71. Alexander B. Murphy, "The Sovereign State System as Political-Territorial Ideal: Historical and Contemporary Considerations," in Thomas J. Biersteker and Cynthia Weber (eds.) *Social Sovereignty as Social Construct* (Cambridge: Cambridge University Press, 1996), 97.
72. See Yosef Lapid, "Culture's Ship: Returns and Departures in International Relations Theory," in Yosef Lapid and Friedrich Kratochwil (eds.), *The Return of Culture and Identity in ir Theory* (Boulder, CO: Lynne Rienner, 1996), 3–20.
73. Gellner, *Nations and Nationalism*, 56.
74. Ibid., 34.
75. Worsley, *Three Worlds*, 292.
76. See Armstrong, *Nations before Nationalism;* and Smith, *Ethnic Origins, of Nations*. Armstrong and Smith both emphasize the importance of ethnicity in the world's political evolution. Ethnic identities are real and widespread; many have a long history, in some cases actually extending into prehistory; and the existence of an ethnic core was critical to establishment of some modern states. Nevertheless, continued ethnic fragmentation remains a major challenge to many present nation builders (and maintainers).
77. Gellner, *Nations and Nationalism*, 55–56.
78. Worsley, *Three Worlds*, 252.

79. This postwar development is not unprecedented. The breakup of the Austro-Hungarian and Russian Empires as a consequence of World War I and the spreading of the "national principle" by Western liberals produced a host of weak and economically dependent states in Central Europe that proved ready prey for Nazi influence in the 1930s. Arguably, the erosion of the Roman Empire had the same consequences.

80. Worsley, *Three Worlds*, 290.

81. Ibid., 290, 289.

82. W. Raymond Duncan, *Latin American Politics: A Developmental Approach* (New York: Praeger, 1976), 121.

83. Alessandro Passerind 'Entreves, *The Notion of the State: An Introduction to Political Theory* (London: Oxford University Press, 1967), 96.

84. Clifford Geertz, *Negara: The Theatre State in Nineteenth-Century Bali* (Princeton: Princeton University Press, 1981).

85. Nettl, "State as a Conceptual Variable," 560.

86. Hinsley, *Sovereignty*, 1. Hinsley's is a brilliant study, by far the best to date, of the historical evolution of the concept.

87. Alan James, *Sovereign Statehood: The Basis of International Society* (London: Allen & Unwin, 1986), 25.

88. Ibid., especially 180 ff.

89. Ibid., 276–77.

90. See especially Robert H. Jackson and Carl G. Rosberg, "Why Africa's Weak States Persist: The Empirical and the Juridical in Statehood," *World Politics* 35, no. 1 (1982), 1–24; Robert H. Jackson, "Negative Sovereignty in Sub-Saharan Africa," *Review of International Studies* 12, no. 4 (1986); 246–64; Robert H. Jackson, "African States and International Theory," paper delivered at the British International Studies Association annual meeting, University of Reading, Reading, U.K., December 16, 1986; and Robert H. Jackson, *Quasi-States: Sovereignty, International Relations and the Third World* (Cambridge: Cambridge University Press, 1990).

91. Jackson, "African States and International Theory," 29.

92. Ibid., 4–7. See also James Mayall, "The Variety of States," paper delivered at the British International Studies Association annual meeting, University of Reading Reading, U.K., December 16, 1986.

93. Jackson, "African States and International Theory," 33.

94. Ibid., 36–38. The reference is to J. D. B. Miller, "Sovereignty as a Source of Vitality for the State," *Review of International Studies* 12, no. 2 (1986), 79–91.

95. Stephen D. Krasner, *Sovereignty: Organized Hypocrisy* (Princeton: Princeton University Press, 1999), 8, 9.

96. Jackson and Rosberg, "Why Africa's Weak States Persist," 13–14.

97. John Gerard Ruggie, "Continuity and Transformation in the World Polity: Toward a Neorealist Synthesis," *World Politics* 35, no. 2 (January 1983), 275–76.

98. Ibid., 776 n.39. We see no need to alter our views.

99. Kenneth N. Waltz, *Theory of International Politics* (Reading, MA: Addison-Wesley, 1979), 96.

100. Ruggie, "Continuity and Transformation in the World Polity," 276n. 39, 276. Emphasis in original.

101. Ibid., 280. Emphasis in original.

102. Thomas J. Biersteker and Cynthia Weber, "The social construction of state sovereignty," in Biersteker and Weber, *Social Sovereignty as Social Construct*, 1.

103. David Strang, "Contested sovereignty: the social construction of colonial imperialism," in Biersteker and Weber (eds.) *Social Sovereignty as Social Construct*, 31.

104. Waltz, *Theory of International Politics*, 91.

105. For a careful analysis of Weber's writings on the state and citations of his major works, see Badie and Birnbaum, *Sociology of the State*, 17–24. We have drawn heavily on Badie and Birnbaum in our discussion of Weber, as well as of Durkheim and Parsons below.

106. Eric A. Nordlinger, *On the Autonomy of the Democratic State* (Cambridge, MA: Harvard University Press, 1981).

107. Badie and Birnbaum, *Sociology of the State*, 23–24.

108. Janice E. Thomson, *Mercenaries, Pirates, and Sovereigns: State-Building and Extraterritorial Violence in Early Modern Europe* (Princeton: Princeton University Press, 1994), 17, 151.

109. Colombia formally turned over two large areas of the country to leftist guerrilla groups, surely a de facto surrender of sovereignty. The government later sought their recovery.

110. Quoted in Badie and Birnbaum, *Sociology of the State*, 12.

111. Ibid., 28, 27.

112. Ibid., 56.
113. Ibid., 49, 60, 62.
114. Ibid., 100–1. See also Howard J. Wiarda, *Ethnocentrism in Foreign Policy: Can We Understand the Third World?* (Washington, DC: American Enterprise Institute for Public Policy Research, 1985). On participation, see especially Samuel P. Huntington and Joan M. Nelson, *No Easy Choice: Political Participation in Developing Countries* (Cambridge, MA: Harvard University Press, 1976).
115. Stephen D. Krasner, *Defending the National Interest: Raw Materials Investments and U.S. Foreign Policy* (Princeton: Princeton University Press, 1978). For a succinct description of the Marxist model of international relations, see Wojciech Kostecki, "A Marxist Paradigm of International Relations," *International Studies Notes* 12, no. 1 (1985), 19–21.
116. Krasner, *Defending the National Interest*, 27.
117. Associated especially with the work of Graham Allison and Morton Halperin. We will examine this approach in chapter 7.
118. Krasner, "Approaches to the State," 224–25.
119. Nordlinger, *On the Autonomy of the Democratic State*, 11. Emphasis added.
120. Ibid., 9–10.
121. Ibid., 8.
122. Ibid., 7.
123. Ibid., 186–87. Emphasis in original.
124. In Great Britain, devices such as cabinet responsibility serve to perpetuate the same myth.
125. Manfred Wilhelmy, "Politics, Bureaucracy, and Foreign Policy in Chile," in Heraldo Muñoz and Joseph S. Tulchin (eds.), *Latin American Nations in World Politics* (Boulder, CO: Westview Press, 1984), 50.
126. See James N. Rosenau, *Along the Domestic-Foreign Frontier*, chap. 6.
127. John Agnew and Stuart Corbridge, *Mastering Space: Hegemony, Territory and International Political Economy* (New York: Routledge, 1995), 80.
128. Robert D. Kaplan, "The Coming Anarchy," *Atlantic Monthly*, February 1994, 46. See also Kaplan, *The Ends of the Earth: A Journey to the Frontiers of Anarchy* (New York: Vintage, 1996).
129. John Markoff, "U.S. Fails to Win Global Accord on Police Internet Eavesdropping," *New York Times*, March 27, 1997, A1, C3.
130. Philip G. Cerny, "Globalization and the Changing Logic of Collective Action," *International Organization* 49, no. 4 (Autumn 1995), 595–625.
131. James N. Rosenau, *Turbulence in World Politics: A Theory of Change and Continuity* (Princeton: Princeton University Press, 1990), 11; quotation on 334.
132. Dina A. Zinnes, "Prerequisites for the Study of System Transformation," in Ole R. Holsti, Randolph M. Siverson, and Alexander L. George (eds.), *Change in the International System* (Boulder, CO: Westview Press, 1980), 5.

CHAPTER 6: THE UNCERTAIN BOUNDS OF BOUNDED RATIONALITY

1. Kenneth N. Waltz, *Theory of International Politics* (Reading, MA: Addison-Wesley, 1979), 77. Some pages later (118), Waltz denies that his theory requires any assumption of rationality. Robert O. Keohane, writing about Waltz, declares, "The link between system structure and actor behavior is forged by the rationality assumption, which enables the theorist to predict that leaders will respond to the incentives and constraints imposed by their environments." Keohane, "Theory of World Politics: Structural Realism and Beyond," in Keohane (ed.), *Neorealism and Its Critics* (New York: Columbia University Press, 1986), 167.
2. Jack S. Levy, "Prospect Theory, Rational Choice, and International Relations," *International Studies Quarterly* 41, no. 1 (1997), 88.
3. Miles Kahler, "Rationality in International Relations," *International Organization* 52, no. 4 (1998), 939.
4. Efforts to study national attributes in order to predict and explain behavior avoid the need to assume rationality. The results of this research have, however, been disappointing to date. Even more importantly, such research is difficult to relate to policy because the variables upon which it focuses tend to be nonmanipulable.
5. John A. Vasquez, *The Power of Power Politics: From Classical Realism to Neotraditionalism* (Cambridge: Cambridge University Press, 1998), 156. Emphasis added. As noted earlier, we do not consider realism a genuine paradigm.

6. Kahler, "Rationality in International Relations," 926.
7. Cited in ibid., 920.
8. Ibid., 921.
9. Hans J. Morgenthau, *Politics among Nations: The Struggle for Power and Peace*, 5th ed., rev. (New York: Knopf, 1978), 5. Emphasis added.
10. Steve Smith, "Theories of Foreign Policy: An Historical View," *Review of International Studies* 12, no. 1 (1986), 14–15.
11. Morgenthau, *Politics among Nations*, 4.
12. Ibid., 5. Emphasis added.
13. Ibid., 7.
14. Ibid., 8.
15. Vasquez, *Power of Power Politics*, 218, 219.
16. For an excellent example of the use of rational choice analysis to examine the causes of war, see Bruce Bueno de Mesquita and David Lalman, *War and Reason* (New Haven: Yale University Press, 1992).
17. Vasquez, *Power of Power Politics*, 219.
18. Ibid., 32.
19. Robert O. Keohane, *After Hegemony: Cooperation and Discord in the World Political Economy* (Princeton: Princeton University Press, 1984), 66. Emphasis added. See also Keohane, "International Institutions: Two Approaches," in Keohane, *International Institutions and State Power: Essays in International Relations Theory* (Boulder, CO: Westview Press, 1989), 168–71.
20. It also assumes that one can differentiate between domestic and foreign arenas, an assumption that is highly dubious in an era of multiple boundaries and identities.
21. Edward A. Comor, *Communication, Commerce and Power: The Political Economy of America and the Direct Broadcast Satellite, 1960–2000* (New York: St. Martin's Press, 1998), 7–8.
22. Sidney Verba, "Assumptions of Rationality and Non-rationality in Models of the International System" in Klaus Knorr and Sidney Verba (eds.), *The International System: Theoretical Essays* (Princeton: Princeton University Press, 1961), 95. This model was always regarded as an ideal type. Neither sufficient information nor information processing capability was believed to be available to individuals for its attainment.
23. For a debate regarding the utility of assuming rationality in deterrence, see *World Politics* 41, no. 2 (1989); specifically, Christopher H. Achen and Duncan Snidal, "Rational Deterrence Theory and Comparative Case Studies" (143–69); Alexander L. George and Richard Smoke, "Deterrence and Foreign Policy" (170–82); Robert Jervis, "Rational Deterrence: Theory and Evidence" (183–207); Richard Ned Lebow and Janice Gross Stein, "Rational Deterrence Theory: I Think, Therefore I Deter" (208–24); and George W. Downs, "The Rational Deterrence Debate" (225–37).
24. Richard W. Cottam, *Foreign Policy Motivation* (Pittsburgh: University of Pittsburgh Press, 1977), 3. The key issues in the debate between science and "traditionalism" are to be found in Klaus Knorr and James N. Rosenau (eds.), *Contending Approaches to International Politics* (Princeton: Princeton University Press, 1969).
25. Thomas C. Schelling, *The Strategy of Conflict* (Cambridge, MA: Harvard University Press, 1960); Schelling, *Arms and Influence* (New Haven: Yale University Press, 1966). For a sophisticated analysis of the variety of games in global politics, see Glenn H. Snyder and Paul Diesing, *Conflict among Nations: Bargaining, Decision Making and System Structure in Inernational Crises* (Princeton: Princeton University Press, 1977). Herman Kahn, *Thinking about the Unthinkable* (New York: Horizon Press, 1962); Kahn, *On Escalation: Metaphors and Scenarios* (New York: Praeger, 1965).
26. Richard J. Barnet, *The Roots of War: The Men and Institutions behind U.S. Foreign Policy* (Baltimore: Penguin, 1973), 44.
27. John D. Steinbruner, *The Cybernetic Theory of Decision: New Dimensions of Political Analysis* (Princeton: Princeton University Press, 1974), 9.
28. Cottam, *Foreign Policy Motivation*, 6. For a penetrating analysis of the effect of Vietnam on American views, see Ole R. Holsti and James N. Rosenau, *American Leadership and World Affairs: Vietnam and the Breakdown of Consensus* (Boston: Allen & Unwin, 1984).
29. Levy, "Prospect Theory, Rational Choice, and International Relations," 87.
30. See, for example, Barnet, *Roots of War*, chap. 2.
31. Steinbruner, *Cybernetic Theory of Decision*, 27.
32. Richard C. Snyder, H. W. Bruck, and Burton Sapin, "Decision-Making as an Approach to the Study of International Politics" in Snyder, Bruck, and Sapin (eds.), *Foreign Policy Decision-Making*

(New York: Free Press, 1962), 14–185. Harold Sprout and Margaret Sprout, "Environmental Factors in the Study of International Politics," in James N. Rosenau (ed.), *International Politics and Foreign Policy*, rev. ed. (New York: Free Press, 1969), 41–56. See also Sprout and Sprout, *Man-Milieu Relationship Hypotheses in the Context of International Politics* (Princeton: Center of International Studies, 1956), *The Ecological Perspective on Human Affairs with Special Reference to International Politics* (Princeton: Princeton University Press, 1965), and *An Ecological Paradigm for the Study of International Politics*, Research Monograph no. 30 (Princeton: Center of International Studies, 1968). Joseph H. de Rivera, *The Psychological Dimension of Foreign Policy* (Columbus, OH: Charles E. Merrill, 1968), 21. Emphasis in original.

33. Paul Dickson, *Official Explanations* (New York: Delacorte Press, 1980), 28.
34. De Rivera, *Psychological Dimension of Foreign Policy*, 43. Emphasis in original.
35. Verba, "Assumptions of Rationality and Non-rationality," 109, 110, 112, 113.
36. See especially James G. March and Herbert Simon, *Organizations* (New York: Wiley, 1957); Herbert Simon, *Models of Man* (New York: Wiley, 1957), and *Administrative Behavior: A Discussion of Decision-Making Process in Administrative Organization*, 2nd ed. (New York: Macmillan, 1961).
37. See especially Charles E. Lindblom, *The Policy-Making Process* (Englewood Cliffs, NJ: Prentice-Hall, 1968), and "The Science of Muddling Through," *Public Administration Review* 19, no. 2 (1959), 79–88. For a careful comparison of the assumptions of the rational model with those advanced by Simon and Lindblom, see William I. Bacchus, *Foreign Policy and the Bureaucratic Process: The State Department's Country Director System* (Princeton: Princeton University Press, 1974), 19–23.
38. Verba, "Assumptions of Rationality and Non-rationality," 115, 116.
39. See Alexander E. Wendt, "The Agent-Structure Problem in International Relations Theory," *International Organization* 41, no. 3 (1987), 335–70. Wendt observes that "'agent-structure,' 'parts-whole,' 'actor-system,' and 'micro-macro' problems all reflect the same meta-theoretical imperative" (338).
40. One must, of course, be alert to the potential for "groupthink" in such a process. Irving Janis, *Victims of Groupthink: A Psychological Study of Foreign-Policy Decisions and Fiascoes* (Boston: Houghton Mifflin, 1972).
41. Jervis, "Rational Deterrence," 204, 205.
42. Graham T. Allison, *Essence of Decision: Explaining the Cuban Missile Crisis* (Boston: Little, Brown, 1971), 10. In order to take account of new information about the missile crisis that became available after the Cold War, Allison and Philip Zelikow published a second edition of the book (New York: Longman, 1999). Allison's model I is vigorously critiqued in Jonathan Bendor and Thomas H. Hammond, "Rethinking Allison's Models," *American Political Science Review* 86, no. 2 (1992) 301-22.
43. Steinbruner, *Cybernetic Theory of Decision*.
44. On this point, see Ronald L. Jepperson, Alexander Wendt, and Peter J. Katzenstein, "Norms, Identities, and Culture of National Security," in Peter J. Katzenstein (ed.), *The Culture of National Security: Norms and Identity in World Politics* (New York: Columbia University Press, 1996), 60–61.
45. Yosef Lapid, "Culture's Ship: Returns and Departures in International Relations Theory," in Yosef Lapid and Friedrich Kratochwil, *The Return of Culture and Identity in IR Theory* (Boulder, CO: Lynne Rienner, 1996), 3.
46. John Keegan, *A History of Warfare* (New York: Knopf, 1993), 3.
47. Jon Elster *The Cement of Society: A Study of Social Order* (Cambridge: Cambridge University Press, 1989), 100.
48. See Jim George, *Discourses of Global Politics: A Critical (Re)Introduction to International Relations* (Boulder, CO: Lynne Rienner, 1994).
49. D. S. L. Jarvis, *International Relations and the Challenge of Postmodernism: Defending the Discipline* (Columbia, SC: University of South Carolina Press, 2000), 22. The term "ontology" has become very fashionable in postpositivist scholarship and has spread to opponents as well. Unfortunately, in many cases it is misused, having lost its original metaphysical meaning of "essence of being," and is equated with little more than what used to be called "units of analysis." In other words, it has been trivialized through being equated with "the furniture" in the shop window.
50. See, for example, Richard K. Ashley and R. B. J. Walker, "Speaking the Language of Exile: Dissident Thought in International Studies," *International Studies Quarterly* 34, no. 3 (1990), 259–66.
51. Steve Smith, "Positivism and Beyond," in Steve Smith, Ken Booth, and Marysia Zalewski (eds.), *International Theory: Positivism and Beyond* (Cambridge: Cambridge University Press, 1996), 23.
52. Chris Brown, "'Turtles All the Way Down': Anti-Foundationalism, Critical Theory and International Relations," *Millennium* 23 (Summer 1994), 216.

53. Arnold A. Rogow, *James Forrestal: A Study in Personality, Politics, and Policy* (New York: Macmillan, 1963). Alexander L. George and Juliette L. George, *Woodrow Wilson and Colonel House: A Personality Study* (New York: Day, 1956).

54. Robert A. Isaak, *Individuals and World Politics*, 2nd ed. (North Scituate, MA: Duxbury Press, 1981). De Rivera, *Psychological Dimension of Foreign Policy*, especially chap. 5. Margaret G. Hermann and Thomas W. Milburn (eds.), *A Psychological Examination of Political Leaders* (New York: Free Press, 1977). Lloyd S. Etheridge, *A World of Men: The Private Sources of American Foreign Policy* (Cambridge, MA: MIT Press, 1978).

55. See, for example, Margaret G. Hermann, "When Leader Personality Will Affect Foreign Policy: Some Propositions" in James N. Rosenau (ed.), *In Search of Global Patterns* (New York: Free Press, 1976), 326–33.

56. See, for example, Harold D. Lasswell, *World Politics and Personal Insecurity* (New York: McGraw-Hill, 1935). Even doodles become the subject of scrutiny as exemplified in the attention scholars pay to the wolves that Stalin drew in the margins of papers and documents.

57. Kahler, "Rationality in International Relations," 928.

58. De Rivera, *Psychological Dimension of Foreign Policy*, 168, 167. The barriers to adequate conceptualization of psychological constructs are epitomized in James David Barber, *The Presidential Character: Predicting Performance in the White House* (Englewood Cliffs, NJ: Prentice-Hall, 1972).

59. On this point, see especially Gunnar Sjoblom, "Some Problems of the Operational Code Approach," in Christer Jönsson (ed.), *Cognitive Dynamics and International Politics* (New York: St. Martin's Press, 1982), 37–74.

60. See, for example, James N. Rosenau, "Pre-theories and Theories of Foreign Policy," in R. Barry Farrell (ed.), *Approaches to Comparative and International Politics* (Evanston, IL: Northwestern University Press, 1966), 27–93

61. Sjoblom, "Some Problems of the Operational Code Approach," 45.

62. Ole Holsti takes strong exception to Sjoblom's argument along this line, but his counter is little more than an assertion that an emphasis on organizations or bureaucracies entails even more severe theoretical problems. It is significant, as Sjoblom and several of the other authors in the Jönsson collection note, that "operational code" was actually coined back in the early 1950s by Nathan Leites to describe aspects of Bolshevik doctrine, rather than individual behavior. See Nathan Leites, *The Operational Code of the Politburo* (New York: McGraw-Hill, 1951).

63. Kahler, "Rationality in International Relations," 926.

64. Philip E. Tetlock and Charles McGuire Jr., "Cognitive Perspectives on Foreign Policy," in Samuel Long (ed.), *Political Behavior Annual* (Boulder, CO: Westview Press, 1986), 147–79.

65. See, for example, Alexander L. George, "The 'Operational Code': A Neglected Approach to the Study of Political Leaders and Decision-Making," *International Studies Quarterly* 13, no. 2 (1969), 190-222; Ole R. Holsti, *Toward a Typology of "Operational Code" Belief Systems*. Final Report to the National Science Foundation (Chapel Hill, NC: Duke University, 1977); Holsti, "The Operational Code Approach: Problems and Some Solutions" in Jonsson (ed.), *Cognitive Dynamics and International Politics*, 75-90; Holsti, "The Belief System and National Images: A Case Study" in James N. Rosenau (ed.), *International Politics and Foreign Policy*, 542–50.

66. Snyder, Bruck, and Sapin, *Foreign Policy Decision-Making*, 5–6. Emphasis in orginal. Robert D. Putnam, "Diplomacy and Domestic Politics: The Logic of Two-Level Games," *International Organization* 42, no. 3 (1988), 427-60.

67. Robert Jervis, *Perception and Misperception in International Politics* (Princeton: Princeton University Press, 1976), 29. See also Jervis's seminal article, "Hypotheses on Misperception," *World Politics* 20, no. 3 (1968), 454–79, his more recent "Introduction: Approach and Assumptions" and "Perceiving and Coping with Threat," in Robert Jervis, Richard Ned Lebow, and Janice Gross Stein, *Psychology and Deterrence* (Baltimore: Johns Hopkins University Press, 1985), 1–33.

68. De Rivera, *Psychological Dimension of Foreign Policy*; Alexander L. George, *Presidential Decision-Making: The Effective Use of Information and Advice* (Boulder, CO: Westview Press, 1980), especially 25-55; Steinbruner, *Cybernetic Theory of Decision*, chap. 4.

69. On this subject see especially, Ernest R. May, *"Lessons" from the Past: The Use and Misuse of History in American Foreign Policy* (New York: Oxford University Press, 1973); Yaacov Y. I. Vertzberger, "Foreign Policy Decisionmakers as Practical-Intuitive Historians: Applied History and Its Shortcomings," *International Studies Quarterly* 30, no. 2 (1986), 223–47; and Yuen Foong Khong, *Analogies at War* (Princeton: Princeton University Press, 1992).

70. Efforts to apply similar insights to studying the Cuban missile crisis may be found in Ole Holsti, Richard A. Brody, and Robert C. North, "Measuring Affect and Action in International Reaction

Models: Empirical Materials from the 1962 Cuban Crisis," in Rosenau, *International Politics and Foreign Policy*, 679–96.
71. Jervis, *Perception and Misperception in International Politics*, 29.
72. Ibid., 20.
73. Raymond Cohen, *Threat Perception in International Crisis* (Madison, Wl: University of Wisconsin Press, 1979), 189; see also 181.
74. Jack L. Snyder, "Perceptions of the Security Dilemma in 1914," in Jervis, Lebow, and Stein, *Psychology and Deterrence*, 153.
75. Jervis, *Perception and Misperception in International Politics*, 62.
76. Charles F. Hermann, "International Crisis as a Situational Variable" in Rosenau (ed.), *International Politics and Foreign Policy*, 409–21.
77. Richard Ned Lebow, *Between Peace and War: The Nature of International Crisis* (Baltimore: Johns Hopkins University Press, 1981), 7–12.
78. Cottam, *Foreign Policy Motivation*, 7, 87. See also William A. Gamson and André Modigliani, *Untangling the Cold War* (Boston: Little, Brown, 1971).
79. Cottam, *Foreign Policy Motivation*, 89.
80. Ibid.
81. See, for example, Jervis, *Perception and Misperception in International Politics*, 102–202 and chap. 12; Alexander L. George, "The Case for Multiple Advocacy in Making Foreign Policy," *American Political Science Review* 66, no. 3 (1972), 751–85; Cottam, *Foreign Policy Motivation*, 11 and 332–33; and Vertzberger, "Foreign Policy Decisionmakers as Practical-Intuitive Historians," 243–44.
82. Steinbruner, *Cybernetic Theory of Decision*, 338.
83. Snyder, Bruck, and Sapin, *Foreign Policy Decision-Making*, 5.
84. Christer Jönsson, Introduction to Jönsson (ed.), *Cognitive Dynamics and International Politics*, 7. Ibid. Jönsson observes. "No 'hard' data on the cognitive beliefs or processes of decisionmakers exist. Nor is there agreement as to what constitutes the best available 'soft' data, or the appropriate categories into which whatever data are available can be coded" (Ibid. 19).
85. Steinbruner, *Cybernetic Theory of Decision*, 136. Emphasis in original.
86. Ibid. 150.
87. Jervis, *Perception and Misperception in International Politics*, 31.
88. Hedley Bull, "International Theory: The Case for a Classical Approach," in Knorr and Rosenau (eds.), *Contending Approaches to International Politics*, 20.
89. See, for example, Mark L. Haas, "Prospect Theory and the Cuban Missile Crisis," *International Studies Quarterly* 45, no. 2 (2001).
90. Raymond Aron, *Peace and War: A Theory of International Relations* (New York: Praeger, 1968), 773.
91. Bruce Bueno de Mesquita, *Principles of International Politics: People's Power, Preferences, and Perceptions* (Washington, DC: Congressional Quarterly Press, 2000), 3.
92. See Jeffry A. Frieden, "Actors and Preferences in International Relations," in David A. Lake and Robert Powell (eds.). *Strategic Choice and International Relations* (Princeton: Princeton University Press, 1999), 39–76.
93. David A. Lake and Robert Powell, "International Relations: A Strategic Choice Approach," in Lake and Powell (eds.), *Strategic Choice and International Relations*, 4. In *Principles of International Politics* Bueno de Mesquita restricts his analyses to individual decisionmakers, whom he believes "are largely motivated by personal welfare" (2).
94. William James Booth, Patrick James, and Hudson Meadwell, (eds.), Introduction to *Politics and Rationality* (New York: Cambridge University Press, 1993), 1, 2.
95. Lake and Powell, "International Relations," 31. Emphasis added.
96. Ibid., p. 7. The authors explicitly deny that their approach is a theory.
97. This assumption has allowed strategic-choice theorists to take advantage of work on perception and misperception such as Jervis, *Perception and Misperception in International Politics*, and Snyder and Diesing, *Conflict among Nations*.
98. Lake and Powell, "International Relations," 31.
99. The use of iterated games has contributed significantly to overcoming the problem of preference. See, for example, Robert M. Axelrod, *The Evolution of Cooperation* (New York: Basic Books, 1984). This work owes much to the earlier analyses of Thomas C. Schelling, who abandoned strict game theory in favor of psychologically informed induction as a way of deriving preferences and allowing for changes in the key variables underpinning formal game theory. See Schelling, *Strategy of Conflict*. For a recent example of application to negotiation, see Rafael Reuveny, "Bilateral Import, Export, and Conflict/Cooperation Simultaneity," *International Studies Quarterly* 45, no. 1 (2001), 131–58.

100. Even this limited version of rationality has severe critics, some of whom strongly believe that the preference schedules of individuals are intransitive and depend heavily on context, which is continually undergoing change.
101. Lake and Powell, "International Relations," 31.
102. Arthur A. Stein, "The Limits of Strategic Choice: Constrained Rationality and Incomplete Explanation," in Lake and Powell, (eds.), *Strategic Choice and International Relations*, 197.
103. Lake and Powell, "International Relations" 33.
104. Stein, "Limits of Strategic Choice," 204.
105. Frieden, "Actors and Preferences in International Relations," 57. Frieden himself recognizes the problem on p. 59.
106. See, for example, Steven J. Brams and D. Marc Kilgour, *Game Theory and National Security* (New York: Basil Blackwell, 1988); and Michael Nicholson, *Rationality and the Analysis of International Conflict* (Cambridge: Cambridge University Press, 1992).
107. Lake and Powell, "International Relations," 35; and Stein, "Limits of Strategic Choice," 210–13.
108. Stein, "Limits of Strategic Choice," 211.
109. See, for example, the articles in K. I. Manktelow and D. E. Over (eds.), *Rationality: Psychological and Philosophical Perspectives* (New York: Routledge, 1993).
110. Stein, "Limits of Strategic Choice," 215–16.
111. Jervis, *Perception and Misperception in International Politics*, 342.
112. Stein, "Limits of Strategic Choice," 216.

CHAPTER 7: *QUO VADIS* FOREIGN POLICY?

1. As with the case of realism, neorealism was taken to task particularly ignoring domestic factors. See, for example, Peter Evans, Harold Jacobson, and Robert Putnam (eds.), *Double-Edged Diplomacy: International Bargaining and Domestic Politics* (Berkeley: University of California Press, 1993).
2. Indeed, many of the putatively scientific analyses of foreign policy have essentially been realist or neorealist as regards assumptions. See John A. Vasquez, *The Power of Power Politics. From Classical Realism to Neotraditionalism* (Cambridge: Cambridge University Press, 1998).
3. See, for example, Yale H. Ferguson and Richard W. Mansbach, "Global Politics at the Turn of the Millennium: Changing Bases of 'Us' and 'Them,'" in Davis B. Bobrow (ed.), *Prospects for International Relations: Conjectures about the Next Millennium* (Malden, MA: Blackwell Publishers, 1999), 77–107; and Richard W. Mansbach, "Deterritorializing Global Politics," in Donald J. Puchala (ed.), *Visions of International Relations: Assessing an Academic Field* (Columbia, SC: University of South Carolina Press, 2002).
4. Sigmund Freud, "Why War?" in Melvin Small and J. David Singer (eds.), *International War: An Anthology and Study Guide* (Homewood, IL: Dorsey Press, 1985), 161.
5. Paul Dickson, *The Official Explanations* (New York: Delacorte Press, 1980).
6. One reason why it was not possible to raise money for an American pavilion at the World's Fair in Hannover, Germany, in 2000 was that American corporations "now see themselves as 'global players'; they do not wish to be associated with a national pavilion." Roger Cohen, "A World's Fair Beckons: The Superpower Declines," *New York Times*, May 29, 2000, A4.
7. Saskia Sassen, *Globalization and Its Discontents* (New York: New Press, 1998), xxvi; see also Paul Knox and Peter J. Taylor (eds.) *World Cities in a World System* (Cambridge: Cambridge University Press, 1995).
8. Helen V. Milner, "Rationalizing Politics: The Emerging Synthesis of International, American, and Comparative Politics," *International Organization* 52, no. 4 (1998), 759.
9. Kenneth Waltz draws an analogy between the state and the system in global politics, and the firm and the market in microeconomics. Waltz, *Theory of International Politics* (Reading, MA: Addison-Wesley, 1979), 89–91. In Waltz's view, the two are not equal; the system (structure) dominates (agency) states. He discounts any alternative as "reductionist." In addition, since Waltz argues that states are functionally alike, there is no need to look within them. Thus, he assumes that states "are unitary actors" (118). John Ruggie was one of the first to criticize Waltz for ignoring domestic structures. See John Gerard Ruggie, "Continuity and Transformation in the World Polity: Toward a Neorealist Synthesis," *World Politics* 35, no. 2 (1983), 273.
10. Steve Smith, "Theories of Foreign Policy: An Historical View," *Review of International Studies* 12, no. 1 (1986), 15.

11. Vasquez, *Power of Power Politics*, 194. Vasquez points to the relative success of examining relations between pairs of states, or dyads.
12. This was as true of early Machiavellians as it is of twentieth-century realists.
13. Sidney Verba "Assumptions of Rationality and Non-rationality in Models of the International System," in Klaus Knorr and Sidney Verba (eds.), *The International System: Theoretical Essays* (Princeton: Princeton University Press, 1961), 111.
14. For an analysis of "unitariness" as a variable, see Richard W. Mansbach and John A. Vasquez, *In Search of Theory: A New Paradigm for Global Politics* (New York: Columbia University Press, 1981), 165–85.
15. Milner, "Rationalizing Politics:" 779.
16. Ibid. 779–82. For a strong form of the realist/neorealist position, see John J. Mearsheimer, "The False Promise of International Institutions," *International Security*, 19, no. 3 (1994), 7.
17. See, for example, Janice Gross Stein, "Political Learning by Doing: Gorbachev as Uncommitted Thinker and Motivated Leader," *International Organization*, 48, no. 2 (1994), 155–83.
18. Smith, "Theories of Foreign Policy," 15. Emphasis in original.
19. Barry Buzan, Charles, Jones, and Richard Little, *The Logic of Anarchy: Neorealism to Structural Realism* (New York: Columbia University Press, 1993), 227. Emphasis added.
20. Waltz, *Theory of International Politics*, and "Reflections on *Theory of International Politics:* A Response to My Critics," in Robert O. Keohane (ed.), *Neorealism and Its Critics* (New York: Columbia University Press, 1986), 322–45. Robert O. Keohane, *After Hegemony: Cooperation and Discord in the World Political Economy* (Princeton: Princeton University Press, 1984). Keohane, of course, does give much more scope to institutions and norms than do typical realists or neorealists. See Immanuel Wallerstein, *The Capitalist World-Economy* (New York: Cambridge University Press, 1979); and *The Politics of the World-Economy: The States, the Movements, and the Civilizations* (New York: Cambridge University Press, 1984). Robert W. Cox, *Production, Power, and World Order: Social Forces in the Making of History* (New York: Columbia University Press, 1987).
21. Waltz, *Theory of International Politics*, 113.
22. Ruggie, "Continuity and Transformation in the World Polity," 270.
23. Keohane, *After Hegemony*, 64. For a critical assessment of regime theory, see Michael P. Sullivan, *Theories of International Relations: Transition vs. Persistence* (New York: Palgrave, 2001), 104–5, 143–47, and 150–61.
24. Wallerstein, *Politics of the World-Economy*, 182.
25. Andrew Moravcsik, "Taking Preferences Seriously: A Liberal Theory of International Politics," *International Organization*, 51, no. 4 (1997), 544.
26. See, for example, Herbert I. Schiller's work on cultural imperialism. Schiller, *Communication and Cultural Domination* (New York: M. E. Sharpe, 1976) and *Mass Communications and American Empire*, 2nd ed. (Boulder, CO: Westview Press, 1992).
27. Robert W. Cox (with Timothy J. Sinclair), *Approaches to World Order* (Cambridge: Cambridge University Press, 1996), 518.
28. Cox, *Production, Power, and World Order*, 6
29. Charles W. Kegley Jr. and Eugene R. Wittkopf, *American Foreign Policy: Pattern and Process*, 2nd ed. (New York: St. Martin's press., 1982), 516–17.
30. Richard J. Barnet, *Roots of War: The Men and Institutions behind U.S. Foreign Policy* (Baltimore: Penguin, 1973), 5, 6.
31. Ibid. 7, 8–9.
32. Robert Jervis, *Perception and Misperception in International Politics* (Princeton: Princeton University Press, 1976), 26.
33. Morton H. Halperin, *Bureaucratic Politics and Foreign Policy* (Washington, DC: Brookings Institution, 1974), 11–12, 14.
34. Robert A. Packenham, *Liberal America and the Third World* (Princeton: Princeton University Press, 1973).
35. Thomas R. Dye, *Who's Running America? The Conservative Years*, 4th ed. (Englewood Cliffs, NJ: Prentice Hall, 1986), 273–74, 267.
36. Ibid, 268. Emphasis in original.
37. Ibid, 271.
38. Ibid, 272–73. Emphasis in original.
39. Comparing 1976 and 1980 samples designed to illuminate the foreign policy beliefs of U.S. leaders, it is interesting that Ole R. Holsti and James N. Rosenau found remarkable stability but "deep cleavages on fundamental issues." See Holsti and Rosenau, "A Leadership Divided: The Foreign Policy Beliefs of American Leaders, 1976–1980" in Charles W. Kegley Jr. and Eugene R. Wittkopf

(eds.), *Perspectives on American Foreign Policy: Selected Readings* (New York: St. Martin's Press, 1983), 196–212.

40. Halperin, *Bureaucratic Politics and Foreign Policy*, 14–15.
41. Richard W. Cottam, *Foreign Policy Motivation* (Pittsburgh: University of Pittsburgh Press, 1977), 9–11.
42. Halperin, *Bureaucratic Politics and Foreign Policy*, 15.
43. See especially Irving L. Janis, *Victims of Groupthink: A Psychological Study of Foreign-Policy Decisions and Fiascoes* (Boston: Houghton Mifflin, 1972). See also Irving L. Janis and Leon Mann, *Decision Making: A Psychological Analysis of Conflict, Choice, and Commitment* (New York: Free Press, 1977).
44. John D. Steinbruner, *The Cybernetic Theory of Decision: New Dimensions of Political Analysis* (Princeton: Princeton University Press, 1974), especially chap. 3; quotations on pp. 13 and 50–51. For a rather frightening analysis of the implications of this approach for strategic deterrence, see Steinbruner, "Beyond Rational Deterrence: The Struggle for New Conceptions," *World Politics* 28, no. 2 (1976), 223–45.
45. Joseph H. de Rivera, *The Psychological Dimension of Foreign Policy* (Columbus, OH: Charles E. Merrill, 1968), 59-60. See also Charles F. Hermann, "Bureaucratic Constraints on Innovation in American Foreign Policy" in Kegley and Wittkopf (eds.), *Perspectives on American Foreign Policy*, 390-409.
46. Steinbruner, *Cybernetic Theory of Decision*, 13–14.
47. De Rivera, *Psychological Dimension of Foreign Policy*, 46.
48. Graham T. Allison, *Essence of Decision: Explaining the Cuban Missile Crisis* (Boston: Little, Brown, 1971), 164, 178. On the governmental (bureaucratic) politics approach, see also especially: Graham T. Allison and Morton H. Halperin, "Bureaucratic Politics: A Paradigm and Some Policy Implications," in Raymond Tanter and Richard N. Ullman (eds.), *Theory and Policy in International Relations* (Princeton: Princeton University Press, 1972), 40–79. Halperin, *Bureaucratic Politics and Foreign Policy;* and Morton H. Halperin and Arnold Kanter (eds.), *Reading, in Foreign Policy: A Bureaucratic Perspective* (Boston: Little, Brown, 1973).
49. Stephen D. Krasner, "Are Bureaucracies Important? (Or Allison Wonderland)," *Foreign Policy.* 7 (summer 1972), 179. Krasner thus defends both approaches to reform—get better leaders and pursue the "right" values—which, as we have noted, cognitive theory suggests are unlikely to be productive.
50. Kim Richard Nossal, "Bureaucratic Politics and the Westminster Model," in Robert O. Matthews, Arthur G. Rubinoff, and Janice Gross Stein (eds.), *International Conflict and Conflict Management* (Scarborough, Ont.: Prentice-Hall of Canada, 1984), 125.
51. Steinbruner, *Cybernetic Theory of Decision*, 147.
52. Robert J. Art, "Bureaucratic Politics and American Foreign Policy: A Critique," in Robert J. Art and Robert Jervis (eds.), *International Politics: Anarchy, Force, Political Economy, and Decision-Making*, 2nd ed. (Boston: Little, Brown, 1985), 470.
53. Halperin, *Bureaucratic Politics and Foreign Policy*, 16. Emphasis added.
54. Allison, *Essence of Decision*, 166. Emphasis in original.
55. Stephen D. Krasner, *Defending the National Interest: Raw Materials Investments and U.S. Foreign Policy* (Princeton: Princeton University Press, 1978), 88–89. Krasner also argues that "even in a weak political system the state is not merely an epiphenomenon: central decision-makers can still resist pressures from private groups; they can still formulate preferences related to general societal goals." What is critical, according to Krasner, is which decisionmaking "arena" is used to decide an issue, and this is "partly a function of [the] inherent nature [of the issue] and partly a function of the way it is defined." In his view, leaders may be able to change "the way societal groups perceive a particular problem" and "thereby the arena in which it is decided and the final policy outcome" (89–90).
56. Stephen D. Cohen, *The Making of United States International Economic Policy*, 2nd ed. (New York: Praeger, 1981), 89.
57. Allison, *Essence of Decision*, 168.
58. Krasner, "Are Bureaucracies Important?"
59. James N. Rosenau, "Capabilities and Control in an Interdependent World" *International Security* 1, no. 2 (Fall 1976), 40–42.
60. Ibid., 42. There is little consensus in the literature even with respect to the classification of issues. John Spanier and Eric M. Uslaner, for example, offer a threefold typology: crisis, security, and intermestic issues. As they see it, crisis issues involve only a few top officials in the executive; security issues involve those actors mentioned by Rosenau, plus Congress because of budgetary considerations; and intermestic issues (energy is the example) "mobilize all the actors that domestic

politics do: the executive agencies whose jurisdiction is basically domestic, Congress, interest groups, and public opinion." Spanier and Uslaner, *American Foreign Policy and the Democratic Dilemmas*, 4th ed. (New York: Holt, Rinehart & Winston, 1985), 17–18.

Despite taxonomic problems, issue analysis has become very popular. See, for example, Theodore J. Lowi, "American Business, Public Policy, Case Studies and Political Theory," *World Politics* 16, no. 4 (1964), 677–715; William Zimmerman, "Issue Area and Foreign-Policy Process: A Research Note in Search of a General Theory," *American Political Science Review* 67, no. 4 (1973), 1204–12; Thomas L. Brewer, "Issue and Context Variation in Foreign Policy," *Journal of Conflict Resolution* 17, no. 1 (1973), 89–115; Michael K. O'Leary, "The Role of Issues," in James N. Rosenau (ed.), *In Search of Global Patterns* (New York: Free Press, 1976), 318–26; and Mansbach and Vasquez, *In Search of Theory*, 28–67.

61. Glenn H. Snyder and Paul Diesing, *Conflict among Nations: Bargaining, Decision Making, and System Structure in International Crisis* (Princeton: Princeton University Press, 1977), 511–23. This is a variant of Arnold Wolfers's fire-in-the-house argument.

62. James N. Rosenau, "Comparative Foreign Policy: Fad, Fantasy, or Field?" in Rosenau, *The Scientific Study of Foreign Policy* (New York: Free Press, 1971), 67.

63. James N. Rosenau, "Pre-Theories and Theories of Foreign Policy" in R. Barry Farrell (ed.), *Approaches to Comparative and International Politics* (Evanston, IL: Northwestern University Press, 1966), 27–93. A good deal of subsequent research in the field entailed investigation and elaboration of the Rosenau pre-theory and its taxonomy.

64. Christer Jönsson, introduction to, *Cognitive Dynamics and International Politics* (New York: St. Martin's press, 1982), 1.

65. James N. Rosenau, "A Pre-Theory Revisited: World Politics in an Era of Cascading Interdependence," *International Studies Quarterly* 28, no. 3 (1984), 246, 247.

66. Patrick J. McGowan and Howard B. Shapiro, *The Comparative Study of Foreign Policy: A Survey of Scientific Findings*, vol. 4 of Sage Library of Social Research (Beverly Hills, CA: Sage, 1973), 215. See also James N. Rosenau (ed.), *Comparing Foreign Policies: Theories, Findings and Methods* (Beverly Hills, CA: Sage, 1974).

67. Linda P. Brady, "A Proposal" in Patrick C. Callahan, Linda P. Brady, and Margaret G. Hermann (eds.), *Describing Foreign Policy Behavior* (Beverly Hills, CA: Sage, 1982), 29. Emphasis in original. The entire volume unintentionally reveals how little the field of comparative foreign policy had advanced by that time.

68. McGowan and Shapiro, *Comparative Study of Foreign Policy*, 218, 214–24. It is remarkable that fully thirteen years after McGowan and Shapiro had argued that "the evaluation of past policy from a normative point of view . . . and the *prescription* of future policy" were an "essential aspect of the comparative study of foreign policy" (223), John Vasquez was again calling for foreign policy evaluation. John A. Vasquez, "The Need for Foreign Policy Evaluation," in. Vasquez (ed.), *Evaluating U.S. Foreign Policy* (New York: Praeger, 1986), 3–16.

69. Bahgot Korany, "Foreign Policy Decisions in the Third World: An Introduction," in Korany (ed.), *Foreign Policy Decisions in the Third World*, topical issue of *International Political Science Review*, 5, no. 1 (1984), 7–8. For an excellent review of the strengths and weaknesses of the research record compiled in the comparative study of foreign policy, see Charles W. Kegley Jr., *The Comparative Study of Foreign Policy: Paradigm Lost?* Essay Series no. 10 (Columbia, SC: Institute of International Studies, University of South Carolina 1980).

70. Kalevi J. Holsti, "National Role Conceptions in the Study of Foreign Policy," *International Studies Quarterly* 14, no. 3 (1970), 233–309. See also Christer Jönsson and Ulf Westerlund, "Role Theory in Foreign Policy Analysis" in Jönsson (ed.), *Cognitive Dynamics and International Politics*, 122–57.

71. Jönsson and Westerlund observe, "As with most prevalent concepts, there exists no one agreed definition of the concept of role." ("Role Theory in Cognitive Analysis," 124.)

72. Henry A. Kissinger, *American Foreign Policy: Three Essays* (New York: Norton, 1969), chap. 3.

73. Nossal discusses these three reasons at some length in his essay, "Bureaucratic Politics and the Westminster Model," 120–21.

74. See especially Jerel A. Rosati, "A Neglected Actor in American Foreign Policy: The Role of the Judiciary," *International Studies Notes* 12, no. 1 (1985), 10–15. The international courts of the European Union and the Council of Europe are also becoming increasingly active in human rights cases.

75. See Wayne Selcher, "Brazil's Foreign Policy: More Actors and Expanding Agendas," in Jennie K. Lincoln and Elizabeth G. Ferris (eds.), *The Dynamics of Latin American Foreign Policies: Challenges for the 1980s* (Boulder, CO: Westview Press, 1984), 103–7. On the relevance of general theories of foreign policy decisionmaking to Latin America, see Yale H. Ferguson, "Analyzing Latin

American Foreign Policies," *Latin American Research Review* 22, no. 3 (1987), 142–64. Howard J. Wiarda explores some of the policy implications for the United States of Latin American "differentness" in his *Ethnocentrism in Foreign Policy: Can We Understand the Third World?* (Washington, DC: American Enterprise Institute for Public Policy Research, 1985).

76. Nossal, "Bureaucratic Politics and the Westminster Model," 146.

77. Cohen, *Making of United States International Economic Policy*, chap. 8.

78. See, for example, David Collier (ed.), *The New Authoritarianism in Latin America* (Princeton: Princeton University Press, 1979).

79. See, for example, Gerhard Lehmbruch and Philippe C. Schmitter (eds.), *Patterns of Corporate Policy Making* (Beverly Hills, CA: Sage, 1982); and Philippe C. Schmitter, "Democratic Theory and Neocorporatist Practice," *Social Research* 50, no. 4 (1983), 885–928.

80. Bernard C. Cohen, *The Public's Impact on Foreign Policy* (Boston: Little, Brown, 1973), 188–89. Emphasis in original. See also Gabriel A. Almond, *The American People and Foreign Policy* (New York: Praeger, 1960); and James N. Rosenau, *Public Opinion and Foreign Policy* (New York: Random House, 1961).

81. Cohen, *Public's Impact on Foreign Policy*, 178. Emphasis in original.

82. Richard L. Merritt, "Public Opinion and Foreign Policy in West Germany" in Patrick J. McGowan (ed.), *Sage International Yearbook of Foreign Policy Studies*, vol.1 (Beverly Hills, CA: Sage, 1973), 271.

83. On autonomy in federalized systems, see Ivo D. Duchacek, "The International Dimension of Subnational Self-Government," *Publius* 14, no. 4 (Fall 1984), 5–31.

84. See, with regard to ethnic-group influences, Louis L. Snyder, *Global Mini-Nationalisms: Autonomy or Independence?* (Westport, CT: Greenwood Press, 1982), *Ethnicity and Regionalism*, topical issue of *International Political Science Review* 6, no. 2 (1985); and Daniel Patrick Moynihan, *Pandaemonium: Ethnicity in International Politics* (New York: Oxford University Press, 1993). For other influences, James N. Rosenau, ed.,*Linkage Politics* (New York: Free Press, 1969).

85. Susan Strange, *The Retreat of the State: The Diffusion of Power in the World Economy* (Cambridge: Cambridge University Press, 1996), 120.

86. John Gerard Ruggie, "Territoriality and Beyond: Problematizing Modernity in International Relations," *International Organization* 47, no. 1 (1993), 172.

87. Edward A. Comor, *Communication, Commerce and Power: The Political Economy of America and the Direct Broadcast Satellite, 1960–2000* (New York: St. Martin's Press, 1998), 98, 110.

88. Joan Edelman Spero, "Information: The Policy Void," *Foreign Policy* no. 48 (fall 1982), 150–51.

89. Cited in Roger Cohen, "Tiffs over Bananas and Child Custody," *New York Times*, May 28, 2000, sec. 4: 1, 4.

90. Ann Marie Clark, Elisabeth J. Friedman, and Kathryn Hochstetler, "The Sovereign Limits of Global Civil Society: A Comparison of NGO Participation in UN World Conferences on the Environment, Human Rights, and Women," *World Politics*, 51, no. 1 (1998), 2. See also Ronnie D. Lipschutz, "Reconstructing World Politics: The Emergence of Global Civil Society," *Millennium*, 21, no. 3 (1992), 389–420; Paul Wapner, "Politics beyond the State: Environmental Activism and World Civic Politics, *World Politics*, 47, no. 3 (1995), 311–40; and Jackie Smith, Charles Chatfield, and Ron Pagnucco, *Transnational Social Movements and Global Politics: Solidarity beyond the State* (Syracuse: Syracuse University Press, 1997).

91. See, for example, Robert O'Brien, Anne Marie Goetz, Jan Aart Scholte, and Marc Williams, *Contesting Global Governance: Multilateral Economic Institutions and Global Social Movements* (Cambridge: Cambridge University Press, 2000); and Margaret Keck and Kathryn Sikkink, *Advocates beyond Borders: Advocacy Networks in International Politics* (Ithaca, NY: Cornell University Press, 1998).

92. John Agnew and Stuart Corbridge, *Mastering Space: Hegemony, Territory and International Political Economy* (New York: Routledge, 1995), 80.

93. This is hardly a new insight. It was explicitly announced more than thirty years by James N. Rosenau when he declared, "Almost every day incidents are reported that defy the principles of sovereignty. Politics everywhere, it would seem, are related to politics everywhere else." Rosenau, Introduction to *Linkage Politics*, 2.

94. James N. Rosenau, "Governance, Order, and Change in World Politics," in Rosenau and Ernst-Otto Czempiel, *Governance without Government: Order and Change in World Politics* (New York: Cambridge University Press, 1992), 5.

95. Ibid. 22–23, 2. For a similar claim that focuses on the relations of multilateral economic institutions and global social movements, see O'Brien et al., *Contesting Global Governance*.

96. Commission on Global Governance, *Issues in Global Governance* (London: Klewer Law International, 1995).

97. For the implications of fragmegration in the context of public administration, see Donald J. Savoie, "Globalization, Nation-States, and the Civil Service," in B. Guy Peters and Donald J. Savoie (eds.), *Governance in a Changing Environment* (Montreal: McGill-Queens University Press, 1995), 82–110. The other essays in this volume are also useful in this context.

98. See J. Ørstrøm Møller, *The End of Internationalism* (Westport, CT: Praeger, 2000), 103–4.

99. Jessica Matthews, "Power Shift," *Foreign Affairs* 76, no. 1 (1997), 50.

100. For analyses of a variety of sources of "private" authority, see A. Claire Cutler, Virginia Haufler, and Tony Porter (eds.), *Private Authority and International Affairs* (Albany, NY: State University of New York Press, 1999); and Martin Hewson and Timothy J. Sinclair (eds.), *Approaches to Global Governance Theory* (Albany, NY: State University of New York Press, 1999).

101. David Held, *Democracy and the Global Order: From the Modern State to Cosmopolitan Governance* (Stanford, CA: Stanford University Press, 1995), 16. See also Richard Falk, *On Humane Governance: Toward a New Global Politics* (University Park, PA: Penn State Press, 1995).

102. Held, *Democracy and the Global Order*, 18.

CHAPTER 8: THE CHALLENGE OF ANARCHY AND THE SEARCH FOR ORDER

1. See Hedley Bull, *The Anarchical Society: A Study of Order in World Politics* (New York: Columbia Univerity Press, 1977) and his earlier article, "Society and Anarchy in International Relations," in Herbert Butterfield and Martin Wight (eds.), *Diplomatic Investigations: Essays in the Theory of International Politics* (London: Allen & Unwin, 1966), 40–48. Bull argues that there is a high degree of order within the apparent anarchy of world politics. See also Yale H. Ferguson, "Hedley Bull's *The Anarchical Society* Revisited: States or Polities in Global Politics?" in B. A. Roberson, ed., *International Society and the Development of International Relations Theory* (London: Pinter Press, 1998), 184–09; and Oran R. Young, "Anarchy and Social Choice: Reflections on the International Polity," *World Politics* 30, no. 2 (1978), 241–63.

2. See Kalevi J. Holsti, *The Dividing Discipline: Hegemony and Diversity in International Theory* (Boston: Allen & Unwin, 1985), 23–27.

3. See Arnold Wolfers and Laurence W. Martin (eds.), *The Anglo-American Tradition in Foreign Affairs* (New Haven: Yale University Press, 1956), especially the introduction, and Mark W. Zacher and Richard A. Matthew. "Liberal International Theory: Common. Threads, Divergent Strands," in Charles W. Kegley Jr. (ed.), *Controversies in International Relations Theory: Realism and the Neoliberal Challenge* (New York: St. Martin's Press, 1995), 107–50.

4. Kenneth N. Waltz, *Theory of International Politics* (Reading, MA: Addison-Wesley, 1979), 77.

5. See, for example, Fred W. Riggs, "International Relations as a Prismatic System," in Klaus Knorr and Sidney Verba (eds.), *The International System: Theoretical Essays* (Princeton: Princeton University Press, 1961), 141–81. The most extreme examples of the disappearance of the two arenas are to be found in the case of "failed states" such as Somalia and Sierra Leone. See Gerald B. Helman and Steven R. Ratner, "Saving Failed States," *Foreign Policy* 89 (Winter 1992–93), 3–20.

6. Kenneth N. Waltz, *Man, the State and War* (New York: Columbia University Press, 1959), 232. Emphasis added.

7. Ernst B. Haas, *The Uniting of Europe: Political, Social, and Economic Forces, 1950–1957* (Stanford: Stanford University Press, 1958), xxiv.

8. See, for example, Peter J. Katzenstein, "International Interdependence: Some Long-Term Trends and Recent Changes," *International Organization* 29, no. 4 (1975), 1021–34.

9. Richard N. Rosecrance, A. Alexandroff, W. Koehler, J. Kroll, S. Laqueur, and J. Stocker, "Whither Interdependence?" *International Organization* 31, no. 3 (1977), 426–27. Emphasis in original.

10. Robert O. Keohane and Joseph S. Nye Jr., *Power and Interdependence: World Politics in Transition* (Boston: Little, Brown, 1977), 9–10, 11–19.

11. Robert O. Keohane, *After Hegemony: Cooperation and Discord in the World Political Economy* (Princeton: Princeton University Press, 1984), 70, 76, 75; see also p.6.

12. Robert M. Axelrod, *The Evolution of Cooperation* (New York: Basic Books, 1984), 174. See also Axelrod and Robert O. Keohane, "Achieving Cooperation under Anarchy: Strategies and Institutions," in David A. Baldwin (ed.), *Neorealism and Neoliberalism: The Contemporary Debate* (New York: Columbia University Press, 1993), 85–115.

13. Axelrod, *Evolution of Cooperation*, 173–74.
14. Ibid., 174. See also Keohane, *After Hegemony*, 76; and Keohane, "Reciprocity in International Relations," in Keohane, *International Institutions and State Power: Essays in International Relations Theory* (Boulder, CO: Westview Press, 1989), 158–79.
15. Kenneth N. Waltz, "Will the Future Be Like the Past?" in Nissan Oren (ed.), *When Patterns Change: Turning Points in International Politics* (New York: St. Martin's Press, 1984), 26. Waltz's definition of interdependence is very similar to Keohane and Nye's.
16. Rosecrance et al., "Whither Interdependence?" 441–44. Differing conceptualizations of Interdependence naturally lead to measurement disputes. See, for example, Mary Ann Tetreault, "Measuring Interdependence," *International Organization* 34, no. 3 (1980), 429–43; Richard N. Rosecrance and William Gutowitz, "Measuring Interdependence: A Rejoinder," *International Organization* 35, no. 3 (Summer 1981), 553–56; and Mary Ann Tetreault, "Measuring Interdependence: A Response," *International Organization* 35, no. 3 (1981), 557–60.
17. Stephen D. Cohen, *The Making of United States International Economic Policy*, 2nd ed. (New York: Praeger, 1981), 85, 89.
18. Keohane, *After Hegemony*, 5.
19. Waltz, "Will the Future Be Like the Past?" 27.
20. See James A. Caporaso (ed.), "Dependence and Dependency in the Global System," special issue, *International Organization* 32, no. 1 (1978).
21. This is perhaps not surprising in view of the potent ideological commitments evident in earlier discussions of this issue. See Osvaldo Sunkel, "The Crisis of the Nation-State in Latin America: Challenge and Response," in Yale H. Ferguson and Walter F. Weiker (eds.), *Continuing Issues in International Politics* (Pacific Palisades, CA: Goodyear, 1973), 352–68; Sunkel, "Big Business and 'Dependencia': A Latin American View," *Foreign Affairs* 50, no. 3 (1972), 517–31; Fernando Enrique Cardoso, *Dependencia y desarrollo en América Latina* (México: Siglo Veintiuno Editores, 1969); and Theontonio dos Santos, *El nuevo carácter de la dependencia* (Santiago, Chile: Cuadernos de CESO, 1968).
22. Alberto van Klaveren, "The Analysis of Latin American Foreign Policies: Theoretical Perspectives," in Heraldo Muñoz and Joseph S. Tulchin (eds.), *Latin American Nations in World Politics* (Boulder, CO: Westview Press, 1984), 8.
23. William E. Brock, "Trade and Debt: The Vital Linkage," *Foreign Affairs* 62, no. 5 (1984), 1045.
24. See Thomas Schelling's enlightening discussion of the tactics used by Chiang Kai-shek in *Arms and Influence* (New Haven: Yale University Press, 1966), 43.
25. Dennis K. Gordon, "Argentina's Foreign Policies in the Post-Malvinas Era," in Jennie K. Lincoln and Elizabeth G. Ferris (eds.), *The Dynamics of Latin American Foreign Policies: Challenges for the 1980s* (Boulder, CO: Westview Press, 1984), 98.
26. David Leyton-Brown, "The Nation-State and Multinational Enterprise: Erosion or Assertion?" in Robert O. Matthews, Arthur G. Rubinoff, and Janice Gross Stein (eds.), *International Conflict and Conflict Management: Readings in World Politics* (Scarborough, Ont.: Prentice-Hall of Canada, 1984), 339. See also Joseph M. Grieco, "Between Dependency and Autonomy: India's Experience with the International Computer Industry," *International Organization* 36, no. 3 (1982), 609–32.
27. Norman Angell, *The Great Illusion* (London: Heinemann, 1914).
28. See Karl W. Deutsch, S. Burrell, R. Kann, M. Lee, M. Lechterman, R. Lindgren, F. Lowenbein, and R. Van Wegen, *Political Community and the North Atlantic Area* (Princeton: Princeton University Press, 1957); and Ernst B. Haas, *Beyond the Nation-State: Functionalism and International Organization* (Stanford: Stanford University Press, 1964).
29. John W. Burton, *Systems, States, Diplomacy and Rules* (New York: Cambridge University Press, 1968), 8–9. See also Burton, *World Society* (Cambridge: Cambridge University Press 1972).. For his elaboration of the ways communication can reduce conflict, see Burton, *Conflict and Communication: The Use of Controlled Communication in International Relations* (New York: Free Press, 1969).
30. Richard N. Rosecrance, *The Rise of the Virtual State: Wealth and Power in the Coming Century* (New York: Basic Books, 1999), xi. Rosecrance also refers to "head" nations as "virtual states" (xii).
31. James N. Rosenau, *Turbulence in World Politics: A Theory of Change and Continuity* (Princeton: Princeton University Press, 1990), especially chaps. 12 and 13.
32. Cited in Waltz, *Man, the State and War*, 183.
33. Jean-Jacques Rousseau, "Abstract of the Abbé de Saint-Pierre's Project for Perpetual Peace," in M. G. Forsyth, H. M. A. Keens-Soper and P. Savigear (eds.), *The Theory of International Relations: Selected Texts from Gentili to Treitschke* (New York: Atherton Press, 1970), 148.

34. See Waltz, *Man, the State and War*, 163 ff. for a discussion of the stag-hare exemplar.
35. Waltz, *Theory of International Politics*, 127.
36. Cited in Herbert Butterfield, "The Balance of Power:' in Herbert Butterfield and Martin Wight (eds.), *Diplomatic Investigations: Essays in the Theory of International Politics* (London: Allen & Unwin, 1966), 144. Burke's argument is reflected in a more recent incarnation, in Richard N. Rosecrance's discussion of bipolarity. Rosecrance "Bipolarity, Multipolarity, and the Future," *Journal of Conflict Resolution* 10, no. 3 (1966), 318.
37. It is frequently claimed that the existence of continental alliance systems in 1914 transformed a local conflict between Serbia and Austria-Hungary into a global one.
38. See F. Parkinson, *The Philosophy of International Relations: A Study in the History of Thought* (Beverly Hills, CA: Sage, 1977), 45–48.
39. Emmerich de Vattel, "The Just Causes of War," in Forsyth, Keens-Soper, and Savigear (eds.), *Theory of International Relations*, 118.
40. Friedrich V. Kratochwil, *Rules, Norms, and Decisions: On the Conditions of Practical and Legal Reasoning in International Relations and Domestic Affairs* (Cambridge: Cambridge University Press, 1989), 62–63, 61. Emphasis in original.
41. Andreas Osiander, *The States System of Europe, 1640–1990: Peacemaking and the Conditions of International Stability* (Oxford: Clarendon, 1994), 11–120.
42. For the classic expressions of the debate, see Karl W. Deutsch and J. David Singer, "Multipolar Power Systems and International Stability." *World Politics* 16, no. 3 (1964), 390–406; Richard N. Rosecrance, "Bipolarity, Multipolarity and the Future"; and Kenneth N. Waltz, "The Stability of a Bipolar World," *Daedalus* 93 (summer 1964), 881–909. A useful anthology of such research is Alan Ned Sabrosky (ed.), *Polarity and War: The Changing Structure of International Conflict* (Boulder, CO: Westview Press, 1985).
43. See, for example, J. David Singer, S. Bremer, and J. Stuckey, "Capability Distribution, Uncertainty, and Major Power War, 1820–1965," in Bruce M. Russett (ed.), *Peace, War, and Numbers* (Beverly Hills, CA: Sage, 1972), 19–48; Michael Wallace, "Status, Formal Organization, and Arms Levels as Factors Leading to the Onset of War, 1820–1964,' in ibid., 49–71; and Wallace, "Alliance Polarization, Cross-Cutting, and International War, 1815–1964," *Journal of Conflict Resolution* 17, no. 4 (1973), 575–604. Such research was responsible for generating important insights into the role of status inconsistency and the onset of war. An excellent synthesis of quantitative analyses of the causes of war is John A. Vasquez, *The War Puzzle* (Cambridge: Cambridge University Press, 1993).
44. Elements of the argument were originally put forward by A. F. K. Organski, *World Politics* (New York: Knopf, 1958). Among the best of the works in this area are Charles Doran, *Systems in Crisis* (New York: Cambridge University Press, 1991); Jacek Kugler and Douglas Lemke (eds.), *Parity and War* (Ann Arbor: University of Michigan Press, 1996); and Ronald L. Tammen, Jacek Kugler, Douglas Lemke, Allan C. Stam III, Mark Abdollahian, Carole Alsharabati, Brian Efird, and A. F. K. Organski, *Power Transitions: Strategies for the Twenty-First Century* (New York: Seven Bridges Press, 2000).
45. J. David Singer, *A General Systems Taxonomy for Political Science* (New York: General Learning Press, 1971), 9.
46. See, for example, Morton A. Kaplan, *System and Process in International Politics* (New York: Wiley, 1957), 22–36; and A. R K. Organski, *World Politics* (New York: Knopf, 1958), chaps. 11, 12, 14.
47. For examples of these positions see, respectively, Ernst B. Haas, "The Balance of Power: Prescription, Concept or Propaganda?" *World Politics* 5, no. 4 (July 1953), 442–77; and Inis L. Claude, Jr., *Power and International Relations* (New York: Random House, 1962), chaps. 2–3.
48. See Donald Reinken, "Computer Explorations of the 'Balance of Power': A Project Report" (459–81); Hsi-Sheng Chi, "The Chinese Warlord System as an International System" (405–25); and Winfried Franke, "The Italian City-State System as an International System" (426–58), all in Morton A. Kaplan, *New Approaches to International Politics* (New York: St. Martin's Press, 1968).
49. Robert J. Lieber, *Theory and World Politics* (Cambridge, MA: Winthrop, 1972), 123. The only exception to this was general systems theory, a highly abstract mode of analysis that posited isomorphisms among variables in very different types of systems. See, for example, Anatol Rapoport's, foreword to Walter Buckley (ed.), *Modern Systems Research for the Behavioral Sciences* (Chicago: Aldine, 1968); and Ludwig von Bertalanffy, "General System Theory," in J. David Singer (ed.), *Human Behavior and International Politics: Contributions from the Social-Psychological Sciences* (Chicago: Rand McNally, 1965), 20–31.

50. Morton A. Kaplan, *Macropolitics* (Chicago: Aldine, 1969), 66. The use of jargon to describe the commonplace did nothing to improve the prose of scholars.

51. Harold Sprout and Margaret Sprout, *The Ecological Perspective on Human Affairs with Special Reference to International Politics* (Princeton: Princeton University Press, 1965), 208.

52. The work of Karl W. Deutsch, perhaps more than that of any other political scientist, reflects a debt to cybernetic theory. See Deutsch, *The Nerves of Government* (New York: Free Press, 1964).

53. A. Hall and R. Fagen, "Definition of a System," *General Systems*, 1 (1956), 18. Emphasis in original.

54. See, for example, Kalevi J. Holsti, *International Politics: A Framework for Analysis*, 4th cd. (Englewood Cliffs, NJ: Prentice-Hall, 1983), 27–64.

55. See, for regionsl subsystems, Michael Banks, "Systems Analysis and the Study of Regions," *International Studies Quarterly* 13, no. 4 (1969), 335–60; Louis J. Cantori and Steven L. Spiegel, *The International Politics of Regions: A Comparative Approach* (Englewood Cliffs, NJ: Prentice-Hall, 1970); and William R. Thompson, "The Regional Subsystem: A Conceptual Explication and a Propositional Inventory," *International Studies Quarterly* 17, no. 1 (1973), 89–117.

    See, for issue-based systems, Oran R. Young, "Political Discontinuities in the International System," *World Politics* 20, no. 3 (April 1968), 369–92, and Donald E. Lampert, Lawrence L. Falkowski and Richard W. Mansbach, "Is There an International System?" *International Studies Quarterly* 22, no. 1 (March 1978), 143–66.

56. Jerome Stephens, "An Appraisal of Some Systems Approaches in the Study of International Systems," *International Studies Quarterly* 16, no. 3 (1972), 328.

57. John Spanier, *Games Nations Play: Analyzing International Politics*, 4th ed. (New York: Holt, Rinehart & Winston, 1981), 10.

58. See Immanuel Wallerstein, *The Capitalist World-Economy* (New York: Cambridge University Press, 1979) and *The Politics of the World-Economy: The States, the Movements, and the Civilizations* (New York: Cambridge University Press, 1984). Useful critiques of Wallerstein include Aristide R. Zolberg, "Origins of the Modern World System: A Missing Link," *World Politics* 23, no. 2 (1981), 253–81; Robert Brenner, "The Origins of Capitalist Development: A Critique of Neo-Smithian Marxism," *New Left Review* 104 (July/August 1976), 25–92; Theda Skocpol, "Wallerstein's World Capitalist System: A Theoretical Critique," *American Journal of Sociology* 82, no. 5 (1977), 1075–90; and Peter Worsley, *The Three Worlds: Culture and World Development* (Chicago: University of Chicago Press, 1984), 312–31.

59. Waltz, *Theory of International Politics*, 98–99, 88, 73.

60. John Gerard Ruggie, "Continuity and Transformation in the World Polity: Toward a Neorealist Synthesis," *World Politics* 35, no. 2 (1983), 281. See also Richard N. Rosecrance, "International Theory Revisited," *International Organization* 35, no. 4 (1981), 691–713; Kenneth N. Waltz, "Letter to the Editor" *International Organization* 36, no. 3 (1982), 679–81; and Rosecrance, "Reply to Waltz," *International Organization* 36, no. 3 (1982), 682–85.

61. Interestingly, it is generally accepted that research in most of the natural sciences is inductive, reducing a problem into components and observing relations among these. This was not the case with the systems approach.

62. Edward Vose Gulick, *Europe's Classical Balance of Power: A Case History of the Theory and Practice of One of the Great Concepts of European Statecraft* (Ithaca: Cornell University Press, 1955), 35.

63. Cited in Lynn Montross, *War through the Ages*, 3rd ed. (New York: Harper & Row, 1960), 315.

64. René Albrecht-Carrié, *The Concert of Europe* (New York: Harper & Row, 1968), 4.

65. See Richard B. Elrod, "The Concert of Europe: A Fresh Look at an International System," *World Politics* 28, no. 2 (1976), 159–74.

66. See Waltz, *Theory of International Politics*,.

67. Although the preference of such scholars for stability is rarely expressed openly, it is implicit in their tendency to evaluate alternative systems in terms of the stability they afford. See, for example, Waltz, *Theory of International Politics*, 161ff.

68. Edward Shils, *Political Development in the New States* (The Hague: Mouton, 1962), 10.

69. Reinhard Bendix, cited in Paul T. McClure, "The Organizational Approach versus the Society Approach to Development in Emerging Nations," Document no. P-3927 (Santa Monica, CA: RAND Corporation, 1969), 26.

70. Leonard Binder, cited in Fred W. Riggs, "The Theory of Developing Politics," *World Politics* 16, no. 1 (1963), 156. For a classic statement that economic development does not assure political stability, infused with a strong bias toward stability and order, see Samuel P. Huntington, *Political Order in Changing Societies* (New Haven: Yale University Press, 1968).

71. Barrington Moore, *Social Origins of Dictatorship and Democracy: Lord and Peasant in the Making of the Modern World* (Boston: Beacon Press, 1966).

72. David Mitrany, *A Working Peace System* (London: Royal Institute of International Affairs, 1943). See also Inis L. Claude Jr., *Swords into Plowshares*, 3rd ed. (New York: Random House, 1964), chap. 17; and James P. Sewell, *Functionalism and World Politics* (Princeton: Princeton University Press, 1966).

73. See Richard A. Falk, *This Endangered Planet* (New York: Random House, 1971); Falk, "Contending Approaches to World Order," *Journal of International Affairs* 31 (fall/winter 1977), 171–98; and Saul H. Mendlowitz, "The Program of the Institute of World Order," *Journal of International Affairs* 31 (fall/winter 1977), 259–66.

74. Sewell, *Functionalism and World Politics*, 3.

75. In effect, functionalists shared the deterministic fallacy with classical Marxists and suffered a similar disappointment.

76. Karl W. Deutsch, "Nation and World," in Ithiel de Sola Pool (ed.), *Contemporary Political Science: Toward Political Theory* (New York: McGraw-Hill, 1967), 218. John H. Herz, a leading realist, came to a similar conclusion about the indefensibility of the nation-state, which led him to believe, like the functionalists, that the state would disappear. He later came to revise this claim significantly. See Herz, *International Politics in the Atomic Age* (New York: Columbia University Press, 1959), and "The Territorial State Revisited: Reflections on the Future of the Nation-State," in James N. Rosenau (ed.), *International Politics and Foreign Policy*, rev. ed. (New York: Free Press, 1969), 76–89.

77. Deutsch et al., *Political Community and the North Atlantic Area*.

78. Both Keohane and Nye in *Power and Interdependence* and Rosecrance et al. in "Whither Interdependence?" view transaction flows as "horizontal interdependence" which "implies only interconnectedness" ("Whither Interdependence?" 427). Genuine interdependence, according to Rosecrance et al., is "vertical" (429).

79. This includes mass media exchange, such as radio, television, newspapers, and films, and interpersonal communications such as mail and telephone calls. Sophisticated methods were developed to measure economic and sociocultural transactions with an eye to discerning the development of transnational society. See, for example, Leon N. Lindberg and Stuart A. Scheingold (eds.), *Regional Integration: Theory and Research* (Cambridge, MA: Harvard University Press, 1970); and Bruce M. Russett, *International Regions and the International System: A Study in Political Ecology* (Chicago: Rand-McNally, 1967).

80. See Karl W. Deutsch et al., *Political Community and the North Atlantic Area;* Bruce M. Russett, *Community and Contention: Britain and America in the Twentieth Century* (Cambridge, MA: MIT Press, 1963); and Richard E. Neustadt, *Alliance Politics* (New York: Columbia University Press, 1970).

81. Richard Meier, "Information, Resources and Economic Growth," in J. J. Spengler (ed.), *National Resources and Economic Growth* (Washington, DC: Resources for the Future, n.d.), 113.

82. See, for example, Haas, *Uniting of Europe*, and N. Leon Lindberg, *The Political Dynamics of European Economic Integration* (Stanford: Stanford University Press, 1963).

83. Robert D. Putnam, "Diplomacy and Domestic Politics: The Logic of Two-Level Games." *International Organization*, 42, no. 3 (1988), 427–60.

84. See Joseph S. Nye Jr. (ed.), *International Regionalism: Readings* (Boston: Little, Brown, 1968).

85. Similarly, American scholarly interest in deterrence and strategic theory waxed during the period when American leaders were seeking to find a coherent NATO defense policy and trying to persuade France that its efforts to establish a national nuclear force were in error.

86. Modernization theory served to justify U.S. foreign aid during much of the 1950s and 1960s.

87. The issue was reprinted as Robert O. Keohane and Joseph S. Nye Jr. (eds.), *Transnational Relations and World Politics* (Cambridge, MA: Harvard University Press, 1972). See also Richard W. Mansbach, and Yale H. Ferguson, Donald E. Lampert, *The Web of World Politics: Nonstate Actors in the Global System* (Englewood Cliffs, NJ: Prentice-Hall, 1976).

88. Keohane and Nye, *"Transnational Relations and World Politics,"* xii, xvii.

89. Ibid, 374–76. See also James A. Field Jr., "Transnationalism and the New Tribe," in ibid., 3–32.

90. For example, ITT involvement in the overthrow of Chile's Salvador Allende, the OPEC oil embargo, the end of the Vietnam War, the intensification of international monetary and debt instabilities, persistent problems of global stagflation, and several ecological disasters.

91. Keohane and Nye, *Power and Interdependence*, 24–37, 25. For the evolution of Keohane and Nye's ideas on this subject, see their "Introduction: The Complex Politics of Canadian-American Interdependence," and Nye, "Transnational Relations and Interstate Conflicts: An Empirical

Analysis," both in *International Organization* 23, no. 4 (1974): 495–607 and 961–96, respectively; Keohane and Nye, "Transgovernmental Relations and International Organizations," *World Politics* 27, no. 1 (1974), 39–62; and C. Fred Bergsten, Robert O. Keohane, and Joseph S. Nye Jr., "International Economics and International Politics: A Framework for Analysis," *International Organization* 29, no. 1 (1975), 3–36.

92. Keohane and Nye, *Power and Interdependence*, 227, 229. Keohane and Nye strongly insist that regimes must be based on mutual interests. See Keohane and. Nye, "Two Cheers for Multilateralism," *Foreign Policy* 60 (fall 1985), 148–67.

93. Keohane and Nye, *Power and Interdependence*, 19. See also Oran R. Young, "International Regimes: Problems of Concept Formation," *World Politics* 32, no. 3 (1980), 331–56; Ernst B. Haas, "Why Collaborate? Issue-Linkage and International Regimes," *World Politics* 32, no. 3 (1980), 357–405; Ernst B. Haas, "On Systems and International Regimes," *World Politics* 27, no. 2 (1975), 147–74; and Stephen D. Krasner (ed.), "International Regimes," special issue of *International Organization* 36, no. 2 (Spring 1982). The contributors to that volume apparently reached a consensus on defining international regimes as "sets of implicit or explicit principles, norms, rules, and decision-making procedures around which actors' expectations converge in a given area of international relations." Stephen D. Krasner, "Structural Causes and Regime Consequences: Regimes as Intervening Variables," in ibid., 186.

94. Robert O. Keohane, "The Theory of Hegemonic Stability and Changes in International Economic Regimes, 1967–1977," in Ole R. Holsti, Randolph M. Siverson, and Alexander L. George (eds.), *Change in the International System* (Boulder, CO: Westview Press, 1980), 133.

95. Keohane, *After Hegemony*, 90, 94.

96. Ibid. 100–1.

97. Keohane argued that regimes could prosper under conditions of imperfect or "bounded" rationality. Ibid., 110–20.

98. Krasner, "Structural Causes and Regime Consequences 185–86.

99. Arthur A. Stein, "Coordination and Collaboration: Regimes in an Anarchic World," *International Organization* 36, no. 2 (1982), 299, 316.

100. Donald J. Puchala and Raymond F. Hopkins, "International Regimes: Lessons from Inductive Analysis," *International Organization* 36, no. 2 (1982), 247. Emphasis added. See also Oran R. Young, "Regime Dynamics. The Rise and Fall of International Regimes," *International Organization* 36, no. 2 (1982), 277–97.

101. Krasner, "Structural Causes and Regime Consequences," 193.

102. Hedley Bull, "The Grotian Conception of International Society," in Butterfield and Wight (eds.), *Diplomatic Investigations*, 52.

103. Krasner, "Structural Causes and Regime Consequences," 187.

104. Keohane, *After Hegemony*, 64.

105. Bull, *Anarchical Society*, 161.

106. Krasner, "Structural Causes and Regime Consequences," 189, 202.

107. Stein, "Coordination and Collaboration," 299, 300. See also Susan Strange, *"Cave! hic dragones:* A Critique of Regime Analysis," *International Organization* 36, no. 2 (1982), 480–86.

108. Strange, *"Cave! hic dragones,"* 487, 481.

109. Ibid., 488, 491.

110. Richard W. Mansbach and John A. Vasquez, *In Search of Theory: A New Paradigm for Global Politics* (New York: Columbia University Press, 1981), 281–328.

111. Recent years have witnessed some ingenious efforts to study this issue empirically. See, for example, Mark J. Gasiorowski, "Economic Interdependence and International Conflict: Some Cross-National Evidence," *International Studies Quarterly* 30, no. 1 (1986), 23–38.

112. Alexander E. Wendt, "The Agent-Structure Problem in International Relations Theory," *International Organization* 41, no. 3 (1987), 358–59.

113. Alexander E. Wendt, "Anarchy Is What States Make of It: The Social Construction of Power Politics," *International Organization*, 46, no. 2 (1992), 394–95. Emphasis in original.

114. Roy Licklider, *Political Power and the Arab Oil Weapon: The Netherlands, Great Britain, Canada, Japan, and the United States* (Berkeley: University of California Press, 1988), 416–17, 419.

115. Ibid, 419.

116. A. W. DePorte, *Europe between the Superpowers* (New Haven: Yale University Press, 1979), vii.

117. Stephen Szabo, *The Successor Generation: International Perspectives* (London: Butterworth, 1983).

118. Regime theorists correctly point out that national bureaucracies occasionally form transnational alliances in support of particular arrangements of mutual benefit. To this extent, they may represent the other side of the coin. See, for example, Raymond F. Hopkins, "The

International Role of 'Domestic' Bureaucracy," *International Organization* 30, no. 3 (1976), 405–32.

119. Licklider, *Political Power and the Arab Oil Weapon*, 429.
120. Analysts argue over the extent to which Cuba's support for Soviet objectives in areas such as Africa and Central America was compelled by dependency on the USSR or stemmed from Castro's own perception of Cuban interests. Contrast, for example, Juan del Aguila, "Cuba's Foreign Policy in Central America and the Caribbean," in Lincoln and Ferris (eds.), *Dynamics of Latin American Foreign Policies*, 251–66, with Cole Blasier, *The Giant's Rival: The USSR and Latin America* (Pittsburgh: University of Pittsburgh Press, 1983), chap. 5
121. For an overview, see among many others, Thomas Friedman, *The Lexus and the Olive Tree* (New York: Anchor Books, 2000); David Held et al., *Global Transformations: Politics, Economics and Culture* (Cambridge: Polity Press, 1999); Richard Langhorne, *The Coming of Globalization: Its Evolution and Contemporary Consequences* (New York: Palgrave, 2001); Saskia Sassen, *Globalization and Its Discontents* (New York: New Press, 1998); Jan Aart Scholte, *Globalization: A Critical Introduction* (New York: Palgrave, 2000); Herman M. Schwartz, *States versus Markets: The Emergence of a Global Economy*, 2nd ed. (New York: St. Martin's Press, 2000); and Susan Strange, *The Retreat of the State: The Diffusion of Power in the World Economy* (Cambridge: Cambridge University Press, 1996).
122. Keohane and Nye, *Power and Interdependence*, 3rd ed. (New York: Longman, 2001), chap. 10.
123. See, for example, Stephen J. Kobrin, "Electronic Cash and the End of National Markets," *Foreign Policy*. 107 (summer 1997), 65–77; Benjamin J. Cohen, *The Geography of Money* (Ithaca, NY: Cornell University Press, 1998); and Susan Strange, *Mad Money: When Markets Outgrow Governments* (Ann Arbor: University of Michigan Press, 1998).
124. See, for example, Christopher Bright, "Invasive Species: Pathogens of Globalization," *Foreign Policy* 116 (fall 1999), 50–64.
125. Benjamin R. Barber, *Jihad vs. McWorld* (New York: Times Books, 1995); Friedman, *Lexus and the Olive Tree*; and James N. Rosenau, *Along the Domestic-Foreign Frontier: Exploring Governance in a Turbulent World.* (Cambridge: Cambridge University Press, 1997).
126. Rosenau, *Along the Domestic-Foreign Frontier*, 80–81.
127. Robert Wright, "Will Globalization Make You Happy?" *Foreign Policy* (September/October 2000), 62.
128. For more on these debates, see Yale H. Ferguson and Richard W. Mansbach, "Global Politics at the Turn of the Millennium: Changing Bases of 'Us' and 'Them,'" *International Studies Review*, special issue 1, no. 2 (1999), 77–107; and Ferguson, Mansbach et al., "What Is the Polity? A Roundtable," *International Studies Review*, 2, no. 1 (2000), 3–31. See also Linda Weiss, *The Myth of the Powerless State* (Ithaca, NY: Cornell University Press, 1998); and Stephen K. Vogel, *Freer Markets, More Rules: Regulatory Reform in Industrial Countries* (Ithaca, NY: Cornell University Press, 1996).
129. See Parkinson, *The Philosophy of International Relations: A Study in the History of Thought* (Beverly Hills, CA: Sage, 1977), 9–25.

CHAPTER 9: THE END THE ELUSIVE QUEST?

1. Patrick J. McGowan and Howard B. Shapiro, *The Comparative Study of Foreign Policy: A Survey of Scientific Findings*, vol. 4 of Sage Library of Social Research (Beverly Hills, CA: Sage, 1973), 214.
2. Morton A. Kaplan, "Problems of Theory Building and Theory Confirmation in International Politics," in Klaus Knorr and Sidney Verba (eds.), *The International System: Theoretical Essays* (Princeton: Princeton University Press, 1961), 23–24.
3. Ibid., 10.
4. Sir Brian Pippard, "Instability and Chaos: Physical Models of Everyday Life," *Interdisciplinary Science Review* 7, no. 2 (1982), 93.
5. Ibid., 101.
6. Kaplan, "Problems of Theory Building and Theory Confirmation in International Politics," 7–8.
7. Robert Jervis, *Perception and Misperception in International Politics* (Princeton: Princeton University Press, 1976), 158.
8. Ibid.
9. Kaplan, "Problems of Theory Building and Theory Confirmation in International Politics," 8–9.

10. Marion J. Levy Jr., 'Does It Matter If He's Naked? Bawled the Child," in Klaus Knorr and James N. Rosenau (eds.), *Contending Approaches to International Politics* (Princeton: Princeton University Press, 1969), 89.
11. Pippard, "Instability and Chaos," 92.
12. Knorr and Verba, introduction to *The International System*, 1–2.
13. Yosef Lapid, "The Third Debate: On the Prospects of International Theory in a Post-Positivist Era," *International Studies Quarterly* 33, no. 3 (1989), 236. In a footnote, Lapid places the debate in a Kuhnian framework, "a genuinely multiparadigmatic international relations discipline" (238 n. 4).
14. Ibid., 237.
15. Kenneth N. Waltz, *Theory of International Politics* (Reading, MA: Addison-Wesley, 1979), 18.
16. Lapid, "Third Debate," 239. Paradigmatism refers to "an enhanced post-positivist concern with meta-scientific constructs which incorporate integral thematic components as a precondition of scientific intelligibility" (240).
17. Ibid., 242.
18. Robert D'Amico, cited in Ibid., 243. Emphasis in original.
19. Lapid, "Third Debate," 243-44.
20. Ibid., 245, 246.
21. Ibid. 248, 249.
22. Robert G. Gilpin, "The Richness of the Tradition of Political Realism," *International Organization* 38, no. 2 (1984), 289. Gilpin is responding to Richard K. Ashley, "The Poverty of Neorealism," *International Organization* 38, no. 2 (1984), 225–86.
23. Peter J. Katzenstein, Robert O. Keohane, and Stephen D. Krasner, "International Organization and the Study of World Politics," *International Organization* 52, no. 4 (1998), 678.
24. On the other hand, Habermasian, Wallersteinian world-systems, feminist, and "critical" theorists (often overlapping categories) generally had their own agendas. Although all theories rest on normative foundations, theirs were overtly revolutionary and reformist.
25. Martin Hollis, *The Philosophy of Social Science: An Introduction* (Cambridge: Cambridge University Press, 1994), 241.
26. Charles Hostovsky, "How to Speak and Write Postmodern." Obtained from hostovsk @GEOG.UTORONTO.CA. We are grateful to Elizabeth Strom for bringing this essay to our attention.
27. For an analysis of the common structure of positivism and postpositivism, see Larry Laudan, *Beyond Positivism and Relativism: Theory, Method, and Evidence* (Boulder, CO: Westview Press, 1996).
28. D. S. L. Jarvis, *International Relations and the Challenge of Postmodernism: Defending the Discipline* (Columbia, SC: South Carolina University Press, 2000), 123.
29. Postmodernists would object to this phrasing because situating them anywhere is an attempt at categorization and co-optation and, therefore, always an illusion. An excellent sample of post-structuralist writings can be found in two collections: Richard K. Ashley and R. B. J. Walker (eds.), "Speaking the Language of Exile: Dissidence in International Studies," *International Studies Quarterly* 34, no. 3 (1990); and James Der Derian and Michael Shapiro (eds.), *International/ Intertextual Relations: Postmodern Readings of World Politics* (Lexington, MA: Lexington Books, 1989). See also by Der Derian: *On Diplomacy: A Genealogy of Western Estrangement* (Oxford: Basil Blackwell, 1987) and *Anti-Diplomacy: Speed, Spies and Terror in International Relations* (Oxford: Basil Blackwell, 1992).
30. For analyses of Derrida and Foucault and bibliography, see chap. 3 (by David Hoy) and chap. 4 (by Mark Philip), respectively, in Quentin Skinner (ed.), *The Return of Grand Theory in the Human Sciences* (Cambridge: Cambridge University Press, 1991). For Jacques Derrida, see his *Writing and Difference*, trans. A. Bass (Chicago: University of Chicago Press, 1978). For Michel Foucault, see his *The Archeology of Knowledge* (London: Tavistock, 1972) and *Power/Knowledge* (New York: Pantheon, 1980). For an argument that Foucault is a positivist, see Peter Dews, *Logics of Disintegration: Post-Structuralist Thought and Claims of Critical Theory* (London: Verso, 1987), 184. Wittgenstein's best-known work is *Philosophical Investigations* (Oxford: Basil Blackwell, 1953). A useful discussion of Wittgenstein can be found in Hollis, *Philosophy of Social Science*, 152–55.
31. Vendulka Kubálková, Nicholas Onuf, and Paul Kowert, *International Relations in a Constructed World* (Armonk, NY: M. E. Sharpe, 1998), 7.
32. See Cynthia Enloe, *Bananas, Beaches and Bases: Making Feminist Sense of International Politics* (Berkeley: University of California Press, 1990); V. Spike Peterson, *Gendered States: Feminist (Re)Visions of International Relations Theory* (Boulder, CO: Lynne Rienner, 1992); V. Spike Peterson and Anne S. Runyan, *Global Gender Issues* (Boulder, CO: Westview Press, 1993); J. Pettman,

Worlding Women: A Feminist International Politics (New York: Routledge, 1996); Christine Sylvester, *Feminist Theory and International Relations in a Postmodern Era* (Cambridge: Cambridge University Press, 1994); and J. Ann Tickner, *Gender in International Relations: Feminist Perspectives on Achieving Global Security* (New York: Columbia University Press, 1992). See also the dialogue in *International Studies Quarterly* 42, no. 1 (1998), 193–210, sparked by Tickner's article. "You Just Don't Understand: Troubled Engagements between Feminists and IR Theorists," *International Studies Quarterly* 41, no. 4 (1997), 611–32.

33. Tickner, "You Just Don't Understand," 614, 619, 629.
34. See Franke Wilmer, *The Indigenous Voice in World Politics* (Newbury Park, CA: Sage, 1993).
35. For an overview and listing of Habermas's writings and critiques thereof (upon which our discussion draws heavily), see Anthony Giddens, "Jürgen Habermas," in Skinner, *Return of Grand Theory in the Human Sciences;* quotation on p. 138.
36. Felipe Fernández-Armesto, *Truth: A History and a Guide to the Perplexed* (London: Bantam, 1997), 222.
37. Steve Smith, "Positivism and Beyond," in Smith, Ken Booth, and Marysia Zalewski (eds.), *International Theory: Positivism and Beyond* (Cambridge: Cambridge University Press, 1996), 30.
38. Krishan Kumar, *From Post-Industrial to Post-Modern Society: New Theories of the Contemporary World* (Oxford: Basil Blackwell, 1995), 66–67.
39. Fernández-Armesto, *Truth*, 204.
40. Kumar, *From Post-Industrial to Post-Modern Society*, 93–98.
41. David Ashley, *History without a Subject: The Postmodern Condition* (Boulder, CO: Westview, 1997), 9.
42. Jim George, *Discourses of Global Politics: A Critical (Re)Introduction to International Relations* (Boulder, CO: Lynne Rienner, 1994), 53.
43. David Campbell, *National Deconstruction: Violence, Identity, and Justice in Bosnia* (Minneapolis: University of Minnesota Press, 1998), 24–25.
44. J. David Singer, "The Incompleat Theorist: Insight without Evidence," in Klaus Knorr and James N. Rosenau (eds.), *Contending Approaches to International Politics* 80.
45. Smith, "Positivism and Beyond," 29. Smith goes on to identify as the three writers who have had the greatest impact on postmodernism Michel Foucault, Jacques Derrida, and Richard Rorty. Postmodernism encompasses several approaches, and there is no simple definition of postmodern scholarship.
46. Fred Halliday, "The Future of International Relations: Fears and Hopes," in Smith, Booth, and Zalewski, *International Theory*, 320.
47. See Yale H. Ferguson and Rey Koslowski, "Culture, International Relations Theory, and Cold War History," in Odd Arne Westad (ed.), *Reviewing the Cold War: Approaches, Interpretations, Theory* (London: Frank Cass, 2000), 149–79.
48. On this point, see Hollis, *Philosophy of Social Science*, 240–47; and Fernández-Armesto, *Truth*, chap. 6.
49. Richard K. Ashley and R. B. J. Walker, "Reading Dissidence/Writing the Discipline: Crisis and the Question of Sovereignty in International Studies," *International Studies Quarterly* 34, no. 3 (1990), 259–268. This appeared in a special issue of *ISQ* that is taken as additional evidence of "ghettoizing" by "dissidents."
50. We welcome the recent return of overtly normative approaches to the field. See Chris Brown, *International Relations Theory: New Normative Approaches* (New York: Columbia University Press, 1993).
51. Quoted in Fernández-Armesto, *Truth*, 203.
52. This does not mean that we believe that compromise is *always* superior to the extremes.
53. Levy, "'Does It Matter If He's Naked?' Bawled the Child," 92.
54. John Gerard Ruggie, "What Makes the World Hang Together? Neo-utilitarianism and the Social Constructivist Challenge," *International Organization* 52, no. 4 (1998), 856. Constructivists disagree about where the line can be drawn between brute facts and social facts. See, for example, Emanuel Adler, "Seizing the Middle Ground: Constructivism in World Politics," *European Journal of International Relations*, 3, no. 3 (1997), 320.
55. Stephen D. Krasner, *Sovereignty: Organized Hypocrisy* (Princeton: Princeton University Press, 1999), 5, 6.
56. For example, Rodney Bruce Hall argues persuasively that British entanglement on the Continent in the Seven Years' War was a result of George II's identity as Elector of Hanover rather than British interests. Hall, *National Collective Identity: Social Constructs and International Systems* (New York: Columbia University Press, 1999), 118.
57. Anthony Giddens, *The Constitution of Society: Outline of the Theory of Structuration* (Cambridge: Polity, 1984). See also John R. Searle, *The Construction of Social Reality* (New York: Free Press, 1995).

58. Frank Ninkovich, *Modernity and Power: A History of the Domino Theory in the Twentieth Century* (Chicago: University of Chicago Press, 1994), xv.

59. See Alexander E. Wendt, "The Agent-Structure Problem in International Relations Theory," *International Organization* 41, no. 3 (1987), 335–70; David Dessler, "What's at Stake in the Agent-Structure Debate?" *International Organization* 43, no. 3 (1989), 441–73; and Walter Carlsnaes, "The Agent-Structure Problem in Foreign Policy Analysis," *International Studies Quarterly* 36, no. 3 (1992), 254–70.

60. Hall, *National Collective Identity*, 116.

61. Katzenstein, Keohane, and Krasner, "*International Organization* and the Study of World Politics," 649. Finnemore and Sikkink argue persuasively that rationality and constructivism need not be incompatible. Martha Finnemore and Kathryn Sikkink, "International Norm Dynamics and Political Change," *International Organization* 52, no. 4 (1998) 910–15.

62. Alexander E. Wendt, *Social Theory of International Politics* (Cambridge: Cambridge University Press, 1999), 1.

63. Katzenstein, Keohane, and Krasner, "*International Organization* and the Study of World Politics," 675. Ruggie defines ontology as "the real-world phenomena that are posited by any theory and are invoked by its explanations." Ruggie, "What Makes the World Hang Together?" 879.

64. Katzenstein, Keohane, and Krasner, "*International Organization* and the Study of World Politics," 678, 682. See Ruggie, "What Makes the World Hang Together?" 867–68.

65. Alexander Wendt, "Anarchy Is What States Make of It: The Social Construction of Power Politics," *International Organization*, 46, no. 2 (spring 1992), 391–426,

66. Alexander Wendt, "Constructing International Politics," *International Security* 20, no. 1 (1995), 71–75. Emphasis in original.

67. Wendt acknowledges his debt to Bull. See *Social Theory of International Politics*, 253.

68. See by Nicholas J. Onuf, *World of Our Making: Rules and Rule in Social Theory and International Relations* (Columbia, SC: University of South Carolina Press, 1989); "Levels," *European Journal of International Relations* 1, no. 1 (1995), 35–58; and "Constructivism: A User's Manual," in Kubálková, Onuf, and Kowert, *International Relations in a Constructed World*, 58–78. See especially Friedrich. Kratochwil, *Rules, Norms, and Decisions: On the Conditions of Practical and Legal Reasoning in International Relations and Domestic Affairs* (Cambridge: Cambridge University Press, 1989). Friedrich Kratochwil and John Gerard Ruggie, "International Organization: A State of the Art on an Art of the State," *International Organization* 40, no. 3 (1986), 753–75.

69. John Gerard Ruggie, "International Responses to Technology: Concepts and Trends," *International Organization* 29, no. 3 (1975), 569–70. Emphasis in original.

70. Ruggie, "What Makes the World Hang Together?" 855.

71. Robert O. Keohane, *After Hegemony: Cooperation and Discord in the World Political Economy* (Princeton: Princeton University Press, 1984), especially 78–80. Keohane seemed to have moved toward a constructivist position when, with Judith Goldstein, he wrote that "ideas *as well as* interests have causal weight in explanations of human action" and that researchers should "investigate not just what strategies are devised to attain interests but how preferences are formed and how identities are shaped." Goldstein and Keohane, "Ideas and Foreign Policy: An Analytical Framework," in Goldstein and Keohane (eds.), *Ideas and Foreign Policy: Beliefs, Institutions, and Political Change* (Ithaca, NY: Cornell University Press, 1993), 4, 6. Emphasis in original. Ruggie argues, however, that in the end Goldstein and Keohane retreat back into neo-utilitarianism. Ruggie, "What Makes the World Hang Together?" 866–67.

72. R. B. J. Walker, *Inside/Outside: International Relations as Political Theory*, (Cambridge: Cambridge University Press, 1993), 179.

73. Onuf, *World of Our Making*, 142. Even where there is an abyss between reality and the idea of sovereignty, sovereignty provides states with a degree of legitimacy denied other actors. See Robert H. Jackson, *Quasi-States: Sovereignty, International Relations and the Third World* (Cambridge: Cambridge University Press, 1990).

74. Thomas J. Biersteker and Cynthia Weber, "The Social Construction of State Sovereignty," in Biersteker and Weber (eds.), *State Sovereignty as a Social Construct* (Cambridge: Cambridge University Press, 1996), 11.

75. Ruggie, "What Makes the World Hang Together?" 870.

76. Jackson, *Quasi-States*, 36. Constitutive rules are contrasted with what Jackson calls "instrumental rules" which "contribute to winning play" (*Quasi-States*, 35) and Ruggie calls "regulative rules" "which are intended to have causal effects" ("What Makes the World Hang Together?" 871).

77. Ruggie, ("What Makes the World Hang Together?" 879–80.

78. One of the authors of this book became a coeditor of the journal with the idea of altering that reputation.

CHAPTER 10: THE QUEST CONTINUES

1. James N. Rosenau, *Turbulence in World Politics: A Theory of Change and Continuity* (Princeton: Princeton University Press, 1990), 21–44, 247.
2. See Hendrik Spruyt, "The End of Empire and the Extension of the Westphalian System," *International Studies Review*, 2, no. 2 (2000), 65–92. The impact of changing norms on institutions in global politics and the ways in which research can have an effect on political reality are highlighted in Margaret Keck and Kathryn Sikkink, *Advocates beyond Borders: Advocacy Networks in International Politics* (Ithaca, NY: Cornell University Press, 1998).
3. Michael Nicholson, "The Continued Significance of Positivism?" in Steve Smith, Ken Booth, and Marysia Zalewski (eds.), *International Theory: Positivism and Beyond* (Cambridge: Cambridge University Press, 1996), 130–34.
4. Donald J. Puchala, "Woe to the Orphans of the Scientific Revolution," in Robert L. Rothstein (ed.), *The Evolution of Theory in International Relations* (Columbia, SC: University of South Carolina Press, 1991), 47. The examples he uses are "state," "society," "international system," "international interdependence," "global economy," "world revolution," and "security community."
5. Rosenau, *Turbulence in World Politics*, 27.
6. Martha Finnemore and Kathryn Sikkink, "International Norm Dynamics and Political Change," *International Organiztion* 52, no. 4 (1998) 892.
7. See, for example, John Dewey, *Characters and Events: Popular Essays in Social and Political Philosophy*, vol. 2 (London: Allen & Unwin, 1929).
8. Stephen D. Krasner, *Sovereignty: Organized Hypocrisy.* (Princeton: Princeton University Press, 1999).
9. Rodney Bruce Hall, *National Collective Identity: Social Constructs and International Systems* (New York: Columbia University Press, 1999), xii.
10. Ole Waever, "The Sociology of a Not So International Discipline: American and European Developments in International Relations," *International Organization* 52, no. 4 (1998), 712.
11. Yale H. Ferguson and Richard W. Mansbach, *Polities: Authority, Identities, and Change* (Columbia, SC: University of South Carolina Press, 1996). See also our "History's Revenge and Future Shock: The Remapping of Global Politics," in Martin Hewson and Timothy J. Sinclair (eds.), *Approaches to Global Governance Theory* (Albany, NY: State University of New York Press, 1999), 197–238.
12. Robert Gilpin, *War and Change in World Politics* (Cambridge: Cambridge University Press, 1981), 7. See also Kenneth N. Waltz, *Theory of International Politics* (Reading, MA: Addison-Wesley, 1979), 66.
13. Waltz, *Theory of International Politics*, 95.
14. Robert W. Cox, "Social Forces, States and World Orders: Beyond International Relations Theory," in Robert O. Keohane (ed.), *Neorealism and Its Critics* (New York: Columbia University Press, 1986), 211. Waltz's metaphors are rarely historical. Rather, like his use of "firm," they tend to derive from microeconomics.
15. John Gerard Ruggie, "Continuity and Transformation in the World Polity: Toward a Neorealist Synthesis," *World Politics* 35, no. 2 (1983), 273. Ruggie argues that Waltzian neorealism lacks any mechanism for system transformation.
16. Edward Hallett Carr, *The Twenty Years' Crisis, 1919–1939: An Introduction to the Study of International Relations* (New York: St. Martin's Press 1946), 229.
17. Barry Buzan, Charles Jones, and Richard Little, *The Logic of Anarchy: Neorealism to Structural Realism* (New York: Columbia University Press, 1993), 85. Emphasis added. See also their "Reconceptualizing Anarchy: Structural Realism Meets World History," *European Journal of International Relations* 2, no. 4 (1996), 403–38.
18. Michael Mann, *The Sources of Social Power*, vol. 1, *A History of Power from the Beginning to A.D. 1760* (Cambridge: Cambridge University Press, 1986).
19. Mann, *The Sources of Social Power*, vol. 2, *The Rise of Classes and Nation-States, 1760–1914* (Cambridge: Cambridge University Press, 1993), 2, 3.

20. See, for example, Hendrik Spruyt, *The Sovereign State and Its Competitors* (Princeton: Princeton University Press, 1994), and Charles Tilly, *Coercion, Capital and European States, A.D. 990–1990* (Oxford: Basil Blackwell, 1990). See also our respective roundtable discussions in Ferguson and Mansbach et al., "What Is the Polity?: A Roundtable."
21. *International Studies Review* 2, no. 1 (2000), 3–31.
22. Felipe Fernández-Armesto, *Truth: A History and a Guide to the Perplexed.* (London: Bantam, 1997), 227.
23. Stephen J. Kobrin, "Back to the Future: Neomedievalism and the Postmodern Digital World Economy," *Journal of International Affairs* 51, no. 2 (1998), 364.
24. R. B. J. Walker, *Inside/Outside: International Relations as Political Theory* (Cambridge: Cambridge University Press, 1993), 161–62. See also Peter J. Katzenstein, *The Culture of National Security: Norms and Identity in World Politics* (New York: Columbia University Press, 1996).
25. See, for example, Yale H. Ferguson and Richard W. Mansbach, "Global Politics at the Turn of the Millennium: Changing Bases of 'Us' and 'Them'," in Davis B. Bobrow (ed.), *Prospects for International Relations: Conjectures about the Next Millennium* (Malden, MA: Blackwell Publishers, 1999), 77–107; and Ferguson and Mansbach, "History's Revenge and Future Shock": 197–238.
26. Yale H. Ferguson and Richard W. Mansbach, "The Past as Prelude to the Future? Identities and Loyalties in Global Politics," in Yosef Lapid and Friedrich Kratochwil (eds.), *The Return of Culture and Identity in IR Theory* (Boulder, CO: Lynne Rienner, 1996), 21–44.
27. Ferguson and Mansbach, *Polities*, 381–82.
28. Hall, *National Collective Identity*, 71. Bruce Bueno de Mesquita argues that the Concordat of Worms of 1122 "created a property right over territory (specifically bishoprics) that adhered to the sovereign as a fiduciary rather than to the sovereign as an individual," thereby hastening the end of feudalism. Bueno de Mesquita "Popes, Kings, and Endogenous Institutions: The Concordat of Worms and the Origins of Sovereignty," *International Studies Review*, 2, no. 2 (2000), 115.
29. Peter Paret, "Napoleon and the Revolution in War," in Paret (ed.), *Makers of Modern Strategy from Machiavelli to the Nuclear Age* (Princeton: Princeton University Press, 1986), 124
30. Yosef Lapid, "Culture's Ship: Returns and Departures in International Relations Theory," in Lapid and Kratochwil (eds.), *Return of Culture and Identity in IR Theory* (Boulder, CO: Lynne Rienner, 1996), 3.
31. Quoted in Larry Rohter, "Maya Renaissance in Guatemala Turns Political," *New York Times*, August 12, 1996, A5.
32. See James N. Rosenau, *Along the Domestic-Foreign Frontier: Exploring Governance in a Turbulent World* (Cambridge: Cambridge University Press, 1997), 28.
33. Rosenau, *Turbulence in World Politics*, 239.
34. Susan Strange, *The Retreat of the State: The Diffusion of Power in the World Economy* (Cambridge: Cambridge University Press, 1996), 197–98.
35. Saskia Sassen, *Globalization and Its Discontents* (New York: New Press, 1998), xxv–xxvii. See also Sassen, *The Global City: New York, London, Tokyo* (Princeton: Princeton University, Press, 1991).
36. Quoted in Joel Greenberg, "Israel Battles New Foreign Foe: Music," *New York Times*, December 20, 1998, sec. 1, 10.
37. United Nations Development Programme, Human Development Office, *Summary: Human Development Report 1999* (New York: UNDP, 1999), 7.
38. Jonathan Boyarin, "Space, Time, and the Politics of Memory," in Boyarin (ed.), *Remapping Memory: The Politics of TimeSpace* (Minneapolis: University of Minnesota Press, 1994), 4, 13.
39. Strange, *Retreat of the State.* See also Peter Dombrowski and Richard W. Mansbach, "From Sovereign States to Sovereign Markets?" *International Politics* 36 (March 1999), 1–23.
40. Miles Kahler, *International Institutions and the Political Economy of Integration* (Washington, DC: Brookings Institution, 1995), xv.
41. Susan Strange, *Mad Money: When Markets Outgrow Governments* (Ann Arbor: University of Michigan Press, 1998), 25.
42. Ibid., 27.
43. Alexander B. Murphy, "The Sovereign State System as Political-Territorial Ideal: Historical and Contemporary Considerations," in Thomas J. Biersteker and Cynthia Weber (eds.), *State Sovereignty as Social Construct* (Cambridge: Cambridge University Press, 1996), 93.
44. Martin van Creveld, *Technology and War: From 2000 B.C. to the Present* (New York: Free Press, 1989), 108.
45. Steven Metz, "Racing toward the Future: The Revolution in Military Affairs," *Current History* (April 1997), 185.

46. The effort to defend realism in the face of a changing reality is reflected in the work of John J. Mearsheimer. See his "Back to the Future: Instability in Europe after the Cold War," *International Security*, 15, no. 1 (1990), 5–56, and "The False Promise of International Institutions," *International Security*, 19, no. 3 (1994), 5–49.
47. Bruno Bettelheim, *Freud and Man's Soul* (New York: Knopf, 1983), 8, 5.

Bibliography

Abraham, Geraldo. *The Chess Mind*. Baltimore: Penguin Books, 1960.

Achen, Christopher H., and Duncan Snidal. "Rational Deterrence Theory and Comparative Case Studies." *World Politics*. 41, no. 2, (1989): 143–69.

Adler, Emanuel. "Seizing the Middle Ground: Constructivism in World Politics," *European Journal of International Relations*. 3, no. 3 (1997): 319–63.

Agnew, John, and Stuart Corbridge. *Mastering Space: Hegemony, Territory and International Political Economy*, (1995).

Aguila, Juan del. "Cuba's Foreign Policy in Central America and the Caribbean." In Jennie K. Lincoln and Elizabeth G. Ferris eds., *The Dynamics of Latin American Foreign Policies: Challenges for the 1980s*, 251–66 Boulder, CO: Westview Press, 1984.

Albrecht-Carrié, René. *A Diplomatic History of Europe since the Congress of Vienna*. New York: Harper & Row, (1958).

———*The Concert of Europe*. New York: Harper & Row, 1968.

Alker, Hayward R. Jr., and Thomas J. Biersteker. "The Dialectics of World Order: Notes for a Future Archeologist of International Savoir Faire." *International Studies Quarterly* 28, no. 2 (1984): 121–42.

Allison, Graham T. *Essence of Decision: Explaining the Cuban Missile Crisis* Boston: Little, Brown, 1971.

Allison, Graham T., and Morton H. Halperin. "Bureaucratic Politics: A Paradigm and Some Policy Implications." In Raymond Tanter and Richard H. Ullman, eds., *Theory and Policy in International Relations*, 40–79. Princeton: Princeton University Press, 1972.

Almond, Gabriel A. *The American People and Foreign Policy*. New York: Praeger, 1960.

Anckar, Dag and Erkki Berndtson, eds. The Evolution of Political Science: Selected Case Studies. Special edition of *International Political Science Review vol.* 8, no. 1 (1987).

Anderson, Benedict. *Imagined Communities: Reflections on the Origin and Spread of Nationalism*. London: Verson, 1983.

Angell, Norman. *The Great Illusion*. London: Heinemann, 1914.

Armstrong, John A. *Nations before Nationalism*. Chapel Hill, NC: University of North Carolina Press, 1982.

Aron, Raymond. *Peace and War: A Theory of International Relations*. New York: Praeger, 1968.

Art, Robert J. "Bureaucratic Politics and American Foreign Policy: A Critique." In Robert J. Art and Robert Jervis, eds., *International Politics: Anarchy, Force, Political Economy, and Decision-Making*, 467–90 2nd ed. Boston: Little, Brown, 1985.

Art Robert J., and Robert Jervis, eds. *International Politics: Anarchy, Force, Political Economy, and Decision-Making*, 2nd ed. Boston: Little, Brown, 1985.

Ashley, David, *History without a Subject: The Postmodern Condition*. Boulder, CO: Westview, 1997.

Ashley, Richard K. "Noticing Pre-Paradigmatic Progress." In James N. Rosenau ed., *In Search of Global Patterns*, 161–66. New York: Free Press, 1976.

———"The Poverty of neorealism." *International Organization*, 38, no. 2 (1984) 225–86.

Ashley, Richard K., and R. B. J. Walker eds. "Speaking the Language of Exile: Dissident Thought in International Studies." Special edition of *International Studies Quarterly* vol. 34, no. 3 (1990).

———. "Speaking the Language of Exile: Dissident Thought in International Studies *International Studies Quarterly* 34, no. 3 (1990), 259–68.

———. "Reading Dissidence/Writing the Discipline: Crisis and the Question of Sovereignty in International Studies." *International Studies Quarterly*, vol. 34 no. 3 (1990) 367–416.

Avinieri, Shlomo. "Hegel and Nationalism." In Walter Kaufmann, ed., *Hegel's Political Philosophy*, 109–36. New York: Atherton Press , 1970.

Axelrod, Robert M. *The Evolution of Cooperation.* New York: Basic Books, 1984.

Axelrod, Robert M., and Robert O. Keohane. "Achieving Cooperation under Anarchy: Strategies and Institutions." In David A. Baldwin, ed., *Neorealism and Neoliberalism: The Contemporary Debate*, 85–115. New York: Columbia University Press, 1993).

Bacchus, William I. *Foreign Policy and the Bureaucratic Process: The State Department's Country Director System.* Princeton: Princeton University Press, 1974.

Badie, Bertrand, and Pierre Birnbaum. *The Sociology of the State.* Trans. Arthur Goldhammer. Chicago: University of Chicago Press, 1983.

Baldwin, David A., ed. *Neorealism and Neoliberalism: The Contemporary Debate.* New York: Columbia University Press, 1993.

Banks, Michael. "Systems Analysis and the Study of Regions." *International Studies Quarterly* 13, no. 4 (1969): 335–60.

Barber, Benjamin R. *Jihad vs. McWorld.* New York: Times Books, 1995.

Barber, Bernard. *Science and the Social Order.* London: Allen & Unwin, 1953.

Barber, James David. *The Presidential Character: Predicting Performance in the White House.* Englewood Cliffs, NJ: Prentice-Hall, 1972.

Barnet, Richard J. *The Roots of War: The Men and Institutions Behind U.S. Foreign Policy.* Baltimore: Penguin, 1973.

Baumberger, Jorg. "No Kuhnian Revolution in Economics." *Journal of Economic Issues* 11, no. 1 (1977): 1–20.

Beal, Richard Smith. "A Contra-Kuhnian View of the Discipline's Growth." In James N. Rosenau, ed., *In Search of Global Patterns.* New York, Free Pree, 1976: 158-61.

Beik, Paul H., and Laurence Lafore. *Modern Europe: A History since 1500.* New York: Henry Holt, 1959.

Bendor, Jonathan, and Thomas H. Hammond. "Rethinking Allison's Models." *American Political Science Review* 86, no. 2 (1992) 301–22.

Bergsten, C. Fred, Robert O. Keohane, and Joseph S. Nye Jr. "International Economics and International Politics: A Framework for Analysis." *International Organization.* 29, no. 1 (1975): 3–36.

Bertalanffy, Ludwig von. (1965). "General System Theory." In J. David Singer, (ed.), *Human Behavior and International Politics: Contributions from the Social-Psychological Sciences*, 20–31. Chicago: Rand McNally, 1965.

Bettelheim, Bruno. *Freud and Man's Soul.* New York: Knopf, 1983.

Biersteker, Thomas J. and Cynthia Weber, eds. *State Sovereignty as Social Construct.* Cambridge: Cambridge University Press, 1996.

Bishop, William W. Jr. *International Law: Cases and Materials*, 3rd ed. Boston: Little, Brown, 1971.

Blasier, Cole. *The Giant's Rival: The USSR and Latin America.* Pittsburgh: University of Pittsburgh Press, 1983.

Blaug, Mark. "Kuhn versus Lakatos, or Paradigms versus Research Programmes in the History of Economics." In Gary Gutting, ed., *Paradigms and Revolutions: Appraisals and Applications of Thomas Kuhn 's Philosophy of Science*, 137–60. Notre Dame, IN: University of Notre Dame Press, 1980.

Bloch, Marc. *Feudal Society.* 2 vols. Trans. L. A. Manyon. Chicago: University of Chicago Press, 1961.

Bloor, David. "Two Paradigms for Scientific Knowledge?" *Science Studies* 1, no. 1 (1971): 101–15.

Bobrow, Davis B., ed. *Prospects for International Relations: Conjectures about the Next Millennium.* Malden, MA: Blackwell Publishers 1999.

Booth, William James, Patrick James, and Hudson Meadwell, eds. *Politics and Rationality.* New York: Cambridge University Press, 1993.

Bourdieu, Pierre. *Distinction: A Social Critique of the Judgement of Taste.* Trans. Richard Nice. Cambridge, MA: Harvard University Press, 1984.

Bowle, John. *Politics and Opinion in the Nineteenth Century.* New York: Oxford University Press, 1964.

Boyarin, Jonathan, ed. *Remapping Memory: The Politics of TimeSpace.* Minneapolis: University of Minnesota Press, 1994.
Boynton, G. R. 1976. "Cumulativeness in International Relations." In James N. Rosenau, ed., *In Search of Global Patterns,* 145–50. New York: Free Press, 1976.
Bozeman, Adda B. *Politics and Culture in International History.* Princeton: Princeton University Press, 1960.
Brady, Linda P. "A Proposal." In Patrick C. Callahan, Linda P. Brady, and Margaret G. Hermann, eds., *Describing Foreign Policy Behavior,* 17–30. Beverly Hills, CA: Sage, 1982.
Braillard, P. "The Social Sciences and the Study of International Relations." *International Social Science Journal,* 102, no. 4, (1984): 627–42.
Brams, Steven J., and D. Marc Kilgour. *Game Theory and National Security.* New York: Basil Blackwell, 1988.
Brecher, Michael. "International Studies in the Twentieth Century and Beyond: Flawed Dichotomies, Synthesis, Cumulation." *International Studies Association* 43, no. 2 (1999): 213–64.
Bremer, Stuart A. "Obstacles to the Accumulation of Knowledge." In James N. Rosenau, ed., *In Search of Global Patterns,* 204–12. New York: Free Press, 1976.
Brennan, William J. Jr. "The Constitution of the United States: Contemporary Ratification." Text and Teaching Symposium, Washington, DC, October 12, 1985.
Brenner, Robert. "The Origins of Capitalist Development: A Critique of Neo-Smithian Marxism." *New Left Review* 104 (July/August 1976): 25–92.
Brewer, Thomas L. "Issue and Context Variation in Foreign Policy." *Journal of Conflict Resolution.* 17, no. 1 (1973): 89–115.
Brierly, J. L. *The Law of Nations: An Introduction to the International Law of Peace.* 5th ed. New York: Oxford University Press, 1955.
Bright, Christopher. "Invasive Species: Pathogens of Globalization." *Foreign Policy* 116 (Fall 1999): 50–64.
Brinton, Crane. *The Anatomy of Revolution.* New York: Norton, 1938.
Brock, William E. "Trade and Debt: The Vital Linkage." *Foreign Affairs* 62, no. 5 (1984): 1037–57.
Brodie, Bernard. *War and Politics.* New York: Macmillan, 1973.
Bronfenbrenner, Martin. "The 'Structure of Revolutions' in Economic Thought." *History of Political Economy* 3, no. 1 (1971): 136–51.
Bronowski, Jacob. *The Origins of Knowledge and Imagination.* New Haven, CT: Yale University Press, 1978.
Bronowski, Jacob, and Bruce Mazlish. *The Western Intellectual Tradition: From Leonardo to Hegel.* New York: HarperCollins, 1986.
Brown, Chris. *International Relations Theory: New Normative Approaches.* New York: Columbia University Press, 1993.
———"'Turtles All the Way Down': Anti-Foundationalism, Critical Theory and International Relations." *Millennium* 23 (Summer 1994): 213–36.
Bryant, C. G. A. "Kuhn, Paradigms and Sociology." *British Journal of Sociology* 26, no. 3 (September 1975): 354–59.
Buckley, Walter, ed. *Modern Systems Research for the Behavioral Sciences.* Chicago: Aldine, 1968.
Bueno de Mesquita, Bruce. "Toward a Scientific Understanding in International Relations." *International Studies Quarterly.* 29, no. 2(1985): 121–36.
———. "Popes, Kings, and Endogenous Institutions: The Concordat of Worms and the Origins of Sovereignty." *International Studies Review* vol. 2, no. 2 (2000): 93–118.
———. *Principles of International Politics: People's Power, Preferences, and Perceptions.* Washington, DC: Congressional Quarterly Press, 2000.
Bueno de Mesquita, Bruce, and David Lalman. *War and Reason.* New Haven: Yale University Press, 1992.
Bull, Hedley. "The Grotian Conception of International Society." In Herbert Butterfield and Martin Wight, eds., *Diplomatic Investigations: Essays in the Theory of International Politics,* 51–73. London: Allen & Unwin, 1966.
———. "Society and Anarchy in International Relations." In Herbert Butterfield and Martin Wight, eds., *Diplomatic Investigations: Essays in the Theory of International Politics,* 40–48. London: Allen & Unwin, 1966.
———. (1969). "International Theory: The Case for a Classical Approach." In Klaus Knorr and James N. Rosenau, eds., *Contending Approaches to International Politics,* 20–38. Princeton: Princeton University Press, 1969.
———. "The Theory of International Politics 1919–1969." In B. Porter, ed., *The Aberystwyth Papers: International Politics 1919–1969,* 30–56. London: Oxford University Press, 1972.

———. *The Anarchical Society: A Study of Order in World Politics.* New York: Columbia University Press, 1977.

Bunge, Mario. *Finding Philosophy in Social Science.* New Haven, CT: Yale University Press, 1996.

Burke, Edmund. *Reflections on the Revolution in France.* Garden City, NY: Doubleday, 1961.

Burnham, James. *The Machiavellians: Defenders of Freedom.* Chicago: Henry Regnery Co, 1943.

Burton, John W. *Systems, States, Diplomacy and Rules.* New York: Cambridge University Press, 1968.

———. *Conflict and Communication: The Use of Controlled Communication in International Relations.* New York: Free Press, 1969.

———. *World Society.* Cambridge: Cambridge University Press, 1972.

Butterfield, Herbert. *The Origins of Modern Science.* New York: Free Press, 1957.

———. "The Balance of Power." In Herbert Butterfield and Martin Wight, eds., *Diplomatic Investigations: Essays in the Theory of International Politics,* 149–75. London: Allen & Unwin, 1966.

Butterfield, Herbert, and Martin Wight, eds. *Diplomatic Investigations: Essays in the Theory of International Politics.* London: Allen & Unwin, 1966.

Buzan, Barry, Charles Jones, and Richard Little. *The Logic of Anarchy: Neorealism to Structural Realism.* New York: Columbia University Press, 1993.

———. "Reconceptualizing Anarchy: Structural Realism Meets World History," *European Journal of International Relations.* 2, no. 4 (1996): 403–38.

Callahan, Patrick C., Linda P. Brady, and Margaret G. Hermann, eds. *Describing Foreign Policy Behavior.* Beverly Hills, CA: Sage, 1982.

Campbell, David. *National Deconstruction: Violence, Identity, and Justice in Bosnia.* Minneapolis: University of Minnesota Press, 1998.

Cantori, Louis J., and Steven L. Spiegel. *The International Politics of Regions: A Comparative Approach.* Englewood Cliffs, NJ: Prentice-Hall, 1970.

Caporaso, James A., ed. "Dependence and Dependency in the Global System." Special issue of *International Organization* 32, no. 1.

Cardoso, Fernando Enrique. *Dependencia y desarrollo en América Latina.* México: Siglo Veintiuno Editores, 1969.

Cardozo, Benjamin N. *The Nature of the Judicial Process.* New Haven: Yale University Press, 1921.

Carlsnaes, Walter. "The Agent-Structure Problem in Foreign Policy Analysis." *International Studies Quarterly* 36, no. 3 (1992): 254–70.

Carr, Edward Hallett. *The Twenty Years' Crisis 1919–1939: An Introduction to the Study of International Relations.* New York: St. Martin's Press, 1946.

Cassese, Sabino. "The Rise and Decline of the Notion of State." *International Political Science Review.* 7, no. 2 (1986): 120–30.

Cerny, Philip G. "Globalization and the Changing Logic of Collective Action." *International Organization* 49, no. 4 (1995) 595–625.

Cheetham, Nicholas. *Keepers of the Keys: A History of the Popes from St. Peter to John Paul II.* New York: Charles Scribner's Sons, 1983.

Chi, Hsi-Sheng. "The Chinese Warlord System as an International System." In Morton A. Kaplan, ed., *New Approaches to International Politics,* 405–25. New York: St. Martin's Press, 1968.

Claessen, Henri J. M. and Peter Skalnik, eds. *The Early State.* The Hague: Mouton, 1978.

Clark, Ann Marie, Elisabeth J. Friedman, and Kathryn Hochstetler. "The Sovereign Limits of Global Civil Society: A Comparison of NGO Participation in UN World Conferences on the Environment, Human Rights, and Women." *World Politics* 51, no. 1 (1998): 1–35.

Claude, Inis L. Jr. *Power and International Relations.* New York: Random House, 1962.

———. *Swords into Plowshares.* 3rd ed. New York: Random House, 1964.

———. "Myths about the State." *Review of International Studies* 12, no. 1 (1986): 1–11.

Coates, A. W. "Is There a 'Structure of Revolutions' in Economics?" *Kyklos* 22, no. 2 (1969): 289–95.

Cohen, Benjamin J. "Balance-of-Payments Financing: Evolution of a Regime." *International Organization* 36, no. 2 (1982): 457–78.

———. *The Geography of Money.* Ithaca, NY: Cornell University Press, 1998.

Cohen, Bernard C. *The Public's Impact on Foreign Policy.* Boston: Little, Brown, 1973.

Cohen, Raymond. *Threat Perception in International Crisis.* Madison, WI: University of Wisconsin Press, 1979.

Cohen, Ronald. "State Origins: A Reappraisal." In Henri J. M. Claessen and Peter Skalnik, eds., *The Early State,* 31–75. The Hague: Mouton 1978.

Cohen, Ronald, and Elman R. Service, eds. *Origins of the State: The Anthropology of Political Evolution.* Philadelphia: ISHI, 1978.

Cohen, Stephen D. *The Making of United States International Economic Policy*. 2nd ed. New York: Praeger, 1981.

Collier, David, ed. *The New Authoritarianism in Latin America*. Princeton: Princeton University Press, 1979.

Commission on Global Governance, *Issues in Global Governance*. London: Klewer Law International, 1995.

Comor, Edward A. *Communication, Commerce and Power: The Political Economy of America and the Direct Broadcast Satellite, 1960–2000*. New York: St. Martin's Press, 1998.

Contamine, Philippe. *War in the Middle Ages*. Trans. Michael Jones. Oxford: Basil Blackwell, 1984.

Cottam, Richard W. *Foreign Policy Motivation*. Pittsburgh: University of Pittsburgh Press, 1977.

Cox, Robert W. "Social Forces, States and World Orders: Beyond International Relations Theory." In Robert O. Keohane, ed., *Neorealism and Its Critics*, 204–54. New York: Columbia University Press, 1986.

———. *Production, Power, and World Order: Social Forces in the Making of History*. New York: Columbia University Press, 1987.

Cox, Robert W., (with Timothy J. Sinclair). *Approaches to World Order*. Cambridge: Cambridge University Press, 1996.

Crick, Bernard. *The American Science of Politics*. Berkeley and Los Angeles: University of California Press, 1960.

Cutler, A. Claire, Virginia Haufler, and Tony Porter, eds. *Private Authority and International Affairs*. Albany, NY: State University New York Press, 1999.

Dahl, Robert. *Modern Political Analysis*. Englewood Cliffs, NJ: Prentice-Hall, 1963.

Davies, James C. "Toward a Theory of Revolution." *American Sociological Review* 27, no. 1 (1962): 5–19.

De Rivera, Joseph H. *The Psychological Dimension of Foreign Policy*. Columbus, OH: Charles E. Merrill, 1968.

Tocqueville, Alexis de. *Democracy in America*, vol. 1. New York: Knopf, 1945.

Denisoff, R. Serge, Orel Callahan, and Mark H. Levine. *Theories and Paradigms in Contemporary Sociology*. Itasca, IL: F. E. Peacock, 1974.

DePorte, A. W. *Europe between the Superpowers*. New Haven: Yale University Press, 1979.

Der Derian, James. *On Diplomacy: A Genealogy of Western Estrangement*. Oxford: Basil Blackwell, 1987.

———. *Anti-Diplomacy: Speed, Spies and Terror in International Relations*. Oxford: Basil Blackwell, 1992.

Der Derian, James, and Michael Shapiro, eds. *International/Intertextual Relations: Postmodern Readings of World Politics*. Lexington, MA: Lexington Books, 1989.

Derrida, Jacques. *Writing and Difference*. Trans. A. Bass. Chicago: University of Chicago Press, 1978.

Dessler, David. "What's at Stake in the Agent-Structure Debate?" *International Organization* 43, no. 3 (1989): 441–73.

Deutsch, Karl W. *The Nerves of Government*. New York: Free Press, 1964.

———. "Nation and World." In Ithiel de Sola Pool ed., *Contemporary Political Science: Toward Political Theory*, 204–27. New York: McGraw-Hill 1967.

Deutsch, Karl W., S. Burrell, R. Kann, M. Lee, M. Lichterman, R. Lindgren, F. Lowenhein, and R. Van Wagenen. *Political Community and the North Atlantic Area: International Organization in the Light of Historical Experience*. Princeton: Princeton University Press, 1957.

Deutsch, Karl W., and J. David Singer. "Multipolar Power Systems and International Stability." *World Politics* 16, no. 3 (1964): 390–406.

Dewey, John. *Characters and Events: Popular Essays in Social and Political Philosophy*, vol. 2. London: Allen & Unwin, 1929.

Dews, Peter. *Logics of Disintegration: Post-Structuralist Thought and Claims of Critical Theory*. London: Verso, 1987.

DiCicco, Jonathan M., and Jack S. Levy. "Power Shifts and Problem Shifts: The Evolution of the Power Transition Research Program." *Journal of Conflict Research* 43, no. 4 (1999): 675–704.

Dickson, Paul. *The Official Explanations*. New York: Delacorte Press, 1980.

Dodds, E. R. *The Greek and the Irrational*. Berkeley, CA: University of California Press, 1964.

Dombrowski, Peter, and Richard W. Mansbach. "From Sovereign States to Sovereign Markets?" *International Politics* 36 (March 1999): 1–23.

Doran, Charles. *Systems in Crisis*. New York: Cambridge University Press, 1991.

Dos Santos, Theontonio. *El nuevo carácter de la dependencia*. Santiago, Chile: Cuadernos de CESO, 1968.

Dougherty, James E., and Robert L. Pfaltzgraff Jr. *Contending Theories of International Relations: A Comprehensive Survey*. 2nd ed. New York: Harper & Row, 1981.

Downs, George. "The Rational Deterrence Debate." *World Politics* 41, no. 2 (1989): 225–37.

Duchacek, Ivo D. "The International Dimension of Subnational Self-government." *Publius* 14, no. 4 (1984): 5–31.

Duncan, W. Raymond. *Latin American Politics: A Developmental Approach.* New York: Praeger, 1976.

Dye, Thomas R. *Who's Running America? The Conservative Years.* 4th ed. Englewood Cliffs, NJ: Prentice Hall, 1986.

Earle, Edward Mead, ed. *Makers of Modern Strategy: Military Thought from Machiavelli to Hitler.* New York: Atheneum, 1967.

Ebenstein, William, ed. *Great Political Thinkers.* 4th ed. New York: Holt, Rinehart & Winston, 1969.

Eckberg, Douglas Lee, and Lester Hill Jr. "The Paradigm Concept and Sociology: A Critical Review." In Gary Gutting, ed., *Paradigms and Revolutions: Appraisals and Applications of Thomas Kuhn's Philosophy of Science,* 117–37. Notre Dame, IN: University of Notre Dame Press, 1980.

Effrat, Andrew. "Power to the Paradigms: An Editorial Introduction." *Sociological Inquiry* 42, nos. 3–4, (1972): 3–34.

Eisenstadt, S. N. *The Political Systems of Empires.* New York: Free Press, 1963.

Elrod, Richard B. "The Concert of Europe: A Fresh Look at an International System." *World Politics* 28, no. 2 (1976): 159–74.

Elster, Jon. *The Cement of Society: A Study of Social Order.* Cambridge: Cambridge University Press, 1989.

Enloe, Cynthia. *Bananas, Beaches and Bases: Making Feminist Sense of International Politics.* Berkeley: University of California Press, 1990.

Etheridge, Lloyd S. *A World of Men: The Private Sources of American Foreign Policy.* Cambridge, MA: MIT Press, 1978.

Eulau, Heinz. *The Behavioral Persuasion in Politics.* New York: Random House, 1963.

Evans, Peter, Harold Jacobson, and Robert Putnam, eds. *Double-Edged Diplomacy: International Bargaining and Domestic Politics.* Berkeley: University of California Press, 1993.

Falk, Richard A. *This Endangered Planet.* New York: Random House, 1971.

———. "Contending Approaches to World Order." *Journal of International Affairs.* 31 (fall/winter 1977): 171–98.

———. *On Humane Governance: Toward a New Global Politics.* University Park, PA: Penn State University Press, 1995.

Farrell, R. Barry, ed. *Approaches to Comparative and International Politics.* Evanston, IL: Northwestern University Press, 1966.

Ferguson, Yale H. "Hedley Bull's *The Anarchical Society* Revisited: States or Polities in Global Politics?" In B. A. Roberson, ed., *International Society and the Development of International Relations Theory,* 184–209. London: Pinter Press, 1998.

———. "Analyzing Latin American Foreign Policies." *Latin American Research Review,* 22, no. 3 (1987), 142–64.

Ferguson, Yale H., and Rey Koslowski. "Culture, International Relations Theory, and Cold War History," in Odd Arne Westad, ed., *Reviewing the Cold War: Approaches, Interpretations, Theory,* 149–79. London: Frank Cass, 2000.

Ferguson, Yale H. and Richard W. Mansbach. *The Elusive Quest: Theory and International Politics.* (Columbia, SC: University of South Carolina Press, 1988).

———. *The State, Conceptual Chaos, and the Future of International Relations Theory.* Boulder, CO: Lynne Reinner, 1989.

———. "Global Politics at the Turn of the Millennium: Changing Bases of 'Us' and 'Them.'" *International Studies Review,* special issue 1, no. 2 (1999), 77–107. Reprint Davis B. Bobrow, ed., *Prospects for International Relations: Conjectures about the Next Millennium,* 77–107. Malden, MA: Blackwell Publishers, 1999.

———. "History's Revenge and Future Shock: The Remapping of Global Politics." In Martin Hewson and Timothy J. Sinclair, eds., *Approaches to Global Governance Theory,* 197–238. Albany, NY: State University of New York Press, 1999.

———. "The Past as Prelude to the Future? Identities and Loyalties in Global Politics." In Yosef Lapid and Friedrich Kratochwil, eds., *The Return of Culture and Identity in IR Theory,* 21–44. Boulder, CO: Lynne Rienner, 1996.

———. *Polities: Authority, Identities, and Change.* Columbia, SC: University of South Carolina Press, 1996.

Ferguson, Yale H, and Richard W. Mansbach et al. "What Is the Polity? A Roundtable." *International Studies Review* 2, no.1 (2000): 3–31.

Ferguson, Yale H., and Walter F. Weiker, eds. *Continuing Issues in International Politics.* Pacific Palisades, CA: Goodyear, 1973.

Fernández-Armesto, Felipe. *Truth: A History and a Guide to the Perplexed.* London: Bantam, 1997.
Field, James A. Jr. "Transnationalism and the New Tribe." In Robert O. Keohane and Joseph S. Nye Jr., eds, *Transnational Relations and World Politics*, 3–32. Cambridge, MA: Harvard University Press, 1972.
Finifter, Ada W., ed. *Political Science: The State of the Discipline.* Washington, DC: American Political Science Association, 1983.
Finley, M. I. *Politics in the Ancient World.* Cambridge: Cambridge University Press, 1983
Finnemore, Martha and Kathryn Sikkink, "International Norm Dynamics and Political Change, *International Organization* 52, no. 4 (1998), 887–917.
Fleisher, Martin, ed. *Machiavelli and the Nature of Political Thought.* New York: Atheneum, 1972.
Forsyth, M. G., H. M. A. Keens-Soper, and P. Savigear eds. *The Theory of International Relations: Selected Texts from Gentili to Treitschke.* New York: Atherton Press, 1970.
Foucault, Michel. *The Archeology of Knowledge.* London: Tavistock, 1972.
——. *Power/Knowledge.* New York: Pantheon, 1980.
Fox, William T. R. "Interwar International Relations Research: The American Experience." *World Politics.* 2, no. 1 (1949): 67–80.
Franke, Winfried. "The Italian City-State System as an International System." In Morton A. Kaplan, ed. , *New Approaches to International Relations*, 426–58. New York: St. Martin's Press, 1968.
Franklin, Julian H. *Jean Bodin and the Rise of Absolutist Theory.* Cambridge: Cambridge University Press, 1973.
Freyberg-Inan, Annette. "Human Nature in International Relations Theory: An Analysis and Critique of Realist Assumptions about Motivation." Paper delivered at the meeting of the International Studies Association, Washington, D.C., 1999.
Fried, Morton H. "The State, the Chicken, and the Egg: Or What Came First?" In Ronald Cohen and Elman R. Service, eds., *Origins of the State: The Anthropology of Political Evolution*, 35–47. Philadelphia: ISHI, 1978.
Frieden, Jeffry A. "Actors and Preferences in International Relations." In David A. Lake and Robert Powell, eds., *Strategic Choice and International Relations*, 39–76. Princeton: Princeton University Press, 1999.
Friedman, Thomas. *The Lexus and the Olive Tree.* New York: Anchor Books, 2000.
Fromm, Erich. *Beyond the Chains of Illusion.* New York: Simon & Schuster, 1962.
Galtung, Johan. "The Social Sciences: An Essay on Polarization and Integration." In Klaus Knorr and James N. Rosenau, eds., *Contending Approaches to International Politics*, 243–86. Princeton: Princeton University Press, 1969.
Gamson, William A., and André Modigliani. *Untangling the Cold War.* Boston: Little, Brown, 1971.
Gasiorowski, Mark J. "Economic Interdependence and International Conflict: Some Cross-National Evidence." *International Studies Quarterly.* 30, no. 1 (1986): 23–28.
Geertz, Clifford. *Negara: The Theatre State in Nineteenth-Century Bali.* Princeton: Princeton University Press, 1981.
Gellner, Ernest. *Nations and Nationalism.* Ithaca, NY: Cornell University Press, 1983.
George, Alexander L. "The 'Operational Code': A Neglected Approach to the Study of Political Leaders and Decision-Making." *International Studies Quarterly.* 13, no. 2 (1969): 190–222.
——. "The Case for Multiple Advocacy in Making Foreign Policy." *American Political Science Review* 66, no. 3 (1972): 751–85.
——. *Presidential Decision-Making: The Effective Use of Information and Advice.* Boulder, CO: Westview Press, 1980.
George, Alexander L., and Juliette George. *Woodrow Wilson and Colonel House: A Personality Study.* New York: Day, 1956.
George, Alexander L., and Richard Smoke. "Deterrence and Foreign Policy." *World Politics*, 41, no. 2 (1989): 170–82.
George, Jim. *Discourses of Global Politics: A Critical (Re)Introduction to International Relations.* Boulder, CO: Lynne Rienner, 1994.
Giddens, Anthony. *The Constitution of Society: Outline of the Theory of Structuration.* Cambridge: Polity, 1984.
——. "Jürgen Habermas." In Quentin Skinner ed., *The Return of Grand Theory in the Human Sciences.* Cambridge: Cambridge University Press, 1991.
Gilbert, Felix. "Machiavelli: The Renaissance of the Art of War." In Edward Mead Earle, ed., *Makers of Modern Strategy: Military Thought from Machiavelli to Hitler*, 3–25. New York: Atheneum, 1967.
Gilpin, Robert. *American Scientists and Nuclear Weapons Policy.* Princeton: Princeton University Press, 1962.

————. *War and Change in World Politics*. Cambridge: Cambridge University Press, 1981.

————. "The Richness of the Tradition of Political Realism." *International Organization*, 38, no. 2 (1984): 287–304.

Gleditsch, Kristian S., and Michael D. Ward. "War and Peace in Space and Time: The Role of Democratization." *International Studies Quarterly* 44, no. 1 (2000): 1–29.

Goldstein, Judith. *Ideas, Interests, and American Trade Policy*. Ithaca, NY: Cornell University Press, 1993.

Goldstein, Judith, and Robert O. Keohane, eds. *Ideas and Foreign Policy: Beliefs, Institutions, and Political Change*. Ithaca, NY: Cornell University Press, 1993.

Gordon, Dennis K. "Argentina's Foreign Policies in the Post-Malvinas Era." In Jennie K. Lincoln and Elizabeth G. Ferris, eds., *The Dynamics of Latin American Foreign Policies: Challenges for the 1980s*, 85–100. Boulder, CO: Westview Press, 1984.

Graebner, Norman A. *Ideas and Diplomacy: Readings in the Intellectual Tradition of American Foreign Policy*. New York: Oxford University Press, 1964.

Greenberg, Jack. "Litigation for Social Change: Methods, Limits and Role in Democracy." *Record of the Association of the Bar of the City of New York*, 29 (1974).

Greenfeld, Liah. *Nationalism: Five Roads to Modernity*. Cambridge, MA: Harvard University Press, 1992.

Grieco, Joseph M. "Between Dependency and Autonomy: India's Experience with the International Computer Industry." *International Organization* 36, no. 3 (1982): 609–32.

————. "Anarchy and the Limits of Cooperation: A Realist Critique of the Newest Liberal Institutionalism." In David A. Baldwin, ed., *Neorealism and Neoliberalism: The Contemporary Debate*, 269–300. New York: Columbia University Press, 1993.

"The Origins of American Psychiatric Epidemiology." *American Journal of Public Health* 75, no. 3 (1985): 229–31.

Guetzkow, Harold. "Long-Range Research in International Relations." *American Perspective*, 4, no. 4 (1950): 421–40.

————. "Sizing Up a Study in Simulated International Processes." In James N. Rosenau, ed., *In Search of Global Patterns*, 91–105. New York: Free Press, 1976.

Guicciardini, Francesco. *The History of Italy*. Trans. Sidney Alexander. London: Collier-Macmillan, 1969.

Gulick, Edward Vose. *Europe's Classical Balance of Power: A Case History of the Theory and Practice of One of the Great Concepts of European Statecraft*. Ithaca, NY: Cornell University Press, 1955.

Gurr, Ted Robert. *Why Men Rebel*. Princeton: Princeton University Press, 1970.

Gutting, Gary, ed. *Paradigms and Revolutions: Appraisals and Applications of Thomas Kuhn's Philosophy of Science*. Notre Dame, IN: University of Notre Dame Press, 1980.

Haas, Ernst B. "The Balance of Power: Prescription, Concept or Propaganda?" *World Politics* 5, no. 4 (1953): 442–77.

————. *The Uniting of Europe: Political, Social and Economic Forces, 1950–1957*. Stanford: Stanford University Press, 1958.

————. *Beyond the Nation-State: Functionalism and International Organization*. Stanford: Stanford University Press, 1964.

————. "On Systems and International Regimes." *World Politics* 27, no. 2 (1975): 147–74.

————. "Why Collaborate? Issue-Linkage and International Regimes." *World Politics* 32, no. 3 (1980): 357–405.

————. "Words Can Hurt You; Or, Who Said What to Whom about Regimes." *International Organization* 36, no. 2 (1982): 207–43.

Haas, Jonathan. *The Evolution of the Prehistoric State*. New York: Columbia University Press, 1982.

Haas, Mark L. "Prospect Theory and the Cuban Missile Crisis," *International Studies Quarterly* 45, no. 2 (2001): 214–70

Halberstam, David. *The Best and the Brightest*. New York: Random House, 1972.

Hall, A. and R. Fagen. "Definition of a System." *General Systems* 1 (1956): 241–70

Hall, David. *Democracy and the Global Order: From the Modern State to Cosmopolitan Governance*. Stanford, CA: Stanford University Press, 1995.

Hall, John H., ed. *States in History*. Oxford: Oxford University Press, 1986.

Hall, Rodney Bruce. *National Collective Identity: Social Constructs and International Systems*. New York: Columbia University Press, 1999.

Halliday, Fred. "The Future of International Relations: Fears and Hopes." In Steve Smith, Ken Booth, and Marysia Zalewski, eds. *International Theory: Positivism and Beyond*, 318–27. Cambridge: Cambridge University Press, 1996.

Halperin, Morton H., *Bureaucratic Politics and Foreign Policy*. Washington, DC: Brookings Institution, 1974.

Halperin, Morton H. and Arnold Kanter, eds. *Readings in Foreign Policy: A Bureaucratic Perspective.* Boston: Little, Brown, 1973.

Heilbroner, Robert. *An Inquiry into the Human Prospect.* New York: Norton, 1975.

Held, David. *Democracy and the Global Order: From the Modern State to Cosmopolitan Governance.* Stanford, CA: Stanford University Press, 1995.

Held, David, et al. *Global Transformations: Politics, Economics and Culture.* Cambridge: Polity Press, 1999.

Helman, Gerald B., and Steven R. Ratner. "Saving Failed States." *Foreign Policy* 89 (Winter 1992–93): 3–20.

Hempel, Carl G. *Aspects of Scientific Explanation.* New York: Free Press, 1965.

Herbst, Jeffrey. "Responding to State Failure in Africa." *International Security* 21, no. 3 (1996–97): 120–44.

Hermann, Charles F. *Crises in Foreign Policy.* Indianapolis: Bobbs-Merrill, 1969.

———. "International Crisis as a Situational Variable." In James N. Rosenau ed., *International Politics and Foreign Policy.* Rev. ed., 409–21, New York: Free Press, 1969.

———. "Bureaucratic Constraints on Innovation in American Foreign Policy." In Charles W. Kegley Jr. and Eugene R. Wittkopf, eds., *Perspectives on American Foreign Policy: Selected Readings,* 390–409. New York: St. Martin's Press, 1983.

Hermann, Margaret G. "When Leader Personality Will Affect Foreign Policy: Some Propositions." In James N. Rosenau, ed., *In Search of Global Patterns,* 326–33. New York: Free Press, 1976.

———. *How Leaders Shape Foreign Policy.* Columbia, SC: University of South Carolina Press, forthcoming.

Hermann, Margaret G., and Thomas W. Milburn, eds. *A Psychological Examination of Political Leaders.* New York: Free Press, 1977.

Hertz, Frederick. *Nationality in History and Politics.* New York: Humanities Press, 1944.

Herz, John H. *International Politics in the Atomic Age.* New York: Columbia University Press, 1959.

———. "The Territorial State Revisited: Reflections on the Future of the Nation-State." In James N. Rosenau, ed., *International Politics and Foreign Policy.* rev. ed., 76–89. New York: Free Press, 1969.

———. *The Nation-State and the Crisis of World Politics.* New York: David McKay, 1976.

Hewson, Martin, and Tomothy J. Sinclair eds. *Approaches to Global Governance Theory.* Albany, NY: State University of New York Press, 1999.

Heyl, John D. "Paradigms in Social Science." *Society* 12, no. 5 (1975): 61–67.

Hinsley, F. H. *Sovereignty.* 2nd ed. Cambridge: Cambridge University Press, 1986.

Hirst, Paul. "The Global Economy—Myths and Realities." *International Affairs* 73, (1997): 409–25.

Hobsbawm, E. J. *Nations and Nationalism since 1780: Programme, Myth, Reality.* Cambridge: Cambridge University Press, 1990.

Hoffmann, Stanley. "International Relations: The Long Road to Theory." *World Politics* 11, no. 3 (1959): 346–77.

Hollinger, David A. "T. S. Kuhn's Theory of Science and Its Implications for History." In Gary Gutting, ed., *Paradigms and Revolutions: Appraisals and Applications of Thomas Kuhn's Philosophy of Science,* 195–223. Notre Dame, IN: University of Notre Dame Press, 1980.

Hollis, Martin. *The Philosophy of Social Science: An Introduction.* Cambridge: Cambridge University Press, 1994.

Hollis, Martin, and Steve Smith. *Explaining and Understanding International Relations.* Oxford: Oxford University Press, 1990.

Holmes, George. *Europe: Hierarchy and Revolt, 1320–1450.* London: Fontana, 1975.

Holsti, Kalevi J. "National Role Conceptions in the Study of Foreign Policy." *International Studies Quarterly* 14, no. 3 (1970): 233–309.

———. *International Politics: A Framework for Analysis.* 4th ed. Englewood Cliffs, NJ: Prentice-Hall, 1983.

———. "Along the Road to International Theory." *International Journal* 39, no. 2 (1984): 337–65.

———. *The Dividing Discipline: Hegemony and Diversity in International Theory.* Boston: Allen & Unwin, 1985.

———. *The State, War, and the State of War.* Cambridge: Cambridge University Press, 1996.

Holsti, Ole R. "The Belief System and National Images: A Case Study." In James N. Rosenau ed., *International Politics and Foreign Policy.* Rev. Ed. 542–50. New York: Free Press, 1969.

———. *Toward a Typology of "Operational Code" Belief Systems.* Final Report to the National Science Foundation. Chapel Hill, NC: Duke University, 1977.

———. "The Operational Code Approach: Problems and Some Solutions." In Christer Jonsson, ed., *Cognitive Dynamics and International Politics.* New York: St. Martin's Press, 1982.

Holsti, Ole, Richard A. Brody, and Robert C. North. "Measuring Affect and Action in International Reaction Models: Empirical Materials from the 1962 Cuban Crisis." In James N. Rosenau, ed., *International Politics and Foreign Policy*. Rev. ed., 679–96. New York: Free Press, 1969.

Holsti, Ole R., and James N. Rosenau. "A Leadership Divided: The Foreign Policy Beliefs of American Leaders, 1976–1980." In Charles W. Kegley, Jr. and Eugene R. Wittkopf, eds., *Perspectives on American Foreign Policy: Selected Readings* 196–212. New York: St. Martin's Press, 1983.

———. *American Leadership and World Affairs: Vietnam and the Breakdown of Consensus*. Boston: Allen & Unwin, 1984.

Holsti, Ole R., Randolph M. Siverson, and Alexander L. George, eds. *Change in the International System*. Boulder, CO: Westview Press, 1980.

Hopkins, Raymond F. "The International Role of 'Domestic' Bureaucracy." *International Organization* 30, no. 3 (1976): 405–32.

Hopkins, Raymond F., and Richard W. Mansbach. *Structure and Process in International Politics*. New York: Harper & Row, 1973.

Hopmann, P. Terrence. "Identifying, Formulating, and Solving Puzzles in International Relations Research." In James N. Rosenau, ed., *In Search of Global Patterns*, 192–97. New York: Free Press, 1976.

Hopmann, P. Terrence, Dina A. Zinnes, and J. David Singer, eds. *Cumulation in International Relations Research*. Denver: Graduate School of International Studies.

Hopple, Gerald W., and Paul J. Rossa. "International Crisis Analysis: Recent Developments and Future Directions." In P. Terrence Hopmann, Dina A. Zinnes and J. David Singer, eds., *Cumulation in International Relations Research*, 65–97 University of Denver Monograph Series in World Affairs. Denver: Graduate School of International Relations, 1981.

Howard, Michael. "Reassurance and Deterrence: Western Defense in the 1980s." *Foreign Affairs* 61, no. 2 (1982–83): 309–24.

Huntington, Samuel P. *The Common Defense*. New York: Columbia University Press, 1961.

———. *Political Order in Changing Societies*. New Haven: Yale University Press, 1968.

Huntington, Samuel P., and Joan M. Nelson. *No Easy Choice: Political Participation in Developing Countries*. Cambridge, MA: Harvard University Press, 1976.

Huntley, Wade L. "Kant's Third Image: Systemic Sources of the Liberal Peace." *International Studies Quarterly* 40, no. 1 (1996): 45–76.

Inglehart, Ronald. *Culture Shift in Advanced Industrial Society*. (Princeton: Princeton University Press, 1990.

———. *Modernization and Postmodernization: Cultural, Economic, and Political Change in 43 Countries*. Princeton: Princeton University Press, 1997.

IPSR Editorial Committee. *Ethnicity and Regionalism*. Topical issue of *International Political Science Review* 6, no. 2 (1985).

Isaak, Robert A. *Individuals and World Politics*. 2nd ed. North Scituate, MA: Duxbury Press, 1981.

Jackson, Robert H. "African States and International Theory." Paper delivered at the British International Studies Association annual meeting, University of Reading, Reading U.K., December 16, 1986.

———. "Negative Sovereignty in Sub-Saharan Africa." *Review of International Studies* 12, no. 4 (1986): 246–64.

———. Quasi–States. Dual Regimes, and Neoclassical Theory: International Jurisprudence and the Third World, *International Organization* 41, no. 4 (1987): 519–49.

———. *Quasi-States: Sovereignty, International Relations and the Third World*. Cambridge: Cambridge University Press, 1990.

Jackson, Robert H., and Alan James, eds. *States in a Changing World: A Contemporary Analysis*. Oxford: Clarendon Press, 1993.

Jackson, Robert H., and Carl G. Rosberg. "Why Africa's Weak States Persist: The Empirical and the Juridical in Statehood." *World Politics* 35, no. 1 (1982): 1–24.

Jacobson, Harold K., and Eric Stein. *Diplomats, Scientists, and Politicians*. Ann Arbor, MI: University of Michigan Press, 1966.

James, Alan. *Sovereign Statehood: The Basis of International Society*. London: Allen & Unwin, 1986.

Janis, Irving L. *Victims of Groupthink: A Psychological Study of Foreign-Policy Decisions and Fiascoes*. Boston: Houghton Mifflin, 1972.

Janis, Irving L., and Leon Mann. *Decision Making: A Psychological Analysis of Conflict, Choice, and Commitment*. New York: Free Press, 1977.

Jarvis, D. S. L. *International Relations and the Challenge of Postmodernism: Defending the Discipline*. Columbia, SC: University of South Carolina Press, 2000.

Jepperson, Ronald L., Alexander Wendt, and Peter J. Katzenstein, "Norms, Identities, and Culture of National Security." In Peter J. Katzenstein, ed., *The Culture of National Security: Norms and Identity in World Politics*, 33–75. New York: Columbia University Press, 1996.
Jervis, Robert. "Hypotheses on Misperception." *World Politics*, no. 3 (1968): 454–79.
———. "Cumulation, Correlations, and Woozles." In James N. Rosenau, ed., *In Search of Global Patterns*, 181–85. New York: Free Press, 1976.
———. *Perception and Misperception in International Politics*. Princeton: Princeton University Press, 1976.
———. "Security Regimes." *International Organization* 36, no. 2 (1982): 357–78.
———. "Rational Deterrence: Theory and Evidence." *World Politics* 41, no. 2 (1989): 183–207.
———. *System Effects: Complexity in Social and Political Life*. Princeton: Princeton University Press, 1997.
Jervis, Robert, Richard Ned Lebow, and Janice Gross Stein. *Psychology and Deterrence*. Baltimore: Johns Hopkins University Press, 1985.
Job, Brian L. "Grins without Cats: In Pursuit of Knowledge of International Alliances." In P. Terrence Hopmann, Dina A. Zinnes, and J. David Singer, eds., *Cumulation in International Relations Research* 39–63. University of Denver Monograph Series in World Affairs. Denver: Graduate School of International Studies, 1981.
Johnson, Allen W., and Timothy Earle. *The Evolution of Human Societies: From Foraging Group to Agrarian State*. Stanford, CA: Stanford University Press, 1987.
Jönsson, Christer, ed. *Cognitive Dynamics and International Politics*. New York: St. Martin's Press, 1982.
Jönsson, Christer, and Ulf Westerlund. "Role Theory in Foreign Policy Analysis." In Christer Jönsson, ed., *Cognitive Dynamics and International Politics*, 122–57. New York: St. Martin's Press, 1982.
Kahler, Miles. *International Institutions and the Political Economy of Integration*. Washington, DC: Brookings Institution, 1995.
———. "Rationality in International Relations." *International Organization* 52, no. 4 (1998): 919–41.
Kahn, Herman. *Thinking about the Unthinkable*. New York: Horizon Press, 1962
———. *On Escalation: Metaphors and Scenarios*. New York: Praeger, 1965.
Kaplan, Morton A. *System and Process in International Politics*. New York: Wiley, 1957.
———. "Problems of Theory Building and Theory Confirmation in International Politics." In Klaus Knorr and Sidney Verba, eds., *The International System: Theoretical Essays*, 6–24. Princeton: Princeton University Press, 1961.
———. *Macropolitics*. Chicago: Aldine, 1969.
———. "The New Great Debate: Traditionalism vs. Science in International Relations." In Klaus Knorr and James N. Rosenau, eds., *Contending Approaches to International Politics*, 39–61. Princeton: Princeton University Press, 1969.
———., ed. *New Approaches to International Relations*. New York: St. Martin's Press, 1968.
Kaplan, Robert D. "The Coming Anarchy," *Atlantic Monthly* (February 1994): 46.
———. *The Ends of the Earth: A Journey to the Frontiers of Anarchy*. New York: Vintage, 1996.
Karns, Margaret P., ed. *Persistent Patterns and Emerging Structures in a Waxing Century*. New York: Praeger, 1986.
Katzenstein, Peter J. "International Interdependence: Some Long-Term Trends and Recent Changes." *International Organization* 29, no. 4 (1975): 1021–34.
———., ed. *The Culture of National Security: Norms and Identity in World Politics*. New York: Columbia University Press, 1996.
Katzenstein, Peter J., Robert O. Keohane, and Stephen D. Krasner. "*International Organization* and the Study of World Politics," *International Organization* 52, no. 4 1998.
Kaufmann, Walter, ed. *Hegel's Political Philosophy*. New York: Atherton Press, 1970.
Kautsky, John H. *The Politics of Aristocratic Empires*. Chapel Hill, NC: University of North Carolina Press, 1982.
Keck, Margaret, and Kathryn Sikkink. *Advocates beyond Borders: Advocacy Networks in International Politics*. Ithaca, NY: Cornell University Press, 1998.
Keegan, John. *A History of Warfare*. New York: Knopf, 1993.
Kegley, Chales W. Jr. *The Comparative Study of Foreign Policy: Paradigm Lost?* Essay series no. 10. Columbia, SC: Institute of International Studies, University of South Carolina, 1980.
———., ed. *Controversies in International Relations Theory: Realism and the Neoliberal Challenge*. New York: St. Martin's Press, 1995.
Kegley, Charles W. Jr., and Eugene R. Wittkopf. *American Foreign Policy: Pattern and Process*. 2nd ed. New York: St. Martin's Press, 1982.
———. *World Politics: Trends and Transformation*. 2nd ed. New York: St. Martin's Press, 1985.
———., eds. *Perspectives on American Foreign Policy: Selected Readings*. New York: St. Martin's Press, 1983.

Kelman, Herbert C., ed. *International Behavior: A Social-Psychological Analysis.* New York: Holt, Rinehart & Winston, 1965.

Kennan, George F. *American Diplomacy 190–1950.* Chicago: University of Chicago Press, 1951.

———. *The Decline of Bismarck's European Order: Franco-Russian Relations, 1875–1890.* Princeton: Princeton University Press, 1979.

Keohane, Robert O. "The Theory of Hegemonic Stability and Changes in International Economic Regimes, 1967–1977." In Ole R. Holsti, Randolph M. Siverson, and Alexander L. George, eds., *Change in the International System,* 131–62. Boulder, CO: Westview Press, 1980.

———. "The Demand for International Regimes." *International Organization* 36, no. 2 (1982): 325–55.

———. *After Hegemony: Cooperation and Discord in the World Political Economy.* Princeton: Princeton University Press, 1984.

———. *International Institutions and State Power: Essays in International Relations Theory,* 132–57. Boulder, CO: Westview Press, 1989.

Keohane, Robert O. "Institutional Theory and the Realist Challenge after the Cold War." In David A. Baldwin, ed., *Neorealism and Neoliberalism: The Contemporary Debate,* 116–42. New York: Columbia University Press, 1993.

———., ed. *Neorealism and Its Critics.* New York: Columbia University Press, 1986.

Keohane, Robert O., and Lisa Martin. "The Promise of Institutionalist Theory." *International Security* 20, no. 1 (1995): (Summer).

Keohane, Robert O., and Joseph S. Nye Jr. "Introduction: The Complex Politics of Canadian-American Interdependence." *International Organization* 23, no. 4 (1974): 39–51. 495–607.

———. "Transgovernmental Relations and International Organizations." *World Politics* 27, no. 1 (1974): 39–62.

———. "Transnational Relations and Interstate Conflicts: An Empirical Analysis." *International Organization* 22, no. 4 (1974): 961–96.

———. *Power and Interdependence: World Politics in Transition.* Boston: Little, Brown, 1977.

———. "Two Cheers for Multilateralism." *Foreign Policy,* 60 (fall 1985): 148–67.

———. *Power and Interdependence.* 3rd ed. New York: Longman, 2001.

———., eds. *Transnational Relations and World Politics.* Cambridge, MA: Harvard University Press, 1972.

Khazanov, Anatoli M. "Some Theoretical Problems of the Study of the Early State." In Henri J. M. Claessen and Peter Skalnik, eds., *The Early State* 77-92. The Hague: edited by Mouton, 1978.

Khong, Yuen Foong Khong. *Analogies at War.* Princeton: Princeton University Press, 1992.

King, M. D. "Reason, Tradition, and the Progressiveness of Science." In Gary Gutting, ed., *Paradigms and Revolutions: Appraisals and Applications of Thomas Kuhn's Philosophy of Science,* 97–117. Notre Dame, IN: University of Notre Dame Press, 1980.

Kissinger, Henry A. *American Foreign Policy: Three Essays.* New York: Norton, 1969.

Knorr, Klaus, and James N. Rosenau, eds. *Contending Approaches to International Politics.* Princeton: Princeton University Press, 1969.

Knorr, Klaus, and Sidney Verba, eds. *The International System: Theoretical Essays.* Princeton: Princeton University Press, 1961.

Knox, Paul, and Peter J. Taylor, eds. *World Cities in a World System.* Cambridge: Cambridge University Press, 1995.

Kobrin, Stephen J. "Electronic Cash and the End of National Markets." *Foreign Policy* 107 (Summer 1997): 65–77.

———. "Back to the Future: Neomedievalism and the Postmodern Digital World Economy." *Journal of International Affairs* 51 no. 2 (1998): 361–86.

Koenigsberger, H. G. *Medieval Europe, 400–1500.* London: Longman, 1987.

Kohn, Hans. *The Idea of Nationalism.* New York: Macmillan, 1944.

Korany, Bahgot. "Foreign Policy Decisions in the Third World: An introduction." In Bahgot Korany (ed.), *Foreign Policy Decisions in the Third World.* Topical issue of *International Political Science Review* no. 1 (1984): 7–20.

Koslowski, Rey, and Friedrich V. Kratochwil. "Understanding Change in International Politics: The Soviet Empire's Demise and the International System." *International Organization* 48, no. 2 (1994): 215–47.

Kostecki, Wojciech. "A Marxist Paradigm of International Relations," *International Studies Notes* 12, no. 1 (1985): 19–21.

Krasner, Stephen D. "Are Bureaucracies Important? (Or Allison Wonderland)." *Foreign Policy* 7 (summer 1972): 159–79.

———. "State Power and the Structure of International Trade." *World Politics* 28, no. 3 (1976): 317–47.

———. *Defending the National Interest: Raw Materials Investments and U.S. Foreign Policy.* Princeton: Princeton University Press, 1978.

——— "Regimes and the Limits of Realism: Regimes as Autonomous Variables." *International Organization* 36, no. 2 (1982): 497–510.

———. "Structural Causes and Regime Consequences: Regimes as Intervening Variables." *International Organization* 36, no. 2 (1982): 185–205.

———. "Approaches to the State: Alternative Conceptions and Historical Dynamics." *Comparative Politics* 16, no. 2 (1984): 223–46.

———. "Westphalia and All That." In Judith Goldstein and Robert O. Keohane, eds., *Ideas and Foreign Policy: Beliefs, Institutions, and Political Change,* 235–64. Ithaca, NY: Cornell University Press, 1993.

———. *Sovereignty: Organized Hypocrisy.* Princeton: Princeton University Press, 1999.

———., ed "International Regimes." Special issue of *International Organization* 36, no. 2.

———., ed. *International Regimes.* Ithaca, NY: Cornell University Press, 1983.

Kratochwil, Friedrich V. *Rules, Norms, and Decisions: on the Conditions of Practical and Legal Reasoning in International Relations and Domestic Affairs.* Cambridge: Cambridge University Press, 1989.

Kratochwil, Friedrich V., and John Gerard Ruggie. "International Organization: A State of the Art on an Art of the State." *International Organization* 40, no. 4 (1986): 753–75.

Kubálková, Vendulka, Nicholas Onuf, and Paul Kowert. *International Relations in a Constructed World.* Armonk, NY: M. E. Sharpe, 1998.

Kugler, Jacek, and Douglas Lemke, eds. *Parity and War.* Ann Arbor: University of Michigan Press, 1996.

Kuhn, Thomas S. "Reflections on My Critics." In Imie Lakatos and Alan Musgrove, eds., *Criticism and the Growth of Knowledge.* Cambridge: Cambridge University Press, 1970.

———. *The Structure of Scientific Revolutions.* Expanded ed. Chicago: University of Chicago Press, 1970.

———. "Second Thoughts on Paradigms." In F. Suppe, ed., *The Structure of Scientific Theories,* 459–517. Urbana, IL: University of Illinois Press, 1971.

———. *The Essential Tension.* Chicago: University of Chicago Press, 1977.

Kuklick, Henrika. "A 'Scientific Revolution': Sociological Theory in the United States." *Sociological Inquiry* 43, no. 1 (1972): 2–22.

Kumar, Krishan. *From Post-Industrial to Post-Modern Society: New Theories of the Contemporary World.* Oxford: Basil Blackwell, 1995.

Kunin, L., and F. S. Weaver. "On the Structure of Scientific Revolutions in Economics." *History of Political Economy* 3, no. 2 (1971): 391–97.

Lakatos, Imre. "Falsification and the Methodology of Scientific Research Programmes." In Imre Lakatos and Alan Musgrave, eds., *Criticism and the Growth of Knowledge,* 91–196. Cambridge: Cambridge University Press, 1970.

———. *The Methodology of Scientific Research Programmes.* Vol. 1. Cambridge: Cambridge University Press, 1978.

Lakatos, Imre, and Alan Musgrave, eds. *Criticism and the Growth of Knowledge.* Cambridge: Cambridge University Press, 1970.

Lake, David A., and Robert Powell. *Strategic Choice and International Relations.* Princeton: Princeton University Press, 1999.

Lampert, Donald E., Lawrence L. Falkowski, and Richard W. Mansbach. "Is There an International System?" *International Studies Quarterly* 22, no. 1 (1978): 143–66.

Langhorne, Richard. *The Coming of Globalization: Its Evolution and Contemporary Consequences.* New York: Palgrave, 2001.

Lapid, Yosef. "The Third Debate: On the Prospects for International Theory in a Post-Positivist Era." *International Studies Quarterly* 33, no. 3 (1989): 235–54.

———. "Culture's Ship: Returns and Departures in International Relations Theory." In Yosef Lapid and Friedrich Kratochwil, eds., *The Return of Culture and Identity in IR Theory,* 3–20 Boulder, CO: Lynne Rienner, 1996.

Lapid, Yosef, and Friedrich Kratochwil, eds. *The Return of Culture and Identity in IR Theory.* Boulder, CO: Lynne Rienner, 1996.

Lasswell, Harold D. *World Politics and Personal Insecurity.* New York: McGraw-Hill, 1935.

Lasswell, Harold D., and Abraham Kaplan. *Power and Society.* New Haven, CT: Yale University Press, 1950.

Laudan, Larry. *Progress and Its Problems: Towards a Theory of Scientific Growth.* London: Routledge & Kegan Paul, 1977.

———. *Beyond Positivism and Relativism: Theory, Method, and Evidence.* Boulder, CO: Westview Press, 1996.

Lebow, Richard Ned. *Between Peace and War: The Nature of International Crisis.* Baltimore: Johns Hopkins Press, 1981.

Lebow, Richard Ned, and Janice Gross Stein. "Rational Deterrence Theory: I Think, Therefore I Deter." *World Politics* 41, no. 2 (1989): 208–24.

Lehmbruch, Gerhard, and Philippe C. Schmitter, eds. *Patterns of Corporate Policy Making.* Beverly Hills, CA: Sage, 1982.

Leites, Nathan. *The Operational Code of the Politburo.* New York: McGraw-Hill, 1951.

Levy, Jack S. "Prospect Theory, Rational Choice, and International Relations." *International Studies Quarterly* 41, no. 1 (1997): 87–112.

Levy, Marion J. Jr. " 'Does it Matter If He's Naked?' Bawled the Child." In Klaus Knorr and James N. Rosenau, eds., *Contending Approaches to International Politics,* 87–109. Princeton: Princeton University Press, 1969.

Leyton-Brown, David. "The Nation-State and Multinational Enterprise: Erosion or Assertion?" In Robert O. Matthews, Arthur G. Rubinoff, and Janice Gross Stein, eds., *International Conflict and Conflict Management: Readings in World Politics,* 330–40. Scarborough, Ont: Prentice-Hall of Canada, 1984.

Licklider, Roy. *Political Power and the Arab Oil Weapon: The Netherlands, Great Britain, Canada, Japan, and the United States.* Berkeley: University of California Press, 1988.

Lieber, Robert J. *Theory and World Politics.* Cambridge, MA: Winthrop, 1972.

Lijphart, Arend. "The Structure of the Theoretical Revolution in International Relations." *International Studies Quarterly* 18, no. 1 (1974): 41–74.

Lincoln, Jennie K., and Elizabeth G. Ferris, eds. *The Dynamics of Latin American Foreign Policies: Challenges for the 1980s.* Boulder, CO: Westview Press, 1984.

Lindberg, Leon N. *The Political Dynamics of European Economic Integration.* Stanford: Stanford University Press, 1963.

Lindberg, Leon N., and Stuart A. Scheingold, eds. *Regional Integration: Theory and Research.* Cambridge, MA: Harvard University Press, 1970.

Lindblom, Charles E. "The Science of Muddling Through." *Public Administration Review* 19, no. 2 (1959): 79–88.

———. *The Policy-Making Process.* Englewood Cliffs, NJ: Prentice-Hall, 1968.

Lindblom, Charles E., and David Cohen. *Usable Knowledge: Social Science and Social Problem Solving.* New Haven: Yale University Press, 1979.

Lippmann, Walter. *The Public Philosophy.* New York: Mentor, 1955.

Lipschutz, Ronnie D. "Reconstructing World Politics: The Emergence of Global Civil Society." *Millennium* 21, no. 3 (1992): 389–420.

Lipson, Charles. "The Transformation of Trade: The Sources and Effects of Regime Change." *International Organization* 36, no. 2 (1982): 417–55.

Long, Samuel, ed. *Political Behavior Annual.* Boulder, CO: Westview Press, 1986.

Lowi, Theodore J. "American Business, Public Policy, Case Studies and Political Theory." *World Politics* 16, no. 4 1964: 677–715.

Machiavelli, Niccolò. *The Prince and The Discourses.* Introduction by Max Lerner. New York: Random House, 1950.

Macrae, Duncan J. *The Social Function of Social Science.* New Haven, CT: Yale University Press, 1976.

Maghroori, R., and B. Ramberg, eds. *Globalism versus Realism: International Relations' Third Debate.* Boulder, CO: Westview Press, 1982.

Manktelow, K. I. and D. E. Over, eds. *Rationality: Psychological and Philosophical Perspectives.* New York: Routledge, 1993.

Mann, Michael. *The Sources of Social Power.* Vol. 1: *A History of Power from the Beginning to A.D. 1760.* Cambridge: Cambridge University Press, 1986.

———. *The Sources of Social Power.* Vol. 2: *The Rise of Classes and Nation-States, 1760–1914.* Cambridge: Cambridge University Press, 1993.

Mansbach, Richard W., "Deterritorializing Global Politics." In Donald J. Puchala, ed., *Visions of International Relations: Assessing an Academic Field.* Columbia, SC: University of South Carolina Press, 2002: 101–18.

Mansbach, Richard W., Yale H. Ferguson, and Donald E. Lampert. *The Web of World Politics: Nonstate Actors in the Global System.* Englewood Cliffs, NJ: Prentice-Hall, 1976.

Mansbach, Richard W., and John A. Vasquez. *In Search of Theory: A New Paradigm for Global Politics.* New York: Columbia University Press, 1981.

March, James G., and Herbert Simon. *Organizations.* New York: Wiley, 1957.

Martin, Wayne Richard. "Cumulation, Cooperation, and Commitment." In James N. Rosenau, ed., *In Search of Global Patterns,* 212–15. New York: Free Press, 1976.

Maslow, A. H. "A Theory of Human Motivation." *Psychological Review* 50, no. 4, (1943): 370–96.

Masters, Roger D. "World Politics as a Primitive Political System." *World Politics* 16, no. 4 (1964): 595–619.

———. "The Biological Nature of the State." *World Politics* 35, no. 2 (1983): 161–93.

Matthews, Jessica. "Power Shift." *Foreign Affairs* 76 no. 1 (1997): 50–66.

Matthews, Robert O., Arthur G. Rubinoff, and Janice Gross Stein, eds. *International Conflict and Conflict Management.* Scarborough, Ont. Prentice-Hall, 1984.

May, Ernest R. *"Lessons" from the Past: The Use and Misuse of History in American Foreign Policy.* New York: Oxford University Press, 1973.

Mayall, James. "The Variety of States." Paper delivered at the British International Studies Association annual meeting, University of Reading, Reading, U.K., December 16, 1986.

McClure, Paul T. *The Organizational Approach versus the Society Approach to Development in Emerging Nations.* Document no. P-3927. Santa Monica, CA: RAND Corporation, 1969.

McGowan, Patrick J. "The Future of Comparative Studies: An Evangelical Appeal." In James N. Rosenau, ed., *In Search of Global Patterns,* 217–35. New York: Free Press, 1976.

———., ed. *Sage International Yearbook of Foreign Policy.* Vol 1. Beverly Hills, CA: Sage, 1973.

McGowan, Patrick J., and Howard B. Shapiro. *The Comparative Study of Foreign Policy: A Survey of Scientific Findings.* Vol. 4 of Sage Library of Social Research Beverly Hills, CA: Sage, 1973.

Mearsheimer, John J. "Maneuver, Mobile Defense, and the NATO Central Fronts." *International Security* 6, no. 3 (1981): 104–23.

Mearsheimer, John J. "Why the Soviets Can't Win Quickly in Central Europe." *International Security* 7, no. 4 (1982): 3–40.

———. "Back to the Future: Instability in Europe after the Cold War." *International Security* 15, no. 1 (1990): 5–56.

———. "The Case for Ukrainian Nuclear Deterrent." *Foreign Affairs* 72, no. 3 (1993): 50–66.

———. "The False Promise of International Institutions." *International Security* 19, no. 3 (1994): 5–49.

Meier, Richard. "Information, Resources and Economic Growth. In J. J. Spengler (ed.) *National Resources and Economic Growth.* Washington, DC: Resources for the Future, n.d.

Meinecke, Friedrich. *Machiavellism: The Doctrine of Raison d'Etat and Its Place in Modern History.* Trans. Douglas Scott. New Haven, CT: Yale University Press, 1957.

Mendlowitz, Saul H. "The Program of the Institute of World Order." *Journal of International Affairs* 31 (fall/winter 1977): 259–66.

Merritt, Richard L. "Public Opinion and Foreign Policy in West Germany." In Patrick J. McGowan, ed., *Sage International Yearbook of Foreign Policy Studies.* Vol. 1, 255–74. Beverly Hills, CA: Sage, 1973.

Merton, Robert K. "Priorities in Scientific Discovery: A Chapter in the Sociology of Science." *American Sociological Review* 22, no. 6 (1957): 635–59.

Metz, Steven. "Racing toward the Future: The Revolution in Military Affairs." *Current History* (April 1997): 184–85.

Meyers, R. "International Paradigms, Concepts of Peace, and the Policy of Appeasement." *War and Society* 1, no. 1 (1983): 43–65.

Miller, J. D. B. "Sovereignty as a Source of Vitality for the State." *Review of International Studies* 12, no. 2 (1986): 79–91.

Milner, Helen V. "Rationalizing Politics: The Emerging Synthesis of International, American, and Comparative Politics." *International Organization* 52 no. 4 (1998): 759–86.

Mitrany, David. *A Working Peace System.* London: Royal Institute of International Affairs, 1943.

Modelski, George. "Agraria and Industria: Two Models of the International System." In Klaus Knorr and Sidney Verba, eds., *The International System,* 118–43. Princeton: Princeton University Press, 1961.

Møller, J. Ørstrøm. *The End of Internationalism.* Westport, CT: Praeger, 2000.

Montross, Lynn. *War through the Ages.* 3rd ed. New York: Harper & Row, 1960.

Moore, Barrington. *Social Origins of Dictatorship and Democracy: Lord and Peasant in the Making of the Modern World.* Boston: Beacon Press, 1966.

Moravcsik, Andrew. "Taking Preferences Seriously: A Liberal Theory of International Politics." *International Organization* 51, no. 4 (1997): 513–53.

Morgenthau, Hans J. *Scientific Man and Power Politics.* Chicago: University of Chicago Press, 1946.

————. *In Defense of the National Interest.* New York: Knopf, 1951.

————. "Another Great Debate: The National Interest of the United States." *American Political Science Review* 46, no. 4 (1952): 961–88.

————. *Politics among Nations: The Struggle for Power and Peace.* 5th ed., rev. New York: Knopf, 1978.

Morse, Edward L. *Modernization and the Transformation of International Relations.* New York: Free Press, 1976.

Moynihan, Daniel Patrick. *Pandaemonium: Ethnicity in International Politics.* New York: Oxford University Press, 1993.

Muñoz, Heraldo, and Joseph S. Tulchin, eds. *Latin American Nations in World Politics.* Boulder, CO: Westview Press, 1984.

Murphy, Alexander B. "The Sovereign State System as Political-Territorial Ideal: Historical and Contemporary Considerations." In Thomas J. Biersteker and Cynthia Weber, eds, *State Sovereignty as Social Construct,* 81–120. Cambridge: Cambridge University Press, 1996.

Nettl, J. P "The State as a Conceptual Variable." *World Politics* 20, no. 4 (1968): 559–92.

Neustadt, Richard E. *Alliance Politics.* New York: Columbia University Press, 1970.

Nickles, Thomas. "Lakatosian Heuristics and Epistemic Support." *British Journal for the Philosophy of Science* 38, no. 1 (1987): 181–205.

Nicholson, Michael. *Rationality and the Analysis of International Conflict.* Cambridge: Cambridge University Press, 1992.

————. "The Continued Significance of Positivism?" In Steve Smith, Ken Booth, and Marysia Zalewski, eds., *International Theory: Positivism and Beyond,* 128–45. Cambridge: Cambridge University Press, 1996.

Nicolson, Harold. *The Evolution of Diplomatic Method.* London: Cassell, 1954.

————. *Diplomacy.* 3rd ed. New York: Oxford University Press, 1963.

Ninkovich, Frank. *Modernity and Power: A History of the Domino Theory in the Twentieth Century.* Chicago: University of Chicago Press, 1994.

Nordlinger, Eric A. *On the Autonomy of the Democratic State.* Cambridge, MA: Harvard University Press, 1981.

Nossal, Kim Richard. "Bureaucratic Politics and the Westminster Model." In Robert O. Matthews, Arthur G. Rubinoff, and Janice Gross Stein, eds., *International Conflict and Conflict Management,* 120–27. Scarborough, Ont. Prentice-Hall of Canada, 1984.

————. "Transnational Relations and Interstate Conflicts: An Empirical Analysis." *International Organization* 23, no. 4 (1974): 961–96.

Nye, Joseph S. Jr. *Bound to Lead: The Changing Nature of American Power.* New York: Basic Books, 1990.

————.,ed *International Regionalism: Readings.* Boston: Little, Brown, 1968.

O'Brien, Robert, Anne Marie Goetz, Jan Aart Scholte, and Marc Williams. *Contesting Global Governance: Multilateral Economic Institutions and Global Social Movements.* Cambridge: Cambridge University Press, 2000.

O'Leary, Michael K. "The Role of Issues." In James N. Rosenau, ed., *In Search of Global Patterns,* 318–26. New York: Free Press, 1976.

Olson, Mancur, Jr. *The Logic of Collective Action.* Cambridge, MA: Harvard University Press, 1965.

Oneal, John R, and Bruce M. Russett. "The Classical Liberals Were Right: Democracy, Interdependence, and Conflict, 1950–1985." *International Studies Quarterly* 41, no. 2 (1997): 267–93.

Onuf, Nicholas J. *World of Our Making: Rules and Rule in Social Theory and International Relations.* Columbia, SC: University of South Carolina Press, 1989.

————. "Levels." *European Journal of International Relations,* 1, no. 1 (1995): 35–58.

————. "Constructivism: A User's Manual." In Vendulka Kubálková, Nicholas Onuf, and Paul Kowert, eds., *International Relations in a Constructed World,* 58–78. Armonk, NY: M. E. Sharpe, 1998.

Oren, Nissan. *When Patterns Change: Turning Points in International Organization.* New York: St. Martin's Press, 1984.

Organski, A. F. K. *World Politics.* New York: Knopf, 1958.

Ortega y Gasset, José. *The Dehumanization of Art and Other Essays on Art, Culture and Literature.* Princeton: Princeton University Press, 1948.

Osgood, Robert E. *Ideals and Self-Interest in America's Foreign Relations.* Chicago: University of Chicago Press, 1953.

Osiander, Andreas. *The State System of Europe, 1640–1990: Peacemaking and the Conditions of International Stability.* Oxford: Clarendon, 1994.

Packenham, Robert A. *Liberal America and the Third World: Political Development Ideas in Foreign Aid and Social Science.* Princeton: Princeton University Press, 1973.

Paige, Glenn D. "On Values and Science: *The Korean Decision* Reconsidered." *American Political Science Review* 71, no. 4 (1977): 1603–9.

Paret, Peter, ed. *Makers of Modern Strategy from Machiavelli to the Nuclear Age*. Princeton: Princeton University Press, 1986.

Parkinson, F. *The Philosophy of International Relations: A Study in the History of Thought*. Beverly Hills, CA: Sage, 1977.

Passerin d'Entreves, Alessandro. *The Notion of the State: An Introduction to Political Theory*. London: Oxford University Press, 1967.

Perry, Clive. "The Function of Law in the International Community." In Max Sorensen, ed., *Manual of Public International Law*, 1–54. New York: St. Martin's Press, 1968.

Peters, B. Guy, and Donald J. Savoie, eds. *Governance in a Changing Environment*. Montreal: McGill-Queens University Press, 1995.

Peterson, V. Spike. *Gendered States: Feminist (Re)Visions of International Relations Theory*. Boulder, CO: Lynne Rienner, 1992.

Peterson, V. Spike, and Anne S. Runyan. *Global Gender Issues*. Boulder, CO: Westview Press, 1993.

Pettman, J. *Worlding Women: A Feminist International Politics*. New York: Routledge, 1996.

Pfaltzgraff, Robert, Jr. "International Studies in the 1970s." *International Studies Quarterly* 15, no. 1 (1971): 104–28.

Phillips, Warren R. "Where Gave All the Theories Gone?" *World Politics* 26, no. 2 (1974): 155–88.

Pippard, Brian. "Instability and Chaos: Physical Models of Everyday Life." *Interdisciplinary Science Reviews* 7, no. 2 (1982): 92–101.

Pirages, Dennis. *A New Context for International Relations: Global Ecopolitics*. North Scituate, MA: Duxbury Press, 1978.

Platig, Raymond E. *International Relations Research: Problems of Evaluation and Advancement*. Santa Barbara, CA: Clio Press, 1967.

Popper, Karl. *Logik der Forschung: The Logic of Scientific Discovery*. London: Hutchinson, 1935.

Porter, B, ed. *The Aberystwyth Papers: International Politics 1919–1969*. London: Oxford University Press, 1972.

Poulantzas, Nicos. *State, Power, Socialism*. Trans. Patrick Camiller. London: NLB, 1978.

Puchala, Donald J. *International Politics Today*. New York: Harper & Row, 1971.

———. "Woe to the Orphans of the Scientific Revolution." In Robert L. Rothstein, ed., *The Evolution of Theory in International Relations*, 39–60. Columbia, SC: University of South Carolina Press, 1991.

———., ed. *Visions of International Relations: Assessing an Academic Field*. Columbia, SC: University of South Carolina Press, 2000.

Puchala, Donald J., and Raymond F. Hopkins. "International Regimes: Lessons from Inductive Analysis." *International Organization* 36, no. 2 (1982): 245–75.

Putnam, Robert D. "Diplomacy and Domestic Politics: The Logic of Two-Level Games." *International Organization* 42, no. 3 (1988): 427–60.

Reinken, Donald. "Computer Explorations of the 'Balance of Power': A Project Report." In Morton A. Kaplan, ed., *New Approaches to International Politics* 459–81. New York: St. Martin's Press, 1968.

Reuveny, Rafael. "Bilateral Import, Export, and Conflict/Cooperation Simultaneity." *International Studies Quarterly* 45, no. 1 (2001): 131–58.

Riggs, Fred W. "International Relations as a Prismatic System." In Klaus Knorr and Sidney Verba, eds., 144–81. *The International System: Theoretical Essays*. Princeton: Princeton University Press, 1961.

———. "The Theory of Developing Politics." *World Politics* 16, no. 1 (1963): 147–71.

Ripley, Brian. "A Lakatosian Appraisal of Foreign Policy Decision-Making." Paper delivered to the meeting of The International Studies Association, Washington, DC, 1993.

Ritzer, George. *Sociology: A Multiple Paradigm Science*. Boston: Allyn & Bacon, 1975.

Rogow, Arnold A. *James Forrestal: A Study in Personality, Politics, and Policy*. New York: Macmillan, 1963.

Rogowski, Ronald. "Rationalist Theories of Politics: A Midterm Report." *World Politics* 30, no. 2 (1978).

Rosati, Jerel A. "A Neglected Actor in American Foreign Policy: The Role of the Judiciary." *International Studies Notes* 12, no. 1 (1985): 10–15.

Rosecrance, Richard N. *Action and Reaction in World Politics: International Systems in Perspective*. Boston: Little, Brown, 1963.

———. "Bipolarity, Multipolarity, and the Future." *Journal of Conflict Resolution* 10, no. 3 (1966): 314–27.

———. "The Failures of Quantitative Analysis: Possible Causes and Cures." In James N. Rosenau, ed., *In Search of Global Patterns*, 174–80. New York: Free Press, 1976.

————. "International Theory Revisited." *International Organization* 35, no. 4 (1981): 691–713.

————. "Reply to Waltz." *International Organization* 36, no. 3 (1982): 682–85.

————. *The Rise of the Virtual State: Wealth and Power in the Coming Century.* New York: Basic Books, 1999.

Rosecrance, Richard N., A. Alexandroff, W. Koehler, J. Kroll, S. Laqueur, and J. Stocker." Whither Interdependence?" *International Organization* 31, no. 3 (1977): 425–44.

Rosecrance, Richard N., and William Gutowitz. "Measuring Interdependence: A Rejoinder." *International Organization* 35, no. 3 (1981): 553–56.

Rosenau, James N. *Public Opinion and Foreign Policy.* New York: Random House, 1961.

————. "Pre-theories and Theories of Foreign Policy." In R. Barry Farrell, ed., *Approaches to Comparative and International Politics,* 27–93. Evanston, IL: Northwestern University Press, 1966.

————. *The Scientific Study of Foreign Policy.* New York: Free Press, 1971.

————. "Capabilities and Control in an Interdependent World." *International Security* 1, no. 2 (1976): 32–49.

————. "A Pre-Theory Revisited: World Politics in an Era of Cascading Interdependence." *International Studies Quarterly* 28, no. 3 (1984): 245–305.

————. "Before Cooperation: Hegemons, Regimes, and Habit-Driven Actors in World Politics." *International Organization* 40, no. 4 (1986): 849–94.

————. *Turbulence in World Politics: A Theory of Change and Continuity.* Princeton: Princeton University Press, 1990.

————. "Governance, Order, and Change in World Politics." In James N. Rosenau and Ernst-Otto Czempiel, eds. *Governance Without Government: Order and Change in World Politics,* 1–29. Cambridge: Cambridge University Press, 1992.

————. *Along the Domestic-Foreign Frontier: Exploring Governance in a Turbulent World.* Cambridge: Cambridge University Press, 1997.

————, ed. *International Politics and Foreign Policy.* Rev. ed. New York: Free Press, 1969.

————, ed. *Linkage Politics.* New York: Free Press, 1969.

————, ed. *Comparing Foreign Policies: Theories, Findings and Methods.* Beverly Hills, CA: Sage, 1974.

————, ed. *In Search of Global Patterns.* New York: Free Press, 1976.

Rosenau, James N., Vincent Davis, and Maurice A. East, eds. *The Analysis of International Politics.* New York: Free Press, 1972.

Rosenau, James N., and Ernst-Otto Czempiel, eds. *Governance without Government: Order and Change in World Politics.* Cambridge: Cambridge University Press, 1992.

Rothstein, Robert J., ed. *The Evolution of Theory in International Relations.* Columbia, SC: University of South Carolina Press, 1991.

Rousseau, Jean-Jacques, "Abstract of the Abbé de Saint-Pierre's Project for Perpetual Peace." In M. G. Forsyth, H. M. A. Keens-Soper, and P. Sauigear, eds. *The Theory of International Relations: Selected Texts from Gentile to Trietschke.* New York: Atherton Press, 1970.

Ruggie, John Gerard. "International Responses to Technology: Concepts and Trends," *International Organization* 29, no. 3 (1975): 557–83.

————. "International Regimes, Transactions, and Change: Embedded Liberalism in the Postwar Economic Order." *International Organization* 36, no. 2 (1982): 379–415.

————. "Continuity and Transformation in the World Polity: Toward a Neorealist Synthesis." *World Politics* 35, no. 2 (1983): 261–85. Reprint Robert O. Keohane, ed., *Neorealism and Its Critics,* 131–57. New York: Columbia University Press, 1983.

————. "Territoriality and Beyond: Problematizing Modernity in International Relations." *International Organization* 47, no. 1 (1993): 139–74.

————. "What Makes the World Hang Together? Neo-utilitarianism and the Social Constructivist Challenge." *International Organization* 52, no. 4 (1998): 855–85.

————., ed. *The Antinomies of Interdependence: National Welfare and the International Division of Labor.* New York: Columbia University Press, 1983.

Rummel, R. I. "The Roots of Faith." In James N. Rosenau, ed., *In Search of Global Patterns,* 10–30. New York: Free Press, 1976.

Russett, Bruce M. *Community and Contention: Britain and America in the Twentieth Century.* Cambridge, MA: MIT Press, 1963.

————. *Trends in World Politics.* New York: Macmillan, 1965.

————. *International Regions and the International System: A Study in Political Ecology.* Chicago: Rand-McNally, 1967.

————. "Apologia Pro Vita Sua." In James N. Rosenau, ed., *In Search of Global Patterns,* 31–37. New York: Free Press, 1976.

————. "The Mysterious Case of Vanishing Hegemony; Or, Is Mark Twain Really Dead?" *International Organization* 39, no. 2 (1985): 207–231.

————., ed. *Peace, War, and Numbers.* Beverly Hills, CA: Sage Publications, 1972.

Russett, Bruce M., and Harvey Starr. *World Politics: The Menu for Choice.* San Francisco: W. H. Freeman, 1981.

Ryan, Alan. *The Philosophy of the Social Sciences.* New York: Pantheon Books, 1970.

Sabine, George H. A *History of Political Theory.* 3rd ed. New York: Holt, Rinehart & Winston, 1961.

Sabrosky, Alan Ned, ed. *Polarity and War: The Changing Structure of International Conflict.* Boulder, CO: Westview Press, 1985.

Sassen, Saskia. *The Global City: New York, London, Tokyo.* Princeton: Princeton University, Press, 1991.

————. *Losing Control? Sovereignty in an Age of Globalization.* New York: Columbia University Press, 1996.

————. *Globalization and Its Discontents.* New York: New Press, 1998.

Savoie, Donald J. "Globalization, Nation-States, and the Civil Service." In B. Guy Peters and Donald J. Savoie, ed., *Governance in a Changing Environment,* 82–110. Montreal: McGill-Queens University Press, 1995.

Schelling, Thomas C. *The Strategy of Conflict.* Cambridge, MA: Harvard University Press, 1960.

————. *Arms and Influence.* New Haven: Yale University Press, 1966.

Schiller, Herbert I. *Communication and Cultural Domination.* New York: M. E. Sharpe, 1976.

————. *Mass Communications and American Empire.* 2nd ed. Boulder, CO: Westview Press, 1992.

Schilling, Warner R., Paul Hammond, and Glenn Snyder, eds. *Strategy, Politics, and Defense Budgets.* New York: Columbia University Press, 1962.

Schmitter, Philippe C. "Democratic Theory and Neocorporatist Practice." *Social Research* 50, no. 4 (1983): 885–928.

Scholte, Jan Aart. "Global Capitalism and the State." *International Affairs,* 73 (1993): 427–52

————. *Globalization: A Critical Introduction.* New York: Palgrave, 2000.

Schwartz, Herman M. *States versus Markets: The Emergence of a Global Economy.* 2nd ed. New York: St. Martin's Press, 2000.

Schweller, Randall L., and David Priess. "A Tale of Two Realisms: Expanding the Institutions Debate." *Mershon International Studies Review* 41, no. 1 (1997): 1–32.

Searle, John R. (1995). *The Construction of Social Reality.* New York: Free Press, 1995.

Selcher, Wayne. "Brazil's Foreign Policy: More Actors and Expanding Agendas." In Jennie K. Lincoln and Elizabeth G. Ferris, eds., *The Dynamics of Latin American Foreign Policies: Challenges for the 1980s,* 101–23. Boulder, CO: Westview Press, 1984.

Senese, Paul D. "Democracy and Maturity: Deciphering Conditional Effects on Levels of Dispute Intensity." *International Studies Quarterly* vol. 43, no. 3 (1999): 483–502

Seton-Watson, Hugh. *Nations and States.* Boulder, CO: Westview Press, 1977.

Sewell, James P. *Functionalism and World Politics.* Princeton: Princeton University Press, 1966.

Shils, Edward. *Political Development in the New States.* The Hague: Mouton, 1962.

Simon, Herbert. *Models of Man.* New York: Wiley, 1957.

————. *Administrative Behavior: A Discussion of Decision-Making Process in Administrative Organization.* 2nd ed. New York: Macmillan, 1961.

Singer, J. David. "The Level-of-Analysis Problem in International Relations." In Klaus Knorr and Sidney Verba, eds., *The International System: Theoretical Essays,* 77–92. Princeton: Princeton University Press, 1961.

————. "The Incompleat Theorist: Insight without Evidence." In Klaus Knorr and James N. Rosenau, eds., *Contending Approaches to International Politics,* 62–86. Princeton: Princeton University Press, 1969.

————. *The Wages of War, 1816–1965: A Statistical Handbook.* New York: Wiley, 1972.

————. "Tribal sins on the QIP reservation." In James N. Rosenau, ed., *In Search of Global Patterns,* 167–73. New York: Free Press, 1976.

————. *A General Systems Taxonomy for Political Science.* New York: General Learning Press, 1971.

————., ed. *Quantitative International Politics: Insights and Evidence.* New York: Free Press, 1968.

Singer, J. David, S. Bremer, and J. Stuckey. "Capability Distribution, Uncertainty, and Major Power War, 1820–1965." In Bruce M. Russett, ed., *Peace, War, and Numbers,* 19–48. Beverly Hills, CA: Sage, 1972.

Siverson, Randolph M. "Some Suggestions for Improving Cumulation." In James N. Rosenau, ed., *In Search of Global Patterns,* 198–204. New York: Free Press, 1976.

Sjoblom, Gunnar. "Some Problems of the Operational Code Approach." In Christer Jönsson, ed., *Cognitive Dynamics and International Politics,* 37–74. New York: St. Martin's Press, 1982.

Skinner, Quentin, ed. *The Return of Grand Theory in the Human Sciences.* Cambridge: Cambridge University Press, 1991.

Skocpol, Theda. "Wallerstein's World Capitalist System: A Theoretical Critique." *American Journal of Sociology* 82, no. 5 (1977): 1075–90.

Skolnikoff, Eugene B. *Science, Technology, and American Foreign Policy.* Cambridge, MA: MIT Press, 1967.

Small, Melvin and J. David Singer, eds. *International War: An Anthology and Study Guide.* Homewood, IL: Dorsey Press, 1985.

Smith, Anthony D. *The Ethnic Origins of Nations.* Oxford: Basil Blackwell, 1986.

Smith, Jackie, Charles Chatfield, and Ron Pagnucco. *Transnational Social Movements and Global Politics: Solidarity beyond the State.* Syracuse: Syracuse University Press, 1997.

Smith, Steve. "Theories of Foreign Policy: An Historical View." *Review of International Studies* 12, no. 1 (1986): 13–29.

———. "Positivism and Beyond." In Steve Smith, Ken Booth and Marysia Zalewski, eds. *International Theory: Positivism and Beyond,* 11–44. Cambridge: Cambridge University Press, 1996.

Smith, Steve, Ken Booth, and Marysia Zalewski, eds. *International Theory: Positivism and Beyond.* Cambridge: Cambridge University Press, 1996.

Smith, Steven B. "Hegel's Views on War, the State, and International Relations." *American Political Science Review* 77, no. 3 (1983): 624–32.

Smoke, Richard. "Theory for and about Policy." In James N. Rosenau, ed., *In Search of Global Patterns,* 185–91. New York: Free Press, 1976.

Snow, C. P. *Science and Government.* Cambridge, MA: Harvard University Press, 1961.

Snyder, Glenn H., and Paul Diesing. *Conflict among Nations: Bargaining, Decision Making, and System Structure in International Crises.* Princeton: Princeton University Press, 1977.

Snyder, Jack L. "Perceptions of the Security Dilemma in 1914." In Robert Jervis, Richard Ned Lebow, and Janice Gross Stein, *Psychology and Deterrence.* Baltimore: Johns Hopkins University Press, 1985.

Snyder, Louis L. *Global Mini-Nationalisms: Autonomy or Independence?* Westport, CT: Greenwood Press, 1982.

Snyder, Richard C., H. W. Bruck, and Burton Sapin, eds. *Foreign Policy Decision-Making.* New York: Free Press, 1962.

Sola Pool, Ithiel de, ed. *Contemporary Political Science: Toward Political Theory.* New York: McGraw-Hill, 1967.

Soule, George. *The Coming American Revolution.* New York: Macmillan, 1935.

Spanier, John. *Games Nations Play: Analyzing International Politics.* 4th ed. New York: Holt, Rinehart & Winston, 1981.

Spanier, John, and Eric M. Uslaner. *American Foreign Policy and the Democratic Dilemmas.* 4th ed. New York: Holt, Rinehart & Winston, 1985.

Spengler, J. J., ed. *National Resources and Economic Growth.* Washington, DC: Resources for the Future, n.d.

Spero, Joan Edelman. "Information: The Policy Void," *Foreign Policy* 48 (fall 1982): 139–56.

Sprout, Harold, and Margaret Sprout. *Man-Milieu Relationship Hypotheses in the Context of International Politics.* Princeton: Center of International Studies, 1956.

———. *The Ecological Perspective on Human Affairs with Special Reference to International Politics.* Princeton: Princeton University Press, 1965.

———. *An Ecological Paradigm for the Study of International Politics.* Research Monograph no. 30. Princeton: Center of International Studies, 1968.

———. "Environmental Factors in the Study of International Politics." In James N. Rosenau, ed., *International Politics and Foreign Policy,* Rev. ed. 41–56. New York: Free Press, 1969.

Spruyt, Hendrik. *The Sovereign State and Its Competitors.* Princeton: Princeton University Press, 1994.

———. "The End of Empire and the Extension of the Westphalian System." *International Studies Review* 2, no. 2 (2000): 65–92.

Stein, Arthur A. "Coordination and Collaboration: Regimes in an Anarchic World." *International Organization* 36, no. 2 (1982): 299–324.

———. "The Limits of Strategic Choice: Constrained Rationality and Incomplete Explanation." In David A. Lake and Robert Powell, eds. *Strategic Choice and International Relations,* 197–228. Princeton: Princeton University Press, 1999.

Stein, Janice Gross. "Political Learning by Doing: Gorbachev as Uncommitted Thinker and Motivated Leader." *International Organization* 48, no. 2 (1994): 155–83.

Steinbruner, John D. *The Cybernetic Theory of Decision: New Dimensions of Political Analysis.* Princeton: Princeton University Press, 1974.
———. "Beyond Rational Deterrence: The Struggle for New Conceptions." *World Politics* 28, no. 2 (1976): 223–45.
Stephens, Jerome. "An Appraisal of Some Systems Approaches in the Study of International Systems." *International Studies Quarterly* 16, no. 3 (1972): 321–50.
Strang, David. "Contested Sovereighty: The Social Construction of State Sovereignty. In Thomas J. Biersteker and Cynthia Weber, eds., *Social Sovereighty as Social Construct.* Cambridge: Cambridge University Press, 1996.
Strange, Susan. *"Cave! hic dragones:* A Critique of Regime Analysis." *International Organization* 36, no. 2 (1982): 479–96.
———. *The Retreat of the State: The Diffusion of Power in the World Economy.* Cambridge: Cambridge University Press, 1996.
———. *Mad Money: When Markets Outgrow Governments.* Ann Arbor: University of Michigan Press, 1998.
Sullivan, Michael P. *Theories of International Relations: Transition vs. Persistence.* New York: Palgrave, 2001.
Sullivan, Michael P., and Randolph M. Siverson. "Theories of War: Problems and Prospects." In P. Terrence Hopmann, Dina A. Zinnes, and J. David Singer, eds., *Cumulation in International Relations Research,* 9–37. University of Denver Monograph Series in World Affairs. Denver: Graduate School of International Studies, 1981.
Sunkel, Osvaldo. "Big Business and 'Dependencia': A Latin American View." *Foreign Affairs* 50, no. 3 (1972): 517–31.
———. "The Crisis of the Nation-State in Latin America: Challenge and Response." In Yale H. Ferguson and Walter F. Weiker, eds., *Continuing Issues in International Politics,* 352–68. Pacific Palisades, CA: Goodyear, 1973.
Sylvester, Christine. *Feminist Theory and International Relations in a Postmodern Era.* Cambridge: Cambridge University Press, 1994.
Szabo, Stephen. *The Successor Generation: International Perspectives.* London: Butterworth, 1983.
Tammen, Ronald L., Jacek Kugler, Douglas Lemke, Allan C. Stam III, Mark Abdollahian, Carole Alsharabati, Brian Efird, and A. F. K. Organski. *Power Transitions: Strategies for the Twenty-First Century.* New York: Seven Bridges Press, 2000.
Tanter, Raymond, and Richard H. Ullman, eds. *Theory and Policy in International Relations.* Princeton: Princeton University Press, 1972.
Tetlock Philip E., and Charles McGuire Jr. "Cognitive Perspectives on Foreign Policy." In Samuel Long, ed., *Political Behavior Annual,* 147–79. Boulder, CO: Westview Press, 1986.
Tetreault, Mary Ann. "Measuring Interdependence." *International Organization* 34, no. 3 (1980): 429–43.
———. "Measuring Interdependence: A Response." *International Organization* 35, no. 3 (1981): 557–60.
Thomas, Hugh. *A History of the World.* New York: Harper & Row, 1979.
Thompson, Kenneth W. "The Study of International Politics: A Survey of Trends and Developments." *Review of Politics* 14, no. 4, (1952): 433–43.
———. *Political Realism and the Crisis of World Politics.* Princeton: Princeton University Press, 1960.
Thompson, William R. "The Regional Subsystem: A Conceptual Explication and a Propositional Inventory." *International Studies Quarterly* 17, no. 1 (1973): 89–117.
Thomson, Janice E. *Mercenaries, Pirates, and Sovereigns: State-Building and Extraterrestrial Violence in Early Modern Europe.* Princeton: Princeton University Press, 1994.
Thucydides. *The Peloponnesian War.* Trans. Rex Warner. Baltimore: Penguin, 1954.
Tickner, J. Ann. *Gender in International Relations: Feminist Perspectives on Achieving Global Security.* New York: Columbia University Press, 1992.
———. "You Just Don't Understand: Troubled Engagements between Feminists and IR Theorists," *International Studies Quarterly* vol. 41, no. 4 (1997): 611–32.
Tilly, Charles. *Coercion, Capital and European States, A.D. 990–1990.* Oxford: Basil Blackwell, 1990.
———., ed. *The Formation of National States in Western Europe.* Princeton: Princeton University Press, 1975.
Tocqueville, Alexis de. *Democracy in America,* vol. 1. New York: Knopf, 1945.
Trilling, Lionel. *Beyond Culture.* New York: Harcourt, Brace, Jovanovich, 1965.

Tuchman, Barbara W. *A Distant Mirror: The Calamitous Fourteenth Century.* New York: Knopf, 1978.
United Nations Development Programme, Human Development Office. *Summary: Human Development Report 1999.* New York: UNDP, 1999.
Useem, Michael. "Government Influence on the Social Science Paradigm." *Sociological Quarterly* 17, no. 2 (1976): 146–61.
Van Creveld, Martin. *Technology and War: From 2000 B.C. to the Present.* New York: Free Press, 1989.
———. *The Rise and Decline of the State* Cambridge: Cambridge University Press, 1999.
Van Klaveren, Alberto. "The Analysis of Latin American Foreign Policies: Theoretical Perspectives." In Heraldo Muñoz and Joseph S. Tulchin, eds., *Latin American Nations in World Politics*, 1–21. Boulder, CO: Westview Press, 1984.
Vasquez, John A., ed. *Classics of International Relations.* Englewood Cliffs, NJ: Prentice Hall, 1986.
———. *The War Puzzle.* Cambridge: Cambridge University Press, 1993.
———. *The Power of Power Politics: From Classical Realism to Neotraditionalism.* Cambridge: Cambridge University Press, 1998.
———., ed. *Evaluating U.S. Foreign Policy.* New York: Praeger, 1986.
Vattel, Emmerich de. "The Just Causes of War." In M. G. Forsyth, H. M. A. Keens-Soper, and P. Savigear, eds. *The Theory of International Relations: Selected Texts from Gentili to Treidschke.* New York: Atherton Press, 1970.
Venable, Vernon. *Human Nature: The Marxist View.* Cleveland, OH: Meridian, 1966.
Verba, Sidney. "Assumptions of Rationality and Non-rationality in Models of the International System." In Klaus Knorr and Sidney Verba, eds., *The International System: Theoretical Essays*, 93–117. Princeton: Princeton University Press, 1961.
Vernon, Raymond. *Sovereignty at Bay: The Multinational Spread of U.S. Enterprises.* New York: Basic Books, 1971.
Vertzberger, Yaacov Y. I. "Foreign Policy Decisionmakers as Practical-Intuitive Historians: Applied History and Its Shortcomings." *International Studies Quarterly* 30, no. 2 (1986): 223–47.
Vital, David. "Back to Machiavelli." In Klaus Knorr and James N. Rosenau, eds., *Contending Approaches to International Politics*, 140–57. Princeton: Princeton University Press, 1969.
Vogel, Stephen K. *Freer Markets, More Rules: Regulatory Reform in Industrial Countries.* Ithaca, NY: Cornell University Press, 1996.
Waever, Ole. "The Rise and Fall of the Inter-Paradigm Debate." In Steve Smith, Ken Booth and Marysia Zalewski, eds., *International Theory: Positivism and Beyond*, 149–85. Cambridge: Cambridge University Press, 1996.
———. "The Sociology of a Not So International Discipline: American and European Developments in International Relations." *International Organization* 52, no. 4 (1998): 687–727.
Wagner, G. D., and J. Berger. "Do Sociological Theories Grow?" *American Journal of Sociology* 90, no. 4 (1985): 697–728.
Walker, R. B. J. "Realism, Change, and International Political Theory." *International Studies Quarterly* 31, no. 1 (1987): 65–86.
———. *Inside/Outside: International Relations as Political Theory.* Cambridge: Cambridge University Press, 1993.
Walker, . Thomas C. "The Forgotten Prophet: Tom Paine's Cosmopolitanism and International Relations." *International Studies Quarterly* 44, no. 1 (2000): 51–72.
Wallace, Michael. "Status, Formal Organization and Arms Levels as Factors Leading to the Onset of War, 1820–1964." In Bruce M. Russett, ed., *Peace, War, and Numbers*, 49–71. Beverly Hills, CA: Sage, 1972.
———. "Alliance Polarization, Cross-Cutting, and International War, 1815–1964." *Journal of Conflict Resolution* 17, no. 4 (1973): 575–604.
Wallerstein, Immanuel. *The Modern World-System: Capitalist Agriculture and the Origins of the European World-Economy in the Sixteenth Century.* New York: Academic Press, 1974.
———. *The Capitalist World-Economy.* New York: Cambridge University Press, 1979.
———. *The Politics of the World-Economy: The States, the Movements, and the Civilizations.* New York: Cambridge University Press, 1984.
Waltz, Kenneth N. *Man, the State, and War.* New York: Columbia University Press, 1959.
———. "The Stability of a Bipolar World." *Daedalus* 93 (summer, 1964): 881–909.
———. "International Structure, National Force, and the Balance of World Power." *Journal of International Affairs* 21, no. 2 (1967): 215–31.
———. *Theory of International Politics.* Reading, MA: Addison-Wesley, 1979.
———. "Letter to the Editor." *International Organization* 36, no. 3 (1982): 679–81.

————. "Will the Future Be Like the Past?" In Nissan Oren, ed., *When Patterns Change: Turning Points in International Politics*, 16–36. New York St. Martin's Press, 1984.

————. "Reflections on *Theory of International Politics*: A Response to My Critics." In Robert O. Keohane, ed., *Neorealism and Its Critics*, 322–54. New York: Columbia University Press, 1986.

————. "Structural Realism after the Cold War." *International Security*, 25, no. 1 (2000): 5–41.

Wapner, Paul. "Politics beyond the State: Environmental Activism and World Civic Politics." *World Politics* 47, no. 3 (1995): 311–40.

Watkins, J. W. N. "Against Normal Science." In Imre Lakatos and Alan Musgrave, eds., *Criticism and the Growth of Knowledge*, 25–37. Cambridge: Cambridge University Press, 1970.

Weiss, Linda. *The Myth of the Powerless State*. Ithaca, NY: Cornell University Press, 1998.

Wendt, Alexander E. "The Agent-Structure Problem in International Relations Theory." *International Organization* 41, no. 3 (1987): 335–70.

————. "Anarchy Is What States Make of It: The Social Construction of Power Politics." *International Organization* 46, no. 2 (1992): 391–426,

————. "Constructing International Politics," *International Security* 20, no. 1 (1995): 71–81.

————. *Social Theory of International Politics*. Cambridge: Cambridge University Press, 1999.

Wesson, Robert G. *State Systems: International Pluralism, Politics, and Culture*. New York: Free Press, 1978.

Wiarda, Howard J. *Ethnocentrism in Foreign Policy: Can We Understand the Third World?* Washington, DC: American Enterprise Institute for Public Policy Research, 1985.

Wight, Martin. "Why Is There No International Theory?" In Herbert Butterfield and Martin Wight, eds., *Diplomatic Investigations: Essays in the Theory of International Politics*, 17–34. London: Allen & Unwin Press, 1966.

Wilhelmy, Manfred. "Politics, Bureaucracy, and Foreign Policy in Chile." In Heraldo Muñoz and Joseph S. Tulchin, eds., *Latin American Nations in World Politics*, 45–62. Boulder, CO: Westview Press, 1984.

Wilkinson, David. *Deadly Quarrels: Lewis F. Richardson and the Statistical Study of War*. Berkeley, CA: University of California Press, 1980.

Wilmer, Franke. *The Indigenous Voice in World Politics*. Newbury Park, CA: Sage, 1993.

Wittgenstein, Ludwig. *Philosophical Investigations*. Oxford: Basil Blackwell, 1953.

Wolfers, Arnold. *Discord and Collaboration: Essays on International Politics*. Baltimore: Johns Hopkins Press, 1962.

Wolfers, Arnold, and Laurence W. Martin, eds. *The Anglo-American Tradition in Foreign Affairs*. New Haven: Yale University Press, 1956.

Wolin, Sheldon S. *Politics and Vision: Continuity and Innovation in Western Political Thought*. Boston: Little, Brown, 1960.

————. "Paradigms and Political Theories." In Gary Gutting, ed., *Paradigms and Revolutions: Appraisals and Applications of Thomas Kuhn's Philosophy of Science*, 160–95. Notre Dame: IN: University of Notre Dame Press, 1980.

Worsley, Peter. *The Three Worlds: Culture and World Development*. Chicago: University of Chicago Press, 1984.

Wright, Robert. "Will Globalization Make You Happy?" *Foreign Policy* 20 (September/October, 2000): 55–64.

Young, Oran R. "Political Discontinuities in the International System." *World Politics* 20, no. 3 (1968): 369–92.

————. "The Actors in World Politics." In James N. Rosenau, Vincent Davis, and Maurice A. East, eds., *The Analysis of International Politics*, 125–44. New York: Free Press, 1972.

————. "The Perils of Odysseus: On Constructing Theories of International Relations." *World Politics* 24, Suppl. (spring 1972): 179–203.

————. "Anarchy and Social Choice: Reflections on the International Polity." *World Politics* 30, no. 2 (1978): 241–63.

————. "International Regimes: Problems of Concept Formation." *World Politics* 32, no. 3 (1980): 331–56.

————. "Regime Dynamics: The Rise and Fall of International Regimes." *International Organization* 36, no. 2 (1982): 277–97.

Zacher, Mark W. "The Decaying Pillars of the Westphalian Temple." In James N. Rosenau and Ernst-Otto Czempiel, eds., *Governance without Government: Order and Change in World Politics*, 58–101. Cambridge: Cambridge University Press, 1992.

Zacher, Mark W., and Richard A. Matthew. "Liberal International Theory: Common Threads, Divergent Strands." In Charles W. Kegley Jr., ed., *Controversies in International Relations Theory: Realism and the Neoliberal Challenge*, 107–50. New York: St. Martin's Press, 1995.

Zimmerman, William. "Issue Area and Foreign-Policy Process: A Research Note in Search of General Theory." *American Political Science Review* 67, no. 4 (1973): 1204–12.

Zimmern, Alfred. *The League of Nations and the Rule of Law 1935–1938*. London: Macmillan, 1939.

———. *The Greek Commonwealth: Politics and Economics in Fifth-Century Athens*. New York: Oxford University Press, 1961.

Zinnes, Dina A. "The Problem of Cumulation." In James N. Rosenau, ed., *In Search of Global Patterns*, 161–66. New York: Free Press, 1976.

———. "Prerequisites for the Study of System Transformation." In Ole R. Holsti, Randolph M. Siverson, and Alexander L. George, eds., *Change in the International System*, 1–21. Boulder, CO: Westview Press, 1980.

Zolberg, Aristide R. "Origins of the Modern World System: A Missing Link." *World Politics* 23, no. 2 (1981): 253–81.

Index